PHOTOPLAY TREASURY

PHOTOPLAY TREASURY

edited by Barbara Gelman

CROWN PUBLISHERS, INC.   NEW YORK

© 1972 by Macfadden-Bartell Corporation.
All rights reserved. No part of this book may be reproduced
or utilized in any form or by any means, electronic or mechanical,
including photocopying, recording, or by any information storage
and retrieval system, without permission in writing from the Publisher.
Inquiries should be addressed to Crown Publishers, Inc.,
419 Park Avenue South, New York, N.Y. 10016
Library of Congress Catalog Card Number: 71-147335
ISBN: 0-517-501341
Printed in the United States of America
Published simultaneously in Canada by General Publishing Company Limited

Contents

Introduction

If anyone had told the quiet countryfolk down home in Hollywood, California, that 1910 would ever be called "the good old days," they'd have thought him a lunatic. These were the bad new days—maybe the end of everything that had ever been good about America.

Suffragettes and the new "working girls," Wobblies, and godless socialists were tearing the nation to bits spiritually and physically. And pretty soon that German bad guy Kaiser Bill would be stirring up an international storm that threatened to engulf us all—to involve us in the strange conflicts of decadent foreigners. It would all erupt into World War I before the decade was out.

Such were the blows to God, mother, and country that were toppling a once unshakable nation and robbing it of its most valued assets—its innocence and self-confidence. And if that weren't enough, those bucolic Hollywood folks were being driven right out of their lemon groves and dirt roads by a wild, brand-new industry—the movies. Why couldn't those ex-bookies and carnies and ragpickers who seemed to be running this new business stay in New York or in the wilds of New Jersey, where the whole thing began?

But real estate was still cheap in California, and those long, sun-filled days were vital to a raw industry that hadn't developed technically to the point where it could use artificial light. And there were even some who suggested that a proximity to the Mexican border might also be vital to the people involved in this not-quite-respectable business—should a quick escape from the long arm of the United States legal system become necessary.

But whatever the reaction of Hollywood citizens, the rest of the nation—mothers and suffragettes, farmers and cityfolk—fell instantly and eternally in love. Wobblies and all, they flooded the nickelodeons to make motion pictures—still so new and unpolished and yet curiously fragile—the fifth biggest industry in the country. Outside strife might divide them, but inside the theatres they were united. They loved the flickers, and best of all they loved the boys and girls who starred in them.

The stars! As yet, they were anonymous. But the audiences quickly began to recognize certain faces—faces they wanted to see over and over again—faces they wanted to know more about. Who was the Biograph Girl and Big Bill and Little Mary?

By the time they discovered that the first Biograph Girl's name was Florence Lawrence, they were already in love with Little Mary, the second Biograph Girl. And they loved her as no audience has ever loved anyone before—or since. They flocked to see her films, mobbed any place she was slated to appear in person, wanted desperately to know her name and everything else about her. And when they discovered that her name was Mary Pickford, the first star and the first fans were born.

And what fans they were! Movie crazy, they wanted to know everything about the flickers—how they were made, who wrote them, how the sets were were constructed, how you could get into them. But above all, they wanted to know all about Mary and all of the other new stars that were rising in that Hollywood firmament.

At first, the studios met this demand themselves by publishing their own magazines that tried to answer these questions. But their publications just sounded like a bunch of made-up, official press releases, with nothing really personal about them. In this sense, they weren't really "fan" magazines at all. How-ever, they frequently are given credit as such, and do serve as the forerunners and even models for the first "fan" books to appear.

But it was a smart New York publisher, James Quirk, who saw the really great business possibilities of this kind of magazine. The growing army of fans would certainly pay, and pay a lot, to learn about the stars and the already growing Hollywood legend, if you could only tell them firsthand—and show them—what was happening. But it all had to sound very intimate and on the spot—as though the writer was really seeing it as it happened and was a friend to whom the stars would tell anything.

Mr. Quirk had already chosen a name for his projected idea—*Photoplay*—the word coined by poet Vachel Lindsay for the movies. His next move was to call a young woman reporter already living in California.

Her name was Adela Rogers St. Johns, daughter of the then-famous Justice Rogers. But more important to Quirk, she had once been a "best friend" to famous comedienne Mabel Normand and knew several other of the luminaries on the cinematic scene. What's more, she was a writer, a reporter for Mr. William Randolph Hearst himself. Mr. Quirk asked if she would consider the possibility of moving to Hollywood, once her home, and working for him. He would guarantee her a certain amount of money for a given number of stories, plus extra cash for any item she could contribute to a feature he wanted to call Cal York's Column—the granddaddy of the gossip columns.

As Mrs. St. Johns tells in her autobiography, *Honeycomb,* she did, indeed, go to live among the stars. Literally. The castles and opulent Oriental lairs that were to give Hollywood its unique architectural character were still very few. The stars lived in ordinary bungalows in ordinary neighborhoods, and Mrs. St. Johns was to find that they would become her beloved neighbors and even intimate friends. It was an attitude that would carry through into her writing and into the pages of *Photoplay*. Why, sitting down to dinner with one of Adela's stories was like dining personally with Wally Reid or John Gilbert or Clark Gable.

Mrs. St. Johns was not the only *Photoplay* writer, of course, but she is the prime example of the kind of firsthand contact James Quirk insisted upon for the first forty years of *Photoplay*'s life. From this point of view, he proceeded to tell the fans everything they wanted to know. Columns, written by the stars themselves, told readers the secrets of success and how to live with it. Articles told the "real" personal stories behind the latest news headlines involving a celebrity. Weddings, births, deaths, divorces were discussed in detail. There were stories on how to—or how not to—get into the movies, all sorts of con-tests, movie reviews, and, above all, pictures, pictures, pictures showing various aspects of the stars' off-screen lives. These were not studio publicity pictures or movie stills. These were photographic essays on their homes, or their husbands, or their families. You could see them cooking dinner, and they even shared their recipes with you. You were practically invited along to be part of their lives—or at least *Photoplay* made it seem that way. And very important were the portraits. Indeed, unlike today, back then and up until the forties, the portrait was one of the most vital ingredients in the fan book. Some fans bought the magazines just for the portraits, which they would cut out and hang on the walls, as though the stars were old friends and relatives. By the forties, star portraits were an indispensable part of the decor of every teenager's bedroom, and it was in this decade that the word "pinup" was born, when soldiers decided to grace every barracks wall with pictures of their favorite female stars.

From the start, *Photoplay* was *the* magazine that tailored itself to the fans' every want and need, and readers were invited to participate in the book that was uniquely theirs. Movie-script contests, beauty competitions, and talent searches all made them and their contributions a part of the magazine. And aside from the usual fan fare, there were even fine fiction stories by such popular writers as Mary Roberts Rinehart, or such distinguished ones as playwright Ferenc Molnár, and frequently movies were written up as stories to be read, with stills of visual highlights.

Mr. Quirk had created a very special book, with a kind of limited viewpoint to be sure, but it was, in general content and handling, as good as any "quality" magazine that existed. As such, *Photoplay* would fast emerge as the most important fan book, the bible of Hollywood, the magazine the stars trusted and wanted to appear in—a position it would never lose. Even today, when many fan books have fallen into disrepute, scorned by stars, *Photoplay* still holds its place as number one.

Critics of the early fan books have accused them all of being no more than uncritical publicity outlets for the big studios. This was blatantly untrue of *Photoplay*—except in one respect.

As we've mentioned, in its infancy, motion pictures were a curiously fragile industry and art. Because they were raw and not quite respectable—and bossed by some questionable folk—they did seem about as solid as a straw in the wind and just as likely to blow far, far away.

For *Photoplay,* whose existence depended on the success of movies, the path was clear. Make it respectable and solid, point out the very real hard work that went into the business, justify its reason for being and succeeding. This was *Photoplay*'s earliest objective—it depended on the industry and the industry depended on it. In a sense, it was this mutual dependence—this marriage—that allowed Hollywood and its stars to place a great deal of faith in the magazine and to cooperate with it unhesitatingly.

Not that *Photoplay* was unreservedly kind or uncritical of the stars at all times. By the end of the twenties, it was telling Clara Bow she sounded like Mickey Mouse and Pola Negri she was washed up. It would do the same for Mary Pickford in the following decade. And by the forties, *Photoplay* would have the biggest, most powerful columnists writing for it—Hedda Hopper, Sheilah Graham, Dorothy Kilgallen, and, of course, the biggest of them all—Louella Parsons. A feud with one of these ladies could hurt·a career badly—even destroy it.

From the beginning, *Photoplay* had a very definite effect on the film industry. And yet, there was something very odd about its connection with the real business of making and selling movies to the public. For it would become apparent, as time passed, that the stars the public wanted to see in a movie and the stars they wanted to know more about were not always the same. In the first half of the twenties, for example, Mary Pickford was still top box office. But fans preferred reading about Clara Bow. Chaplin was the undisputed genius who could pull them into the theatres. But Rudolph Valentino and his troubles made for much more popular reading material—even when he was flopping at the box office or not making films at all—or even after he'd been dead for years. Oh, not that Charlie didn't get into the books. His strange marriages and divorces and ultimate scandal could not be ignored after all. But Valentino didn't have to do anything to warrant headlines.

This same attitude would hold true into the forties when when Cary Grant, for example, was very popular. Yet in spite of all his marriages, he did not make for great copy, whereas Lana Turner did. Perhaps it was because Cary was so discreet, never saying much about his problems—not spilling over and talking about personal things the way that Lana or Bogey or Gable did. Later on, when whispers about Cary's troubles did leak out, it did make for copy. But by then, his troubles bordered on scandal, and the fan magazine had become a much different animal from the one we are describing. For we are, in a sense, only talking about a certain period in the life of the fan books in general and *Photoplay* specifically. These were the golden years, a time when the fan books, as we said, had a protective attitude toward the industry on which they depended for their lives. It was an attitude that would prevail from the teens right through the forties. There were some scandals, of course, that were too well publicized not to comment on—like Fatty Arbuckle and Mabel Normand and Mary Miles Minter—toward whom a very protective air was taken. And there was the Charlie Chaplin paternity suit which, together with his political beliefs, won him much censure in *Photoplay* and about drove him from these shores. Errol Flynn had legal problems with young girls—minors—even then. Again, the attitude was protective, and *Photoplay* could scarcely bring itself to describe the charges against him in plain terms. In the final years of the fan magazines as they were—1949—it was impossible to ignore Ingrid Bergman and Roberto Rossellini. Again, the story was told very circumspectly by Louella Parsons, but it blighted a great part of Miss Bergman's career anyway. However, she would be the last fatality of such scandal, for only a few days later, a magazine named *Confidential* would hit the stands. It made scandal a high-paying business and a commonplace thing among the stars. Indeed, the fact that it did seem so commonplace, together with changing moral attitudes on the part of the public, guaranteed that mere scandal would no longer destroy anyone's career in films, at any rate. In fact, readers were so drawn to sex, sin, and related subjects that they stopped reading fan magazines and started buying *Confidential.* That spelled the death of the fan magazines as we once knew them. For in self-defense, they, too, began dealing in scandal. The trust between the magazines and the industry was broken. It was the end of an era—and it is this era of trust, from the teens through 1949, that we cover. That's when *Photoplay* got its stories straight from the horses'—or stars'—mouths. They were invited to christenings and weddings, privy to personal problems, invited to homes, confided in, given exclusive stories. One actress even deliberately delayed a divorce so *Photoplay* could adjust its press time and scoop everyone with the exclusive story. But with the advent of the fifties, *Confidential,* and the need for the fan magazines to compete, the big divorce was definitely between the magazines and the industry.

However, in all fairness and as we've tried to suggest, it did become clear at a very early age that the fan books and the film industry itself were seperate entities. Tops at the box office didn't mean tops in the fan books. Frequently, they did coincide—but not always. But it wasn't scandal that made the difference. In those days, scandal meant professional death, so that scandalous happenings were treated silently in the protective magazines. But trouble, problems, tragedy—such as you and I have, only much, much bigger—now they were the stuff of life and great fan-magazine reading. Spectacular suffering or an obvious potential for the same—the kind of thing that seemed to haunt Lana Turner and Rita Hayworth and Judy Garland—was what made a great star in the magazines. How comforting to know, even then, that beauty and money and fame couldn't buy happiness any more easily than our ordinary means could, and that on some days the stars actually wished they were in our place.

And so, separating the stars the fans wanted to read about from the stars they wanted to see in the movies, *Photoplay* began developing a history of its own. Certainly it reflected a large part of the movie history of its day, but there was something else. Just as movies recorded, in their own peculiar way, their own times, so did the fan magazines. Not that they faithfully recorded the physical reality that existed—there are times when neither the films nor the magazines seemed to have any connection with reality at all. But the fantasies, the hopes, the dreams, the escapes were all there—or at least they were for the incurable moviegoer and dyed-in-the-wool fans, which in those days meant an entire nation.

This then is a record, a re-creation, of the hopes and dreams of a people. It includes the movies and it includes the stars and it even includes the very real world they lived in. But we have tried to show it to you in a very special way, by giving you what seemed most important and relevant in the first four— and perhaps best—decades of *Photoplay*. Each of the decades in this book begins with the portraits of the most important stars and editorial comment reflecting the temper of the times. Then follow the alternating picture stories, full-length articles, columns, fillers, and ads that gave the magazine its look and its pace. And finally, the portraits again—this time of some of the new faces that were emerging and would become important in the following decade. But in following this format, and in attempting at the same time to choose the very best and most interesting stories and pictures, we have had to sacrifice a strict chronological order within the decades themselves. We tried not to stray too far, but when it came to a choice between what seemed the most interesting way to present the essence of *Photoplay* or following the calendar, we felt the subject matter and the look of the book were more important. When it came to choosing portraits, for example, we had to opt for the most popular in the decade as opposed to some rage of the week, month, or year, even though the star chosen might not have emerged at the very beginning of that period. But in making these choices, we also tried very hard to keep the shape of the decade, to reflect what was happening. The twenties, for example, began with a brand-new and relatively free attitude toward sex and morality that swept the nation and was epitomized in its heroes and heroines, the stars. But by mid-decade, the new freedom had bogged down into scandal and disillusionment, the death of some very important careers. The advent of the movies' most technological advance to date—sound—would add to the graveyard knell. And the new freedom with money would by the end of the decade become the Depression. This was the shape of the twenties and we tried to reflect it. Each of the decades had a unique sequence of events and a shape all its own. It was the order of events we strove to keep despite the chronological jumps dictated by subject matter. But most important, it was the attitude of the movies and, above all, the fan books, toward these events that we tried to keep intact. In terms of attitudes then, and in the long-range emotional and philosophical development of films and their audiences—the real world and its fantasies—this is a kind of history. But it is seen very specially through the eyes of a very special group of people—the fans—on the pages of their bible *Photoplay*.

*I*T looks as though Mary is up a tree. Is she wondering whether she ought to accept that $20,000 a week recently offered her, or is she merely figuring out how to get down gracefully? We wish we had problems like $20,000 a week.

Introduction to the Teens

Mary—that's all you had to say and everybody knew precisely who you meant. She was Mary Pickford —the first and most popular star ever—and definitely *the* Mary of the era. A tiny, Victorian valentine of a girl, Mary seemed the perfect replacement for suffragettes, working girls, and other threats to womanhood as it had been known. Yet the breed of working girl loved Mary, too. Utterly feminine or not, she obviously had one of the shrewdest business heads in Hollywood and had made herself its highest-paid star.

But that's how it was, to a certain extent, with all of the beribboned, becurled beauties gracing the new silver screen. They all seemed throwbacks to some Victorian and/or romantic rural era in our past —a return to innocence. Yet they were pioneering and surviving in what even then must have looked like the toughest business in the world. It would be some years before the cracks born of living that kind of life would begin to show—when lovely, fragile Olive Thomas would marry Mary's own brother Jack Pickford and die bizarrely in a Parisian hotel room. The scandalous headlines almost threatened to end the movie business right then and there. But *Photoplay* had already begun to understand this curious new field it had bound itself to. Even now, its aim was protective; it extolled the very real hard work most stars did, explained the tragedy that always seemed to lie just beneath the surface of fame. But at this point, everybody was much more intrigued with the innocence of little, incredibly young Mildred Harris, Chaplin's newest leading lady. They were crazy about waifish, adorable Mabel Normand, sometimes partner to Fatty Arbuckle, and one of the prettiest and most talented comediennes ever. That she would one day suffer a fate nearly as tragic as Olive's—with practically nobody but *Photoplay* on her side—seemed inconceivable during the teens. The wholesome Talmadge sisters—Constance and Norma would never disappoint their audiences with a scandal. Their popularity and box-office power was second only to Mary's.

But even now, there were events in the world that threatened to change both the movies and life irrevocably. Kaiser Bill's high-handed ways in Europe had erupted into World War I, and, like it or not, we would inevitably become involved. The movies would prove themselves part of the mainstream by becoming involved as well. On the production side, there were happy movies with happy endings, which the studios insisted upon so that the public could have come respite from trouble. And the stars themselves were proving to be responsible citizens, even heroes such as those they portrayed, by going off to war.

Meanwhile, *Photoplay* was keeping an insatiably curious public apprized of all these events, and of those still taking place on the home front, via a new concept called gossip column. The magazine was starting to satisfy the public need for "intimate glimpses" into the lives of the famous with "exclusive" and "firsthand" stories. They covered the main events in the lives of all the stars—even Broadway stars —when there wasn't enough news in Hollywood. There was Anna Held's death on the East Coast and Charlie Chaplin's first marriage to Mildred Harris on the West Coast. Charlie was delighted to pose for pictures and talk about his marriage. For the newspapers had been hounding him and his bride, and insisting that little Mildred, scarcely out of her teens, was pregnant. Not *Photoplay*, however, and by its very discretion it would win the trust of Chaplin and the rest of the stars for a long time to come. Actors and actresses would seek to tell their side of the story to *Photoplay*, to give the magazine "intimate," if controlled, glimpses into their lives. This way, they at least had some veto power. Why, even Doug Fairbanks himself—the very epitome of all the American self-confidence that seemed to be slipping away from us—bared his soul, expounded his philosophies, and even wrote his own column for *Photoplay*. And he was the King of Hollywood. And Mary Pickford, who would shortly become his queen, took *Photoplay* readers on a personal shopping tour—showing them how a star bought clothes and just what she meant to add to her wardrobe. She even allowed them to explore the fairy tale romance and ultimate marriage she would have with Doug.

But the war was changing even Hollywood, which seemed so bent on showing a Victorian face to the public. New, foreign-type exotics, like the mysterious Nazimova, were beginning to make their appearances. And a little word—vamp—was fast becoming part of the American language.

Yet it was still the innocents that the public loved—the incredibly fragile-looking Lillian Gish, who could wring your heart with a flutter of her eyelids; her impish sister Dorothy; those crazy, childlike comedians who were still the mainstay of the business. And because it still was a new business readers wanted to know all of the technical magic that took place behind the scenes. How did Fatty Arbuckle write comedy? How were scripts written and finally made into movies? What did happen to those endless letters they sent the stars? But most of all, how did a nice, talented boy or girl get into the movies?

Photoplay tried to help by giving the inside scoop on what it was like to be an extra—the traditional starting place for the stars. They gave continual tips on what every girl wanted to know—how to be discovered. And they even ran contests—beauty as well as writing contests—for those who wanted to be involved in any way. What's more, they reported on how success was changing the face and life-style of Hollywood, and making it incredibly attractive to the star-struck. There was Fannie Ward's new home—a castle practically—that was changing the bungalow colony which had been Hollywood into one of the most sumptuous, if somewhat gaudy, places on earth. Fannie's was one of the first of the palaces, followed very quickly by Mary Pickford's. And with those two unbelievable monuments the race to build aeries and lairs and temples and Babylonian splendor was on.

By the war's end, both Hollywood and films had become very different from what they had been in 1900. From little pie-throwing or shoot-'em-up two-reelers made outdoors with equipment stored in shacks, movies were now feature-length and often serious stories made in substantial studios. A man named D. W. Griffith had shown how to make films that could have a profound effect on the public. Movies began justifying themselves on more than just an entertainment level. Technically and artistically, they began to realize their great potential—and telling the world about it via the pages of *Photoplay*. There was the time, for example, when the movies recorded a war situation and showed it as it really happened, thereby foiling enemy lies and propaganda and keeping the good guys fighting for democracy. And there were socially significant films dealing with such issues as bigotry, like *Broken Blossoms* and *The Squaw Man*, which could yet change some of the evils still existing in this world. Now even Broadway luminaries, who once scoffed at the screen, were taking it seriously. People like Ethel and John Barrymore and Tallulah Bankhead were getting into movies. Broadway was becoming inextricably wed to this growing art form.

Nevertheless the movies were still producing their own peculiar heroes and phenomena. And looking back to better times was still part of the game. Pretty little heroines like Blanche Sweet, all-American heroes like handsome, clean-cut Wallace "Wally" Reid, and the comedians were still the reigning kings and queens. Still, it was obvious that things were changing. Theda Bara did make sin on screen very, very popular. And vamps, or vampires who were not quite the same thing as Dracula, were now a staple of the movie business. And they were heralding a whole new morality—a whole new era and life-style both on screen and off—that we would come to know as the Roaring Twenties.

Edna Goodrich

Olive Thomas

Olive Thomas, sprightly Ziegfeld Follies' queen, now Triangle star and Mrs. Jack Pickford.

Edna Goodrich won fame as a stage beauty. Now she is immortalizing it on the screen.

Marjorie Rambeau, famous beauty and brilliant actress. Her screen career has hardly begun.

Mildred Harris, erstwhile starlet for Lois Weber, plays with Fairbanks in his "Modern Musketeer."

Alfred Cheney Johnston

*M*ABEL NORMAND *will soon give us a new conception of "Sis Hopkins." Mabel left Keystone slap-stick for Goldwyn drawing-room drama. Now the little dramatic yearn has died, leaving Mabel again content as a cut-up.*

8

Pictures from Home

Over there, with thousands of miles of sea and land between them and home, are Our Boys, smiling and fighting—fighting with bullets, against a dogged foe; with smiles, fighting homesickness and dread monotony.

It's a part of the nation's job to-day to keep those boys cheerful, to hold fast the bonds between camp and home, to make light hearts and smiling faces—and these things pictures can help to do—pictures of the home folks and the home doings, pictures of the neighbors, pictures that will enliven their memories of the days before the war—simple Kodak pictures, such as you can make. These can help.

EASTMAN KODAK CO., ROCHESTER, N. Y.

THE WORLD'S LEADING MOVING PICTURE MAGAZINE

PHOTOPLAY

VOL. XIII   DECEMBER, 1917   NO. 1

The Happy Ending

*E*VERY *human action is based upon the desire for happiness.*
The baby cries for something it thinks will make it happy; the miser hoards his gold because he thinks it will make him happy.

Nowhere in the world is this desire more intense than in America. This continent, from its discovery, has been peopled by men and women who came to its shores believing happiness nearer of attainment under its free skies.

Americans believe happiness not merely desirable, but possible. Many have achieved it. It has become the national ideal.

Consequently, American art, to reach the hearts of Americans, must be happy art. Good must triumph over evil. Love must find a way.

Hence — the happy ending.

The moving picture, coming closer to the millions than any other form of art, was quick to reflect the universal demand. Creators of the photoplay soon learned that their work succeeded best when it depicted happiness resulting from some sort of struggle.

In the older, European civilizations, the millions are not so certain of the fulfillment of the great desire. Battling for centuries, for the most part unsuccessfully, against oppression, their art has taken upon itself a tragic color. The European novel, painting, drama, and lately the cinema, is tinged with pessimism.

The American artist and author holds the European art traditions in highest reverence. And so it is, that upon the older forms he has endeavored to engraft the newer faith. He has not learned the technique of happy art.

This, and this alone, is why the happy endings of so many moving pictures seem banal and sentimental.

There is nothing wrong with the happy ending. The fault lies with the craftsman.

This, then, is the mandate of America to the photoplay — to exercise its high privilege and opportunity of making an art of happiness, and a happiness of art.

On "Active Duty" with

By K. Owen

LONG before Uncle Sam dipped into the European mess, a company of volunteer soldiers was organized in Hollywood, the capital of the Western film empire. Nearly all of the troopers were connected with the picture studios, actors, extra men, grips, electricians, cameramen, etc. They were known as the Seventeenth Company of the California Coast Artillery Corps.

When war against Germany was declared and there seemed a good chance of getting some real fighting to do, the company was swamped with applications. And they were federalized and sent to Fort MacArthur at Los Angeles Harbor and from there were despatched to Long Beach, Cal., for active duty, guarding the water front and the shipbuilding plants where submarines are being constructed for the navy.

The company is commanded by a former Lasky player, Captain Ted Duncan. Walter Long, the famous Griffith and Lasky heavy who played the chief villains in "The Birth of a Nation," "Intolerance," "The Little American" and other famous photoplays, is first lieutenant. Two of the sergeants are Tom Forman, one of the best juvenile leads in the films and for three years a Lasky favorite, and Ernie Shields, former Universal leading man.

Among the privates in the company who joined when war was declared is James Harrison, erstwhile American and Fine Arts juvenile and later in Christie Comedies. Jimmie will be remembered for his portrayal of the ukulele playing fellah in "Madam Bo Peep," the last of the Fine Arts pictures.

There have been so many inquiries about the boys now with the colors that PHOTOPLAY asked its staff photographer, Raymond Stagg, to visit the camp at Long Beach and "get" the boys.

Sergeant Tom Forman looks 'em over. From his inscrutable countenance it's hard telling whether it's an auto load of alien enemies he's giving the once over, or a load of visiting film actresses.

When there is nothing else to do, Lieutenant Walter Long takes some of his reformed actors out and shows them how to dig trenches. That's the Lieutenant with the map. At his right is Sergeant Tom Forman, at his left Sergeant Ernie Shields. Private Jimmie Harrison is the busy little fellow with the spade in the foreground.

Left: Lieut. Long at revolver practice.

Private Harrison in the trenches.

Right: Private Harrison "walking post" and keeping an eye out for suspicious characters.

Center: "Signal Drill" in quarters. Sergeant Forman has just misread a signal and his partner, Private Harrison has lost a trick. Lieut. Long is seeing to it that the drill is properly conducted according to the Articles of War and the Hoyle book of tactics.
Below: Sergeant Shields beginning a "fade out" in his mosquito proof apartment.

"You wouldn't believe it" says Jimmie, "but this is just as much fun as playing a ukulele if you have a good washboard and warm water.

Chaplin's New Contract

Charles Chaplin and Mildred Harris, from a photograph made six days before their late October wedding. At this time the comedian was having an outing on Catalina Island after finishing "Shoulder Arms."

from a burning block house. For this, I was given ten dollars a day when I worked."

She made two pictures for Vitagraph and then joined Thomas Ince at "Ince-ville" in the Santa Monica canyon. Here, her salary was $25.00 a week and all her days were taken up with Indian fights and rides down bumpy roads in "prairie schooners." Afterwards, she was featured in a series of child pictures. Before starting in moving picture work, she went to a dramatic school for two years. She had wanted to go on the stage since she was three years old. Now, at eighteen, and a star, she is still stage struck. This does not mean that she is uninterested in her work. On the contrary, she has expended

Stagg

M ILDRED HARRIS, today, is the most fortunate young woman in the world. At least several million fannettes think so.

Charles Chaplin is the world's premier buffoon. But his portraits, without the mustache, have caused no end of feminine heart fluttering. So when the rumor of his marriage to Mildred Harris was confirmed, half the feminine population of this and other countries vowed that their hearts were broken —and immediately went out to see Mildred Harris, now Mrs. Charles Chaplin, in her latest picture.

To say nothing of the Harris devotees, whose hopes were smashed at the announcements of the Chaplin nuptials, and who bitterly resolved never to laugh at Chaplin again.

Mildred Harris is only eighteen years old. She grew up with the movies. She is the first real product of the studios, the first child actress to grow up to play big dramatic roles. What is more fitting than that she should become the bride of the greatest personality the screen has produced?

She likes ice-cream and Chaplin extra special fruit cocktails —(you make them with pineapple and watermelon and a berry or two)—and Worcestershire sauce flavored with a little steak; all of which, a psychologist might say, goes to show that she is very girlish—like ice cream—very naive, and sometimes poses a little in a very natural and entirely pretty way, like a fruit cocktail, and likes to be startling, like Worcestershire sauce.

Once when Charles Chaplin announced that he was going to make seven more pictures and then leave the screen, she is said to have remarked, thoughtfully, "Then you'll be on the screen for seven more years, won't you, Mr. Chaplin?"

Mildred has been in pictures for about six years, starting in when she was eleven. Her first picture was made with the Western Vitagraph and was called "How States are Made."

"I was chased by Indians," she said, "and, I think, rescued

The future Mrs. Chaplin in her first picture engagement, with 101 Bison. She was twelve years old at the time. But all of this was many, many years ago — to be exact, five.

*e has signed up with a woman,
e agreement is for life, and
e will go in for domestic drama*

By
Elizabeth Peltret

o much effort in reaching her present
ace in the film firmament to give it up
htly. But, naturally, she feels "the
re of the far away." She has spent
actically all her life in the studios
ound Los Angeles.

"I'd like to see the curtain go slowly
when there is a crowd of people out
ont and you don't know whether the
ay is good or bad," she said, "I'd like to
ar applause and, most of all, I'd like to
e New York; the greatest regret of my
e is that I've never seen New York."

Once, when she was with Majestic-
eliance, Douglas Fairbanks volunteered
take her to New York as a member of
s company. It was the happiest moment
her life. She went home, packed up,

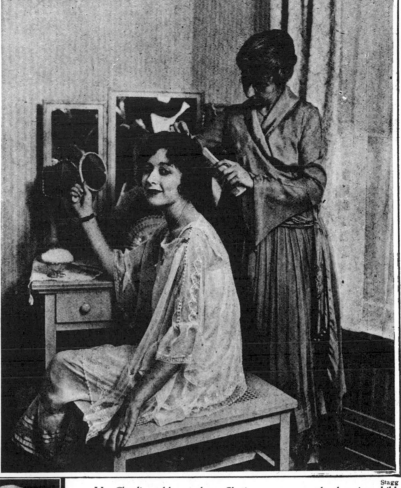

Stagg

Mrs. Chaplin and her mother. She is, as you see, a rather luxurious child, and cultivates the feminine arts of lingerie or lounging most enthusiastically.

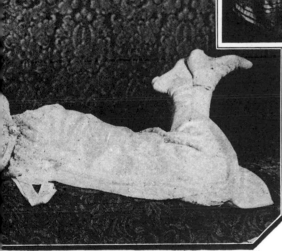

A year after her
Bison days she
joined Kay Bee,
and played var-
ious child and
little girl parts.
This photograph
was taken about
the time she first
attracted Mr.
Griffith's atten-
tion.

Witzel

and then went back to tell Frank Woods, the studio manager.

"Don't you know that you can't leave this studio without Mr. Griffith's permission?" he said, sternly. Mr. Griffith was in the East, somewhere. When they finally located him, he said that she could not go until she had made one more picture —"The Bad Boy"—with Robert Harron. The result was that she never did go; ("That was the greatest disappointment of my life!") Her eyes fill with tears when she mentions it now.

She speaks very quietly. Perhaps the most noticeable thing about her is her perfect poise. She was sitting in a chair of some dark wood the high curved back of which formed a sort of oval frame for her face. She is very lovely—but every-one knows that. Her eyes and hair are brown; her hair has golden glints in it; and her skin is very soft and fair.

From "Inceville" she went to D. W. Griffith's studio where she did little else but rehearse under Griffith and appear briefly in "Intolerance."

Some of the pictures in which she appeared were "Old Folks at Home," with Sir Herbert Beerbohm Tree, and "Enoch Ar-den." She is now with Lois Weber. Her later pictures are "The Price of a Good Time," "The Doctor and the Woman," "The Man Who Dared God," "For Husbands Only," and "The Forbidden Box" and "Borrowed Clothes."

She became the bride of Chaplin when she was not quite eighteen. (She was born in Cheyenne, Wyo., on Thanksgiving Day, 1901.) She married Chaplin on October 23. They en-deavored to keep the marriage a secret by continuing their work as usual—Mildred reported the next day to the Universal studios, and Chaplin to his own Hollywood plant, where he makes comedies for First National. To reporters they denied it emphatically. Mildred is quoted as saying, "I'm not married. I don't want to be married for quite awhile. And anyway, I won't marry until I've seen New York."

But she changed her mind.

Anna Held is Dead!

A biographical note on the French-woman who began her remarkable career as a child singer in Paris streets.

ANNA HELD died in New York August 12th, after a seven-months' battle against pernicious anaemia. She was forty-five years old.

Only women like Bernhardt, Lillian Russell and Mary Pickford have so completely gained the attention of the American people. Anna Held was more than a talented Frenchwoman, or a mere comedienne; she was a national figure.

Her first celebrity, here, was of a daring sort. It was born of her world-famous song hit, "Won't you come and play wiz me?" and the flirtatious use of the singer's eyes as an accompaniment. Anna Held quickly became the most brilliant personage among the *figurantes* of beauty and laughter on the metropolitan boards; and to the outlands, the last word in a risque playgoing adventure when "seeing New York."

But as the years went on, and her popularity remained, other qualities than stage abandon and personal charm be-

White

Anna Held and a good view of her eyes, made famous through her song "Won't You Come and Play Wiz Me?" At lower left—a scene from her only photoplay appearance "Madame La Presidente."

gan to be recognized. Her private career was exemplary. She was a woman, not only of culture, but of far sight where all stage matters were concerned, a keen insight into what the public wanted, and not a little practical business ability.

Married to F. Ziegfeld, Jr., she was instrumental in shaping his early career, and there are some who claim that it was Miss Held who inspired his distinct and successful line of showmanship as manifested year after year, now, in the annual Ziegfeld "Follies." Married in 1897, they were divorced in 1913. She did not marry again. He married Billie Burke. Miss Held's friends say that "Flo" was the one love of her life, and that she never forgot.

In all the later part of her life Miss Held was renowned for her charities, and for her sensible, practical advice to young girls on the stage, scores of whom actually looked to her as a mother.

Plays and Players

Facts and Near-Facts About the Great and Near-Great of Filmland

By CAL YORK

WELL the draft has done its worst. It has singled out Wallie Reid, Charley Ray, George Walsh, and Irving Cummings. The last named was about the only film player of prominence drafted in the East. It was in the West where most of the damage was done. At this time it is impossible to state whether or not Wallie and George will be called out to do real fighting as each is possessed of a wife and child, while Ray and Cummings are supplied with a wife each. Although each has a wife who is a professional and may be adjudged capable of supporting themselves and children. Reid is married to Dorothy Davenport and Walsh to Seena Owen. It would be an awful blow, however, to the feminine contingent of the great army of film hero worshipers should the quartet be taken. Of course they would still have J. Warren Kerrigan and Harold Lockwood who escaped the draft and Francis X. Bushman, who wasn't in danger at any time.

THE comedy studios of the West Coast were hit particularly hard, although Charley Chaplin was not among those called who will form the first army. Jay Belasco and James Harrison, leading men in Christie Comedies were selected among the first. At Fox's, Victor Potel, the "Slippery Slim" of old Essanay days and Director Charles Parrot saw their names posted early on draft day. At Keystone, Business Manager George Stout was drawn and at L-KO, Director General Jack G. Blystone was in the first thousand. At Universal City William Franey and Milton Sims, comedians led the list followed by Directors Craig Hutchinson and George Marshall. Francis McDonald, husband of Mae Busch, Lloyd Whitlock and J. Webster Dill of the dramatic branch of the Big U. Bud Duncan, junior member of the former comedy firm of Ham & Bud, also felt the draft early in the day. Horsley's studio offered Comedian Neal Burns and his director Horace Davey.

LASKY'S studio was hit the hardest. In addition to Wallie Reid, several minor players and a number of technical employees were drafted. Roy Marshall, assistant to Marshall Neilan, Mary Pickford's director and Lucian Littlefield, well known young character actor, were among

Marjorie Daw, caught in the act of "coming back". This popular little player who gained international fame as the protege of Geraldine Farrar when the diva made her motion picture debut at the Lasky studio, has been absent from the studio for many months as she has been devoting her time to studies. She returned to the screen, however, in support of Sessue Hayakawa in a recent Paramount Picture.

them. Littlefield didn't wait for the draft. He left a month previously for France with the Pasadena Ambulance unit. Tom Forman, also a well known Laskyite, likewise declined to wait for the draft and joined the Seventeenth Company of Coast Artillery which is composed almost wholly of motion picture men. Triangle will contribute Lynn F. Reynolds, recently acquired from Universal where he won distinction as a Bluebird director. Victor Fleming cameraman in Douglas Fairbanks' company resigned to join the colors as soon as he saw his name among those drawn and Pliny Goodfriend, Vitagraph cameraman and husband of Mary Anderson, will also take the trip abroad.

MAE MURRAY is now a Bluebird star. The little blonde deserted Lasky several months ago and her director Bob Leonard quit at the same time. He will continue as her director at Universal City.

TRIANGLE, now running full speed ahead with H. O. Davis, erstwhile boss of Univeral City, at the throttle, has been despoiling the latter concern of some of its best known stars. Ruth Stonehouse, Ella Hall, Roy Stewart are among the players and Lynn Reynolds and Jack Conway head the directors who made the switch.

ADMIRERS of the little French comedian will be pleased to learn that Max Linder has so far recovered that he is contemplating a comeback to the screen sometime in November. He recently left the sanitarium in Southern California to which he was removed when he collapsed while making comedies for Essanay.

DW. GRIFFITH has completed one of his war pictures made on the battlefields of Europe and is now working on the second one, according to words from London. He had planned to return home after one picture but decided to do at least one more. It is understood that neither will be completed until the return to America as scenes are to be made on this side. Robert Harron and the Gish sisters, Lillian and Dorothy, have the principal parts in the pictures.

NO little surprise was caused in studio circles last month when it became known that Geraldine Farrar would

Plays and Players

leave Lasky's at the termination of her contract which has been in existence three years. Miss Farrar has just completed her fourth photoplay, a spectacular DeMille production based on the Spanish conquest of Mexico, and she is now engaged on a modern film play. Lou-Tellegen, husband of Miss Farrar, who had a brief career as a Lasky director, will appear with Miss Farrar in her new productions, according to report.

WANDA PETIT, one of the prettiest of Fox ingenues, has transferred her affections, and likewise her baggage from Fort Lee to Hollywood. She will probably be seen opposite George Walsh if that hirsute gentleman manages to retain his civilianship.

REGINALD BARKER who has been making pictures with Thos. H. Ince for a period dating about three years before Billie Burke and her pajamas appeared at Inceville, and who made the first Triangle picture "The Coward" has deserted both Triangle and Ince. He is now a member of the Paralta Company's directing forces and his first picture will be a picturization of Harold McGrath's book "Madame Who." Bessie Barriscale will be the star.

CLARA WILLIAMS has also packed her bandanna handkerchiefs, ear-rings, riding habits and her famous forty ball room frocks and left Triangle for Paralta. Clara made quite a hit recently by her rendition of the old military song, "You're in the Army Now," for the enlisted men at the Presidio, San Francisco.

JIMMY YOUNG has settled down on the Coast once more and has become a regular member of the studio colony. He attends the fights at Jack Doyle's arena every Tuesday, competes in all the fox-trot contests and has issued an open challenge to wrestle "Bull" Montana "Doug" Fairbank's athletic trainer. That is the result of having too much time on his hands; Jimmy only works at directing pictures 18 hours a day.

NORMA TALMADGE has a new director. He is Charles Miller who sprang into sudden prominence by virtue of the really remarkable picture "The Flame of

Meet Mr. Montezuma, who was some pumpkins in his day. It is Raymond Hatton at his old job of kinging in Geraldine Farrar's new picture of Aztec days—you know, when they had so much gold they used to make automobiles out of it.

the Yukon" with Dorothy Dalton. Miller is a nephew of Henry Miller and before entering upon motion picture work was an actor and stage director of prominence.

HOW the years fly by. Why it seems as if it were yesterday that Theodore Roberts won the tennis championship of the Alimony Club at the Ludlow St. Jail and now we find after one day's military drill at the Lasky Studio he became so exhausted he had to be carried home. He has just returned to work after a month on the sick list.

MOLLY MALONE has married a minister's son. Now comes the question: If a motion picture studio is no place for a minister's son, how about a minister's son's wife? Molly says no matter what the answer is she is going to stay at Universal City and continue to act before the camera. The smiling, trusting and courageous young man who stepped up to the altar with Molly is Forrest Cornett, the son of the Rev. W. H. Cornett of the First Presbyterian Church of Venice, California. Mrs. Forrest Cornett is 20 years of age and her husband is one year older.

They made quite an occasion of it when Elsie Ferguson arrived at Fort Lee for her first day's screen work. Director Tourneur was right out in front to open the limousine door, and that's going some for a high-priced director. Yes, of course she knew her picture was being taken.

NAZIMOVA

See her in "Revelation"
See her in "Toys of Fate"
See her in "Eye for Eye"
See her in "Out of the Fog"
and soon in

THE RED LANTERN

Then tell us who is the really
great artist of the Screen

NAZIMOVA PRODUCTIONS

METRO

NEW YORK   PICTURES CORPORATION   LOS ANGELES

MAXWELL KARGER *Director General*

Clothes

SOME NEW *AND*
CHARMING COSTUMES
DESIGNED *FOR*
MARY PICKFORD

*Posed exclusively for
Photoplay Magazine*

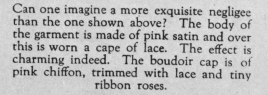

Can one imagine a more exquisite negligee
than the one shown above? The body of
the garment is made of pink satin and over
this is worn a cape of lace. The effect is
charming indeed. The boudoir cap is of
pink chiffon, trimmed with lace and tiny
ribbon roses.

Magnificent, is the word which best describes the gorgeous robe of Royal ermine
shown at the right. Hundreds of skins
perfectly matched were used in the making.
It is lined with pink brocaded satin. The
hair ornament, so becomingly worn by
Miss Pickford, was designed by Lucille.
It is made entirely of ribbons, lavender,
pink and gold.

(Above) Quite wonderful is this little evening gown of white net, trimmed daintily with rows and rows of ruffles. At the waistline a touch of color is supplied by a narrow band of blue ribbon and a spray of pink and blue roses. The shoulder straps are fashioned of iridescent beads.

At the right, a Madame Frances gown suitable for informal evening wear. The material chosen was soft, pink taffeta; the trimming, fluted ruffles. The yoke is of flesh-colored chiffon, and a pleasing color contrast is made in the girdle, of Alice blue velvet.

It would be hard to find a lovelier frock for summer afternoons than the one shown above. It is of sheer white organdie effectively trimmed with wide lace insertions and little groups of daisies. The hat worn with this dainty dress is also of organdie, a bit uncertain of line and trimmed simply with pale blue satin ribbon.

Stagg

THE sunny-haired Gish, snapped at her South Serrano street home in Los Angeles, is appearing on the celluloid in "The Greatest Thing in Life" (Griffith-Artcraft), in which we would say Lillian assumed the title role.

DOUGLAS FAIRBANKS' *Own* PAGE

IF YOU are familiar with baseball—and the chances are nine in ten that you are—you know the meaning of the expression, "the breaks of the game." Given two baseball teams of equal strength, victory will invariably perch on the banner of the side which "gets the breaks."

It's much the same on the stage or in business. Many a good player has been sedulously avoided by whatever fate it is that deals out fame, because the "breaks" have been against him. Conversely, many a mediocre—or even worse—player has tasted all the fruits of victory because he "got the breaks," as they say on the diamond. But don't think I'm going to classify myself, because I'm not. Give it any name you like—even modesty.

Just where I would have wound up had it not been for a strange quirk of fate, of course no one can tell, but it was the misfortune of a fellow player that gave me the big chance I was looking for. Perhaps it was an indiscretion rather than a misfortune. But whatever it was, the victim of the circumstance found himself in jail on the day we were scheduled to treat the natives of Duluth, Minn., to a rendition of "Hamlet."

Now I'm not going to tell you how the star couldn't show up and I stepped into the breach and soliloquoyed all over the stage to the thunderous applause of the Northmen; that would be too conventional. Strangely enough I hadn't set my sights that high. But I *did* want to play Laertes and my colleague having run afoul of some offense which was the subject of a chapter of the Minnesota Penal Code, I played it that night.

Well to make a long story short, I played the part so well that it only took about ten years more to become a star on Broadway, the ultimate goal of all who choose the way of the footlights. Seriously, however, that was my chance and I took full advantage of it. In succeeding articles I will tell more about the climb to the top.

Perhaps the greatest pleasure I get out of my work for the screen is contained in the daily mail bag. And from time to time, I intend on this page to refer to some of the most interesting letters that come to me from all over the country—not only this country, but from such far off places

"Doug" and His *Highest* Honor

You'd never know this was a scene from a christening, would you? "Doug" has just had a mountain named after him and is registering appreciation in his characteristic manner. D. G. Desmond was the United States Government's official godfather, and the christening took place while the Fairbanks Artcraft picture, "Down to Earth" was being filmed. Douglas Fairbanks' Peak is one of the most picturesque of the steep granite crowns that dot the Yosemite Valley. There is a comfortable hotel on its summit where visitors take the stage for the trip to the Big Trees.

as Australia. By the way, I believe they are more enthusiastic over the screen in the Antipodes than they are in this country, proportionately speaking.

One of the most frequent questions I am asked to answer is that relating to success in athletics.

It may sound strange to some of those who have been following my work on the screen, but I was a failure as an athlete. In college at the Colorado School of Mines I did not excel in any particular branch of sports. I went in for nearly everything, but the student body never wrote or sang any songs about me. I never came up in the ninth with the score three to nothing against us, with three men on base and put the ball over the fence. I never even ran the length of the whole field with the pigskin and scored the winning touchdown with only fifteen seconds of play left.

Then when I went to Harvard later I still was active in athletics but while just about able to get by in most of the games, I never got the spotlight in any specific instances. It might have been different had I remained, but the call of the footlights was too insistent.

There is one rule which every athlete must follow to be successful. Be clean in mind and body. For a starter, I know of no better advice.

I am not much given to preaching, but if I ever took it up as a vocation, I would preach cleanliness first and most.

The boy who wishes to get to the front in athletics must adopt a program of mental and bodily cleanliness.

Perhaps the greatest foe to athletic success, among young college men is strong drink. Personally I have never tasted liquor of any sort.

It was my mother's influence that was responsible for that as I promised her when I was eight years old that I would never drink. I might state, parenthetically and without violating a confidence, that my family tree had several decorations consisting of ambitious men who had sought valiantly, if futilely, to decrease the visible supply of liquor. I do not wish to take a great amount of credit for my abstention. Really, more credit is due the person who has fallen under its influence and fought his way out; but I know that the keeping of this promise has had a powerful effect on my life and my career.

A PHOTO INTERVIEW *with* DOUGLAS FAIRBANKS

By Alfred A. Cohn

Let's Go!

"Are you set, Al?" said Mr. Fairbanks.

"Yup!" answered Mr. Cohn.

"Aw-right; start your pencil."

"I believe that the motion picture industry has a wonderful future. I like it particularly because it keeps one out in the open."

"If it's all the same to you, let's stroll around the lot; I can talk better in motion. We won't waste any time going around to the stairs".

A Pair of Suspenders "As an art, the photoplay has not begun to come into its full fruition. More and more the public, now initiated into many of the mysteries of cameraland, demands not only artistic photography but suspense and surprise; and a good seasoning of comedy".

"Just drop easy-like. Nothing can happen that a bottle of arnica won't fix".

Look Out Below! "The chief difficulty these days is the lack of suitable stories, although half the world is writing so-called scenarios".

"Now let's hike over to the Subway".

5745 Minutes from Broadway "California offers exceptional opportunities to the producer of photoplays. (Los Angeles papers please copy.) Every conceivable locale in the world can be duplicated here, and so forth. We loll in Venetian gondolas or take the subway for Harlem, 3500 miles away".

Drawing by D. Fairbanks. "In this game of life the fortunate ride" (Hear! Hear!) "at the expense of the less fortunate. The big idea is to do it cheerfully no matter how humble the task".

Steady: On the Right!
"What we, as a nation, need most these days, is more balance—more poise. We Americans are too susceptible to panic and hysteria, particularly in a time when absolute balance is required".

"Let's take a spin in the little old boat—got ninety out of her yesterday out in the country—and go for a swim up in my back yard. Got a lot more to tell you and a swim would put you in shape for it".

They're Off at Hollywood! "Another great fault with us, as a people, is our insatiable demand for speed. We want it everywhere—we even dine too rapidly because of our fear that we will miss something somewhere. Why can't people take it easy? Speed merely serves to speed the end of existence. Funny I can't get more than 80 out of her today".

The Ole Swimmin' Hole. "What do I think of the future of the moving pictures? Well, I think none of us can visualize it. In a few years—as a matter of fact the industry is now merely in its infan—" "Better look back and see if I didn't say that once before." "According to the rules, it goes only once in an interview. Some pool, isn't it? Had it built to save beach trips".

At the End of the Rope

"Good cheer and real companionship do not come in bottles and the door to fame is never swung on double hinges." "Gee, Billy Sunday couldn't do better than that, could he? And talking about Billy—"

A Sunday Stunt on Saturday

"The man with a message for the world will get it over if he is earnest and conscientious, and can impress his sincerity on those who listen." "It's mighty handy to have a press agent and a valet around (standing, left to right); one can always be sure of their enthusiastic applause at the right time".

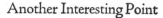

Another Interesting Point

"I aim to have some real purpose, some theme behind each photoplay I produce; not a lesson conveyed in some conventional way but with a coating of sugar as it were, over it."

"Come on over. These are only wooden spikes anyhow and couldn't hurt much".

Off (or over) To the Front

"There is a fallacious belief that pull is required to make a success on the shadow stage. That belief is rapidly being—"

"Don't holler or you'll drop the pencil. Beyond this shack lies Flanders".

PETITS CHAUD 2 FOIS PAR JOUR

EPICERIE

In the Wake of the Boches

"With many who get up in the world, the big problem, though they do not realize it, is to get down again—down to the level of the man who views life—"

"Now don't get nervous. The bombardment is over and these Belgian buildings are sturdy affairs. It won't fall unless I shake it".

268

The End of a Perfect Day

"As I was saying, when you fell, life is just a game of give and take and—"

"Call up the Receiving Hospital, Naka, after we slide him in, I want to go a few rounds with Spike".

All They Say Is: "See Our Lawyer!"

*Photograph
by Stagg*

DOUG and Mary and David Wark and Charlie. Read it the other way and it will be just as impressive: Charlie and David Wark and Mary and Doug.

We wonder if the nonchalant geranium and the darned old bench realize that they are having their picture taken in company with the most universal (no apologies to Carl Laemmle) amusement quartet ever drawn together?

The secession of Bill Hart from the Big Five left this Big Four. They haven't announced very many plans yet, except to assert that their "United Artists' Distributing Association" will begin to print from worth-their-weight-in-platinum negatives as soon as various and sundry existing contracts are finished. For the rest—consult their lawyer, Mr. McAdoo.

This is the first really large job William Gibbs McAdoo has had on his hands. He was, for a spell, director-general of the railroads of the whole country, and Treasurer of the United States, but the railroads and the treasury were at best only a two-star combination, whereas now he has four.

It seems that one learns the moving picture business pretty fast in California. In November Carl Laemmle offered Mr. McAdoo the directorship of Universal, at a salary of $50,000 a year, to which Mr. McAdoo replied in his letter of declination: "I doubt my qualifications for the position you offer." And he went on to say, plainly, that he knew nothing of the making of pictures. Further, he intended to come to New York to practice law. But then, you see, Mr. McAdoo moved to the artistically infectious Coast and it's all different now. His salary with the Mammoth Quartet may reach a quarter of a million a year, in place of the measly fifty thousand he declined when he didn't know anything about the motion picture business.

Following the stellar injunction, we will permit the Big Four's lawyer to speak for them. He says: "They have determined not to permit any trust to destroy competition, or to blight or to interfere with the high quality of their work. They feel that it is of the utmost importance to secure the artistic development of the motion picture industry, and they believe that this will be impossible if any trust should get possession of the field and menace the business."

This one was so funny it will probably go on the screen because the rehearsal got such a laugh. No one was shot as Roscoe interrupted the feud by "crowning" Buster with the bottle.

Fatty thought this would be much funnier if they reversed the order and had him at the top. His motion was beaten two to one.

"Cummon, it's time to get to work," says Buster Keaton. Buster is the keeper of a wild west dance hall and gambling house and Roscoe is his drink dispenser. Buster's watch, it will be seen, is equipped with skid chains.

Fatty Arbuckle

HEREWITH is presented a bunch of "gags" that you probably won't see on the screen. They are merely being tried out to see if they're funny— if they can "get a laugh."

What is a "gag"?

Why, a "gag" is a bit of "business"—a situation, that will shake a laugh out of the casual looker, because of its incongruity, its abrupt contrast, or its physical humor. It may be a subtle piece of work or a sudden bit of rough stuff.

Now comedy making is largely inspirational. Most of the "gags" are evolved on the scene, so that the "writing" of the vehicle is largely a matter of physical experimentation.

Many times the screen comedian keeps his entire company on the set for hours, just to provide him with the atmosphere necessary to work out his "gags."

"The gag's the thing" is the gospel of the makers of slapstick comedy. And very often when the "gags" are coming good, the plot—if there happens to be one—is tossed into the scrap heap to make room for the "gags."

Roscoe Arbuckle, like Charlie Chaplin, likes to dope out his funny stunts right in front of the camera, even if it is not in operation, but "Fatty" is more generous with his footage so far as his colleagues are concerned—he lets them "get" the laugh if it improves the completed product.

Photograph by Stagg

"Now this is an old gag, but we'll try to get a new angle on it. When I swing Al ducks and Buster gets the broom on the jaw. We'll try it once—"

The way it worked.

DANCE WITH ONE WOMAN AT A TIME

This picture is defective in only one particular — it doesn't show Buster's banjo. It might be entitled "When—and why—the jazz band stopped playing." The Salvation Army lass is Alice Lake, Fatty's leading lady.

Whenever we see a pergola we think of what the rich old lady from Iowa said to the architect who
one of those things. She answered; "No, sir! I like tea as well as anybody—but I ain't a Russian

Above, a view through
the sitting room and the
dining room, taken from
the drawing room. The
sun-dial at the right, is,
according to its owner's
declaration, one of the
absolute necessities of her
domestic happiness.

Fannie Ward's

A NUMBER of motion picture women have
larger incomes than Fannie Ward, but she is
the only one of her kind, so far, to manifest
the possession of a generous independence in the
European fashion of a thoroughly imposing establishment. Miss Ward's handsome house in Hollywood—
previously half-toned in these pages—was a sumptuous residence, but it, and especially its grounds, are
not to be compared with her new home and its artistic
gardens at 255 South New Hampshire street, Los
Angeles. Only Julian Eltinge's Italian palace can beat
it as a regal dwelling. Fannie Ward's love of a fine
house is not the frantic determination of a newly-rich
ingenue to put it over her neighbors and associates.

Her theatrical career was crowned with
complete artistic and financial success
abroad before "abroad" blew to pieces;
hence her well-paid movie career has
merely meant the realization of long-
cherished dreams.

The sunken garden and
the marble balcony over-
looking it. Directly be-
neath this balcony is the
garden's tenderest inhab-
itant, a huge-leaved
banana plant, so suscept-
ble to slight cold that few
of them endure even in
the mild airs of California.

Napoleon used to sleep in this bed—when it belonged to his Empress, Josephine. Miss Ward purchased it in Paris for 75,000 francs.

asked her if her projected home would have
and I make it in a plain, old-fashioned tea-pot."

New Home

Excepting Julian Eltinge's Italian palace the most sumptuous photoplayer's domicile in the world.

At the foot of the marble stairs leading to the terrace and the sunken garden. These steps are a replica of a flight belonging to a villa in Florence.

Miss Ward in her study, whose wide portiered doors, as you see, open into her own simple sleeping apartment.

Marcia Manon, one of the three extra girls at Lasky's who, out of thousands of aspirants, have become established in "stock," which means their pay check is regular.

What Every Girl

In the last year thousands have striven and a million have yearned for motion picture success. Yet not the twinkle of one new star has been seen. This story likely explains it. Perhaps it also tells what you—young lady—have been wondering.

covered in the film firmament in the past twelve months—not one aspiring becurled or marcelled beauty has fought or cajoled her way into the spotlight's beam. Yet thousands have striven.

Truly the trail of film stardom is a long one and it is white with the bleached bones (almost said hair) of blasted hopes.

The stars of today, for the most part, have been recruited from the stage, or have worked their way up through the

MUCH has been written in recent years about the relative chances of attaining film success. It has been a popular subject with some 23,456,112 young women (according to the U. S. Census Bureau) residing within the boundaries of this nation who are properly qualified,—as to age,—for a screen career.

Much will be written in the future on the same fascinating subject, no doubt; but each subsequent writer if he has any regard for the verities, will be increasingly discouraging to the aspiring feminine youth of the land.

Of course not all of the 23,456,112 properly-qualified-as-to-age young women yearn to see themselves as they see their favorite stars—probably not more than 23,456,000 aspire to gaze on their shadowed counterparts. It's nothing to be ashamed of; in fact it is a very laudable ambition. In passing we might credit the screen with administering a knockout to the old fashioned temptation of pre-film days. The girl of today, as compared with her sister of preceding generations, has it "on" the latter from relish to roquefort, as it were, when it comes to having something for which to wish and dream and work. It is a golden lighted road to fame and fortune that had a dim counterpart yesterday in the way to stage success.

As indicated in the foregoing the desire for screen fame is not only laudable but it has been a source of beneficent advantage to the girlhood of the nation. Obviously, therefore, it would be in the same degree injurious to our best interests to discourage that ambition.

So the writer disclaims any intention of bringing sorrow to these millions of potential film stars in endeavoring to set forth existing conditions. Every one of them has a chance to be a Mary Pickford or a Norma Talmadge, or a Theda Bara, if their aspirations take that direction, but—

How many new faces have you seen on the screen during the last year?

Not many, were there? And those could be counted on the fingers of one hand.

Yet there were millions who aspired and thousands who actually tried.

By new faces, of course I do not refer to the girls who play "atmosphere" or bits that are just barely visible to the naked eye. Yet even in these humble places the new face is a rarity.

As to new stars not one new twinkle has been dis-

Many of the society "extras" posing in New York and Los Angeles studios lookout for the sort of young woman who can walk through a drawing

Wants to Know

By

ALFRED A. COHN

various strata of studio drudgery. There are those too who, just glided into stardom through the easily swung door of the early days of filmdom—just pretty girls to begin with, who developed as the business grew from store-show to the million dollar theater.

But even the number of this latter class has dwindled steadily. The fittest, only, have survived.

There are scores—perhaps thousands of possible stars who may never have an opportunity of exhibiting their beauty or talent. Geographically, screendom's limitations are even more restricted than the stage's. The girl in Salt Lake or Louisville or Pittsburgh who had histrionic ability found an

are young women of means and breeding. Producers are always on the room without spilling the statuary or doing a keystone over a bookcase.

outlet in the local stock companies—and still does for that matter; though the aspirant of the smaller town is deprived now of the opportunities provided by the one-week-stand-repertoire company. The screen has completely ousted the old "rep" show.

The girl who would be a film star must either go to New York or to Los Angeles; the latter preferably as something like 85 per cent of the world's "visible" supply of celluloid is prepared in that city and its environs,

Then what chance has she when she gets there?

If she is one in a million or two, she may attain stardom—in a year or two.

But the girl who is just "pretty"—you know the kind whose friends tell her "My dear, you should be in the movies"—why she has about as much chance of "getting by" as Ole Hanson, the mayor of Seattle, has of being elected chief of the I. W. W.

The girl without experience who has been led to believe that stardom may be reached overnight is doomed to certain disappointment.

The producer of today not only cannot afford to experiment where stars are concerned, *he cannot even experiment in the assignment of small parts.*

On each round of the ladder to screen fame is stamped the word "experience."

There was a time when stars were made overnight, when favoritism figured largely but those were the days when only youthful, ingenuous beauty was demanded. Acting ability was not required, or even recognized. But of those stars, only they survived who had that rare gift designated as screen charm or personality, combined with adaptability and inherent talent.

Today, the first step forward of the aspirant is to "get by" the employment or casting director.

That gentleman knows all the symptoms. He looks at the applicant and he tells immediately whom she aspires to succeed. She invariably apes, in some manner, her film favorite—the Mary Pickford curls, Blanche Sweet's charming disarray of coiffure or the Theda Bara ear loops. They are as quickly dismissed as catalogued. The quickest passport out of a casting director's sanctum is a bunch of Pickford curls. The producer of today doesn't want another Pickford —he knows *it ain't.* Besides there couldn't be another one made because all the material required in making the existing and only Mary—the story material—has been exhausted. That is why Mary herself is now paying $40,000 for stories.

34

Says Mack Sennett, father of the pretty-girl-comedy: "There are girls, not specially beautiful, whom you could not lose in a crowd. There are other girls, apparently perfect in beauty, who seem to melt into insignificance."

The girl who would attract the attention of the employment czar must be unusually beautiful or a striking type—not just physically, but intelligently beautiful. She must have that same indefinable something that people call personality, or character. And she must know how to wear clothes because the employment man is more eager to get young women who can dress than he is to get stars. Anyhow he isn't on the lookout even for potential stars.

There really is a demand for girls who can, as one employment director put it, "look like ladies." They are always on the lookout for "class" in feminine apparel. By "class" he does not mean flashy or up-to-the-minute-in-style appearance— it's more a matter of carriage and the look of breeding—the sort of young woman who looks as though she could walk through a drawing-room without spilling the statuary or doing a Keystone fall over a bookcase.

It is a matter of record that most of the young women who are employed because of this "class" quality are of the class which are not "acting" when they play the lady. Many of the "atmospheres" in New York and Los Angeles are young women of means who "work" in the studios "just to be doing something." But for the sake of argument suppose they *were* dependent upon their studio work for their livelihood!

The pay for atmosphere varies. In ordinary "mob stuff" the pay is usually $3 per day. For this grade of employment there are no especial requirements. The next step is the "dress" or "society stuff" mentioned in the preceding paragraph. This pays $5 per day where the studio provides the gowns and $7.50 where the young woman furnishes her own wardrobe. Some studios prefer to supply the dresses.

The average employment of the extra girl is something like three days a week. Figure that out at $3, $5 or $7.50 and you can see the average earning of the girl who starts out on the road to fame via the celluloid route.

Despite the thousands who apply for admittance into the magic realm of the make-believes, few are selected even to play "atmosphere." The casting director in one of the largest Los Angeles studios told me that so far as his records had it there were only about sixty young women in Southern California who were available for "society stuff." He warned me also that if such a statement were published there would be

a mad dash to California of girls who just "thought" they knew how to wear clothes with a resultant call for more funds by the Y. W. C. A. to ship them back home.

Countless others will write to the various studios setting forth their accomplishments and perhaps enclosing their photographs. It may be of interest to this class to learn that casting directors never hire anyone as the result of a letter or a photographers' work or art. The still photograph, to him means little. Moving pictures cannot be retouched for the removal of blemishes or defects.

Nowadays the producer never comes into contact with the inexperienced applicant having shifted that burden to his casting director so that the latter having made a study of his studio's needs and the material to supply them is perhaps the best authority on the subject of the outside girl's chance to enter.

"It isn't so hard to get the chance if the girl has some quality of beauty or type which immediately enlists the attention of the employment man," says L. M. Goodstadt, casting director at the Lasky studio; "it's far more difficult to remain in. But the girl who leaves home to 'break into' motion pictures without any experience whatever has a hard row to hoe. I have watched hundreds, perhaps thousands of them, come and go and the best advice I can offer is for the pretty aspirant *to stay home unless she has enough money to provide for her wants for at least a year.*"

Of the thousands of girls who have entered the portals of the Lasky studio as extra girls during the five years of its existence and have been given a chance, only three of them have graduated to "stock" which word is synonomous with a weekly pay check. They are Marcia Manon who played so splendidly the character role in "Stella Maris" with Mary Pickford, Edna Mae Cooper and Julia Faye.

However, the Lasky studio is known as the most conservative of all the Coast film emporiums in taking a chance with new material.

Another girl who started in at Lasky's as "atmosphere," is Irene Rich who in less than a year became Dustin Farnum's leading lady at another studio. But she is a notable exception as is Katherine MacDonald whose natural beauty and inherent talent enabled her to skip all the usual preliminaries and jump into the limelight as a principal. She becomes a full-fledged

Photo by Witzel

Julia Faye is another of the three extra girls who entered the portals of the Lasky studio as an extra.

star in Hugh Ford's production of "The Woman Thou Gavest Me" recently completed at the Lasky studio. Miss MacDonald had the advantage however of some stage experience. It may be added incidentally that she is Mary MacLaren's elder sister. Another new face in important roles is that of Doris Lee who has been playing opposite Charles Ray in Ince pictures. Doris got her first chance as an extra girl less than two years ago doubling for Mary Pickford in "Rebecca of Sunnybrook Farm." Of the Universal stars Priscilla Dean and Ruth Clifford graduated from the extra benches at Universal City and Carmel Myers began as an extra girl at Griffith's studio. One could go back farther and enumerate many of the stars who began as bits of atmosphere but this article is dealing only with recent times in filmdom annals.

Not a few girls have entered the ranks of dramatic stars and leads via the comedy route. Screen comedy must have youth and beauty to offset its Ben Turpins and Mack Swains. Comedy does not demand intelligence or brains of its feminine beginners, yet the girl who smiles her way through the sacred portals of the fun canneries must have that same filmable quality hereinabove mentioned before she can rise above the $25 weekly pay check.

When asked about his views on the pretty girl question and what qualities she must possess to be successful, Mack Sennett, that connoisseur of feminine beauty said to the writer:

"The truth is, no one can tell with exactitude what it is in a girl's face that places her in the category of screen beauties.

Priscilla Dean began at Universal as an extra.

Photo by Witzel

"There are a few general rules, but they are about as general and as vague as the rules for the kind of man that makes a great writer.

"For instance, they say that a girl cannot screen well unless she has even well formed teeth; that wrinkles down the sides of her lips from the outer rim of the nostrils are fatal; that large animated eyes are essential; that a face should be round and soft of contour, etc.

"As a matter of fact, these rules mean very little. They mean just as little as any rule one could make as to what constitutes beauty off the screen.

Girls who believe screen success can be aided by an ability to dance will be interested to learn that whenever dancers are desired, experienced stage artists are available. The pupils of Ruth St. Denis' school have appeared in scores of productions and scores of musical companies have been used in pictures dealing with the stage.

"As a general thing a horse with three legs isn't likely to win many derbies; but the possession of four legs doesn't imply that they are derby winners either.

"There are certain defects that a girl must not have; but the lack of these defects is no sign that she has that mysterious something else that makes for personality on the screen.

"There are girls, not specially beautiful, whom you could not lose in a crowd; they would stand out from any number. There are other girls, seemingly perfect in beauty, who seem to melt into insignificance. What they lack cannot be put into words."

Yet it has been said that inasmuch as screen comedy has to do largely with bathing or athletic suits of smallish dimensions, the demand for beauty in the laugh foundries is largely a matter of form.

There is a large class of girls scattered throughout our forty-eight states and the District of Columbia as well as places not contiguous to us, who believe that the way into the movies would be easier for them because they are good dancers or riders or something else that calls for exceptional ability. It would interest them to learn that whenever dancers are desired experienced stage artists are available for picture purposes. The pupils of Ruth St. Denis' school have appeared in scores of productions and the choruses of musical comedy shows have been utilized for pictures dealing with the stage.

Perhaps no individual is in closer touch with the situation as affecting the girl aspirant to movie honors than Miss Edna Harris, Y. W. C. A. secretary in charge of the Hollywood Girls' Studio Club, one of the most novel organizations in the country where star and extra girl mingle on even footing, and the refuge of the struggling aspirant who has learned her fate at about the same time that her available funds have been exhausted.

"If the movie-struck girl could foresee just a bit of the hard road to success as a film player, she would hesitate a long time before leaving home," says Miss Harris, who is a graduate of Northwestern University and an experienced social service worker.

"Girls have come to Los Angeles with just enough money to make the trip. They are usually the most difficult to convince that they are not fitted for the screen and inevitably we must obtain positions for them in other lines or get them back to their homes. The employment directors of the various studios are splendid and are always willing to help us with the girls who are badly in need of work but they are in a highly organized business and not a philanthropic work. It is a hard game even for the girl who comes prepared for a long and arduous artistic siege."

35

Announcement *of* Winners
Film Corporation

*Two of the four prize winners are
now being made into photoplays*

H. O. Davis, vice-president and general manager of the Triangle Film Corporation.

WE offer our heartiest congratulations to the winners of the prizes in the PHOTOPLAY MAGAZINE-Triangle Film Corporation scenario contest.

Over 7,000 scenarios were submitted in this contest, and we hardly need to say how prodigious has been the task of selecting from these 7,000 the four that were best. But Mr. H. O. Davis, vice-president and general manager of the Triangle Film Corporation, has made good on his promise to give us the news for this issue, working overtime to do it. Everything has come by means of telegrams as there wasn't time to wait for the mails. The magazine is going to press as this article is being written and for that reason we can't tell you very much this month about the prize winners. We'll give you what we have learned at the last minute, and next month we'll try to do better.

Mrs. Kate Corbaley, who wins the first prize of $1,000, is the wife of a successful construction engineer, and the mother of four beautiful children. Although she lives in

Los Angeles, the world's film capital, Mrs. Corbaley has never been in a motion picture studio, nor has she ever met a player. So you see, any sort of initiation is not essential to success, for Mrs. Corbaley has sold several comedies to the Sidney Drews although she has only been trying to write scenarios for a year and a half. She says, "The trouble with most photoplays we see is that they are just motion pictures. I have tried to write about real people, acting as real people would act in real life."

That she succeeded is especially indicated by Mr. Davis' comment regarding her play, "Real Folks,"—"It is a story of American life which for sheer characterization recalls the wonderfully distinct types of William Dean Howells' novels."

Mrs. Corbaley is a graduate of Stanford University, and is a daughter of California pioneers.

The winner of the second prize of $500, Katherine Kavanaugh, was formerly leading woman with Valerie Bergere, in vaudeville, is thirty-five years old and admits it. She has been writing photoplays for one year and in

in the Photoplay-Triangle Scenario Contest

Selections prove that best stories come from real life.

that time has sold six. Two of hers, "The Wheel of the Law" and "Peggy, the Will o' the Wisp" have been produced. She has also written for the vaudeville stage. In "Betty Lends a Hand," the part of Betty will be taken by Olive Thomas, the famous beauty, and former Follies star.

Now we have a story which will surely spell wonderful encouragement to the faint-hearted. Mabel Richards, who is going to be surprised by a check for $300, never wrote a photoplay before in her life. She saw the announcement of the competition in the PHOTOPLAY MAGAZINE, and conceived "The Tree of Life." She is a girl in her twenties, and goes to work every morning, just like thousands of other girls in moderate circumstances. Miss Richards is a stenographer and has for years cherished an ambition to be a short story writer. She has worked diligently along these lines, but without success, hardly encouragement. The photoplay opens for her a new field of endeavor.

Mrs. Byrd Weyler Kellogg, the winner of the fourth prize of $200, sends us a telegram which is about as illuminating a bit of "color" as we've ever seen. We quote it verbatim: "Age thirty-six. Newspaper aspirations killed by matrimony. Occupation, mothering family. Recreation, amateur theatricals. Husband banker. 'Skipper Fly' conceived with the desire to give mature bachelors a chance on the screen."

Honorable mention has been awarded seven other stories, some of which will be purchased by the Triangle Film Corporation. They are "His Brother's Keeper," by Frances E. Russell, Marquette, Mich.; "The Panther," by Clara McCorkle, Seattle, Wash.; "Cupid Picks a Lock," by W. Russell Cole, San Francisco, Calif.; "The Doctor," by Mrs. Sophie W. Newmeyer, Cleveland, Ohio; "A Man of Resources," by Madeline Rice, Holliston, Mass.; "Tempering Justice," by Gizelle Wohlberg, Waco, Texas, and "The Alien Strain," by Katherine Kavanaugh, winner of the second prize.

The stories winning first and second prizes are already being filmed, and the authors will shortly have the pleasure of seeing the plots of their own creating enacted upon the screen. The pictures will be made under the personal supervision of Mr. H. O. Davis, and no expense or pains will be spared to make them the best that the resources and experience of the Triangle Corporation can produce—and that's saying a great deal.

We want to emphasize one fact which this contest indicates so clearly: that there are golden opportunities in this age of the photoplay, opportunities just waiting for men and women to come along and pick them up. Photoplay writing is going to be recognized as a legitimate branch of literary endeavor—it is already so recognized; see the comment of Mr. Davis.

The Winners

First Prize, $1,000

"Real Folks"

KATE CORBALEY, 2227 West Twenty-fourth St.,
Los Angeles, Calif.

Second Prize, $500

"Betty Takes a Hand"

KATHERINE KAVANAUGH, 3434 Belair Rd.,
Baltimore, Md.

Third Prize $300

"The Tree of Life"

MABEL A. RICHARDS, 3402 Flournoy Street,
Chicago, Ill.

Fourth Prize, $200

"The Moth and the Skipper Fly"

MRS. BYRD WEYLER KELLOGG, 1006 Humboldt Street, Santa Rosa, Calif.

PHOTOPLAY MAGAZINE congratulates the winners, but it does not forget those who tried and lost. Perhaps there were in those thousands of stories many others which fell just a little short of success. The experiences of those who have won offer hope and inspiration to the less fortunate ones.

NEXT MONTH We will publish articles about the winners and how they came to write the plays which won prizes, in the hope that these accounts will prove of value to those who have not yet won success. We have talked with Miss Richards, and feel safe in saying that her story will be one of the most interesting and human documents you have ever read.

"Uncle Ca

Harriet Beecher Stowe's anti-slavery classic—perhaps the greatest piece of democracy propaganda ever conceived—has now been done into moving pictures.

Marguerite Clark as "Topsy," the amusing little pickaninny who "just growed." You remember "Topsy" is befriended by "Little Eva," who gives her her freedom.

Walter Lewis as "Simon Legree," the brutal overseer—whose tyranny over Uncle Tom established him as the ideal villain of melodrama. Will they hiss him on the screen?

"PROPAGANDA" today is a powerful and familiar word. Mrs. Stowe never used it, perhaps, in connection with her "Uncle Tom's Cabin," yet who shall say it was not the purest and most successful propaganda exploited?

Written ten years before the Civil War, "Uncle Tom's Cabin" acquainted the entire world with the futility of slavery, produced a finer appreciation of humanity—a belief in democracy that germinated the ideals for which we are today fighting.

And now, thanks to the camera, "Uncle Tom's Cabin" has reached another vehicle of expression. It is astonishing that the enterprising film people never before thought of it as a screen possibility. Paramount sent a company to Louisiana to make "Uncle Tom" on the original site. J. Searle Dawley is in charge of the direction of this classic. Famous Players is starring Marguerite Clark in both roles—"Topsy" and "Little Eva." Read by millions, seen in theatres by as many, a hundred million, perhaps, will see "Uncle Tom" on the screen.

Tom's bin"

Above, in oval—Marguerite Clark as "Eva St. Clair," the lovely little daughter of a wealthy plantation owner. She meets Uncle Tom—as pictured at left, above—and persuades her father to buy him. St. Clair promises to free Uncle Tom—but neglects to do so; and little Eva dies in the old negro's arms.

Frank Losee as "Uncle Tom," the lovable negro murdered by the oppression of slavery as typified by Simon Legree. Forgotten after Little Eva's death, Uncle Tom is bought by Simon Legree; and when at last they come to set him free, it is too late—-Uncle Tom is dead.

Florence Carpenter as "Eliza," the beautiful mulatto. Her escape with her child over the ice, tracked by blood hounds, is a memorable bit of stage history. It is even more thrilling on the screen.

The Shad

This man's stock in trade is that he looks like a fool — and is as far from being a fool as Rockefeller is from being a spendthrift. Mr. Arbuckle's most recent portrait.

Sylvia Breamer, beautiful, dusky and fervent, yet on occasion possessing the tender charm of an ingenue, is one of the acting finds of the year.

Robert Harron has increased his scope in characterizing, and his resource in small details — but his charming simplicity and unaffected boyishness have remained.

An Analytical Review of the Year's Acting

THERE are fewer memorable acting performances in the screen records of the past year than in any twelvemonth since the photoplay became the great national art; but if you are going to put all the blame for this on the actors you might as well blame the unmined anthracite for any emptiness in your family bin next winter. The photoplay actors are here, just as the coal is there, but unless you give an actor a play, or the coal a miner and a gondola, what can they do to warm your heart and your home?

The facts must be told to thwart the very pessimists and knockers who would profit by their concealment. If you have an infection on your little finger clean it out — don't let it give your whole healthy body a case of general blood-poisoning. The photoplay industry today is at the peak of favor and material prosperity. It is a national necessity and a war utility. It is run mainly by honest men — Tory authors please note. Its future is certain because the world's need of it grows greater and greater. The mysteries of science are as open to it as the sack of wealth — and here is the sore little finger: worthless plays.

The play situation is extremely complex, and I have no patience with the man or woman who finds all the answer in one place. Overproduction is a cardinal sin, a sin for which the manufacturers can honestly refuse to accept more than half the blame. Chasing the new thing is the national vice of the speediest nation, and as long as the American public had rather hop from house to house, lightly skimming the silversheet for a new sensation instead of exploring human life and dwelling upon details — as s t r a n g e l y enough they seem willing to do in novels and spoken dramas — we shall have quantity production with all but the third gear sealed. No author's golden age has ever been or will be in which competent pens and typewriters might even keep in sight such joyriders as today's cameramen. The managers and the authors need a President Wilson to bring them together on an equitable and productive basis. The managers say that the real authors are contemptuously giving them only by-products, and the authors insist that in any event what happens to their scripts renders original writing not worth while. There is abundant prejudice, misrepresentation —

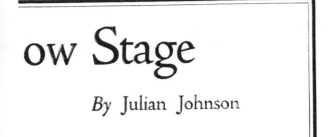

ow Stage

By Julian Johnson

Unity, as played by Mary Pickford in "Stella Maris," was unquestionably the most remarkable single acting performance of the year, and the most startling Pickford character.

and truth—on both sides. The directors act like little czars, and the stars like big ones, but the star-director problem is not half as big as it was a year ago. The scenario-writers are accused of factory output—but is not the average scenario-writer a factory hand?

Here is the streak of dawn which makes rosy the whole eastern sky: every really big man in the film business has come to a deep, sincere realization that the play's the thing. The problem of making a man do the right thing, however hard it may be, is as nothing to making a man wish to do the right thing. A year ago you couldn't have told the celluloid king that the story was the main event; he was too busy expanding his distribution, making gorgeous productions, signing every star in the milky way. Today you don't have to tell him. He is trying to tell you. He is a bit helpless. Most of the authors are making selfish demands instead of co-operatively studying a big problem. The audiences are just as restlessly demanding a perfect barrage of thirty-thousand-dollar productions. The war has added its intricacies and anxieties. Nevertheless, we are on the way to curtailment of quantity and an unmeasured rise in quality, just as surely as America is on the way to military victory.

However, this is no complete alibi for the actor. Some players, by characterizing power and force of will, have risen above mediocre material this year in notable assumptions. Others have only made their material a little worse: there are some so-called stars in America who are insincere and presumptuous cheats, throwing a little personality and no dramatic labor into every assignment. No accident of temporary popularity can make these permanent survivors.

Extraordinary Performances

I seldom use the word "great." One can so seldom enunciate it truthfully or sincerely. It is, like fame, one of the most abused words in the language. Nevertheless, "great" is the only adjective I can attach to Mary Pickford's performance of Unity, the little crippled slavey in "Stella Maris." Locke himself, a master of all the pastel emotions, never struck a finer note of grim though quiet tragedy than Miss Pickford found in her representation of this loyal, forlorn, plaintive, terrible character. A play which by its fabric tricked the audience into a logical end-

In Carmel Myers Universal possesses a young star of luxurious physique, lovely face and a sort of elfish personal charm. What are they going to give her to play?

Roy Stewart's western hero is the simple, good-natured but sternly virile plainsman as he used to be found in real life—all of which accounts for his general popularity.

Griffith has a habit of giving his people astounding single parts. Let us hope that the verve and fire Dorothy Gish poured forth as "The Little Disturber" will find another medium.

ing, tragic and yet "happy." A play which accounts definitely for Mary Pickford's Victorian (so to speak) reign as Queen of the Movies.

Here goes "great" again. This time, pasted upon Norma Talmadge. This wee American is all at once a shadow Bernhardt, a Duse, a Rejane—and a delightful comedienne. In her universality she is a young girl David Warfield. There is no limit in her ability to rise in any dramatic situation. Speaking in professional parlance, there seems to be no situation and no actor that, in the limitless heights of emotion, she cannot top. It will be a very real tragedy if this magnificent youngster is allowed to waste her wonderful twenties upon a succession of inferior materials.

Mr. Chaplin is the miniaturist of laughter. His humanity makes him a world-relief, and his perfection of detail should be—and is not—a lesson to all his acting brothers. I commend Chaplin's slowness of output; it is the true artist's determination, in the face of a temptation consisting of literal barrels of gold, to do nothing not worth while. "A Dog's Life," though only a grimy little backyard tableau, ranks with the year's few real achievements.

As a rule, Alla Nazimova is as bad on the screen as she is good on the stage. She overacts, on the screen, to an absurd degree. But in "Revelation" she did not overact! Here was a study of an elfinlike *grisette* which DuMaurier or Henri Murger might have been proud to claim in writing. A performance unequalled, in kind, on either stage or screen during the year.

It is hard to tell, in any rendition under the Griffith baton, how much of the appeal is Griffith's, and how much the player's. Sometimes I have thought that we never see Griffith's people at all—we see only David Wark himself, in a protean performance under a set of male and female masks. However that may be, Dorothy Gish's "Little Disturber," in "Hearts of the World," is one of the brightest splashes of vivid human sunshine in the whole gallery of Griffith impressionism.

Raymond Hatton has gone along at an unvarying gait, always resultful, no matter how much or how little he has had to do. Morbid and depressing, "The Whispering Chorus" found him, and his truly colossal conception of its self-doomed central character, its chief redeeming feature.

Among Notable Achievements

I hardly think anyone will gainsay the statement that Elsie Ferguson is the screen's most valuable acquisition this year. True, she has had no flawless scenarios, nor has she ever risen to such heights as did Mary Pickford in "Stella Maris," or Nazimova in "Revelation." But she has vouchsafed a personality of combined mental and material beauty, has brought a certain well-defined originality into the shadows, and has left an impression of fineness, of detail, of real womanly character in each of her roles which baffles exact description. "Barbary Sheep," one of the most satisfying and atmospheric narratives ever rolled up on reels, is to me her star accomplishment, though I admit that those who give "The Rise of Jennie Cushing" first place have ground for argument.

Marguerite Clark has done the best work of her picture life. "Prunella" is not wholly responsible, though assuredly this was a pliant script in her sensitive hands. Miss Clark's advance as a serious artist has been a very definite one. Witness the "Sub-Deb" stories—quite unsatisfying as to scenarios—and "The Seven Swans."

Kathlyn Williams has thoroughly re-established herself as a mature woman of graphic, poignant charm. Her Charity Cheever, in "We Can't Have Everything," did honor to that fastidious author, Capt. Hughes.

Elliott Dexter has developed a proficiency and a following in what we may call heavy virility. He is one of those players here in classified as "coming along."

Viola Dana has quite grown up, mentally, and still looks the child. She is much, much better than the plays they have given her.

Theodore Roberts might sink out of sight in the parts he draws were he not such a consummate actor. How completely he stole every honor, including even a bit of the director's, in "Old Wives For New!"

Much more difficult than Roberts' is George Fawcett's position. He has done scarcely anything in the year—and yet each little part he gets is cameo-like in its lustrous definition. How superb he was in his unnamed bit in "Hearts of the World." There's a lesson for young actors who think their toil is definitely measured by the number of "sides" in their scripts!

Eugene O'Brien has accomplished one task for the

whole craft. He has proved, in part after part, that a leading man may remain a human being, and that a gentleman is not known by his dress-suit.

Robert Harron has more sympathy and spontaneity than any juvenile in films. In every part he is not primarily a hero, a lover or an adventurer, but a real boy, with a boy's foibles, ambitions, loves and hates.

A year has gone by since Edward Connelly pulled from popular tradition, the newspapers and a few directions by Herbert Brenon his barbaric, ferocious, mystic Rasputin, in "The Fall of the Romanoffs." If you think this character played itself, recall Montagu Love's queer impression of the same part.

For surprising and unexpected novelty, Robert Anderson's "M'sieu Cuckoo," in "Hearts of the World," probably takes the 1918 movie cake.

Newcomers

We have already considered Miss Ferguson.

Then there is Sylvia Breamer—dusky, sensuous, sweet, a facile mirror to all the voluptuous and most of the tender emotions. "Missing" was her high mark, but Cecil De-Mille utilized her admirably as the luxurious foil in "We Can't Have Everything."

You almost have to consider Shirley Mason and Ernest Truex together—Viola Dana's extraordinary smart and pretty little sister (right name, Leonie Flugrath) and the energetic, kiddish, moustached, serious little comedian who plays with her. Miss Mason is, after all, not so much a newcomer, except in her new effectiveness.

Robert Gordon may be classed as a characterizing lead. He proved a definite and distinct appeal in "Missing."

Mr. Chaplin in his newest expression, a human and timely farce called "Shoulder Arms!" Chaplin is one of the hardest workers and the most painstaking artist on the screen.

Madge Evans, thanks to the plays she has been given recently, is to-day the foremost child star in films. She will hold her place as long as she has proper vehicles—and no longer.

Bert Lytell appeared first in "The Lone Wolf," last year, but his establishment came only with this season. Still, he has had no such vehicle as his initial one.

Madge Kennedy acts well and naturally in her comedies, but, somehow, she doesn't stick in one's memory. Why, I wonder?

Betty Blythe, a tall and strikingly handsome girl, has lent a good deal of feminine force to Vitagraph.

Texas Guinan's beauty, recruited from musical comedy, was found briefly in Triangle plays. In "The Gunwoman," she created a female Bill Hart, and would have started new Western vogue, had a line of these plays been put forth by a management which proved too timid to take a chance.

Roy Stewart—speaking of Westerners—has played cowmen just a year, and by his naturalness, good-natured sincerity and force stands as Hart's one real challenger.

Carmel Myers may have been put in "Sirens of the Sea" for her lovely legs, but since then she has shown such a refined, racial beauty, and such acting ability that one wonders what sort of material they will give her.

Jane Cowl brought a gracious presence, and much interpretative ability, to a screen which rewarded her by giving her "The Spreading Dawn." At that, there was an idea here, which totally failed to materialize.

Any list of newcomers ought also to include Agnes Ayres, the sweet little girl of the O. Henry stories; Mildred Harris, placid little creature who seems such an excellent hypnotic subject for Lois Weber, and Evelyn Greeley, now arrived as a World leading woman. Barbara Castleton, another World leading woman, has not made good the promise exhibited in her first picture or two a year ago.

Coming Along

Ann Little, in 1918, has slowly developed from horsewoman to actress. "Nan of Music Mountain" gave her perhaps her best opportunity.

Elliott Dexter has developed a proficiency and a following in what we may call heavy virility. Don't know what else to call it. Witness "Old Wives."

Jack Holt, Tom Moore, Norman Kerry, John Bowers—a quartette of excellent leading men of widely divergent capacities in widely separated fields.

At Triangle, Olive Thomas became a comedienne—and is dropping out of sight through no releases. Pauline Starke had a good play or two, best of all, "Until They Get Me." Alma Rubens, genuinely classic beauty, is a hypnotic subject awaiting a director; without one, she is quite expressionless.

The Shadow Stage

As They Were

Add to or subtract from this list as you will. Here, in all probability, two like opinions could not be found.

Excepting "The Land of Promise," Billie Burke has had nothing on the screen this year justifying her unique talents. Ethel Clayton, whose gifted director-husband, Joseph Kaufman, died a few months ago, has found no especially fitting vehicle. Mr Bushman and Mrs. Bayne-Bushman put in an artistically declining twelvemonth until two or three summer comedies pulled their stock back toward par. Thomas Meighan is invariably cast in supporting roles only more or less well-fitting; an actor of his sympathy and power of expression deserves better assignments. William S. Hart is at the famine stage for plays. Tully Marshall seems to have subsided into small bits. John Barrymore has been mainly absent from the screen. Also, Lewis S. Stone. All of Metro's scripts for Edith Storey have been at least five sizes too small. William Farnum, except for his well-remembered Jean Valjean, has been treading the dreary path of seek and ye shall not find. Constance Talmadge is still growing up—I don't mean physically; "Up the Road with Sallie" was so delightful that she has had a hard time trying to equal it—and hasn't.

Holding their own, all of them, but fighting to hold it! For another instance, Alice Joyce, a woman whose sensibilities, subtleties and sense of humor place her among the very finest actresses in this country; she has had practically no worthy material. Clara Williams shone splendidly through "Carmen of the Klondyke." Bill Russell, just pounding along. Like Clara Williams, Harry Morey's average was pulled up by one piece, "All Man." Frank Losee, acquitting himself admirably always, but certainly miscast as Uncle Tom.

Florence Vidor has had bigger parts, but not one so good or impressive as her emotional flash of a year ago in "A Tale of Two Cities." Tony Moreno—marking time. Bill Desmond—one fine play, in "The Sea Panther," and before, and after, undeserved mediocrities. Even Pearl White has made no strides in the past year, but she has held on. Frank Keenan's very best work, I think, was not in serious plays, but in a Pathe comedy called "More Trouble." Hayakawa—bound like Mazeppa to a single dramatic theme, the unescapable tragedy of the yellow man in a white man's world.

All these, mind you, are the solid, established backbone of the film acting business.

A Poor Year

—for these, now: most of them through the sheer lack of opportunity.

Dorothy Phillips, for instance, has not had a role which equalled her abilities since H. O. Davis left Universal. Dorothy Dalton has had impressive publicity, but neither her parts nor her performances in them have measured up to her old standard—a case in which poor scripts have not been wholly to blame.

Tsuru Aoki is nearly out of sight. So is Emmy Wehlen. Franklyn Farnum is another Davis discovery who has gotten nowhere without his finder. Where are King Baggott and Spottiswoode Aitken and Seena Owen and Miriam Cooper and Julia Swayne Gordon and Margery Wilson and Mary Alden? One might almost ask the same about Creighton Hale and Henry Walthall and David Powell.

Mae Marsh, save for "The Cinderella Man," a brilliant and delightful interlude, has been just one Goldwyn experiment after another. Mabel Normand, the ex-queen of comedy, is still a disembodied spirit trying to find her merry shell. Clara Kimball Young needs help. Alice Brady, ditto. Mary Miles Minter has been playing the darling child a drearily long time. J. Warren Kerrigan, save for "A Man's Man," has been out of it, through an accident and bad management.

Anita Stewart—a case of legally suspended animation.

Douglas Fairbanks has never found such plays as Anita Loos used to write for him. Romantic acrobatics are a poor substitute for romantic satire.

Bessie Barriscale—still there when she has a chance, but where have her chances been? Also, when has there been a convincing piece for Fannie Ward?

Ethel Barrymore, apparently, cannot be put right in light and shadow.

Charlie Ray is a better actor than he was last year—and he has been seen to less advantage.

Cecil DeMille lost his grip on Geraldine Farrar, but it looks as though Goldwyn would bring her back.

Pauline Frederick, despite hard work, has made no appreciable advances. In public favor it is doubtful if she stands where she did a year ago.

Here, One Asks Why?

Why, for instance, does that master of almost everything, George M. Cohan, fail to get across on the screen? When he made "Broadway Jones" we were all delighted—he had transferred his snap, speed and Americanism to celluloid, and he needed only a play or two to fully arrive. "Seven Keys to Baldpate" was a good surprise melodrama, yet, as an embodiment of Cohan, it didn't even come up to "Broadway Jones." And "Hit the Trail Holliday," save as a Bevo advertisement, was quite inefficient.

Why the utter dreadfulness of the great Mary Garden as a picture actress?

Why must Olga Petrova be so vastly unreal in her silversheet impersonations?

Why must Mae Murray, one of the daintiest of comediennes, perform such weird but not wonderful emotional vagaries as have puzzled even her best friends this season?

Why does that very fine stage actress, Rita Jolivet, act like a singer of Donizetti opera when she gets before a camera?

Why, at all, such pictures as those we have seen featuring Lina Cavalieri, Edna Goodrich and Kitty Gordon?

Why such a complete catastrophe as that mangler of history, Theda Bara?

Cleopatra has always been more or less wronged, but never more than in the Fox Production Sennettizing her tragic life.

Why such plays as Gladys Brockwell has had?

The Comedy Question

Roscoe Arbuckle shares comedy honors this year with Chaplin, though no comedian, it must be admitted, even approaches Chaplin in personal variety and appeal. But Arbuckle's material—his own make—has, in the main, been consistently funny and human. He has surrounded himself with good people. He has made good productions. He has kept moving. "The Bell Boy," it seems to me, was his year's ace.

Harold Lloyd, in miniature fashion, has brought in a lot of laughs, just as his little side-partner, Bebe Daniels, has contributed a lot of beauty. But one of Lloyd's heaviest reliances has been his snappy title-writer, H. M. Walker.

Sennett's screen Follies keeps Ziegfelding it along the celluloid white way, but we've been looking vainly all year long for such a satire, for instance, as Mack's own "Villa of the Movies."

Directors

The problem of directors, and their responsibility or lack of it in placing ultimate praise or blame for any studio's output, is too big a question to receive more than the barest mention here.

Personally, I think that Cecil DeMille has in the past year been unfortunate in his choice of personal material, and that Tom Ince will never return to his pristine glories until he once more takes a hand at directing himself. The same is true of Sennett, the most successful comedy director who ever walked on a set. Sidney Drew, now back on the stage, was a successful director of his own pieces, and it is to be hoped that his absence is only temporary.

Ince's situation is complicated by the collapse of his scenario department. Once the finest source of original material in filmland, it is now a factory of mediocre scripts. The superhumanly industrious C. Gardner Sullivan appears to be written out; the hand that penned that masterpiece, "The Cup of Life," has for a year ground out the most trivial banalities.

Current Releases

Much was expected of Mr. Griffith's first Artcraft, "The Great Love." Although replete with the little intimacies and touches of human life which he alone knows how to give such a story the piece was, on the whole a mediocre effort—not all of which is to be charged to Mr. Griffith, however, for he had a British war-subject with many photographs of actual people and places, and these were not the easiest thing in the world to fit into a fiction without jarring its sense of proportion. Robert Harron, Lillian Gish and others of the familiar Griffith crew passed over the canvas. Henry Walthall returned to his old master's direction, playing a rather unconvincing heavy.

Other Paramount-Artcraft pictures include an interesting Cecil De Mille production, "Till I Come Back to You"; "In Pursuit of Polly," with Billie Burke, and Enid Bennett in "The Marriage Ring." John Barrymore, badly lighted and made up to look 108, cavorts familiarly through Willie Collier's old piece, "On the Quiet," changed somewhat to suit the material restrictions of war times. "Heart of the Wilds," with Elsie Ferguson, is a strange make-over of Edgar Selwyn's "Pierre of the Plains," done into a woman star play in which the quaint original centerpiece Pierre, is quite submerged. "The Hun Within," an output of the Griffith studio—the year's first Griffith "supervise"—is a stirring melodrama.

Metro's heaviest offering for the month is a dramatization of Edith Wharton's gloomy and powerful story, "The House of Mirth," rather well handled considering the difficulties of popularizing such a subject. Metro has given it a splendid cast and careful staging. However, other offerings step right along. There is Ethel Barrymore in a very fair screen version of "Our Mrs. McChesney"; Viola Dana in "Flower of the Dusk," a play to which she is charmingly suited, and Bert Lytell in "Boston's Blackie's Little Pal." "In Judgment Of," however, is below par.

"Her Only Way," Norma Talmadge's Select offering, is enjoyable only in that it reveals Miss Talmadge's extraordinary dramatic powers. Her scene outside the window of her own house, before the murder, is without any physical action—and absolutely thrilling. The production is excellent; the story, a very trite matter. Clara Kimball Young, in "The Savage Woman," visualizes a French novel.

World's best picture this month is "Inside the Lines," a very realistic story of the British secret service. If there were space, much might be offered in criticism of scenario and general treatment, but in a sentence it may be said that as a whole it is pleasing entertainment.

Vitagraph's programme includes two vehicles for Harry Morey: "All Man," reviewed at length last month, and "The Green God." Gladys Leslie is to be seen in "Wild Primrose," Hedda Nova in "The Changing Woman," and Corinne Griffith in "The Clutch of Circumstance."

Tom Moore's first star picture, "Just for Tonight," heads the Goldwyn programme. Mae Marsh is to be seen in "Money Mad," Mabel Normand in "Peck's Bad Girl," and Geraldine Farrar in "The Turn of the Wheel."

Pathe puts forth "The Ghost of the Rancho," a comedy-melodrama of Mexico, starring Bryant Washburn; "Winning Grandma," a mild vehicle for Baby Osborne, and Elaine Hammerstein, in "Her Man."

Blue Bird vouchsafes "Fires of Youth," with Ruth Clifford, and "The Love Swindle," with Edith Roberts.

Triangle's releases include "Alias Mary Brown," with Pauline Starke; "The Ghost Flower," with Alma Rubens; "Daughter Angela," with Miss Starke; and "Wild Life," with William Desmond. A wretched vehicle for Desmond.

45

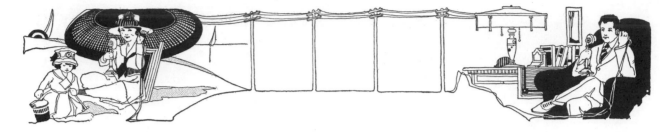

Lending Enchantment to Distance

A neat reversal of the old formula by getting Billie
Burke on the far end of a thousand-mile telephone wire.

By Julian Johnson

THIS periodical's publisher, vice-president, general manager, screen supplement director and all-around factotum should have been an artist. In fact, he is one.

He rushed into the editor's office—on his return from a recent trip to New York—without stopping even to put down the demi-tasse typewriter which constitutes the main portion of his travelling luggage.

"I've brought a beautiful cover of Billie Burke!" he exclaimed. "We've got to match it up with a story—"

"Excellent for early summer," affirmed the editor. "Billie Burke has just gone to Palm Beach, so of course—"

"Early summer rats!" interposed the P., V. P., G. M., S. D. and A. A. F. "The time to use this Billie Burke cover is *now*. And the story accordingly."

He reminds me of the Russian Emperor who, discovering an interminable wrangle between two factions of engineers on the course of a railroad between Petrograd and Moscow, took a ruler and a pen, drew a straight mark between the two cities, and said: "There gentlemen, is your line!"

A little more than eleven years ago I saw Billie Burke for the first time. She was then the adorable ingenue leading-woman for that sleek, svelte gentleman who has since become stout— John Drew. She was playing "My Wife," and all of you who recall that footlight sensation of 1907 must remember the roguish, pink-haired, blue-eyed girl who romped away

with hearts male and female, old and young, from New York's Battery to 'Frisco's Bay.

Since then, many interesting things and many high honors have happened to Billie Burke—and how very, very, very much has happened to the world and all the rest of us!

It is quite a new Billie Burke that the pictures found, two seasons ago; a Billie Burke no longer an ingenue, but in the prime of fine young womanhood, with a personality as elusive and distinctive in sunshine as in the upshine of floor-sunk electrics—

—and considerably more elusive, and just as distinctive, no doubt, in these February days when she was basking in Florida sands with all the reporters a thousand miles away to the north in cold and rain and influenza.

I happened to remember that one of Billie Burke's adventures in these ten years has been the quite usual feminine adventure of marriage; the other party to the contract being Florenz' Ziegfeld, Jr., creator of Follies and Frolics and Chief Justice in the World's Court of Pretty Girls.

One Leon Friedman has, during the whole Ziegfeld regime, been the mouthpiece and publicist of the follies-maker—therefore what less could be expected from him than an easily procurable reminiscence, based upon association and information, of Mr. Ziegfeld's charming and celebrated wife?

Leon was highly accessible—he thought it could be done.

Mrs. Flo Ziegfeld (Billie Burke) and her daughter, Patricia, on the sands at Palm Beach.

47

Above, Billie Burke, as she looked at the time of her first stage appearance. In the center of the page, with her husband, Flo Ziegfeld, in golfing garb, at Palm Beach.

And so we sailed on the ship of easy hope until two days before press time, when—utter consternation in a message from Mr. Friedman, still holding on like the Americans in the Argonne, but with even less on which to hold.

"I'm a walking dictionary"—w i r e d Mr. Friedman from St. Louis—"on the Follies, alphabetically arranged, from Dolores to Pennington. I can give you an essay on peace problems, for while I don't know much about Alsace, I know all about Lorraine. But I'll be darned if I can tell you anything about the boss's wife, because he won't mix Hastings-on-the-Hudson with the New Amsterdam theatre. He wires me to go ahead with the story—and won't give me a fact or a picture to go ahead on."

So much for so much. Sheridan is at Winchester, twenty miles away—without a horse or a Nieuport or a Curtiss. Not time enough even to go to Palm Beach, even if such a desperate expedient were to be considered.

No recourse left but the telephone.

And don't believe them when they give you these saccharine, smooth-flowing accounts of long-distance interviews. So far, I'd never had one that had even the least traces of success. You're bothered with cut-offs, bad connections, and what you might call wire-fright at both ends of the line. My subjects have always been bored, and the only thing I've ever been able to think of—while endeavoring to ask snappy questions in a bright way—was the auditor's blasphemy when he came to look over the expense accounts at the end of the month.

However—

The mail and telegraph address was simply Palm Beach, but Alfred Cheney Johnston, the benevolent old black-box Rembrandt whose ornate photographs anon appear upon these pages, suggested that I try the Vanderbilt's cottage, in which, he believed, the Ziegfelds were wintering.

A long wait after the call, then an assortment of clicks and monosyllables, a servant's somewhat querulous questioning, then a long silence, and then—the voice I first heard in "My Wife."

I couldn't think of anything to say, after introducing myself, and receiving a pleasant but risingly-inflected "Yes?" by way of reply and recognition. But at some dollars a minute, you simply must make conversation. I took from the colloquial shelf bromide No. 1.

"How's the weather?"

"Oh, fine!" came the silvery and surprisingly clear answer. And then, derisively, "Did you expect me to say that the ocean was frozen and the oranges were banked up under the snow-drifts? I suppose that's the sort of weather you're in?"

Center Photograph by Apeda

Photo at left by Sarony

Below, Billie Burke at the age of fourteen.

Here was my chance.

"You're wrong. I'll bet our weather up here is as nice today as yours down there. We've got sunshine and little birds hopping round and everything."

"How nice!"

Three dollars, and I hadn't bought a cent's worth of interview yet.

"What are you going to do this spring? stage play or more pictures?"

"Well, I'm going to do some more pictures—"

"And no play?"

"Not just at present. I'm going to come to New York in a new play about the first of October, but I can't give you any definite news on that yet."

"Going to England, or Europe, this year?" (Almost everybody will say "yes" to that one.)

"No. There is so much to do in Europe, and so many people in the way, it seems to me. I don't want to go to Europe until I have a definite thing in mind, or until I can actually do some good over there. Crowds and crowds of visitors, everywhere! I shudder when I think of it. It reminds me of a mob around an accident. I do hope to go to England, though, a year from this Spring. So you see I shall make pictures here, and I hope to have a successful play, too, in America in the seasons that's coming."

"You sure you aren't slacking on art to be a patriot in the household?"

"No! No! Please tell PHOTOPLAY's readers how important it is for a woman who has ever had a career to keep right on loving her work even though she's married. And by a career I don't mean, necessarily and exclusively, a celebrated career. I mean a woman who has done any useful thing well. And by useful thing I mean any service that has helped the world to be a nicer place to live in in any way. It might be baking an apple pie, it might be watching a business—just as well as it might be amusing an audience. It seems to me that we're in a time where everybody who can do anything —man or woman—is needed in his or her particular line."

Suddenly another voice sounded in the telephone; a voice very much like Billie Burke's; a small edition of Billie Burke's.

"I hear somebody butting into our tete-a-tete," ventured the Chicago listener. "Do I guess right?"

"You do—if you guess Patricia. My small daughter is calling me to lunch—no, I'm not hungry, but she is. She lunches at least eight times a day, and my attendance on her numerous meals is mainly a matter of form, not eating."

"Has Patricia ever been interviewed—to speak of something which might be a change from the pleasures of her small table?"

"Not yet, and I doubt if you could get her away from her bread and jam just now by telling her that President Wilson wished to converse with her. But I'll say this— she's quite capable of expressing her opinion on any subject. She has—oh, ever so many more positive opinions than her mother!"

"And will she be an actress, too?"

"I'm sure I don't know what she'll be. I'm not one of those mothers who say 'None of my career for my child!' I think that's just silly. Inevitably a child indicates, if it doesn't determine, its own career. I want to help my little girl to the work she can and ought to do in the world, that's all. Just now—and always—she is entranced with music. I hope some day it will be a big factor in her life. If she wishes to become a musician I shall help her in every way—but she must realize that it means work, not trifling play."

"And you can tell me nothing of your stage plans?"

"Not just yet. Except that next season I hope to do some real work—bigger, better work than I have ever done—on the stage. And I shall devote the summer to pictures. This butterfly existence is very charming, and I needed the rest—but how glad I'll be to see the Cooper-Hewitts and the open arcs again, and to hear my director call 'Camera!'"

"Well . . . . . good luck to all your hopes, and Patricia's."

"Thank you—and what can we say that isn't good-bye? I hate good-bye!"

"We might try an absolutely original expression—So Long!"

"All right—so long!"

"So long!"

Click . . . . . click.

And Palm Beach was once more in Florida, while Chicago had suddenly returned to Cook county, Illinois.

As to biography, one can write as much or as little as he pleases. This young woman has had a very busy and varied career, and her activities of a decade rival many another's enterprises of a lifetime.

But first of all, I think you should know that Mrs. Ziegfeld was christened not Billie, But Ethel. Ethel Burke was born in Washington August 7, 1886. Her father, the late William E. Burke, was a well-known actor of that day. He was known only as "Billie" Burke, and thus, when his daughter came to follow his career, she affectionately decided to keep her father's name alive.

Miss Burke was educated in France, and toured through Austria, Germany and Russia. She was engaged at the London Pavillion, subsequently appeared in pantomime in Glasgow and Sheffield, and made her first appearance on the regular stage at the Prince of Wales' Theatre, London, on May 9, 1903. Her first essays were parts in musical comedy. Her great venture on the dramatic stage began at New York's Empire theatre Aug. 31, 1907, when she played Beatrice Dupre in John Drew's production, "My Wife." Her debut as a star was made just a year later, when, also in New York, she played Jacqueline in "Love Watches."

"Gloria's Romance," a serial, marked her entrance into films.

She was last seen on the stage in Henry Miller's revival of "A Marriage of Convenience."

"Movy-Dols"

Announcing a series of famous stars of the screen presented in paper-doll form.

BEGINNING with the next, the June, issue, PHOTOPLAY MAGAZINE will contain a beautiful page of "Movy-Dol" cut-out figures—paper-doll size likenesses, in colors, of motion picture favorites. This forthcoming PHOTOPLAY feature will have an irresistible appeal to every child in America. "Movy-Dols" will become a playroom favorite in thousands of homes.

These paper-dolls were painted by a well known artist and are reproduced by offset process, in dainty pastel coloring on heavy paper.

The first subject is Mary Pickford and besides a color likeness of Mary herself, will include several changes of costumes, modelled after some of Mary's best known screen characterizations. All of the subjects of this series are the best known screen favorites, popular because of their constructive appeal to children.

Be sure and get the first—order your copy of June Photoplay at once from your nearest newsdealer.

Symbols

By Julian Johnson

LIKE Rachmaninoff's best-known prelude, John Barrymore's acting symbolizes the lofty tragedy of human life. A beginning in faint sounds that are very ghosts of silence, a swirl to the clamor of noisy young confidence, a crash into the discord of maturity, a trembling into the uncertainties of age . . . a fadeout into chorded nothings.

A SYMBOL of all the ladies of embattled England, is this Sylvia Breamer: suave, yet ardent; poised, but passionate, with the tide in her veins as red as it is steady. Her image might well be the dusk figurehead of any ship in the vast blue court of the Mistress of the Seas—indomitable, inflexible, invulnerable, indefatigable.

MARIE PREVOST must be the old marble that Pygmalion loved and made warm ivory. Surely a sculptor wrought those round arms and perfect legs! Anyway, she's a Greek girl—a vision of the youth of the world, when there weren't any motion picture censors and it wasn't considered naughty to be gorgeously healthy and beautiful all over.

DO YOU think of a glacier on an infinitely-patient volcano when you look at Katherine McDonald? She ought to play nothing—absolutely nothing—but those regal cool wives with Babylonian eyes who are always saying "Mine has been a marriage of convenience, George . . . I understand . . . but you must never try to see me again . . ."

RICHARD BARTHELMESS is a symbol of Delight Evans' juvenescent ideal. On her fair figurative knees she begged me to write an "impression" of him, but I told her cheap competition had driven me out of the impression business. Some day she'll go to chant a Grand Crossing rhapsody about him. Please omit flowers. I'll tell the Coroner she died of joy.

PHYLLIS HAVER, chicken-incarnate, is the standard sample of Misses'-size America. Looking at Phyllis, one thinks of so many, many wonderful things! However, it's a safe bet that Phyllis is thinking only that she's hungry, or of that dance last night at The Ship, or of the new hat she's going to buy next week at Robinson's.

DOROTHY DALTON is as much an emblem of the Middle West as a sorority-pin from the U. of I. Looking into her pictured eyes I see grain elevators and moonlight on Lake Michigan; I hear French spoken with a State street twang; I think of a millionaire's home in Lake Forest where they have a stack of wheats for breakfast.

CRIME in three shades—pink, pinker, pinkest; that's Priscilla Dean. If you are ever robbed by Priscilla you must, surely, do one of two things; love her yourself, or get some one else to do it. If you don't want to, you know my address. She's the 1919 model of all the bad babies who have to be made good by kissing.

THE PEOPLE who don't govern themselves because they're too busy governing everybody else have a statue that moves and talks and everything. Its name is Tom Moore. They took his eyes for lakes, his brogue for a language, his smile for sunny skies, dumped them over a lump of land in the North Atlantic Ocean, and called it Ireland.

YOU'RE Russia, Alla; Russia with all her potentiality for art, power, anarchy. As a Chinese girl, an American mother, an Arabian adventuress, you are always that same symbol—brooding, fantastic, incomprehensible. In the tropics you suggest a background of snow on the steppes, yet in a Moscow *droshky* you seem a veritable Sirocco. You're Russia.

PEARL WHITE is the image of a creature she has never played—not one of these Chinee-chased serial queens, but a grand adventuress in diplomacy; a high-sexed schemess who, a year ago, would have set all the young Vons in the Wilhelmstrasse fighting wildly to protect her when some entirely old Hindenburg turned her up to Pa Hohenzollern as a spy.

FRANK KEENAN, more than any other interlocutor of the vertical platform, symbolizes the Original Stalwart American. Why? Because said O. S. A., never one of these sweet juveniles, was there forty ways at fifty, a rugged oak sheltering some great cross-roads of life. Good man or bad man, Keenan plays them all, and truly.

How *the* Motion Picture Saved *the* World!

*When our government used film to cement the morale of France —
the insidious use of our unclean pictures by the Hun — the
tragic failure of the motion picture mission to Russia.*

By William A. Brady

TO a great many otherwise intelligent people the motion picture is only an entertainment, never anything more than a toy, no more important than the comic paper with which you kill time in a barber-shop.

I want to tell such people in particular, and the readers of PHOTOPLAY MAGAZINE in general, just how important the motion picture is, how powerful it has proved itself to be, what a world-factor it has become.

A little more than a year ago the motion picture saved the world. *Saved the world!*

That sounds big, and it is big, because it is not soap-box oratory. It is truth, a matter of government record. This magazine, I think, makes known the fact for the first time, and it is the biggest piece of news the picture business ever let loose. Here's the story of that salvation.

It was the darkest hour of the war. France and England were bent, but not broken. America had come in, but she was only getting ready, and struggling Europe had little more than her word and her good will. It was the exact moment for a great German psychological drive. German whispers, German arguments, German persuasions, German discouragements drifted all over France on every wind that blew from the North.

"All you will ever get from America is promises. The United States is not and can never be a military nation. Her people are entirely commercial—she'll sell you munitions, but she will not fight. They can't get ready across the Atlantic for they've nothing to get ready with. They have no gun-works, small-arms factories, or army organization. They can't build ships fast enough, and if they could, we'd sink them. Don't count on America as a material ally, for she couldn't get ready to begin to fight in less than ten years!"

That's what the French army got in one way, what the country people got in another, what was told pityingly to the French mothers, what the commercial agents told the bankers, the news brought to the mercantile men of the cities by their correspondents. There has never been such an insidious stream of propaganda-acid directed against the heart of a whole people. And it began to take effect!

France did not weaken or grow cowardly. That is not the spirit of France. But its people saw gathering above them the clouds of hopelessness—which is more fatal than weakness or cowardice. Probably—they reasoned—the Germans told the truth, for their arguments seemed based on facts that convinced.

At this moment the whole bridge of the Allied Cause trembled. France is not the entire bridge, but it is the keystone, the central arch.

There could be but one response: to *prove* to the whole people of France that *the Germans lied*. Not merely to convince a few statesmen, a visiting commission. It was up to America to show Jacques and Marie, from Belfort to Bordeaux, from Rheims to the Spanish border, that *we were coming to them*, right away and millions strong.

In its five thousand recorded years humanity has contrived only one device to make such an exposition possible: The Motion Picture.

Not thousands, but millions of feet of film were rushed across by our government, and were shown in all parts of France simultaneously.

And what did the almost-disheartened French people see?

Gun-works like Krupp's, or their own Papa Creusot's, roaring through the day, blazing through the night. Shipyards, with great carriers building in quartets and octettes. Shell factories, with literal miles of workers. Great naval stations, and thousands of young sailors. Army camps, with hundreds of thousands of splendidly-drilled troops. Small-arms factories the like of which are nowhere. The vast organization of the army and navy, actually at work in Washington. The conservation of food for every part of the world except Kaiserdom—France saw a moving, living, rushing negative of every vicious argument Wilhelm's agents had put forth.

France drew a long breath. It smiled. It cinched up its belt. And —with its American brothers—it began to give their answer to the Germans at Chateau Thierry.

GERMANY told France — and half-convinced her—"All you will ever get from America is promises!"

There could be but one response: to prove to the whole people of France that the Germans lied.

Not thousands, but millions of feet of film were rushed across by the United States Government, and were shown in all parts of France simultaneously. France saw a moving, living, rushing negative of every vicious argument Wilhelm's agents had put forth. France drew a long breath. It smiled. It cinched up its belt, and — with its American brothers — began to give their answer to the Germans at Chateau Thierry.

That is how the motion picture saved the world.

Anything which can be a great power for good can also be a great force for evil. That's a natural law as applicable to the motion picture as it is to fire and water.

About the time America was getting its myriad celluloid tongues ready to call the Germans liars—and before that time —Germany itself was a great believer in and purchaser of American films.

Unclean pictures; morbid stories; vampire tales; gangster and gunmen reels—every sort of cheap, suggestive, sensational, unnatural melodrama and prurient sex-story that it could pick up in the neutral countries around it, or that its American agents could smuggle to those neutral countries. To these pictures, especially among neutrals where it still had free access, Germany gave the widest circulation possible.

"Here," sneered the representatives of Potsdam, "is 'the saviour of civilization!' This is America—typical America— who is going to preserve the world for democracy. They abuse our Kultur; here's theirs. These gunmen and thugs are only average Americans. These vampires represent their women of leisure. Now then, which do you want in Europe—our civilization, or what these barbarians think is civilization?"

Needless to say, these dirty and desperate arguments were not wholly convincing to the intelligent citizens of Sweden, Switzerland and Spain. But they did damage enough.

I have given you merely an advance summary of two chapters of war history that remain to be written.

One more such chapter will concern the great film propaganda prepared here for Russia before she slipped into anarchy—a complete system of friendly argument and exposition, held up and completely thwarted by one man. I can't give you his name. I can only say that we were as ready to save Russia as we had been to reassure France—when into the machinery went just one monkey-wrench. But it was enough.

The film men of America have responded quietly and instantly, on government demand, without comment or press-work.

One day, Washington called for 2,500,000 million feet of film immediately, for emergency use across the water. Presumably, this great quantity had to be shipped in a week. Actually, it was all shipped in twenty-four hours.

The motion picture is the greatest enthusiasm of my life. There is nothing like it in power, in versatility, in range of expressiveness, in the whole world.

As Americans, we should be proud of the fact that the world knows only one standard of film—made in America. American film is today and will continue to be what German dye used to be and never can be again—the irritating, incomparable and inimitable mystery of science and commerce.

Ever since the dawn of history the people of the earth have been seeking some common bond of communication. Here it is: the first answer to the Tower of Babel; the Universal Language.

The greatest friend of the motion picture in a place of authority today is the President of the United States. Mr. Wilson realizes more keenly than most film manufacturers the power of the film in war and peace. He knows what a lot of his subordinates never realized—that the screen is a code which makes neighbors and brothers of all nations.

When I remember what Mr. Wilson has said and written about the motion picture—what he has said and written to me—I cannot but smile at the clumsy stupidity of a treacherous attack like that of George Kleine in his recent letter to the War Industries Board; in which he, not engaged in the manufacture of new photoplays but in the marketing of old ones, artfully recommends a shut-down of all productive activity for a year as a matter of war-time welfare!

The great evils of the photoplay industry today are ignorance, selfishness and suspicion. It takes charity to make progress. You must let the other fellow live to get the larger life yourself. You have got to give today to make tomorrow. Yet those are the things the majority of picture men refuse to do. They sit tight, grab everything in reach, and glare at each other. Ignorance is a tremendous but youthful folly of this business. Ignorant, narrow-minded, uneducated men have been its curse. More especially, men without imagination. Illiterate men with imaginations have sometimes moved the world.

I am such an enthusiast over the screen as an educational, civilizing factor that I see this as the great field of the future, rather than mere picture-play production.

Can you fancy anything greater than Woodrow Wilson's "History of the American People" on the screen? So visualized, this work will—I say "will," because it certainly will be picturized—make us a people 100 per cent patriotic, and give every boy and girl an inspiring and personal acquaintance with every incident of consequence since the landing of Columbus, and an understanding of the national purposes and faiths not to be had in a thousand texts. The motion picture will breathe the breath of life into every other study, from geography to botany, and even into higher mathematics. It will be the first genuine college of trade, because it will show one people's real needs, and another's faculty to supply. It will be an international preacher of peace, and a more solemn warning against war than any coalition of statesmen.

51

PITY THE POOR "EXTRAS!"

THE slightly bored extra-ladies-and-gentlemen to the rear have been sitting in a warm sun atop a Fifth Avenue motor bus for about an hour now. It's noon and they have been at it since nine that morning—and no sandwiches in sight. The director with his inevitable 'script is to blame—he's showing Edward Earle and Agnes Ayres how to act on a motor bus; and it's all for a Vitagraph picture, "Sisters of the Golden Circle," from O. Henry's story. Practically the entire picture was filmed on top the bus. Of course the extras get paid for it—but heavens, whattabore!

Cleopatra *Plays* a Return Date

Photographs by Stagg

Cleopatra in her twentieth century reincarnation goes over the script at the end of each day on the porch of her six-room dressing room bungalow.

It is not generally known that Admiral Peary has fallen a victim to Theda's wiles, but he has. This particular Admiral Peary however is not the one who discovered the end of the earth, but he's just as well satisfied.

OUT on the desert which adjoins the bean fields of Ventura County, California, they have builded the Pyramids and the Sphinx. On a pseudo Nile, almost within the corporate limits of Los Angeles, they have restored the ancient walls and temples and water front of Alexandria, Egypt. Sixty miles away, on the beach at Balboa they have constructed a fleet of war craft and already have fought a desperate battle for the possession of Alexandria.

At these various "locations" and within the Fox studio at Hollywood, Cleopatra has lived again in the person of Theda Bara. She has "vamped" Caesar, who has again been slain at the foot of Pompey's statue; she has lured Antony from Octavia, only to fall desperately in love with her prospective victim; and she has again taken the deadly asp to her bosom with the same fatal effect. Director-general J. Gordon Edwards has been in personal charge of the direction throughout. The accompanying photographs were taken especially for PHOTOPLAY MAGAZINE.

The press agent snapped this just before Cleopatra left to despoil the tomb of some ancient ruler of Egypt. You may recall that she found enough jewels on the mummy to show Antony an awfully good time

"I think you're wrong" said Cleopatra to Rameses Edwards, as she consults the script. You will notice that Marc Antony is just going into a clinch with the siren of the Nile. Note the famous Peacock feather costume.

Cleopatra enters her four-horse power touring car and starts to Alexandria to call Caesar's bluff.

An exact reproduction of the historic monument with the face restored to what is thought to have been its original contours.

The Confessions of

According to what Lew Cody says, the "rag and bone" siren doesn't know nearly as much about men as the "chocolate-coated cave man" understands about women.

Mr. Cody's case it's an advantage. Also, there was orange pekoe tea and other things to sustain one during the ordeal of listening to the confessions of the original male vampire (screen species).

"First," I said, when the penitent had arranged himself as comfortably as possible, with a glowing cigarette between his fingers and a pagan grin on his lips, "why is a male vampire?"

"A male vampire exists because all women want to be a man's last love, not his first," began Mr. Cody. "A man may tell a woman he has never loved anyone in his life before he met her. She accepts it with a sweet smile because she thinks it's only a figure of speech and she doesn't believe him. If she discovers he has told the truth, it's generally 'curtains' for him. Women dislike amateurs. They don't care to be practiced on.

"Life began with a man and a woman in a garden. The game goes on, that's all. A male vampire is merely an expert in the great battle of wits between the sexes. He's the only man who isn't hopelessly outclassed before he starts.

"Incidentally, I've noticed it didn't take Eve long to get out of the garden when she found there was only one man there.

"The ideal male vampire would combine the American's punch, the Englishman's subtility and the Frenchman's suavity."

(I happen to know that Lew Cody was born in America of French parents and that his right name is Cote with accents over the "o" and the "e.")

Now, there are marrying men and bachelors. The difficulty is to tell the difference after Life scrambles them about a bit. Lots of married men are

ALL women want to be a man's last love, not his first. And that, says Mr. Cody, is the secret of the male vampire.

We have come far since the day of "a rag and a bone and a hank of hair." That lady is now considered a rank amateur. She has been followed by the baby vamp, the intellectual vamp and the person who slings slightly obese charms in your face with a freedom ridiculous or disgusting according to your sex and disposition.

Now—enter the male vampire. And, while, to quote once more from Mr. Kipling, "the female of the species is more deadly than the male," the deadliness of the masculine variety is not to be underrated. I know, for I have been mother confessor to the eminent authority on vampires—he and she vampires, vamping a la celluloid and au natural—Mr. Lewis J. Cody, the originator of the male vampire upon the screen.

Mr. Cody insists that the male vampire, as portrayed by him in that delightfully subtle thing of Lois Weber's, "For Husbands Only," is a necessary evolution of the screen in its progress toward realism, a real human being who has landed in a hitherto sadly vacant spot somewhere between the saccharine hero of the thousand virtues and the dreadful hero of the seven deadly sins. He is a sort of chocolate-coated cave man, and after seeing Lew on his own vamping ground in screen versions from real life, a mere spectator is filled with gratitude for his creation.

Our confessional was a charming little luncheon table. The candles, one must admit, wore intimate, silken red shades. And the penitent had the advantage of being seen—at least in

In the topsy-turvy oval at upper left Lew Cody is demonstratin[g]
Mildred Harris is the vampee and the name of the picture
scene from "A Branded Soul," in which Mr. Cody "vamped

a Male Vampire

As told to
Adela Rogers
St. Johns

bachelors by instinct. Lots of bachelors become married men by training. The real male vampire is essentially a bachelor. His freedom is his most cherished possession. He desires wide fields in which to rove and he doesn't care to cheat. His heaven is anticipation. His hell is a woman he is tired of.

"The male vampire is necessarily frivolous—at heart. The moment a man becomes earnest he bores a woman to tears. You cannot harness most men. That is why marriage as an institution is too often a failure.

"There is only one really bad man—the man who desires innocence. That is why the male vampire is not bad—he is only a little humanly wicked. He doesn't really care to waste his time on inexperience. The battle of wits is more engrossing when played with a skilled opponent. The thrill is lost unless the foeman is worthy of one's steel."

He paused and flashed me that companionable little smile and between you and me I began to have a degree of sympathy for the wife in "For Husbands Only" who so nearly was vamped by him.

"Go on," I said. "Just how much does he know about women?"

"Do I have to do that?" he asked.

I nodded solemnly. "What is the ideal woman?"

"The ideal woman is the one a man would never grow tired of. She hasn't been discovered as yet. But the most dangerous woman is the one who is clever enough not to let you know how clever she is. Like a masked battery, her fire is more deadly.

"Women today are doing their best to kill romance. They have grown too clever. Nothing kills a romance like brilliancy in a woman. She ceases to kneel gracefully. And yet, an intelligent man likes an intelligent woman. But the reason that so many intellectual men marry brainless dolls is because the clever woman flaunts her knowledge so brazenly. It doesn't make a great deal of difference what a woman says if it isn't humiliating to a man and she looks attractive while she says it.

"Daintiness is the one physical essential. If a woman has that she may be dark or light, tall or short, thin or fat and still be adorable.

"The two unforgivable sins for a woman in the eyes of the

"Women today are doing their best to kill romance. They have grown too clever. Nothing kills a romance like brilliancy in a woman."

55

A new portrait of Lewis J. Cody.

e masculine theory of vampiring.
Borrowed Clothes." Above is a
posite Gladys Brockwell.

optimistic pessimist we are calling a male vampire are affectation and superiority. Nagging is the one reason I know for justifiable homicide. The possessive case is such a feminine favorite and it ruins more charming women than anything else in the world. The silliest woman can handle the cleverest man if she only lets him think he's having his own way."

"Now," I demanded sternly, "what are the rules of this great game, the rules he has worked out through his experience?"

"There isn't a woman in the world who wouldn't be flattered if you made love to her. But that won't always gain your point. Hold her off a bit. Add the fillip of indifference to the spice of danger. Make her feel that you are a volcano beneath a crust of ice and the sheer perversity of her sex will make her try to break through to see what it's like underneath. If she finds out too soon that you are eager, she will play with you as a cat toys.

"The real male vampire is essentially a bachelor. His freedom is his most cherished possession. His heaven is anticipation. His hell is a woman he is tired of."

"Never roast a man she has cared for or still seems to admire. It disparages her taste and rouses her to the defense of what is or was her property. Rather praise him for the virtues he doesn't possess. Nothing will call her attention to his faults so quickly. On the same principle, never underestimate another beautiful woman to her. Admit her beauty, but suggest that she isn't your style.

"Never talk about yourself to a woman. It arouses in her the critical faculty at once. The law of supply and demand works in this game, as in all others. Give her what she hasn't. Find out where the other fellow fails. Never force the issue. Be aloof, courteous, cool. Above all, don't fall in love with her, or you're gone.

"Ah, women are like moods. They must be changed often to be attractive. Women forgive vices of the flesh more readily than sins of the disposition. They will forgive anything easier than cowardice and sneer at the man who, wont defend her.

"Always remember this—that flattery is the most powerful weapon for either sex. That is where the average woman and the average man make their biggest mistake. Subtle, clever flattery, founded upon enough truth to make it acceptable, scores as nothing else can.

"For instance I told a woman the other night that she should always wear Oriental effects. 'If you did, you would be surpassingly beautiful,' I said. She shrugged it aside, but the next time I saw her she was wearing jade earrings down to her knees and enough Chinese embroidery to start a temple of Buddha.

"'And I learned about women from her,'" he quoted, with that superabundant joy of living, that warmth of color and delight in the actual world that makes him so forgivable in his screen "other men."

"Now, the benediction," I said, as the fervor of his "axioms" burned out.

"Since you're a mother confessor—" he remarked suggestively.

"Absolution, if you never do it again!" I pronounced.

"But, dear lady, I must earn my living," he cried.

"Oh, yes," I said weakly, "I forgot. Sentence suspended." Well, what did you expect of a mere woman?

Resorting to facts, Mr. Cody made his first screen venture opposite Bessie Barriscale in "The Mating," an early Inceville production after a considerable stage career. Since that time he has played with many of our best feminine stars, including Mae Murray, Edith Storey, Gail Kane, Fannie Ward, Mildred Harris, Louise Lovely and others. His latest work, at this time not released, was in "Don't Change Your Husband," a C. B. deMille production, characterized as a companion piece to "Old Wives for New." This picture story is narrated and illustrated elsewhere in this issue.

Alfred Cheney Johnston

THIS profile belongs to the only Young American Actor who is equally at home in Tolstoi or Augustus Thomas. "Jack" is doing "Peter Ibbetson" for Famous, assisted by sister Ethel and brother Lionel Barrymore.

Charlotte Fairchild

*BLANCHE SWEET reappears on the silver-sheet in "The Hushed Hour."
Following this she plays the heroine in Rupert Hughes' novel of the war,
"The Unpardonable Sin," in which she is directed by Marshall Neilan.*

TALLULAH BANKHEAD is a candidate for screen stardom. Only sixteen, she is the daughter of Congressman Wm. B. Bankhead, and the granddaughter of Senator John H. Bankhead. The town of Tallulah in Alabama was named after her.

60

White

" LET'S do something original," said Ethel Barrymore, so they did "Camille,"
while Metro gave its Contessa de Cinema a leave of absence. "Camille" was
rewritten by Edward Sheldon, who made it quite a snappy play; Conway Tearle
played Armand Duval. It is the longest run the Dumas drama ever had in America.

*T*HE most recent portrait of America's f a m e d dancer-actress, Irene Castle, who is in mourning for her aviator - husband, Captain Vernon Castle. She left the studios to go to England, there to devote her terpsichorean talents to war-work.

Alfred Cheney Johnston

The Five Funniest Things

A director who can produce a laugh-getter need not think he will escape the income tax. And here is revealed the secret of successful screen comedy.

A cohesion of dignity and water never fails to arouse hilarity. Sometimes you see it in the form of a bath room so flooded that the occupant uses the tub as a row-boat.

UNKNOWN to the world at large and faithfully guarded by motion picture comedy directors, is a list of five things guaranteed to make people laugh. Comedy directors have built themselves conservatories and joined yacht clubs by reason of their knowledge of this list, for in motion pictures there is nothing so commercially profitable as laughter. A director who can manage a laugh, or an actor who can inspire cachinnatory approval, need not concern himself about the sugar situation. He can go ahead and make plans for his seashore drive.

Audiences are always amused by something that is anticipated. (Lower right). The audience always feels sure that in another moment the powder will blow the victim four ways from the post office.

The funniest thing in the world is for one person to hit another with a pie. Crude as this may sound it has made more people laugh than any other situation in motion pictures. It was first discovered twelve years ago and has been a constant expedient ever since without, so far as can be discovered, any diminution of appreciation. It has made millions laugh and tonight will make a hundred thousand more voice their appreciation in laryngeal outbursts. It is the one situation that can always be depended on. Other comic situations may fail, may lapse by the way, but the picture of a person placing a pie fairly and squarely on the unsuspecting face of another never fails to arouse an audience's risibilities. But the situation has to be led up to craftly. You can not open a scene with one person seizing a pie and hurling it into the face of an unsuspecting party and expect the audience to rise to the occasion; the scene has to be prepared for. There must be a plausible explanation of why one person should find it para-

in the World

By Homer Croy

mount to hurl a pie into another's face. He must have been set on by the other—preferably by somebody larger than himself—and then suddenly the worm turns and sends the pie with unerring accuracy into the face of the astonished aggressor. To this an audience never fails to respond.

The second funniest thing in the world is for a waiter to fall down stairs with a tray of dishes. Over and over the situation has been worked and yet it never grows old. Sometimes he is craning his neck to see a pretty girl and lands at the newel post; sometimes it is because he has been out the night before and is too sleepy

A scene that can always be counted on to make an audience laugh is for a man to assume woman's clothes.

Another of the five funniest things in the world is for a waiter to fall down with a tray of dishes.

to have the necessary care; sometimes he is being pursued by his wife and in his eagerness to get away makes a misstep that ends calamitously. The pretenses and improvisations for the contretemps are legion, but the scene never fails to get a response. Sometimes a reverse twist is given by having the waiter stumble and the diners scurry to escape the threatening crockery, but with the dishes never quite falling. The reverse of the situation is just as humorous as the scene's accepted version.

In experimenting with the sense of humor it was discovered that there was something irresistibly amusing in seeing some one fall into water. Particularly amusing it was found by comedy directors to see a dignified, silk-hatted individual going along and then to have him meet with an unfortuitous catastrophe such as stopping on a bridge to lean against the banister to admire the graceful swans and then to have the banister give quickly and unexpectedly

The funniest thing in the world is for one person to hit another with a pie. Crude as it may seem, it has made more people laugh than any other situation in pictures.

away. Knowing well that a fall of six or eight feet into water would not hurt him, audiences gave themselves up to the full enjoyment of the situation.

Every day of the year this scene in different guises is given to theatre audiences and it never fails to arouse a pleasant sense of anticipation. Sometimes it may be that a bathroom is so flooded that the comedy occupant finds it necessary to make of the tub a temporary rowboat with a long handled bath brush pressed into service as an oar. Sometimes Mary Pickford uses it in comedy more refined when she gathers up mud and hurls it at some person who

has aroused her disapproval. Whether played as burlesque or as high comedy, a water scene rarely ever fails to arouse appreciation.

Audiences are always amused by two things: by something unexpected and by something anticipated. A waiter takes a piece of pie and, standing behind a swinging door, waits to reek revenge on a fellow waiter when the door opens and instead of the other waiter in comes the manager of the restaurant. The manager gets the pie. The scene never fails to arouse the desired laughter; it succeeds by reason of its element of surprise. On the other hand the element of anticipation is just as strong and is made use of almost wholly in situations employing explosives. A set is erected with a number of bottles labeled "nitro-glycerine" or "dynamite" and an actor comes in in comedy make-up and begins to smoke. Throwing his match aside it sets fire to a fuse. The fuse begins to splutter while he smokes on unmindful. On such an occasion an audience never fails to give vent to its sense of the incongruous. If it should stop to reason that real explosives were not being used and that in reality the labeled bottles were empty, it would see the evident pretenses of the scene; but it never does. It always feels sure that in another moment the powder will blow the innocent person four ways from the post office and as a result pounds its palms in approval.

The fifth scene that can always be counted on to make an audience laugh is for a man to assume a woman's clothes. If the man happens to be stout all the better and if he should happen to so manipulate his skirts as to show a flash of underwear still better. But strange as it may seem the placing of a woman in man's apparel is not funny. Many directors staked their pictures and their reputations on this reverse to find that an audience will not laugh at a woman in overalls. If she is the possessor of a pretty face they will think her cute, but never funny. Nor must she stay too long in overalls. If she does her appeal is gone and the scene is lost. Just a flash and then back to more conventional attire.

On these five, fortunes have been made and lost. Directors who are hired to produce laughs have tried to put out films in which none of the scenes appeared—and when their efforts were shown in the picture company's private projection room the directors have been handed their contracts and their hats with a prayer on part of the managers that the men would be employed by their competitors. The scenes have been blacklisted and yet when the directors have tried every other situation wherein a laugh might be aroused they have come thankfully back to the funny five.

Oh, Learned Judge!

SPEAKING of beauty and brains combined, have you heard of this beauteous young person, Frances Marion, who rattles the typewriter to the tune of $10,000 a year while still finding time to doll herself up in Paris plumage that stirs most of the femininity of picturedom to frenzies of envy? Earning $10,000 a year would make a frump of almost any woman. But not Frances Marion! Her clothes, as Mary Pickford, for whom Miss Marion writes scenarios, expressed it, "are simply, gorgeously—*speed!*"

Just the other day Miss Marion was summoned to appear before a stern court to explain the whys and wherefores incident to her bowling her big roadster along at a mere forty-seven miles an hour.

When she stepped up and faced him, the judge tried

valiantly to mix sternness and reproof with a gaze that was inclined to be admiring.

"Young lady," he asked, "why was it necessary for you to go ripping through traffic on Hollywood Boulevard at this unholy rate?"

"Judge," answered Miss Marion with deep seriousness, "I was late for an appointment to try on a perfectly exquisite new evening gown, and—there were four flivvers and a truck and a Chinese peddler's wagon ahead of me. I just *simply had* to get around them, Your Honor."

The judge tried to hem and haw away a smile that began to flicker around his lips. The smile grew into a grin.

"You may go this time," he said. "Er—h'm—er-r—I drive a car myself, and I am afraid I understand."

AN expert likeness of our best-known Younger Son, William Wallace Reid. He plays those sons of fortune with too many millions, who always, always get the Girl. Mrs. Reid is Dorothy Davenport. There's a William Wallace, Jr.

The
SQUAW
MAN

*Narrated, by Jerome Shorey,
from the photoplay.*

IT was not to save his cousin, Henry, Earl of Kerhill, from disgrace, that Jim Wynnegate was leaving England, and by his sudden and unannounced departure tacitly pleading guilty to the embezzlement of charity funds of which he and Henry were joint custodians. Truth was, he despised Henry, not merely because he knew that his cousin was a thief, but because the remainder of his character was in harmony with this fact. Nor was it with any Quixotic idea of sheltering the family name, that he allowed the world to think he, rather than the Earl, was guilty. As the shores of England merged with the horizon he mused bitterly upon the pleas that had been made for him to take the blame upon his shoulders, for the sake of the family. And they all thought it was for the family he had done it. How little they understood!

All Jim hoped, all he asked, was that his action should restore to Diana her peace of mind, if it were not too late. Diana was Henry's wife, and Jim loved her. That was all right. Jim had infinite capacity for concealing his emotions. He never had hinted the truth to Diana, but when Henry, one day in a jealous rage, accused his wife of being too fond of Jim, she became confused and betrayed the fact that Jim's affection was returned. Jim discovered this accidentally, and realized that nothing but unhappiness for the woman he worshiped could result from his remaining in England. He had already decided to go away when the fact of Henry's peculations was discovered. So much the better. Jim could use this as the excuse for his departure, and, he believed, undermine Diana's faith in him so that her love, if it had come to that, would be killed. Diana could not love a thief.

Night closed in about the ship, and still Jim Wynnegate stood at the rail, peering through the gloom for his last glimpse of England. As the land and the sea became one vast mass of grey, shapeless and impenetrable, the face of Diana seemed to take form in the empty spaces, the beautiful face of Diana, proud yet kind, and to Jim it seemed that she smiled, and that in the smile there was a promise.

Two types of men are drawn irresistibly to the western plains—those who find in the arduous life a challenge to their courage and determination, and those who find in its wide, untraveled spaces, opportunities for undetected crime or opportunities for escape when crime is detected. Cash Hawkins was one of the latter. Like all of his kind, he was at heart a coward, blustering only when accompanied by his wolf-like gang. He was known to be a cattle-rustler, but in that remote corner of Wyoming there was not a sufficiently strong organ-

ization of law to attempt conviction and capture. It was rather openly hinted that the Sheriff himself was receiving money from Cash to pay no attention to complaints. When Jim Wynnegate dropped off at the little cow town and announced his intention of becoming a rancher, Cash Hawkins marked him for his special victim. It was inevitable that they should be enemies. The mere fact of two men of such opposite character, the one with the keenest sense of honor, the other with nothing but a sneer for whatever was honorable, living in the same neighborhood, was a guarantee that they must clash.

The feud was one-sided for a long time simply because Jim

Jim was considering whether it would be worth the

refused to recognize the fact that such a person as Cash Hawkins existed. He learned through his own cowboys that Cash was "laying for" him for no reason that anyone could discover. But he went his way unperturbed only being careful not to turn his back toward Cash when they happened to meet. The feud did not become really active until Jim, riding the range one day, came upon Hawkins and his gang, cutting out some of his cattle and branding them with Hawkins' mark. The gang jumped on their horses and fled, swearing vengeance upon Jim for interrupting the theft of his own stock. Not long after this Jim interfered with a deal Hawkins had framed up to cheat the old Ute chief, Tabywana, in a cattle transaction, earning the gratitude of the Indian and the renewed hate of Hawkins. And when, soon after, Jim rescued Tabywana's daughter, Naturitch, from Hawkins' insults, Cash was counting the days lost that gave him no opportunity to kill his enemy.

But if Jim had made Hawkins his blood-enemy, he had won a friend whose faithfulness and almost doglike worship was to stand him in good stead. Naturitch looked upon him as little short of a god.

The Continental Limited pulled into the little town one day with a leaking boilertube, and the passengers were informed that they might as well look about and enjoy some wild western scenery, as it would be several hours before the repairs could be made. Two men and a woman left one of the Pullmans, and strolled about the town. The curious travelling caps the men wore, told that they were English, and they stared at everything with true British curiosity, not unmixed with superciliousness. They were attracted by the dance hall-saloon-

"You too, Queenie," he commanded. "Come on in and get your liquor."

In an instant Jim was at Hawkins' side.

"Put up that gun," he commanded.

Hawkins looked up at him, with a surly snarl. But it was no time for dispute. Jim was facing him, and there was fight in his eyes. With a curse he dropped his gun back in its holster and slunk out of the saloon.

"By Jove, if it isn't our friend the embezzler," exclaimed Applegate.

The Earl looked away uneasily. Diana gave a little cry, and

ace to reach for his own gun, when a sharp report was heard, and Hawkins dropped where he stood.

gambling house, and after some debate decided to investigate. Cash was there with his gang. Spotting the strangers, and recognizing them as of the same caste as his sworn foe, he ordered them up to the bar.

"Cash Hawkins is buying for the house," he yelled, and brandished his gun.

Jim was at the other end of the long bar, with Big Bill and Grouchy, two of his most trusted cowboys. At the commotion he looked down the line and saw—Diana. Jim's cousin, the Earl, was swiftly obeying the bully's command to approach the bar. Sir John Applegate, their traveling companion, was hesitating between a desire to protect Diana from the insult of this barbarian, and the realization that resistance would be futile. Diana alone was defiant. Standing straight and motionless, she looked at Hawkins as Marie Antoinette looked upon the mobs that dragged her to the guillotine. But the scorn that would have withered a civilized being had no effect upon Hawkins.

then controlled herself.

"What's that?" demanded the Sheriff, who had been a witness of the incident.

"Oh, come on, Sir John," the Earl said petulantly. "We'll be missing our train."

"No yuh don't," said the Sheriff, blocking the way. "If this here Britisher's an embezzler, I want to know about it."

"Then find out about it for yourself," the Earl snapped. "Out of my way."

The outburst was so unexpected that the Sheriff, openmouthed, obeyed, and the visitors started for the door. But not until Diana had found opportunity to whisper in Jim's ear:

"Oh why did you go? I know you are innocent."

Just that, and she was gone, but to Jim it was as if the heavens had opened for an instant. It reawakened his courage, that she should have this faith in him.

The Sheriff, always on the alert in the interests of his friend

68

Naturitch had slipped into the house and after crooning for a moment over some of the boy's toys, stealthily departed.

Cash Hawkins, would not allow the incident to be closed without asserting his authority a little further.

"What's this about you being an embezzler?" he demanded of Jim.

"Haven't the slightest idea," Jim replied with a smile. "Never saw the people in my life. Mistaken identity, I suppose. Any objection?"

The Sheriff took a long look into Jim's eyes, and decided he had no further comment to make. There would have been no time, in any event. While Jim's attention was engaged with the Sheriff, Cash Hawkins had flung open the door of the saloon, and flanked by half a dozen of his followers, guns in every hand, shouted:

"Hands up."

It was no time for parley, and Jim obeyed. Cash had the drop on him, and hesitation meant death. He doubted that Cash would have the nerve to shoot him in cold blood, but still the situation unquestionably was ticklish. Cash was in a rage over Jim's interruption of his sport a few minutes earlier, and the old scores remained unsettled. Besides, Cash was secure in his knowledge that the Sheriff was his friend. The tendency in those days was to take for granted that every man was capable of looking out for himself, and except for flagrantly unprovoked murder, invoking the processes of law was looked upon with disfavor. These things all flashed through Jim's mind as he stood facing Cash, whose bestial features were lighted with unholy triumph.

Cash's right hand twitched a little. It looked as if he was about to fire. Jim was considering whether it would be worth the chance to reach for his own gun, when a sharp report was heard, and Hawkins dropped where he stood. A quick examination showed he had been shot through the heart.

The Sheriff, whose zeal for his friend was out of all proportion to his intelligence, wanted to arrest Jim, but an examination of Jim's gun, as well as that of his men, Bill and Grouchy, showed that every chamber contained a loaded cartridge, that the weapons were cold and the barrels clean and bright.

"Well, somebody must 'a killed him," the Sheriff insisted.

"That seems a reasonable conclusion," Jim assured him, "and it's up to you as Sheriff to find out who did it. But I don't believe anybody around here will mourn if you don't, especially owners of cattle."

That night Jim strolled away from his cabin, out under the stars. His mind was filled with thoughts of Diana, and of her faith in him. How splendid she was, as she stood there in the saloon, defying Hawkins, proud and fearless! How pitiful that she should be chained to the weakling Henry! Well, that was all past. He would never see either of them again. Henry would take good care that they never came that way.

As he stood on a slight rise of ground, Jim saw a figure approaching swiftly toward him through the darkness.

"Who's that?" he called, with his hand on his gun.

"Me—Naturitch," a woman's voice replied.

"Are you looking for me, Naturitch?" he asked.

She did not answer until she was close beside him.

"Me kill him," she whispered.

"You!"

"You save me from him, me save you," she explained, simply.

"But where were you?"

"Me watch—side room—he ready shoot —me shoot first," and she handed him a little revolver, hardly more than a toy beside the artillery of the plains.

"I'll keep this," Jim said. "If they find the little bullet, and see this gun, they'll know you did it. I don't suppose there's another this size in Wyoming. But how can I ever repay you?"

For reply she whispered a few words in her own language and slipped away as silently as she had come. Jim could only guess the purport of her remark, but he sensed something to the effect that she was his slave and would serve him whenever he needed her.

Jim's debt of gratitude to Naturitch was soon redoubled. Riding along a treacherous canyon trail one day, in search of stray cattle, his horse slipped, and he fell into a chasm known as Death Hole. Strange mineral springs sent off poisonous vapors in this narrow and almost inaccessible gorge, and animals and men shunned it. The Indians surrounded it with superstitions, and would make long detours to avoid it. As Jim fell his head struck a boulder, and he lay unconscious at the bottom of the Hole. An Indian tracker had been his companion, and hurried back to the camp to inform Tabywana of Jim's plight. But while Tabywana would have done anything in reason for his friend, he was of the older generation, and he would neither venture to defy the superstition, nor order

The Squaw Man

any of his tribe to do so. Naturitch heard the news, and, unseen by her father, hurried away. She too believed in the superstition of Death Hole, but something stronger than superstition drew her on. There was no time to warn the cowboys—the poison fumes would have done their work before they could be brought. So she sped through the steep defiles, and with almost superhuman strength, dragged the object of her devotion to safety.

Nor was this all. When, with the aid of her tribesmen, who were willing enough to help when Jim had been extricated from the Hole itself, she had taken Jim to his cabin, she refused to leave him. The poison had entered his system, and there was no doctor to be had. So she brought to bear all the lore of the aborigines, and nursed him back to health. When he had recovered sufficiently to be about, Jim went to her one day and said:

"Time for you to go back to your father now Naturitch."

She shook her head. "Me no go back again," she said, and no argument could alter her determination.

Jim was lonely. The comradeship of Big Bill, Grouchy, and the other cowboys did not suffice. The thought of his loss of Diana never left him. But the gentle ministrations of Naturitch, through his illness, seemed to supply something of the need that was growing within him. She was not of his race, but she was adaptable, and was willing to forego all to be with him. She asked nothing but to be permitted to serve her selfchosen master, and her face, which was beautiful with all the unspoiled beauty of nature, would light up with joy at the least word of praise from him. But Jim, knowing what it would mean for her to stay, did his best to force her to go, and even appealed to her father. But the old chief only shook his head, a little sadly. So Naturitch stayed, and when a few months later Jim saw her working on a tiny pair of moccasins, he sent for a minister.

Thus Jim Wynnegate, cousin of an Earl, became a squaw man. Ordinarily it was a term of reproach. Men who married Indian women were, frequently, outcasts from their own kind, and by their adoption of an Indian mate they still further isolated themselves. But Jim commanded the respect of the community, and while many looked askance at his marriage, they still held him in respect, although avoiding him a little, that there might be some slight indication of their disapproval of these mixed marriages.

If the few years which followed did not bring Jim actual happiness, they brought something perhaps a little more positive than contentment. He

The Squaw Man

NARRATED, by permission, from Beulah Marie Dix's scenario of the same name, adapted from the famous play of Edwin Milton Royle, and produced by Artcraft, with this cast:

Jim Wynnegate	Elliott Dexter
Henry, Earl of Kerhill, his cousin	
	Thurston Hall
Diana, Henry's wife	Katherine MacDonald
Sir John Applegate	Tully Marshall
Tabywana	Noah Beery
Naturitch	Ann Little
Big Bill	Theodore Roberts
Little Hal	Pat Moore
Grouchy	Jim Mason
Cash Hawkins	Jack Holt

was fairly successful and he had his son. Little Hal was his one joy in life. Naturitch seemed less like his wife than a superior servant, who came and went, intruding as little as possible into his life. She appeared to feel that only through the boy had she any claim to a part in Jim's existence. She made little attempt to learn to speak English fluently in spite of Jim's oft repeated urging that she should do so for the sake of Hal. If he had been firm with her, she doubtless would have obeyed, but he could no more scold her than he could scold his dog or his horse, she took all his words to heart so deeply. So rather than wound her he allowed things to drift along.

Suddenly everything seemed to go wrong. The fair measure of prosperity that had been his, evaporated almost overnight. An epidemic afflicted his cattle, his favorite horse broke its leg in a gopher hole, the whole ranch seemed to be overtaken by some perverse fate. To add to these very real troubles, there came an annoying incident that might have far reaching results. The Sheriff, seeking re-election, had been informed by the friends of Cash Hawkins that they would vote against him unless he discovered and arrested the slayer of their ringleader.

"Need I tell you that I will care for him as if he were my own son?" Diana asked impulsively.

The Squaw Man

A coincidence came to the aid of the officer of the law. He happened to be in the side room of the saloon where Hawkins was killed, when part of the flooring was being torn up to make repairs. There, under the boards, an Indian bead pouch containing a number of small calibre cartridges was found. Naturitch had dropped it through an opening beside the partition, the day she shot Hawkins.

The Sheriff went to his office and compared the cartridges with the bullet that had been taken from Hawkins' body, and they corresponded. No one but an Indian woman would have carried cartridges in a beaded pouch. No Indian woman but Naturitch would have had any motive for killing Hawkins. So the Sheriff reasoned, and swiftly called several of his deputies into council. It was necessary to proceed with caution against so resourceful a person as Jim, especially as it was important to avoid unnecessarily antagonizing old Tabywana, father of the suspected woman, and chief of a tribe of Indians that might be difficult to handle unless the Sheriff had plenty of evidence to back his accusation.

Meanwhile, events at Jim's ranch were swiftly taking another turn. That same afternoon Jim, looking down the road toward town, saw a cloud of dust approaching, which soon resolved itself into the one public conveyance of the vicinity, and its occupants, besides the driver, were Diana and Sir John Applegate. Diana was dressed all in black. Jim's heart leaped to his throat, and he smothered a groan. This was a contingency he had not foreseen. Henry was young, in good health, and Jim had never considered such a possibility as Diana being left a widow. Then, as the buckboard neared the gate, another thought leaped up and almost sent him reeling. If Henry and Diana had no children, he, Jim Wynnegate, was Earl of Kerhill.

It was true. He never had considered the possibility of coming into the title. Although he was next in line, he was only a cousin, and it had seemed absurd. He took for granted that Henry would have an heir. He hardly heard the story that Sir John told him of his own exoneration.

"Your cousin was never quite himself, after that time we saw you in the saloon," Sir John said. "He wanted to travel incessantly—never seemed to be satisfied. We did not understand then, but of course we know now it was his conscience that was driving him. Finally he took to hunting big game, and seemed to enjoy accepting the most dangerous chances. He did it once too often, and a lion got to him before we could save him. He was terribly mangled, and knew he was going to die. Then he confessed about the embezzlement, and insisted that it should be written down and that he should sign it in the presence of the Countess and myself. We have let the facts become known, very diplomatically, among those who knew of your leaving England and the circumstances, so now there is nothing to stand betwen you and your proper place as the Earl of Kerhill."

Jim looked over at Diana, and her eyes were shining. He turned away. Naturitch was standing in the doorway.

"There *is* something between me and that place," Jim said, slowly, and indicated Naturitch with an almost imperceptible motion of his head. "Be very careful what you say. She is faithful, and I do not want to hurt her feelings."

The silence that followed was broken by the voice of a boy calling, "Daddy, daddy," and Hal came running in and flung himself into his father's arms.

"You son?" Sir John asked.

"My son, and hers," Jim replied, adding, that there might be no mistake, "We are married."

"Then he is your heir, the heir to the title," Sir John went on.

Jim only drew the boy closer to him. He knew he could not take Naturitch to England. He knew it would be a violation of his entire code of honor to desert her and go himself. But he knew also that he had no right to deprive his son of the birthright he himself must put aside. Hal Wynnegate, Earl of Kerhill that was to be, was entitled to education, to a place among men who would one day help to rule the British Empire. He was entitled to an opportunity to become one of those rulers himself. As against this, what had life in Wyoming to offer the lad?

"If you insist upon remaining here," Sir John was saying, "at least you must let us take the boy back."

"Need I tell you that I will care for him as if he were my own?" Diana asked, impulsively.

Jim drew a deep breath. He knew how hard it would be for him to give up his son, and that it would be ten times harder for Naturitch. For he knew why the boy was going, what opportunities were awaiting him. To Naturitch it would be as if he were dead, or even worse, for though he was living she would be unable to see him. Still, the boy must go.

"Come for him tomorrow. He will be ready," he said, and Sir John and Diana rose to go.

As they departed, Diana took Jim's hand and looked steadily into his eyes.

"I want you to feel that I understand, and fully sympathize with you," she said, and he pressed her hand, not daring to trust his voice.

When they had gone, Jim explained to Naturitch as gently and patiently as he could, the honors to which their son was heir, that he would be big chief far across the great water, and they must let him go. Whether Naturitch understood or not, she at least realized that her son was being taken from her, and with all the pride of her race she crept away and hid her grief in an all night vigil under the stars.

With this new and unexpected turn of events, everyone had forgotten that the Sheriff had sent word that he had evidence that Naturitch had killed Cash Hawkins, and would arrest her forthwith. Everyone, that is, except Tabyawana. The old chief had informed the Sheriff that if Naturitch killed Hawkins, she had full cause, and if the Sheriff attempted to arrest her there would be war, for he would call out his tribe to defend her. The Sheriff regarded this as mere bluff, and went on with his plans, organizing a strong posse of friends of Hawkins to visit Jim's ranch and bring away Naturitch.

The stoical mother did not come back to the house to say goodbye to her son. Again she knew she would be unable to conceal her emotion, and she watched from a hiding place as the cowboys loaded him with gifts. Jim's heart was breaking too, and he hurried Sir John and Diana away. He had no desire to prolong the leavetaking. No one noticed that Naturitch, during the excitement, slipped into the house, and after crooning a moment over some of the boy's toys that were too big to be taken on the journey, found her little revolver and a pair of the boy's moccasins, and as stealthily departed.

When they had gone, Jim went in and flung himself on a couch. His life was now utterly empty, it seemed. His boy had been his one salvation when he lost Diana, and now he had lost them both. Yet his pity for Naturitch made his own grief seem small in comparison. As he pondered, he heard Big Bill's voice calling for him.

"Here comes the Sheriff and a posse," Bill shouted. "Guess they're after Naturitch."

Jim ran out, and was astonished to find that with the Sheriff was the wagon containing Diana and Sir John and Hal.

"What does this mean?" he demanded.

"It means that this here lady and gent was in town the day Cash Hawkins was killed. I'm here to arrest Naturitch, and they've got to stay for the trial as witnesses. Can't tell how they may hook up with the case," the Sheriff replied, confident of his position, with twenty heavily armed men behind him.

"You let that lady and gentleman go, or—" Jim began.

"My God, boss, what's that," Big Bill shouted, and pointed across the valley.

It was a great cavalcade of Indians in full war paint, Tabywana at their head. At a signal from the chief the line stopped, ranged across the rise like splendid statues. Tabywana rode on to the house where Jim was parleying with the Sheriff.

"I told you I would call my people," Tabywana said, facing the Sheriff sternly. "Will you leave my daughter——"

A shot interrupted the chief. A change came over his features. Some instinct seemed to tell him what had occurred. He spurred his pony and rode around behind the stables. A few minutes later he came back, bearing in his arms the body of Naturitch, his voice quavering in the death chant of his tribe. Naturitch herself had severed the bonds that confined the Earl of Kerhill.

All Aboard!

CLEVELAND exhibitors declare that the lightless nights are having a grievous effect on theatre attendance. "I have been told by more than a dozen women," comments one of them, "that they are afraid to come out onto the darkened streets Monday and Tuesday evenings."

Why cannot exhibitors follow the classic plan of the energetic political candidates who insure a full vote by bringing out the voters in tallyhos and busses? An exhibitor could round up a jolly big crowd of darkness-fearing patrons in that way. Patrons afraid of lightless streets, could be furnished by enterprising exhibitors with a postcard form, to be filled out in some such fashion as

Mrs. J. Rufus Wallington and nine children will be ready for the Elite theatre bus when it calls Monday evening at 739 Darkalley road.

Photo by White

Underwood & Underwood Photo

Stars *of the* Screen *and* Their Stars *in the* Sky

By Ellen Woods

Nativity of Mary Pickford, Born April 8th.

WE do not wonder why she is called "The World's Sweetheart." She has Venus, which provides beauty and grace; Mercury, fertile mind; Sun, power over all, and Jupiter, justice and honor, all in her ascendant.

There are so many good things to say about her nativity that if the Editor would allow me the whole of his magazine, I would be unable to tell the half.

First, she was born with the power to sway the whole world, as Aries was intercepted in the First with Mars, Lord thereof, ruling the other eight planets.

She was born fortunate financially, but the best of all, is her great love for her mother and religion. When Venus rises with the ascendant, as it does in her chart, it gives an inclination for music, singing, dancing and the theatre. There are some players who show only one indication of dramatic ability, viz. Venus and Mars in aspect, but "little Mary" has eight.

To go into Theosophy, I would say this is her eighth reincarnation as an actress.

She has excellent business ability and should follow her own intuitions in this respect.

If everybody were as pure minded as she, there would be no sin in this world.

Nativity of William Farnum, Born July 4th.

AT this gentleman's birth, July 4, midnight, the Sun was in the cardinal sign Cancer, with the artistic sign Taurus on the Eastern horizon. Taurus is the day house of Venus, which is found in the sign Cancer in conjunction with Mars, lord of the Seventh.

The Seventh house is said to rule the marriage partner, and those with whom we do business; therefore, I would say this gentleman would live happy in married life and could go into partnership with any one and do well.

Jupiter, as the Great Jehova, the God of the Hebrews, is located in the Seventh, which rules also the public in general, and Jupiter being there is the reason that Mr. Farnum is loved so well.

Of course we find the indications of the good actor, viz. Mars and Venus in aspect, and there are two other indications that help wonderfully in this direction. First, Uranus in the Fifth house, the house of theatres, in good aspect to three planets: Mercury, the mental planet; the Moon, that rules the female portion of the world, and Venus, Lady of the ascendant, which represents himself; second, Neptune, the God of the Briney Deep, and the God of Inspiration and Intuition, rising with the ascending degree.

Mr. William Farnum has the power from Neptune to judge correctly between truth and error.

CLARA and the whale. That's the way it began for little Miss Bow. She and the whale put over "Down to the Sea in Ships." The whale then retired from public life but Clara kept right on going up. Now she is one of our flippest flappers.

Introduction to the Twenties

"Would you like to sin with Elinor Glyn,
Or err with her on a rug of fur?"

That was the ditty that ushered in the twenties and a whole new era. In her novel *Three Weeks,* Elinor Glyn had done the impossible. She had popularized sex. Imported to Hollywood to do the same for them, she not only wrote—for *Photoplay* as well as the screen—she single-handedly created the "It" Girl, symbol of flaming youth, freedom, and heretofore unmentioned sex appeal. The essence of that creature was her own discovery, the acme of all flappers, Clara Bow.

The counterpart to the new woman was Rudolph Valentino—exotic, sexy, faintly cruel—everything the previous decade's hero wasn't. A whole new kind of hero was born—Ramon Novarro, Rod La Rocque, etc.

The times were changing and nowhere was it more apparent than on the pages of *Photoplay*. Bessie Love herself taught a million little flappers to do the latest rage, or outrage, the Charleston. Rudy, so remote on screen, told the girls firsthand what he wanted in a woman. *Photoplay* ran contests to find new faces for the silver screen. A little wide-eyed flapper named Joan Crawford told the most intimate details of her life as she began one of the longest careers in pictures. Hollywood's swimming pools grew more and more elaborate.

But what of those becurled child-women, those clean-cut men, the little clowns—those innocent folk heroes of only yesterday? Trouble was, they weren't too innocent. And while folks in the twenties might find sexual freedom right in principal and scandal amusing in fiction and on the screen, any hint that it was real spelled death for the star involved. And the scandals of the twenties looked as if they might spell death for the whole movie business.

The first victim was lovely Olive Thomas, found dead in a Paris hotel room from an apparent overdose, clad only in a sable cape. The next scandal followed quickly. Fatty Arbuckle was charged with manslaughter in the death of call-girl starlet Ina Rappe, at a so-called orgy arranged by himself. Then handsome Wally Reid, confined to an asylum by a jealous wife and a studio afraid that his drug habit would be publicized, died. Next came the murder of notorious director William Desmond Taylor. The discovery of his friendship, one apparently intimate, with Mabel Normand and Mary Miles Minter spelled their doom.

"Drugs, sex, scandal!" screamed the daily press. "Tragedy, injustice, big trouble for big people," insisted *Photoplay*. It was the fan magazine's first brush with scandal, and its reaction—total protection when possible, silence if that didn't work—would set the tone for the next thirty years. Silence, *Photoplay* soon learned, usually spelled death for the star involved. But better the death of one star than the whole industry—which seemed very possible at that moment.

So Hollywood started its moral housecleaning, and the government, just to help them along, sent a fellow called Will Hays there to see that it went all right. Thus was born the Hays Office and Hollywood censorship. Nobody loved it, but it was better than total death. And Hollywood set out to prove it was just a small, hardworking town that was just too much in the spotlight, and that its bizarre behavior could happen anywhere.

It was a depressing time, but there was still Chaplin, soon to be followed by troubles of his own, cheering them up. Beautiful Gloria Swanson had married a marquis and became Hollywood's first peeress. And little Mary Pickford, together with Doug, was right up there with the best of them. But Mary, still bewitching, though a bit bothered and bewildered by the same old roles, came to her friends at *Photoplay*. What kind of roles did her fans want her to play? *Photoplay* ran a contest, and the answers came back loud and clear—the same old roles. She didn't listen, and that was the beginning of the end. And two new fads moved in to make it look as though it were the end of everything—radio and the crossword puzzle. So great was the listening and the doodling that folks were staying home from the movies —but just for a while.

Photoplay solved the problem neatly by figuring radio favorites were stars and by printing their own crossword puzzle.

But the barrage was not yet over. In 1926, Rudolph Valentino died, and it must have seemed to a host of fans that the movies died along with him.

Hollywood had learned, however, in this very decade, how to recover. "Youth" again became the cry. A new young fellow named Gary Cooper was so natural you wouldn't believe it. It was a quality that would make him a legend. And there was a young girl being touted as the most beautiful girl in Hollywood, Loretta Young. But the greatest beauty was yet to come, the Stockholm Venus Greta Garbo. Together with Jack Gilbert, she would keep the spirit of the Hollywood romance alive. Jack went off and married Rod La Rocque's old wife Vilma Banky, but Greta ————.

Photoplay was by now firmly entrenched in the business of making legends. But it couldn't have been aware, at the time, that it was just starting to promote the greatest legends of them all. Everything was too shaky, everything that happened seemed like such a threat. Suddenly, there was a new invention in town—the vitaphone—which meant that movies were now going to talk. The very word "Talkies" struck terror to the most famous of hearts. It was the thing, goes the legend, that started Jack Gilbert off on a drinking binge only matched by beautiful Barbara La Marr, who beat him to the grave. The one thing that saved Hollywood from the scandal was the presence of her adopted little boy, quickly adopted by her friend, ZaSu Pitts. Gloria Swanson asked *Photoplay* readers what they thought she ought to do. Radio stars like Rudy Vallee were taking over. Was the whole film business going to make musicals?

And to top it all off, poor Mabel Normand, whom *Photoplay* never thought guilty of anything—murder or sexual indiscretion—was deathly ill. Neither silence nor words would help her now.

In 1929, the stock market crashed. And the decade which had started with a bang was going out with a whimper—a very audible, Mickey-Mouse-sound whimper in Hollywood. But *Photoplay* was quick to point out that somehow princes and society girls still wanted to be movie stars, and that the loyal fans still weren't missing a movie.

The SHEIK

The
popular romance
lives again
on the screen,
with
Agnes Ayres
and
Rudolph Valentino
in the
leading roles.

Photography by Donald Biddle Keyes.

Below—A scene from
"The Sheik," with
Valentino and Agnes
Ayers.

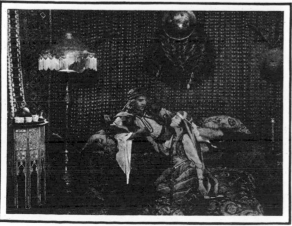

HAVE you read it? The chances are that you
have. The story of a handsome Arab Sheik,
and the English woman whom he kidnaps and
holds for his own, is peculiarly adaptable to
pictures. For the glamor and the beauty of the
desert, the colorful costumes, the real love story lend
themselves to the shadows. Rudolph Valentino, the
Latin lover of "The Four Horsemen," plays the
Sheik. Agnes Ayres is *Diana*, the heroine. The
whole is more or less a tangible version of "Pale hands
I love, beside the Shalimar, where are you now, who
lies beneath thy spell?" But we wonder what the
censors will do to it.

Everybody's Doing It Now

You have never really danced until you have learned the fascinatin' rhythm of the Charleston. Here's a lesson by Hollywood's champion.

IT took place at a party given recently by Mr. and Mrs. Rudolph Valentino—the great Charleston Contest of Hollywood. The two contestants were Ann Pennington and Bessie Love. Now Ann is the undisputed champion of the stage and her fame had spread before her to Hollywood. However, Hollywood backed its own Bessie Love and the movie colony votes that Bessie has a slight shade of advantage on Penny.

When PHOTOPLAY heard of the contest, it asked Bessie to give its readers a few lessons in the intricacies of the steps. Bessie consented to pose for pictures illustrating the most important steps. There are, of course, many variations but if you have mastered the principles of the dance, the rest will come easy.

STEPS Nos. 1, 2 and 3. No. 1. Place arms on hips, bend body forward and step forward with the knees stiff. Then give a double dip on each knee before taking the next step and then on to number two. No. 2. Swinging arms in opposite directions, body bent forward, point right foot forward. Then heel-toe to side and back. Next heel-toe to front, changing to left foot and repeat. No. 3. Bend body forward, knees slightly bent, and place hands on knees while moving knees inward and outward, alternate crossing arms with hands on knees in scissors fashion.

BESSIE LOVE Shows You How

STEPS Nos. 4, 5 and 6. With arms swung to opposite side, skip to right, pointing the toe. Swing body slightly back, raising the hands upward. Point right foot forward and point heel, bending the body far back with the hands extended, palms outward, above the head

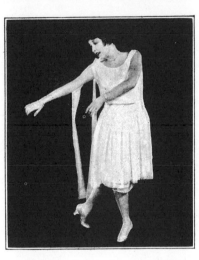

STEP No. 7. Start by repeating Step No. 2 and duplicate, with the exception of kicking forward from the knee only, instead of pointing forward with the toe

STEPS Nos. 8 and 9. This is a twist from front to back by placing the right foot point forward over the left and swinging the body in complete half circle. Repeat with the left foot over the right and swing back to front in position again for finish of the Charleston. A good finish to the dance is to point the right foot forward, extending the right arm to the side and raising the left hand over the head with the palm outward

The Charleston is one of those things that, like a striking slang phrase, seems to come from nowhere, yet is instantly everywhere. It may be said, almost literally, to have broadcast itself. It just came naturally, like time or space, no beginning and, apparently, no end.

It's hard to remember where and when you heard jazz music the first time, isn't it? Well, the Charleston is just like that. So new and yet, oh, so universal!

Maybe you came upon it first in a cabaret, maybe you saw it at a theater, maybe you had got tired a bit of stepping the old steps, and then one of your friends dragged you out of your shell and over to a ballroom floor where the Charleston was giving everyone that peppy old dance thrill you used to enjoy with the old steps.

Well, anyway, who cares? Especially the dancers.

Everyone's doing it. Everyone's enjoying it.

And that's enough.

The Charleston is the one big hit, the grand national performance. More people know the steps now than ever could sing the words to the "Star Spangled Banner." If you're one of those who've never danced before you've got a treat in store for you.

Don't try to do the dance fast at first. If you do, you'll get into difficulties. It is better, says Bessie, to go slow at first and be sure to get the steps accurately. While the steps themselves aren't extremely difficult, the Charleston requires a lithe and active body and it takes a little training. Incidentally, it is a good dance to learn if you want to reduce or to keep in trim.

The Charleston has given the studio orchestras something to do when they are not supplying music for the scenes. Above, on the opposite page, you see a picture of Anna Q. Nilsson and Shirley Mason "doing their stuff" between scenes. To their right is Ann Pennington, champion of the stage.

All Hollywood is now spending its spare time mastering such steps as "The Turkish," "Falling Down Stairs" and "Picking Cherries." And it is also predicting that some musical comedy producer will sign up Bessie Love to do her Charleston in a New York revue.

What is

"IT is Anglo-Saxon hypocrisy," *says* Joseph Schildkraut

By Mark Larkin

Joseph Schildkraut, one of the films' most orchidaceous leading men. According to Joe, *IT* is an Anglo-Saxon hypocrisy used to cover the honest phrase, sex magnetism. Which, of course, sounds very Schildkrautian

"'IT'," said he, "is an Anglo-Saxon hypocrisy to cover up the honest phrase, sex magnetism."

There, ladies and gentlemen, is the Schildkraut definition of "IT." Elinor Glyn herself could have done no better!

"If people in America would only treat sex a little more casually," he went on. "If they did not accent it, if they did not attach unnatural significance to a natural thing. Sex is as fragile as a flower. It should be regarded as a flower in a garden, not a thing to be pulled apart, wantonly dissected, ruthlessly destroyed.

"NOT only am I tired of hearing 'IT,' I feel that the word never should have been created." He shook his head, grimaced. "It suggests nothing, has no meaning, is cooked-up, enigmatic. It has a tiger skin twang."

He paused, looked about, then subsided into his chair.

"Perhaps I am too violent," he hazarded. "I am a one-sided person—what you call, perhaps, a wet blanket. I don't smoke, I don't drink, I don't gamble, I don't dance. I like my home. I do not like boldness, lack of restraint.

"But one should not be too critical here in America. America is very young, Europe is very old. In America you are having a sex awakening. It is all a matter of youth. This country is in a state of puberty so far as sex is concerned. America now makes its romances in taxicabs. Later that will change. As contrasted against the age-old background of Europe, America is like a magnificently gifted young person just learning the ways of the world.

"The madness for romance now upon America shows in all her films. No picture can succeed unless sex is intimated. A glorious picture like 'The Patriot' is mildly acclaimed—rated primarily an artistic success—because it has no love story. A tawdry romance from Poverty Row mops up because of its hugs and kisses and its inevitable clinch at the end.

"American women are more sensually inclined than American men. They are romance-starved because the men here do not know the art of love-making. They laugh foolishly to see a man kiss a woman's hand. They do not understand this gesture of gallantry. They misinterpret it. They condemn the man who does it. Nevertheless, in spite of the reputation it has given me, I shall continue to kiss the ladies' hands.

"American men do not like foreigners because they are too adept at romance.

"AMERICAN men lack imagination. They are practical, matter-of-fact, they possess no fantasy. They cannot smile. The American man can laugh loudly, he can cry salt water tears, but he is not subtle. The smile is a thing that comes only with age, generations of age. The American man dies sixteen deaths inside him before he says, 'I love you.' Yet he resents and fears the delicacy, the innate subtlety of the foreigner." A shrug from the great Schildkraut suggested contempt.

"We need a little more of the old-fashioned romance," he pursued. "Fewer saxophones, more violins. We need to get away from the bold, the blatant, back to the delicate. Less

THE most potent word in the English language today is IT.

Clara Bow is responsible for its current popularity, Elinor Glyn is credited with coining it, but Rudyard Kipling really invented it years ago.

Opinions as to its importance vary. Some say it stands as a symbol of sex, others maintain it is merely a vulgar colloquialism usurping exaggerated importance.

Its arch-enemy in Hollywood at present is Joseph Schildkraut. He thinks we should strip the ugly meaning from the word and restore it to its original place in our vocabulary, that of neuter pronoun, denoting the gender *without* sex.

"Why don't you ask me the meaning of 'IT'?" he demanded when I broached the subject. He was sitting in his library, fine etchings on the walls, interesting books about him. He got up, began to pace the floor. Then he answered his own question:

IT used to be a neuter pronoun—now it

IT?

"IT is a jazz name for personality," *says* Lewis Stone

tuxedos, more costumes. I am eager to know how people take my performance in 'Showboat'. There is nothing 'IT-ty' about it, nothing sexy. It is lavender and old lace—old-fashioned romance.

"In Europe sex is accepted as a matter of course. We don't point at it, don't discuss it. No one is consciously aware of the presence of 'IT'. America, however, seems ashamed of its sex, even though it is the most beautiful thing nature has given us. Perhaps the reason too much attention is paid to the matter of 'IT' here is because the subject is so new. That possibly accounts for the trick names, the subterfuges, the disguises. The word 'IT' is all of these.

"WOMEN in this country go by types. I would say there are three types: The flapper, exemplified by Clara Bow; the purely spiritual type, like Alice Joyce, and the strictly domestic type which in America is becoming more extinct every day, while the American domestic man becomes more distinct.

"The ideal woman, whom I have not met yet—yes I have—has a dash of all three types. But an all-around, finished woman is rare in America."

At that moment Elise Bartlett walked into the room. She had just come from rehearsal at the President. In private life, Elise Bartlett is, of course, Mrs. Schildkraut. I do not know this to be a fact, but as I watched her, as I observed her natural, unstudied ease, I suspected that she represented the "yes I have" part of her husband's remark about the ideal woman.

"I do not see Garbo as the symbol of 'IT' at all," said Schildkraut. "I know her well, and to me she is the very antithesis of sex. Highly spiritual, highly intellectual, yet unfortunately always in strained parts.

"When we start commercializing sex in America, when we take our 'IT' as easily as our baseball or our golf, then will there be no more obnoxious petting parties in the high schools, and the nasty viewpoint of a beautiful subject will be corrected. Just now 'IT' is America's new toy. In time she will tire of playing with it."

OF course the Schildkraut viewpoint represents the outside perspective. Let us turn now to a domestic reaction. Let us listen to Lewis Stone, to his opinions, his conclusions, his philosophy concerning the all-absorbing American topic.

" 'IT'," says Mr. Stone, "is merely a jazz-age name for personality."

Perhaps it will surprise you to note that this definition suggests nothing of sex. Yet it is like the man. Quiet, reserved, self-contained, he is exactly in real life the sort of man that authors picture in fiction. You feel, somehow, that Lew Stone is always master of any situation. And he is inscrutable enough to be intriguing. They call him "The only man on the screen past fifty with 'IT'."

His reserve, his discrimination, his resentment at the mere suggestion of affairs of the heart, give you the impression that he hails from the gallant South. And you are surprised when you discover that he was born near Boston.

But if you think you will get any advice from Lew Stone

Lewis Stone, the good grey actor who has never given a bad performance in his long screen career. Lew says that *IT* is just another word for personality, popularized by the jazz age. And a dignified thought it is, too!

regarding the efficient way in which to conduct an amour, you are doomed to disappointment. The man's facility for changing the subject is little short of genius. He even shies at generalities.

When I told him that "IT" was the text of his interview, an expression of horror crossed his face.

"I'm afraid you've come to the wrong person." He shook his head emphatically, to convince me, no doubt, that he was not well informed on the subject and that any other topic would be infinitely more welcome.

But we persisted. We got out the reportorial gimlet and began to bore in. We knew the information was there, it was merely a matter of getting it. The process was difficult, for we were discussing the matter behind a Russian railroad station on one of the M.-G.-M. stages during the making of "Wonder of Women." Every time we got going,

is the most abused word in our language

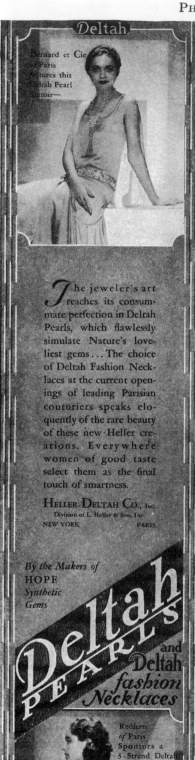
What Is IT?

good, Clarence Brown called Mr. Stone away to make another "take." I began to suspect it was a frame-up.

In time, however, we did garner a few crumbs of information, a few opinions, a conclusion or two.

"IT," according to Mr. Stone, includes all of the characteristics that make up personality. These qualities are sufficiently diversified to satisfy all individual requirements.

"Charm, genuineness, the faculty of being engaging or interesting or cheery, of being quiet, reposeful, languid—all have value, all embrace the ingredients of personality. What appeals to one does not, you know, necessarily appeal to another. It is altogether a matter of satisfying individual needs. What a mess we would be in it we were all cast to a standard."

But Mr. Stone indicated quite plainly that he much preferred to talk about what the Bostonian said when he told him that he, too, was a Bostonian.

The man refused to believe it, absolutely, because Lew had none of that characteristic New England accent which clings from the cradle to the grave.

With difficulty we again detoured back to the subject in hand.

"Is there any particular age, Mr. Stone, at which man appeals to woman?"

He hesitated a moment, weighing the matter, or else reluctant to commit himself.

"No-o-o, I think not. People appeal to each other at all ages. Youth responds to youth, and so on. It depends upon what spectacles we are wearing at the time. Then, too, you may be very charming in the eyes of one and not in the eyes of another. Personality has no universal law. In fact, the idea of 'IT' is like looking at a log fire. Five persons give you

five different impressions. It depends entirely upon what you read into it."

"Is an older man more interesting to women —say a man in his fifties? Is maturity an advantage, does the fruition of experience stand him in good stead?"

"How can we tell that? We cannot think with the feminine mind. Personally, I would say age does not enter into it. But after all that is a lot of peas in a barrel again—for it is an individual thing, depending upon the point of view. We can't all have the same outlook, you know, the same tastes."

THEN for no good reason at all, and yet for the best reason in the world, Lew Stone changed the subject.

"Why do people insist that a man in real life is the character he portrays on the screen? In his home he may be an unbearable grouch and on the screen a light comedian. If, however, he is a light comedian on the screen, then in the public mind he is a humorist in his private life."

Which reminds one of the fact that the parts Mr. Stone portrays on the screen are notable for their generous proportions of "IT." And his comment, therefore, may have been an adroit means of proclaiming his modesty.

At any rate, Mr. Schildkraut said of the typical American man: "He can laugh, but cannot smile; he is practical, matter of fact, has no imagination; he is not subtle; he dies sixteen deaths inside him before he can say, 'I love you'."

And after trying vainly to pierce the inscrutable reserve of Lew Stone, after glimpsing the smouldering fires that he quickly hides in the depths of his eyes, after watching him shield the faintest and most enigmatic of smiles, we concluded that he at least is not a typical American man.

Do you live out in the country or in one of those tangled suburbs? And do your guests frequently get lost the first time they visit your house? Then have a road map printed on top of your letter-paper, so that when you extend an invitation people will know you really mean it. The Gleasons—Russel, Lucile and Jimmy—use this road map to guide their friends to their bungalow

New
Pictures

Ira Hill

EVER since his *Rupert of Hentzau* brought him into the lenslight in "The Prisoner of Zenda," Ramon Novarro has been a storm center of debate. Is he or isn't he a big find? His pagan *Motauri* in "Where the Pavement Ends" is a definite affirmative answer, it seems to us

© Rayhuff-Richter

No international society wedding received more public attention than the marriage of Vilma Banky and Rod La Rocque. And no young couple ever started in married life with more sincere good wishes for their future happiness.

TERRIBLE influence of Hollywood on a nice little Chinee girl. Anna May Wong wears this costume—or lack of costume—in "The Chinese Parrot." What do you suppose the folks in the old country will have to say about it?

84

TOM MIX has quit being a cowboy for one picture at least. As Dick Turpin, film fans will see just what a versatile chap he is. And if you don't believe that he is versatile just read his life story which starts on the following page. He has been nearly everything—a cowboy, a soldier in the U. S. Army and a coal mine worker

*Jean Haskell,
Seattle Society Girl,
Wins the
Photoplay-Goldwyn
New Faces Contest*

Photo
Witzel

The Winner

JEAN HASKELL is abandoning a career in the most fashionable society circles of the west when she enters moving pictures.

When notified that she had won the Photoplay-Goldwyn New Faces contest, she left the big opening ball of the season at Del Monte, where she was dancing with young Spencer Morgan, Jr., and dashed fifty miles an hour to catch the train for Culver City.

Jean Haskell was born nineteen years ago in Chicago.

When she was four years old, her parents moved to Seattle where she was raised. For the past five years she has been a pupil at the fashionable Santa Barbara School for Girls at Santa Barbara, California. She was graduated from that institution last year.

Her father, J. Austin Haskell, is president of Carston and Earl's, investment bankers, of Seattle.

Jean is a talented musician, speaks French fluently, and has spent a great deal of time studying classic dancing.

She rides well and has shown her father's horses, at several western horse shows.

Marshall Neilan saw her walking across the lot a day or two after her first test had been made. "There's the prettiest girl I've seen on this lot in many a day," said the famous director.

She played the leading rôle in the school plays for several years, but had never had any professional experience before the fortunate date, May 8th, on which she entered her picture in the Screen Opportunity Contest.

She is five feet five and a half, has hazel-brown eyes under very long, deep lashes, short curly brown hair and a slim, girlish figure. Typically American, she promises to delight American audiences by displaying to them all the fresh, feminine charm of the best type of American girlhood.

The fact that a selection was very difficult to make and that decision was delayed to the last possible hour is responsible for the brevity of this announcement.

Every ambitious girl who is struggling for success against odds should read this story of Joan Crawford's brave fight

"To any woman, if she be honest with herself and her Creator, Life is a series of men—men who have influenced her growth, her career, her ambitions. Whatever we feel toward the man of the moment, it is he who is our very life and soul"

WRITE my Life Story?

But how can any woman write her Life Story?

A woman's life is not a matter of "I was born here" or "I was educated there!" It is a matter of thoughts, longings, temptations succumbed to, or temptations repudiated. It is a series of sorrows which have carried her to the depths of woeful despair; it is a series of joys which have wafted her to such heights that the very clouds in their mystic, colorful glories have seemed to float in the heavens *beneath* her!

And to any woman, if she be honest with herself and her Creator, Life is a series of men—men who have influenced her growth, her career, her ambitions. Men! We may hate them; we may love them. But whatever we feel toward the man of the moment, it is *he* who is the very life and soul of a woman during that period when he dwells in her thoughts with her.

How, then, are we to write the Life of Woman?

There is only one Life Story I know which has been written honestly, without apology, by a woman. That is by Isadora Duncan. And it was not printed until after she was buried. After we are dead, what does it matter?

PHOTOPLAY has asked for my Life Story? It is an honor and I appreciate it. They wish me to write it in the first person. I have argued, I have said "No," I have tried half-way measures. So now I say to you, who are to read it, I have succumbed after weeks of meditation. I have consented to write it as I have felt it, for to me life *is* feeling. But with

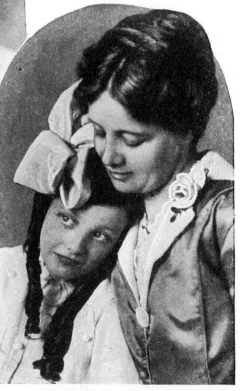

Joan Crawford, at the age of nine, with her mother. At this early age, Joan was waiting on tables and washing dishes to help pay for her meager schooling

The Story of a Dancing Girl

As told to
Ruth Biery
By Joan Crawford

certain reservations. Everything that you will read in these pages is the truth as far as I know; but not all of the truth is printed.

Why should I camouflage about it?

There are certain memories buried deep within woman that she cannot drag out even though she wills it. The innermost corner of a woman's soul is a dark, dank, secret prison. Sometimes in the night she may awaken and feel a ray of light penetrating the walls of that prison. A memory awakens! She turns over, writhes in torture at the suggestion of it. She arises, turns on the light, gets a book, a bit of sewing. Anything to shut out that light which, through her subconsciousness, has penetrated her memory-prison. She pushes it back, refuses to listen; finally eradicates all thought of it!

Why should she listen? She is living; she is happy. Why should buried secrets be allowed to stalk, like ghosts, beside the road of Life with her? To every woman I say: Never allow the past to molest the present. Your life is your own: Live it.

I do not remember anything about being born. That was an event into which I was not taken into consideration. I am glad that it happened, although there have been many times when I wished it had not happened. I know nothing about my first father. I say *first* because I do remember a father. He was not my own but I did not know it.

My earliest memories circle around this man whom I thought was my father. At this time I was called Lucille Cassin. His name was Henry Cassin. He owned a theater in Lawton, Oklahoma.

It is to this theater as much as to my innate nature that I owe the birth of my desire to become a dancer. Night after night, I would slip down to the show with my father and stand in the wings watching

Miss Crawford at the door of her Hollywood home. From a childhood as cheerless as any depicted by Charles Dickens, Joan has grown into one of the most fascinating women of the movies. Her frank story will be an inspiration to girls who, like Joan, want "to make something of themselves"

the chorus. My little feet, sometimes bare—sometimes in sandals, would unconsciously at first imitate the steps of the girls who were dancing. It was here that I learned not only my first steps but learned that in dancing I could find an outlet for my baby pent-up emotions. As I danced I forgot everything but the exhilaration of my swaying body. An exhilaration which has never left me.

Back of our house was a large, old-fashioned barn with a peaked roof. It was here that father kept his left-over stage scenery. It was here that my brother and I established amateur theatricals for other neighborhood youngsters. I was the star dancer, showing off the steps I had learned in the wings, concocting new ones to the music the boys whistled.

I HAVE promised to write this story from feelings! In these days when I was so young that I cannot remember many casual happenings, I recall I was often miserably unhappy. I wanted to play with the boys. I did not like girls. But my mother and my brother, who was two years my senior, would not let me. There were so many things that my mother and brother would not allow me! How foolish it is for mothers to say to their children, "No! You can not do it!" without an adequate explanation. If they had told me *why*—but they didn't. So I used to run away and play with the boys anyway.

I was stubborn. I thought my mother loved my brother best, felt she had no right to let him boss me. Although I was stubborn by nature, this imagined preference of my mother for my brother made me more stubborn. I remember one day mother sent me to my room as a punishment. When she came for me an hour later, I was standing in the corner stamping my feet and screaming "I didn't do it—I didn't!" Whether I had done it or not, I do not remember. But that was my story and I was going to stick to it!

My comfort came from my daddy, my dancing and my doll babies. Isn't it strange that little girls who are not happy always turn to dolls with that instinctive longing to play mother so that they can make *their* children happy? Much has been written about my doll room. It is all true. I have one entire room in my home in Hollywood filled with little girl-babies, boy-babies and soft woolly animals. Even to this day, when I am unhappy, I go to this room, sit on the floor, and talk to my babies. Even to this day when life is all topsy-turvy I go out and dance until I am exhausted. To this day, I long for my Daddy Cassin and wish I could climb on his lap and pour out my troubles as I did when I was a baby.

MY next memory is a mere shadow. But a very black shadow. It began, like most of those baby-shadows, by my disobeying my mother. A bunch of boys came whoopeeing down our alley in their Indian suits calling for me to come and play with them. I must have been seven. In my hurry to get out before my mother or brother could stop me, I stepped on a broken bottle. It cut through my shoe, dug deep into my foot. There were three operations. That bottle explains why I have never been a toe-dancer. To this day that foot bothers me.

I was shut in the house for weeks. I would hobble around with my dolls, poke my nose into this, into that. One afternoon I found a funny bag in the cellar under the cover of one of those old-fashioned empty cisterns. I pulled it out and worked for what was probably an hour to get it open. When I did, a great heap of bright, shiny, gold flat things rolled onto the cold, dirt floor. I screeched with joy as I played with them. Mother heard, came down, grabbed the bag from me. Then she sat down and cried and cried and cried. I couldn't understand. They were so pretty! I tried to comfort my mother. She wouldn't let me.

Shortly after that I was sent with my brother to visit my grandmother in Phoenix, Ariz. I remember how hot and stuffy the train was and that I was crying because I did not want to leave my daddy. Suddenly, my brother opened his suitcase and pulled out a picture of a tall man with black curly hair. Even now, I remember how curly his hair looked in that faded old picture.

"THAT'S your real father, kid," my brother told me. "Cassin is not your father. Your name, sis, is Le Sueur, not Cassin."

And that is the way I was introduced to my *first* father! I have never seen him. They told me he was dead but I know he was alive a year ago because I traced him. That is one reason I decided to write this story. I thought maybe he might read it and come to me.

When we returned home something terrible had happened. I never really understood about it and my mother has never told me. But the bright things I had found in the bag proved to be money. Daddy Cassin had been taken to prison. But he didn't stay there because he didn't steal them. But he had hidden them for another who had taken them. I knew my daddy was innocent.

Soon after that we moved to Kansas City. I felt that something was wrong between my mother and daddy but I never knew anything definite about it. They put me in a convent—St. Agnes Academy.

I suppose all this sounds very strange coming from Joan Crawford, the gay dancing girl of Broadway, as you have seen and read about her. That is the reason I was afraid to tell it to you. You have one idea of Joan Crawford, now you are going to form another. For I have never been a really happy person. Why even now, two women are suing their husbands for divorce, naming me as corespondent. One of them is a musician who plays for my pictures. How can I be happy when things like that are always happening to me? There should be a law in this country forbidding people to name corespondents unless they have some proof against them! I am innocent!

I suppose I should have been happy in the convent. But I was so sensitive. If I thought the girls didn't like me, I would go and hide rather than ask them to play with me.

I was there about a year when mother came for me. There was no money; she and daddy had separated.

But I didn't want to go home with mother if daddy wasn't there. I begged so hard to stay that they let me wait on tables to pay my tuition. I finished grammar school in that manner.

I do not need to tell you that it wasn't easy. There are none so cruel as small children. At least I had been their *equal*. Now I was just their *waitress!*

MOTHER was running a cheap little hotel. An ugly place. Ugh! How I hated to go home to it. As I'd leave the school Saturday and start for home, I'd walk up and down every street looking for my daddy. I didn't look at the people's faces. I was afraid I might miss him! I'd look at their shoes. You can see so many more shoes than faces. Daddy always wore the same kind of shoes. I knew I'd recognize them because I had taken them off every evening and brought his slippers for him.

One day I saw them. "Daddy!" How I screamed it. We went into a drug store and he bought me an ice cream soda. That is one of the happiest memories of my childhood—sitting on a drug store stool eating a ten cent ice cream soda with daddy Cassin!

Mother couldn't keep the hotel; she didn't have enough money. Just about the time I finished grammar school she took a laundry agency. It was in one of the poorest districts of Kansas City. My God, how I hated it! Bad men; terrible women. I couldn't cross the street without men trying to speak to me and looking at me strangely.

Mother couldn't keep me there. She had to find a place for me. She put me in a fourteen room combination boarding and day school that catered to the wealthy children in the residential district. I was to take care of the small kiddies, wash them and dress them in the morning, put them to bed in the evening, clean the house and get the family dinner in the evening. For this I was to get my high school education.

HOW often have I wondered if the wealthy folk who sent their children to that school would have continued had they known the way I was treated. I must be careful what I say for the woman who ran the school may still be living. But she deserves every bad word I could write about her. There was scarcely a day that I did not receive a beating. One time I was half dead from work. Another girl offered to help me. She got the dust pan for me. This woman saw her! She dragged me down two flights of stairs by the hair, then not only beat me but kicked me.

The kiddies were my only comfort. After I got them to bed I would read them stories and wonder why their mothers left them in a school like this when they had money enough to keep them at home and take care of them.

I thought I couldn't stand it. I ran away. I walked the streets of Kansas City one entire day. I *couldn't* go home to mother in those dingy little three rooms at the back of that laundry. It began to grow dark. I had to go somewhere—a policeman stopped me. I returned to the school, took off my shoes and tried to sneak in. I can see myself now in my little blue skirt and blue sweater. That was the only dress I had, two skirts and one sweater. She heard me! And she dragged me into the kitchen, threw me on the floor and kicked me and kicked me!

How I longed to go home and tell mother about it. Every Saturday I would start for home with that feeling, "Now, I am *going* to tell mother." And every Saturday as soon as I'd get in the door she'd tell me to watch the laundry. Then she'd go out with somebody.

As I grew older, things were a little better. The wealthy boys who came to the school liked me. That woman used to let me go out and dance with them so they'd keep coming to the school! It was then that it began to dawn on me that men might be useful to a woman.

There wasn't any particular boy at this time. I went out with them all. Always dancing. It was about this time that I began to wonder if I couldn't make money from my dancing. One night I won a dancing contest at the Jack O'Lantern Cafe in Kansas City. You can imagine what that meant to me. It strengthened my idea that I might make money at something besides sweeping floors and washing dishes.

At the end of three years they said my high school education was finished. Mother took me to Stevens College at Columbia, near the State University. I waited on tables. But tables or no tables I never missed a fraternity dance at the University. The thought that I could become a professional dancer was growing stronger and stronger. I was tired of waiting on table. I didn't see what good college would do me.

I ran away. Daddy Woods, the Dean, caught me at the railway station. He took me back and had a long talk with me. I will never forget it. "Billy, if you are not happy, we do not want you to stay. But leave in an honorable way." He gave me an honorable dismissal. I went home to the laundry. What else could I do? But mother said if I couldn't stay in school, I couldn't go out dancing. What! Take my dancing from me?

ON top of that I found mother was to be married. This time it was to a man named Hough. My third father! Just one more man to help boss me. I couldn't stand it. One day while they were out hunting an apartment, I packed up my clothes and few belongings. I was serious this time. I could dance! Nothing—mother, fathers, schools, men—there wasn't anything in this world big enough to keep me from being a famous dancer. I was going to Broadway. I didn't know how I would get there. I didn't have any money. But that didn't matter. I was started now and Broadway was going to recognize Lucille Le Sueur and make something of her!

And so Joan Crawford, nee Lucille Le Sueur, starts out for Broadway—and gets as far as Springfield, Mo. In the October issue of PHOTOPLAY, Miss Crawford will tell of her experiences in the road companies and cabarets of the middle west. And she writes, too, of her first love affair. Watch for the next installment of her colorful and vivid story.

Shakespeare Is His Middle Name

YOU have often wondered what that "S" in William S. Hart stood for. And now you know. It really is "Shakespeare." There's some reason for it, too. For William S. Hart—he wasn't known as plain Bill then—actually was Romeo to Julia Arthur's Juliet; Armand Duval to Modjeska's Camille. He was Pygmalion, Claude Melnotte in "The Lady of Lyons," Ingomar, Benedick, Iago, Orlando, Bassanio. "I played everything but little Eva and Little Lord Fauntleroy," he says, "they hadn't been written yet"!

Bill, the good bad man of the west; Bill, the two-gun hero, was the original Messala in "Ben Hur," Patrick Henry in "Hearts Courageous"; and he created the first western "bad man" on the American stage when he played Cash Hawkins in "The Squaw Man", in 1905. He was a matinee idol at twenty-one.

We hope this isn't going to prove too much of a shock to those who believe that Hart was born in a saddle and cut his teeth on a six-shooter. He did—figuratively speaking. But he went east and on the stage at nineteen. No real cowboy could step from his cows to the screen and make such a good cowboy as Hart. Realism is never so effective as art in drama.

The Bill Hart of the screen—the hard-shootin', hard-ridin' hero of a thousand western dramas. On the stage, he claims, he played everything except "Little Eva" and "Little Lord Fauntleroy." "They hadn't been written yet," he alibis.

The William S. Hart of the stage—in one of his favorite roles—Patrick Henry in "Hearts Courageous."

It's hard to believe, but Bill really looked like this when he played Messala in Ben Hur.

The Swimming Pools of Hollywood

The Carter de Havens bathe in tropical luxury—palms and weeping willows and all that sort of thing. They—there are four of them, including the two children—look surprisingly unaesthetic. But we wouldn't be surprised to learn that a Hawaiian orchestra was strumming away, concealed somewhere in the background

Norma Talmadge's pool, on the other hand, is almost puritanical in its chaste dignity. Edged with white it is; and very, very simple in design

Harold Lloyd's swimming pool, like his every comedy, is a pleasant jumble of slides and apparatus, of life preservers and pretty girls. It will be noticed that Harold takes his little pleasures straight, and without the aid of his famous specs

Looks like a canal, doesn't it? But it's just cut on the bias to make the picture seem more difficult. In reality it is the one and only pool on the Beverly Hills estate of Doug and Mary. The little picture, at the left, shows the two film favorites trying to cheer up a poor fish— and not succeeding very well!

92

The Reid pool seems homiest of all, somehow. Mrs. Reid declares that her house was designed around it; and it does occupy the center of the sloping hillside estate. The low stucco building is filled with dressing rooms and showers. And the cement walk is brightly hued

Charles Ray may be a simple country boy in pictures, but at home! Opulence-plus is his motto. Pale green tile and a water lily pond makes his swimming pool into a thing of almost unbelievable beauty. Charley and Cora don't swim in the clothes they're wearing—no indeed! They're going out to dine. The synthetic beach is also a part of the Ray estate, the brick stove is for the preparation of make believe shore dinners, and the blond baby is merely atmosphere

93

Carl Laemmle
presents

"OUTSIDE THE LAW"

directed by
TOD BROWNING
Universal-Jewel
Production de Luxe
starring

PRISCILLA DEAN

*T*HIS is a story so startling and a picture so marvelously acted and photographed as to make you forget you are in a theatre. What grips your interest right at the start is its revelation of the perfectly desperate work which is always going on below the surface of society — drama so flamingly passionate in its loves and hates and merciless revenge as to seem to you impossible—until you realize that only your sheltered life has made these things seem unreal—that people are undergoing just such terrific moments right now, today—while you read this page—and that some few will live to tell the tale. And this, as you well know, is just the kind of picture that Priscilla Dean can play better than any other actress in the whole wide world. Supporting her — Lon Chaney, that wonderful character actor who played in "The Miracle Man" and "The Penalty"—Wheeler Oakman, who was the hero in "The Virgin of Stamboul"—E. A. Warren, Ralph Lewis and a great company. Ask your theatre when you can see "OUTSIDE THE LAW." You'll have one crowded hour of entertainment.

Do you want to get in the Movies? Write Dramatic Mirror, 133 W. 44th St., New York

94

WHO filches our purse needs will explode, for the lining is bare. Who filches our heart trespasses, for East is East and West is West and even in pictures the Coast-lines should not knot.

But they do, for the other day—

We were enjoying an asterisk argument with an unseen telephone operator who insisted we had waited only nine and a half minutes for a number, while we insisted ten was correct. Suddenly, the door of our office, which in nowise resembles John D. Rockefeller's, swung wide and in pranced Boy Cupid, a cunning gill of mischief with guileless eyes and Singer Midget bow and arrow.

"Hello," saluted our visitor with moonshine infection.

"For cryin' in low. How are you, Cupe?" We shook hands and placed the receiver on the desk.

"I feel like the last rose of autumn and spring has just came. Think of my being so low when mortals are being knocked for bars of Lohengrin marches."

"What's on your cerebellum, T. N. T.?"

"I can't make heads or torsos of the movie stars," he deplored. "No sooner did I decide Connie Talmadge would marry Buster Collier than she springs a nifty and yesses Captain Alastair Mackintosh from Scotland."

"Scotch über alles," we murmured.

"Cut the split infinitives," he wailed. "I'm all bewildered. Do you know anything about the flicker favorites' romantic doings?"

"Cupe," we elucidated, "what the Oracle was to Athens, we are to Movieopolis."

"I can see modesty is at the root of your poverty," he psychoanalyzed. "But girl, not all my secretaries and file systems can keep abreast of these picture whatnots. Why don't you scribble what you know and help me check up?"

"Have you five tons of asbestos in stock?"

"Yes."

"Very well. Now go to the movies, Cupe, and call again tomorrow morn. Goo'bye and look out for the subway crowds."

We slip a sheet of typewriter, but our es discordantly.

"Hey . . . ," we pick it think you waited more than for that number you're the loon's shadow," the operator was finishing.

"Right you are, Gloria Swanson. Take a sleeping potion, ole bean, and nightmare over your signals. The War's just beginning."

Silence, except for noise everywhere. Our fingers gallop over the keys. They spill:

Syncopated heart strings, a racing romance of the cinema folk which we hereby dedicate to a palpitating world with malice toward none and fun for all.

Be there man amongst you who, to himself, never has exclaimed: My ideal is a jewel and my fingers yearn to be of the butter-and-egg variety, but canst not, for Rudolph Valentino has breathed into Latin type life and love; King

Words
by Dorothy Herzog
Music
by the Spheres

Rudy

Red hot romance. Sizzling romance. Rudy's and Natacha's. Icy dislike. Courts and lawyers. Divorce Rudy and Natacha. And now comes Pola. Hey! Hey!

Natacha

Pola

paper into the w. k. telephone receiver buzz-

up. '. . . and if you nine and a half minutes

So Sharlee went to ried Lita and the divine speedily on her exhilheart throbs. larized the Lorelei in vated Rod La Rocque, "Craney" Gartz, William Haines, and Dr. Daniel C. Goodman, Sharlee welcomed an infantile Junior to his family and Rudolph Valentino endeavored to obliterate his second matrimonial mishap.

La Negri's piercing slate-gray eyes espied the suave Rudy, appraised him, and sparkled with pleasure. What cared she for the blank cartridge report that Valentino and Vilma Banky were linked together by casual gossip in a 101 degree Fahrenheit way? Piff, nothing.

Did Rudy care when we popped the question at him: "Is it true?"

"What?"

"That you are among the elect? That the divine Pola has crowned you?"

Vidor has immortalized "The Big Parade"; and the perfect lover is made only by a sagacious press-agent.

There may be an un-common conception amongst many that the picture cavorters are individual dots in an individual art. The common conception should be they are heterogeneous bodies, good mixers and, ofttimes, good stayers. Look ye to your newspaper headlines.

Boy Cupid rants and raves over the w. k. game of heart throbs as played in cinema-land. Therefore—

We raise the asbestos curtain of love and reveal to you first that rare cosmopolite triumvirate: Rudolph Valentino, Pola Negri, and Charlie Chaplin.

Let the syncopated heart strings jazz forth romantic bars. Prosit! The play is on.

Charlie Chaplin bemoans he is not a lad of pleasure but just plain poisonous. The gentle sex bows to his artfulness and the fire in his eyes. He may be the Pagliacci of the silver sheet, but he is an Adonis in continuity.

While footing it debonairly in Germany, he met the smouldering Pola Negri. Flint struck spark and evoked a blaze. Pola came to America to hunt big game and eagles as an avocation, and Sharlee rushed her *a la* the famous Yale-Harvard football game of whynot. Newspaper scribes flocked to their Elysium where *charlotte russe* reigned supreme and chicken was *a la* comedy king.

Throughout the world, enthusiastic readers absorbed the story of La Negri and her Sharlee.

At the peak of the delicious suspense, Sharlee betook himself to his studio and his projection room, whilst Pola snapped ringed fingers and *fini* to an 8,000 mile romance of hurricane force but puny endurance.

The world refused to do its stuff on its pivots until Sharlee eventually started "The Gold Rush" and Lita Gray skyrocketed into prominence. She did more than skyrocket. Lita had a screen mama who knew that two and two, added or multiplied, made four. Mexico and married Pola continued arating game of While Pola popuHollywood and capti-

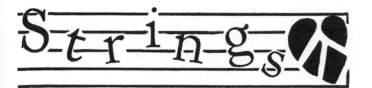

The wedding march is a jazz tune in Filmland. Every little marriage has a triangle all its own

95

He shrugged, oh, so Latin-ish and un-Cicero-ish. "I do not know. I do know that I shall not marry again."

So he returned from New York to the Coast, after a gay vacation on Continental soils. And he was nearly met in Albuquerque by the tempestuous Pola. We say nearly. La Negri was enticed back to Los Angeles in time to avert too many newspaper headlines.

Hollywood promptly fell into a state bordering on hysteria. Could it be true? Sh-h-h, hark. Pola and Valentino go a-visiting the Gouverneur Morrises in Coronado Beach. As suddenly, they disappear.

"Hear they've hastened to Mexicali, Mexico, married, and are honeymooning in Palm Springs, Calif.," exclaimed a news-maddened city editor of a L. A. paper.

Oh, dear, how perfectly luscious. Precisely Rudy's Odyssey when he eloped with Natacha Rambova. Foiled again. Truth is not stranger than fiction; only more expensive. So it is, Vilma Banky again heroines for Valentino in his new picture, "Son of the Sheik." Rumors are rife. Poor Boy Cupid . . . Sharlee is now a married man with a Junior in the family and a second offspring due to arrive. Rudy and Pola continue jazzily on their syncopated heart string route, with junctions up and down the lines but tracks barring the perfect understanding.

We fade-out and -in to Constance Talmadge, reckless daughter of a cautious family. La Negri stoked her way into men's hearts. Connie danced, chided, and entranced her reign there.

Connie's fluttering life is one heart milestone after another. She chucked Irving Berlin to run away and marry John Pialoglou five years ago via the double wedding, yes with Dorothy Gish and James Rennie on the successful receiving end. Berlin was floored for the count. He chirped up when Connie lost interest in her husband and a separation, followed by a divorce, occurred p. d. q. John resumed his Beau Brummel activities on the street called Broadway.

Connie betook herself West, where she annexed William Collier, Jr., better known as Buster. Buster was a laugh a second. They had hilarious times together for almost four years. Marriage was around the next week. Buster was younger than Connie, but that was a trivial detail.

After one of her cyclonic visits East, Irving Berlin, with hopes burning high again, saw Connie off. Farewells made him melancholy. "What'll I do, Dutch, when you are gone?" Dutch is Connie's nickname, originating because of her blue eyes and blonde hair. "By jove, that's a great title for a song," Berlin caught himself saying. So he wrote "What'll I Do," dedicat-

Florence   Eleanor

Cupid's big four. Florence Vidor, King Vidor, Eleanor Boardman, George Fitzmaurice. Divorce, King and Florence. Engagement, George and Florence. Now George is free, King engaged, maybe, to Eleanor Wow!

King   George

IF John Brown, the Millville, Pa., street cleaner, is divorced by Mrs. Brown, 50 people hear of it; if a local celebrity of Chicago is involved in an escapade, 100,000 people are interested. If a film star is divorced the whole world wants every detail. Picture folks live under a giant spotlight of publicity. Their hearts, broken or blissful, become the hearts of humanity

riage inspired by Berlin's ditto? Boy Cupid, check up your files.

We iris-out and -in to Florence and King Vidor. Florence, years ago, was just a little girl in Texas, where men are men and women—well, ladies. King Vidor, a youth with tortoise glasses and genial manner, arrived in the home town to shoot a picture. Would the Texas 400 extra for a thrill? They would and did.

King espied Florence, slim, girlish, beautiful. Florence espied King, good-looking, self-possessed, capable. Palps. Love at first sight. Marriage. The girl with a comfortable roof over her head left it to gamble with her husband; career and thousands versus flop and pennies.

Florence was a lovely flower devoid of tropical warmth. King missed this yet lived in happy domestic isolation until one day—

Well they just separated. Who can tell just why? After all there are just two people in the world who know the inside of any marriage—the man and the woman. The real trouble rarely ever gets to the judge. Everybody likes Florence. King is hard to know, but when you do know him he's a regular citizen in addition to being one of the few directors with brains and balance.

He met another girl, tall, slender, moody. This girl came from Philadelphia, which also boasts the Liberty Bell and Wanamaker's. She strived for a career in pictures. King appreciated her ambition and her talent. Sympathy. Friendship.

King had moved to new quarters. Florence, with their little daughter, remained in the house that had once been home. Months stumbled by. All

ing it, it has been reported, to Connie.

Gradually, he forced himself to lose his infatuation for the charming, though frosted, Connie. He proceeded to fall headlong in love with Ellin Mackay, daughter of the big Postal click and collect man. He bombshelled a slumbrous world by eloping with Miss Mackay. A month and a half later, Connie sprang a ditto surprise by taking on a second "worser half" in Captain Alastair Mackintosh, "unoccupied professionally" member of a wealthy Scotch family. Connie halfway confesses to having met her latest about three years ago through William Rhinelander Stewart, an ex-society swain of hers.

That, however didn't minimize Buster Collier's forlornness at being left a romantic orphan, as badly floored by Connie's unexpected desertion as Irving Berlin had been, so many years before. Was Connie's sudden marriage inspired by Berlin's ditto? Boy Cupid, check up your files.

this time, King kept the key to his former residence, though by now he was a successful director come into his own while Florence was just winning a niche for herself as an actress.

"Yes, it is a pity," Florence admitted to us once. "We did struggle through the early days together and now . . . ," a shrug that conveyed oh, so much.

Florence became acquainted with herself. Ye gods, she had sex appeal and all these years had been unaware of that alluring fact. She commenced to gather friends around her. One day, King returned to the house to get what mail there was for him. He let himself in with his key. A youth accompanied him. The house was homey and comfy and cheery. King sighed.

"You love Florence," the youth, who was a friend, accused.

KING admitted there was some truth and much poetry in the accusation. Why not? Differences of opinion do not necessarily make folks enemies. He gazed out of the window at the tennis court where Florence, beautiful and gay, was playing a love set with George Fitzmaurice.

So divorce followed leisurely on the heels of separation. Was King of "The Big Parade" going to marry Eleanor Boardman? Denials. Folks shook befuddled heads. They couldn't make heads or tails of the mixup.

Florence and George Fitzmaurice, Ouida Bergere's ex-husband and also a director, announced their engagement and forthcoming marriage.

"I give you odds that never comes off," an acquaintance sprang on us.

"Spurned," we retorted, being suspicious of the ways of the impossible.

Boy Cupid doesn't know. Ouida Bergere was supposed to have yessed Basil Rathbun, the actor, months ago. The marriage was postponed and explanations also. Ouida was once mad about Fitzmaurice.

Jack Pickford, restless brother of Mary, married Marilyn Miller several years ago and the optimists offered odds it wouldn't take.

"Give 'em six months and then we're being generous."

They lost, by nearly eighteen months. Then along trotted Ben Finney, reported scion of a well-to-do southern family. Ben Finney had once edged Ben Lyon out of an impassioned love. The tables turned. Ben Finney departed for China, evidently to learn if China-eggs were manufactured by cartloads or carloads. Ben Lyon breezed in.

Marilyn and Ben, the Jungle Crown Prince, swapped ideas, ideals, and I-don't-knows.

"They're engaged," ejaculated the blase, stirred to enthusiasm. (Note: when you're married and separated, it is legitimate to be engaged in the flicker world just as much as if your name appears in the social register.)

"Marilyn is going to Paris this summer to get a divorce from Jack, and Ben will meet her there and they'll be spliced," opines the street of the White Lights and tired hearts.

Boy Cupid, we turn to you. Please wire, collect.

Eyes focus smartly ahead and concentrate on Lillian Gish, purveyor of emotional hysteria in celluloid. Now that Lillian has made the varsity and won her "Scarlet Letter," who will be her next heart victim?

When D. W. Griffith allowed the elder Gish to leave his fold, there were those who sighed and said: "That's over."

When Charles Duell crossed the stormy Atlantic to join his "White Sister" in Florence, the cables agitated a la Vesuvius and steamed stories across the deep. Mrs. Duell was going to divorce her husband because he was engaged to a Gish.

"Romola" brought the law courts and the carrots into prominence. Lillian sued the erstwhile assaulter of her heart and won. He was broken. Joseph Hergesheimer penned a glowing article about the mouse-y Lillian for a ritzy magazine. Ah, ha-a-a-a, breathed the breathers. But it was not Mr. Hergesheimer. It was George Jean Nathan, one of the editors of this periodical.

Where Mr. Nathan went, Miss Gish went. His people were her people. Mr. Nathan re-signed from the magazine with which he had been so long associated. It was said that he would write original screen stories for Miss Gish. Suddenly, they broke. Perhaps the clever Mr. Nathan was too wise to try the movies. Lillian eventually went West to make pictures. Mr. Nathan remained East. A nice guy, this Nathan boy, very nice, and he doffs his highbrow when he leaves his typewriter. Will the quiet Lillian, with her peculiar brand of vamping, break loose again?

Boy Cupid, please respond.

FLICKER-LAND'S latest reel of inside shootings reveals Norma Shearer and Jack Gilbert are finding much in common. Can it be? It can and it can't. Norma has never attempted a matrimonial sail. Jack is a veteran.

Jack was once married to Leatrice Joy who prided her career above wifeliness and forsook the domestic roof every time she made a picture for Cecil De Mille. Since their divorce, Leatrice goes around now and then, but shuns the cooing dove act. Jack seems determined to be fancy free.

Is Richard Barthelmess going to give his Mary a divorce? He is not. He spurns any such move. Yet Dick's name was news paperly associated with Millicent Rogers, the Countess Salm. Whilst on the Coast, he has been seen with Barbara Bennett, tempestuous sister of that erstwhile heart-slayer, Constance, who is now Mrs. Phil Plant, a social princess with millions. Dick cannot make a move but they try to plant him in matrimony. It's part of the price of success.

Boy Cupid must certainly have a feverish time re-vamping the files devoted to the cinema colony. For in this silent drama realm, which is as silent as a nest of hungry baby blackbirds, romance stalks day and night. Personalities meet, tread on others, flare, only to chill and part and continue playing blindly and debonairly the jazz of syncopated heart strings.

Oh, dear, we do so pity poor Boy Cupid and his complicated job of keeping apace of starry heart palps.

RICHARD BARTHELMESS, Mary Hay Barthelmess and their boss—Mary Hay Barthelmess Jr. Being a girl, she naturally turns to Dick

Mr. Valentino with Agnes Ayers in ":The Sheik"

Mr. Valentino Demonstrates cave-man love and tenderness. His article tells his preference

With Gloria Swanson "Beyond the Rocks"

Woman and Love

By RUDOLPH VALENTINO

WHEN you ask me to write for you what I think about woman, I feel that I must produce for you something that would look like the Encyclopedia Britannica. Yet when I should be through with this great work, I shall still have said less than nothing about woman.

We cannot know woman because she does not know herself. She is the unsolvable mystery, perhaps because there is no solution. The Sphinx has never spoken—perhaps because she has nothing to say.

But since woman is the legitimate object of man's thoughts, and mine have been somewhat distilled in the alcohol of experience, I may be able to give to you a little draft of truth.

English is not my own tongue as you know. In Italian, French, Spanish, I might express myself better, for there we have such little words that have fire and understanding and delicate shades of meaning to which I know not yet the English translations.

My point of the view on woman is Latin—is continental. The American man I do not understand at all. I have lived much in Paris, in Rome, in New York, and from this traveling, which is of the finest to develop the mind and understanding soul, I have composed my little philosophy about woman.

For there is only one book in which you may read about Woman. That is the Book of Life. And even that is written in cipher.

But those who refuse to read it are generally more deeply wounded than those who digest it thoroughly.

What comes to my mind first as I try to put into some order my ideas on this all-important subject, I will tell you.

It is this. Which of the

women I have known, have perhaps loved a little, do I remember instantly, and which have I forgotten, so that I must think and think to recall them at all?

The most difficult thing in the world is to make a man love you when he sees you every day. The next is to make him remember that he has loved you when he no longer sees you at all.

Strangely enough, I remember the women who told me perhaps their little lonelinesses, who spoke in close moments true and sweet and simple heart throbs.

Even the highest peak of emotion is finished. It has flamed, gone out, and told us very little about life. It was to enjoy, to drink deeply. But never is even that treasured in the heart as are those moments of simple, tender confidences, when a gentle, loving sigh opened the treasure house of a woman's heart and she spoke truly of those things within.

A man likes even the bad women he knows to be good.

To a woman who has revealed her soul, who has given a brief glimpse of her heart, no man ever pays the insult to forget; he pays her homage. I remember a little Italian girl I once knew. She was very beautiful —so young. We used to sit in a tiny cafe we knew in Naples, and hold hands quite openly. I do not think I ever kissed her. We talked little, for she was not educated. It was not her magnificent eyes, nor the glory of her hair that was like a blackbird's wing, nor the round white curves of her young body—I remember her because of those little intimate moments when our thoughts were bound together by her simple, tender, gentle words. We were intimates, and the soul is such a lonely thing that it treasures those moments of companionship.

I do not like women who know too much.

The modern woman in America tries to destroy romance. Either it must be marriage or it must be ugly scandal.

No other woman can ever mean to a man what his children's mother means to him.

A love affair with a stupid woman is like a cold cup of coffee.

I would not care to kiss a woman whose lips were mine at our second or third meeting.

One can always be kind to a woman one cares nothing about.

The greatest asset to a woman is dignity.

And this, surrender to confidence, to real intimacy of the soul and heart, speaks a much greater surrender to love, a much deeper capacity to love, than all the passion of a Cleopatra.

There was another woman in France, an older woman, the wife of a painter. I loved her because she was the only grave woman I ever have known who did not depress. I never saw her smile. But beneath that smooth, impartial beauty, that pearl-like, moon-like loveliness of hers, flowed a mólten lava of shy, strong, sentimentalism, which her mind condemned. It has remained with me like the perfume of a cathedral.

THERE was a little artist's model, too, in Paris. Oh, of such a saucy, impudent, swift little creature you have not heard. She had eyes like black coals and round little cheeks where hung the scarlet banner of her youth and *joie de vivre*. She was enchanting. She danced like a bacchante. Her red lips were always laughing and singing and flinging teasing little mots at you. And she had a little hat which she herself made over every day, so that I thought she must have at least a dozen hats, and I was madly jealous of the man who must make this extravagance possible. Now it is not her coquetry, nor her vivid young beauty nor her wild youth that makes her live in my memory, but the sweet little incongruity of that little hat that her nimble fingers changed each day.

Tenderness is absolutely the strongest, most lasting, most trustworthy emotion that a woman can arouse in a man. It is a great force that modern woman disregards.

All women are divided into two classes in the mind of a man. Often they are so mixed up that you do not know which is which until you go down very deep. Then it does not matter, for in an affair of amour a counterfeit is often better than the real thing.

In my poor English, let me say that there are what I would call joy-women and duty-women. Now understand, the joy woman may be very good and the duty woman might even be bad. That is just their relation to man. The first kind are the kind that you want to take with you on your joyful care-free wanderings into life's highways and byways. The others are the women who are possibilities to share the principal things of life—home, family, children.

For a wife, a man should pick out a woman who is pretty, has a good disposition, and is domestically inclined. They are very rare, now, I admit. One is too apt to be deceived by their easy method of comradeship. Let her be your inferior, if possible. Then she will be happy with you. It is much more essential to marriage that a woman be happy in it than a man. I do not mean a butterfly that flits from beauty parlor to beauty parlor. But a good woman who has the old-fashioned virtues.

We Europeans do not expect too much of one woman.

The difficulty with love and marriage in this country is that the man has let the game get out of his hand. A woman can never have a happy love affair with a man unless he is her superior. It just can't be done. The love affair where the woman is the stronger in mind and knowledge is always a tragedy or a farce.

I do not like women who know too much. Remember, it

Elinor Glynn, the famous English writer, believes Rudolph Valentino is the "Great Lover" of the screen. She used to prefer Wally Reid

was from the serpent that Eve was given that apple from the Tree of Knowledge. Just so would I make the Tree of Knowledge of Life today—forbidden to women. If they must eat of it, let them do so in secret and burn the core.

Do not misunderstand this that I say. I do not mean this in regard to intelligence, to education, even to position. The more cultured and accomplished a woman is, the more exquisite she is to love, the more like gold that is soft to touch and handle. With her, all is delicate and attractive, all is beautiful and fine, her mind is attuned to beauty —and beauty is of itself a religion.

No, when I speak thus of an inferior—a superior—I mean in experience of life, in power to do, in ways of love. The man may be a digger in the ditch, and the woman a teacher in the school, but he is the master of her if he knows more of the world than she does. It is not becoming that a woman should know the world. It is not proper that a lady should go to places or to things where she acquires this knowledge.

If she knows these things, she must be clever enough to conceal her knowledge, like the girl who can swim a mile, yet with much grace and helplessness she allows me to teach her swimming.

How completely the modern woman in America tries to destroy romance. How ugly and cut-and-dry it has become—love. Either it must be marriage or it must be ugly scandal. The brilliant, absorbing, delightful, dangerous, innocent—sometimes—sport of love, how it goes. She knows too much about life and too little about emotion. She knows all of the bad and none of the good about passion. She has seen everything, felt nothing. She arouses in me disgust.

Sometimes a man may feel that he would rather a woman had done many, many bad things—real bad things—and yet been delicate, and quiet and dignified, than to see her common. If the bloom has been rubbed from the peach, let her paint it back on with an artistic hand.

SHOULD I try again to find me a wife, I say, let me find one who wishes to have children and who when she has had them, wishes to take care of them. That is the proper test for the good woman who is to share the side of your life. No other woman can ever mean to a man what his children's mother means to him—if she does not let herself get fat and ugly and old. No man can love a woman who lets herself get fat, and careless and unpleasant. He must then constantly make comparisons of her with the beautiful young girls about. A wife's first duty is to keep her husband from making comparisons.

A man is always intrigued to see a woman with a child. The Sistine Madonna is as famous and as beloved as Mona Lisa.

But—for a sweetheart. Ah, that is different. To me, I have been won always by the woman who has great ability to feel. I have never yet seen a cold woman who interested me. A reluctant woman, yes. But reluctant only as a flower is reluctant to bloom in winter. Place it in the hot-house of proper wooing—and it blossoms. She must have intelligence.

A love affair with a stupid woman no matter how beautiful, is like cold coffee for breakfast.

98

Woman and Love

It is coffee of course—but one would almost rather do without. The ancient Greeks taught the art of love to their damsels. They understood the necessity of doing well and wisely the things that are important to life. Today, every man is seeking the woman who is intelligent about love, who understands instinctively those fine, sensitive cords that make up passion. Love is as delicate as an orchid.

A WOMAN must have curiosity. I have been most captivated by the sight in a woman's eyes of that infinite curiosity about life. Curiosity is not a fault. It is the cocktail of the emotions.

In one point do I disagree greatly with the American man's philosophy of love. I believe that the most irresistible woman in the world is the woman who is madly in love with you. I can resist any temptation except the incense of adoration. Nothing is so flattering to a man as a woman's adoration. More men are attracted and held by a woman's passion for them than by theirs for her. It is the emotion he is able to arouse in a woman that thrills him most, not the emotion she is able to arouse in him.

The experienced man of the world returns again and again to the warm flame of a woman's passion for him. It is the one form of romance of which a man never tires. He may tire of the particular flame and see a new one, but difference in object will not change singleness of passion.

The less experienced man, the man who doesn't need to seek new sensations, is thrilled by the coquette who plays with him. But he has not yet discovered that the most enthralling thing in the world is an influence over the emotions and actions and heart beats of another—when it is genuine.

The most dangerous woman in the world is a pretty woman who has deep wells of passion in her nature but who has never loved.

Of all the women I have known, the Frenchwomen are the most nearly perfect. No matter what their age or class may be, they have that touch of domesticity, that sweet and gentle something that lends a delicacy even to the wildness of the senses. Thy know how to amuse, how to touch the heart, they have the sixth sense of pleasing a man with their perfection. And they are so very well dressed. All of them.

American women are terribly pretty. Even when they are quite ugly, they are pretty. They are always rather well dressed. And they always behave as though they were beautiful. Which gives them great poise. But they lack softness, they lack feminine charm and sweetness. You cannot imagine them doing their bits of sewing, washing, mending, and what not. They dazzle but they do not warm. They are magnificent when they are dressed up, but I never have seen one who was likewise at ease and delicious and feminine in the kitchen or the nursery.

They are so restless, too. Nothing interferes with romance like restlessness. It destroys those subtle shadings that are the very breath of its life.

I do not blame the women for all this. I blame the American man. He cannot hold a woman, dominate and rule her. Naturally things have come to a pretty pass. He is impossible as a lover. He cares nothing for pleasing the woman. He is not master in his own house. He picks and nags about little things, and then falls down in big ones. He expects to feed a woman on the husks

left from business and golf and money, and satisfy her. He has learned nothing about love and yet he expects to bestow upon her everything she should desire.

In his blindness therefore, he despises the young European who comes here. He laughs at him, makes fun of him, calls him insulting names. Why? Because this man, versed and trained in all that goes to make everything from the lightest philandering to the deepest amour, exquisite and entertaining and delicate, this man—what is it you say —shows him up? Yes.

A woman will flirt with anybody in the world so long as there are lots of other people looking on. That is natural. But to flirt in private without boredom and without offending her delicate sensibilities, she desires a partner whose experience of these things is greater than her own.

The caveman method I abhor, and I do not believe that it is ever successful with the woman who is worth having. Who could desire a woman taken by force? Who would gain any pleasure from loving or caressing a woman who did not give in return? The giving of love to me is not half so wonderful as the receiving. It may be more blessed but it is not nearly so exhilarating.

The mental caveman—ah, that is again different. By cleverness, by diplomacy, by superior mental force, by skill—that is the way to win a woman. It is only a woman who must be so won, but difference in object won can give great ardor to a love affair, who proves attractive.

Even a woman whose passions are never returned has a better chance of keeping her illusions than the woman who has a love affair with a man who is brutal and uncouth. I have never known a woman in my life who was not modest, who did not have in her a certain feeling of delicacy and a regard for herself if allowed to express it.

A man who is brutal and direct and uncouth in his advances to a woman—and you would be surprised to learn how many men today push aside all the ordinary conventions when they see a woman who attracts them—looks at that woman and his purpose with her is written in his eyes. It is plain and ugly and it offends her at once, even though the man himself attracts.

The second or the third time he sees her, he—again I am American—he gets fresh. Maybe he tries to kiss her. Then if she is a woman worth having, she slaps his face and says to him, "How dare you?"

QUITE right. I would not care to kiss the woman whose lips were mine at our second or third meeting.

The preliminaries of a love affair are the most enticing part of the game. Let a woman in them be sweet but cool, promising but never encouraging, never exhibiting brazenly her familiarity with life.

Now we come to the skilled lover—the European lover. He veils his purpose. Back in his mind may be the same thought the same desire to kiss that woman. He does not let her see it. No, no. He is gentle, he is sweet. He is deferential. He flatters her, because all woman love flattery, though not so much as men. He tells her that she is beautiful, that she is good, that she is wonderful beyond all woman.

He pets her, caresses her a little to let her become accustomed to his touch. He lets her see that he enjoys her company, even when they sit the length of a room apart. He lets her know that he likes to be near her, to speak of books and music and paintings. He reads poetry to her.

Then when he kisses her, she gives him back his kiss. No caveman can ever know the sweetness of that returned kiss. What she does, she does for love. So she is happy in it, and makes neither herself nor him miserable with reproaches. Even if he never sees her again, she will cherish a fond memory of him. She has not lost her self-respect. The affair may last a long time, and much happy companionship is possible to them.

A woman loves finesse. In Europe, we are taught to be most polite, to be courteous, to entertain the ladies. When we go into a drawing room, we talk of art, music, books, we tell a witty remark or two. Everyone is happy, and amused. One is never rude but tries to show the greatest attentions and charms he possesses. Then when he goes, the ladies—and maybe one upon whom he has his eyes, says, "What a charming and amusing person."

You see women love with their ears, men with their eyes.

Ah yes, in the small matters one is a slave. But in the big things—he is master. To argue about little things with a woman, to get angry, is one thing that no man versed in the arts of love ever does. After all, it is the woman who decides whether she finds you charming. It is only after you have won her love that you dare be master.

One can always be kind to a woman one cares nothing about—and to a woman by whom one is attracted. But only cruel to a woman one loves or has loved.

THERE are several kinds of women, several kind of methods of wooing on their part that are irresistible to me.

I love the dainty, little woman, who plays seriously at being domestic. She fascinates me. Everything womanly, distinctly feminine, in a woman, appeals to me. I adore her bird-like ways, her sweet pretenses, her delicious prettiness. I love her almost as one loves a cunning child, and when to this is added the filipe of sex, she becomes perfect. I do not like in her flippant, cold-blooded little tricks, but those soft, lovable ways of a little woman, those melting, helpless little ways of hers—that bring tears to your eyes and fire to your lips.

Then there is the silent, mysterious woman who fences divinely. Who knows silently and secretly the secrets of the couquette— that last art of woman, in always leaving herself an opportunity to retreat. Who has always at hand that last weapon of woman —surrender.

The greatest asset to a woman is dignity. It is her shield. With it, she may commit indiscretions that a vulgar puritan could never attempt. Dignity in a woman always puzzles a man. He likes it. He admires it. He feels confidence in the woman who displays it. He knows that she will never make a fool of herself or of him.

Nothing so fascinates me as the ability of a woman to get great pleasure from life. It is so short. The tragedy of age is not that one grows old, but that one's heart stays young. Life that develops the soul, slowly disintegrates the body. Therefore, let us make merry while we can. I cannot stand a woman who is afflicted with ennui. My countrywomen possess the gorgeous quality of enjoying life, of loving it, of getting from it all that there is to get, more than all other women. But they are never hoydenish, nor restless. They have grace and poise and polish.

Love is honey. It is a flower. It may be fierce as a tiger lily, but it must be beautiful, delicate, gentle too.

Hartsook

The Unhappy Ending of Wally Reid's Life Story

Wally Reid is pictured above in one of his most famous characterizations, opposite Geraldine Farrar, in "Joan the Woman." At the right, Wally is seen in the happy old days romping with his son, Bill, and his dog, "Spike"

A TRIBUTE

From a Friend

HE was the exemplar of American youth. Reckless, genial, carefree and democratic, with an unfailing sense of humor and a spirit that never said die.

In appearance a young god, with all the gifts that the gods could bestow and yet with the great lovable good nature that made him —just Wally.

He didn't take himself seriously. He didn't take life seriously. He lavished his gifts freely and offered his hand to all.

An athlete, a musician, an artist, an actor —and yet he would laugh at his own accomplishments. There was no ego in Wally Reid.

He accepted everyone as a friend and his door was open to all. Who you were or where you came from never mattered to Wally. He was not only a hero to the millions who saw him in films, he was a hero to his own valet and to every extra around the studio.

Whenever charity called Wally Reid came. He never spared himself; he never considered his prestige; he was the friend of every man.

Yet few people knew the real Wally Reid, who once said to me, "They would laugh at you if you told them I ever had a serious thought, but just between you and me I'd like to do something worth while some day— give something to the world beside my face and figure."

And now he has.

He lived to delight millions.

Wally, his wife, Dorothy Davenport Reid, and their son, William Wallace Reid, Jr., at the door of their Hollywood home

He died with the whispered hope that he might save at least a few from the agony that was his.

His last role was the greatest he ever played. Never on the screen did he wage such a brave and splendid fight.

The loyal love of millions will follow the star that is forever— just Wally.

HERBERT HOWE

A snapshot of Wally and his wife, taken at Universal City a few hours after their wedding

Gossip
East
&
West

By Cal York

Mary and Doug attended the motion picture circus, held in the Hotel Ambassador horse show arena in Los Angeles, and created something of a three ring sensation themselves. The circus was given for the benefit of the Children's Hospital

THERE have been temperamental romances before, but we predict that of all the temperamental, hectic and exciting love affairs ever before known, the Charlie Chaplin-Pola Negri engagement will win in a walk.

It's kept all Hollywood busy try to 'stay posted on the latest status of the famous engagement.

Charlie Chaplin and Pola Negri are engaged. They aren't. They are.

The very latest is a complete reconciliation, following a violent tiff, and the wedding is to take place very soon.

It happened like this.

Charlie, chatting to a newspaper reporter, and asked for the date of his wedding, laughingly declared that he'd have to finish one picture first, because he was too poor to marry.

Pola saw the little story the newspaper man wrote. Yes, indeed.

Followed three days of tears and three sleepless nights.

Miss Negri could not work, she could not see anyone. She was prostrated. She refused to see Charlie or to tell him why she wouldn't see him.

Then, she saw the reporters and with a pitiful little smile, admitted that her great romance lay in dust and ashes about her feet. She was no longer engaged to Mr. Chaplin. And she used a dignified little printed statement to the effect that though she was Mr. Chaplin's good friend and would always wish him well, they were no longer engaged.

Off stage, in a trembling voice, she said, "Three days I have thought I would do thees thing. I have not slept. Oh, it was a thousand little things. He was so—so. Oh, I don't know. It was just experience. A woman must learn by experiences. I have not tell it to Mr. Chaplin to his face. I could not face that. I have sent my best friend to him. I will live only for my work. Happiness is over for me. The dear days at Del Monte and Santa Barbara, they can be no more."

The official statement, issued immediately, read: "I consider I am too poor to marry Charlie Chaplin. He needs to marry a wealthy woman and he should have no difficulty in finding one in the United States—the richest and most beautiful country in the world. Therefore I give Mr. Chaplin back his freedom, and release him from his engagement. I wish him the best of luck and I will always be his devoted friend.

Pola Negri."

Most of the time you'll find Viola Dana a half hour's ride from the Metro Hollywood Studios. She spends all her spare moments on the Santa Monica Beach

Moral House-Clean

What's It All About?

THE governor of a great state is sued for seduction by his stenographer—a leading banker is accused by his wife of illicit love affairs—a well-known minister with a family is arrested for white slavery—an eminent lawyer is mutilated by a husband for home-breaking. . . .

But does the world conclude that governors, or bankers, or ministers, or lawyers—*as a class*—are therefore rotten, that the whole profession is given to those practices of which one of its members has been accused or found guilty?

No! The thinking world is too just—too sane.

And yet, because two prominent figures in motion pictures have recently been the center of scandal, the entire profession has been put under a cloud.

The reason for this iniquity is manifold:

To begin with, Hollywood is the most talked-of city in America; it is a small community populated by famous people who exist in the white glare of a merciless spotlight. They have as much privacy in their work or lives as a Broadway traffic policeman.

Moreover, the men and women who work in pictures are the most popular and intimately familiar figures in the nation's life.

Also, the dishonest, scavenger press, seeing temporary profit in sensational smut, proceeds to butcher the motion pictures to make a journalistic holiday. Motion-picture scandals are exaggerated and dwelt upon, given exorbitant space, and played up with pictures and banner heads.

Then again, certain despicable seekers for cheap and lurid publicity, in the motion-picture ranks, rush into print with their ideas, tales, suppositions and opinions.

Furthermore, the public, too, is in large part to blame. It is human nature to create an idol and then to tear it down. From time immemorial idols were made to be raised and shattered.

And so, as a result, a great industry is irreparably injured; the reputations of thousands of decent men and women are sullied; an entire community is dragged into the mire!

It is a colossal and unforgivable injustice! I have personally visited Hollywood many times. I am thoroughly familiar with the motion-picture industry. I know as many of its people as anyone in this country. And this I can truthfully say:

Never have I seen the immoral conditions to which the newspapers refer. And while there are members of the motion-picture profession who are addicted to vicious practices, the men and women—*as a whole*—are as decent and self-respecting as the men and women of any other profession.

PHOTOPLAY is not posing as a defender of the motion pictures. It holds no brief for the purity of Hollywood. It prefers, in fact, to refrain from all discussion on the subject. But it can not sit by silently and behold both public and press besmirch with lies the entire rank and file of a great industry. This is why PHOTOPLAY has refused the recent frantic demands from newspapers for photographs of eminent actors and actresses, knowing the use to which they would be put.

Vice is to be found everywhere—in every profession and in every city in the world. The motion-picture profession is neither better nor worse than any other.

PHOTOPLAY asks nothing for motion pictures but justice—that simple, fine justice which the American public knows so well how to exercise.

—JAMES R. QUIRK.

ing In Hollywood

An Open Letter to Mr. Will Hays

DEAR MR. HAYS:

You have just accepted a position which makes you the representative head of the motion picture art and industry. You are the ideal man to occupy that position. Your traits of character and your proven ability, sanity, directness and fearlessness qualify you for this great responsibility.

I am taking the liberty of writing you a letter; and the things I am going to say to you are the outgrowth of a six years' undivided association with the motion-picture industry—its leaders, its directors, and its stars.

You are confronted by the biggest job in America. You hold in your hands, as a sculptor holds a piece of clay, an industry which wields perhaps a more direct and personal influence upon the public than any other in the United States.

It has become a necessity in the lives of many millions, and because of its vastness and influence, is almost a public utility.

You have it in your power to do a greater and finer service for this country than any other man today. You are, indeed, not merely face to face with a gigantic task—you have a sacred duty to perform as well.

In motion pictures, as in all great industries, there are undesirables—selfish vicious persons who work injury to everyone with whom they are associated.

There is the unscrupulous producer who, for a temporary profit, makes his appeal to the baser instincts in human nature.

There is the actor and the actress who live loose, immoral lives, and who thrive on scandal and lurid notoriety.

And there is the exhibitor who attempts to capitalize this scandal and to benefit by this notoriety. (In Los Angeles, while the press was at the height of a recent orgy of sensationalism, a local theater threw across its entrance a large canvas banner bearing the words: "I love you; I love you; I love you!" quoting a note which Mary Miles Minter wrote to Taylor, the murdered director.)

There are the self-appointed guardians of public morals, who forget the spirit of our form of government and in their frenzy of egomania, busy themselves in bringing about censorship, or exercise it in such an autocratic manner that compared to them, the kaiser was a benign and humble ruler.

Whenever a crime or a scandal connected with motion pictures has come to light, there have been those in various branches of the business who have at once rushed in and sought, through one means or another, to profit by it at the expense of the industry's reputation, scattering lies and accusations and innuendoes broadcast.

These are the facts. What, then, can be done?

Viewing the situation broadly, I believe that what motion pictures need at the present time, more than anything else, is a moral house-cleaning. They need it for their own good, as well as the public's. And you are the one man who can bring this about. It is you alone who can rehabilitate the good name of a great industry which has been dragged through the mire.

First of all, you should call on producers to discharge all persons whose private lives and habits make them a menace to the industry. This is vital. When the Stillman scandal broke, the National City Bank dropped Stillman. Surely the picture industry can do as much for its own good name.

Furthermore, you should eliminate all those persons who are eager to take advantage of the sensational publicity offered by any motion-picture scandal which gets into the papers.

Moreover, in every motion-picture contract there should be a clause similar to the one in the new Goldwyn contracts, providing for the immediate discharge of any actor whose private life reflects discredit on the company.

Your problem is to restrain not only the exhibitor, but the producer and the actor as well.

It is a general moral house-cleaning that is needed.

Then there is another point. One of the cardinal reasons why scandals like the Arbuckle and Taylor cases are possible, is that the motion-picture business has built up great public characters, thus making them easy targets for sensational journalism.

This method of production has been wrong; for the publicity, advertising and expenditure should be spent on the pictures and not on the stars.

And here again you can help by focusing interest and attention on the *art* of motion pictures and not merely upon *personalities*.

Indeed, the time will probably come when personalities will be almost entirely obliterated, although you can never succeed in overshadowing the individual ability of the really great actress and actor.

There is no need to go into the causes for the unfortunate condition of affairs which at present exists in the motion-picture industry. No one is directly to blame, for the industry and its problems are new, and certain recent results could not be foreseen and met. Both cause and effect are without precedent.

Perhaps everyone has been a little to blame—the producer, who sat apathetically by and did nothing; the actor and actress, who were suddenly loaded with riches, and sought to enjoy them without counting the cost; the exhibitor, who gave no thought except to the box office; the newspapers, who played up the scandals for personal aggrandizement; the public, which was willing, even eager, to believe whatever it heard or read.

But whatever the causes, the facts exist; and it is these which you, Mr. Hays, must face—and face fearlessly. The time has come to act, and I believe that you are capable of organizing the many factors of influence in America—producers, actors, directors, exhibitors, press and public—to join hands and work with you for a new ideal in motion pictures.

PHOTOPLAY, for its part, will refuse to print any personality story about any motion-picture star, who is notoriously immoral, or whose actions are such as to reflect unfavorably on the industry.

It is a Herculean task you have undertaken.

You are going to find in the motion-picture industry the same trouble that has always existed—selfishness and cut-throat methods. Side by side with men of the highest principles, you are going to find men who are the scum of the earth.

But you will succeed. Neither you, nor anyone else will be able to make the motion-picture business perfect, any more than the railroad business, the steel business, the banking business, or the government is perfect.

After all, just as sorrow and hardship build up character, so out of these tribulations will come a stronger and better business.

JAMES R. QUIRK.

Here Comes the Kid!

THE KID—a big eyed, wistful youngster of five or thereabouts.

His Father—not really his father, only a tramp—a funny little man with a black brush on his upper lip, feet that are all wrong, a cane, and a derby.

And Charlie Chaplin's century plants bloom again!

The great comedian's first screen appearance for many months occurs in this six-reel First National feature—perhaps the most widely heralded, expensive, and mysterious of all productions. It is an original story by Chaplin himself, and in it, as a lovable tramp, he shares honors with his five-year-old dramatic discovery, little Jackie Coogan, who, incidentally, shows more poise and camera-presence than many adults of the screen.

THE characters in the story are the Man, the Woman, the Tramp, the Kid, and the Policeman. The Woman leaves her child, hoping it will be adopted by wealthy people. Instead it is found and cared for by the Tramp. Together they roam, the Kid breaking windows and the Tramp happening along to mend them. There are many adventures, among them an allegorical episode in Heaven, which is the excuse for much clever satire. All through "The Kid" there are touches of pathos as well as characteristic Chaplin comedy. The Kid is finally restored to his mother, now a celebrated opera-singer, and the Tramp is asked to become the Kid's real father. In these pictures you see the Kid and oh, you know the other chap!

Sure Fire

What the public wants in religion, sports, radio and amusements— and why

© Underwood & Underwood

Dr. S. Parkes Cadman—A clergyman with box-office appeal. Neither a conservative nor an extremist. The Answer Man of the pulpit. He knows that Babbitt has a soul

© Underwood & Underwood

Marie Jeritza—A bounteous blonde with a strong voice and good legs. Can sing standing up, lying down or on her head. Lots of temperament, but a winning smile. Opera's pet

Harold Lloyd— Held in affectionate esteem wherever movies are shown. Every comedy a sure success. No temperament, no high-hat, no pose. A boy who really earns his money

© Underwood & Underwood

"Good evening, ladies and gentlemen of the radio audience. Graham McNamee speaking." Gets sex appeal in his station announcements. Pronounces foreign composers correctly. Our radio idol

Jack Dempsey— Breathes there a man—or woman— with soul so dead who wouldn't dig up fifty hardearned dollars to see this handsome lad step into the ring to defend his crown?

© Underwood & Underwood

"Babe" Ruth— Home-run king and favorite prodigal son. His batting average and the state of his morals are subjects of vital interest. The hero of our great summer drama

© Underwood & Underwood

"Red Grange"—He turned a college sport into a national industry. He glorified the American iceman. Just one of the boys who is always sure of landing neatly on the front page of every daily

Suzanne Lenglen—The red hot mamma of the courts. As uncertain as the French franc. As fascinating and as charming as her native country. A great actress playing a triumphant rôle

© Underwood & Underwood

PHOTOPLAY

March, 1925

Speaking of Pictures

By James R. Quirk

THE motion picture theater owners are lying awake nights worrying about the effect of radio on their box office receipts. They should be thinking instead of worrying. Thinking will bring them new business. Worrying will give them apoplexy.

I'LL wager that the cross-word puzzle epidemic which is sweeping the country is losing them more money than the radio. I saved the price of two theater tickets this week by trying to find the names of the Bow of Vishnu, and a rare disease among African elephants. But I made a First-of-February resolution that I would never look at one again, because they made me miss a reel of "Peter Pan," which I have only seen four times. I gather up children in the neighborhood, and take them to see "Peter Pan," using them as an alibi in the same way that I excuse myself for going to the circus every year.

IF radio and cross-word puzzles kept anyone away from "Peter Pan" any place where it has been shown, the theater managers haven't noticed it. It's one of those things that make you proud that you are in the motion picture business. We should all be grateful to Herbert Brenon and Jesse Lasky, not forgetting J. M. Barrie and Betty Bronson.

PETER PANS are not written or produced every week, but there is a deep instinct in all of us that is satisfied by the silence and romance of the motion picture, and many millions of us are jumping into automobiles or walking half a mile every night to escape the complexities and irritations of everyday life, and of the radio and cross-word puzzle. Folks get tired of sitting at home nights and indulging in the household battles over the rival entertainments.

WATCH some wide-awake young business man start a rage on "Peter Pan" hats.

THIS month's prescriptions:
To restore your youth, see "Peter Pan."
For that blue, depressed feeling—one ticket to "The Narrow Street" or "Forty Winks."
For that blase condition—see that horse race in "The Dixie Handicap."

CECIL B. De MILLE has broken his twelve-year connection with Famous Players-Lasky, because he felt that his style was being crabbed. Well, best of luck, Cecil, but if your style was crabbed on "The Golden Bed," your first independent offering will be a wow. What you need is not a change of producers, but a change of thought.

A CHAP, who has been studying speech defects of children in Vienna for five years, returns and denounces our little Jackie Coogan as a bold and dangerous creature, and a sinister influence. The little Austrian boys are mimicking Jackie Coogan, he says. They pull their hats down over one eye and saunter along the streets, hands deep in their pockets, just as he does.
Terrible! Jackie should be sentenced to solitary imprisonment for life.

THIS is the second anniversary of the death of Wally Reid, and the number of letters that come to me calling attention to it proves that his memory is cherished by countless thousands to whom his screen personality and his pictures brought happiness.

Wally was intensely human, and lovable in his own personality. He had human weaknesses. He was no saint. But I never heard of him intentionally hurting anyone, and all that Mrs. Reid says about him in her article on another page of this issue is true. His end was unfortunate, but up to the time he was stricken, he was one of the realest and most companionable human beings I ever knew.

I never have ceased to marvel how the camera caught that lovable quality in the man and reflected it on the screen. Handsome, accomplished, successful, there wasn't an ounce of personal conceit in him, and the amount of work he could and did perform would be inconceivable to most men.

HE broke down under the strain. His case reminds me of a famous surgeon who worked twelve hours a day at his practice, and was so sought after for his charming companionship, and so willing to be agreeable to his friends, that he collapsed much as Wally did. He never thought of himself, never took the advice he gave his patients, to conserve their physical and mental resources. He would perform half a dozen important operations, spend endless wearing hours in his work of life or death, and at the end of the day I have known him to fall asleep at a bridge table rather than disappoint his friends.

WALLY brought happiness into thousands of lives in every country where his pictures were shown. His screen personality was his own personality, and the public sensed it. I am thinking not only of the young women who looked on him as the incarnation of their dream hero, or the boys who, in fancy, lived the dashing, romantic and humorous episodes of his pictures, for I can never forget one lonely old lady who once said to me: "I am always happy when I see Wally's pictures. I never had children, but I keep thinking that he is my boy."

$500.00 In Prizes for Solutions

Cross Word Puzzle No. 1

VERTICAL

1. You never hoot at this actor.
2. Either.
3. Name of automobile.
4. A vine.
6. Noted humorist.
7. Tease.
8. Part of verb to be.
9. Where pictures are made.
13. Period of time.
15. His first name is Richard.
17. Small pie.
19. Near.
21. Street (abbr.).
25. Exclamation.
26. Male offspring.
27. Not young.
28. Charles' last name.
31. First name of noted male star (spelled backwards).
32. Sound reflection.
35. Demonstrative pronoun.
36. Man's name (Spanish).
38. Preposition.
39. Mary's last name; dried grass.
40. Exclamation.
45. Isle (simplified spelling).
46. Terrace (abbr.).
47. Gone, past.
48. Block.
50. Part of verb to be.
52. Exist.

HORIZONTAL

1. First name of actress.
5. Last name of actress.
10. Minister (abbr.).
11. Of (Fr. plural).
12. Beside.
14. Exclamation (Yiddish).
16. Prefix meaning from.
17. You (Latin).
18. Ocean.
20. What baby wears.
21. Unhappy.
22. A grain.
23. Three (prefix).
24. Northern railroad (abbr.)
25. Like.
27. Either.
29. A preposition.
30. A magazine.
31. You (old style).
33. Indefinite article.
34. Day (abbr.).
35. Initials of a president.
37. What some film players don't do
40. Exclamation.
41. Pronoun.
42. Body of water.
43. Not her.
44. Negative.
45. Pronoun.
47. Bachelor's degree.
49. Southeast (abbr.).
50. A prohibited beverage.
51. Loose talk.
53. An important thing in pictures.
54. An actor born in Spain.

HERE is an opportunity for the entire family to make money—and to have fun while doing it.

On this and the adjoining page are two cross word puzzles—mental twisters that will make you hunt up your dictionary and, better still, make you read and re-read PHOTOPLAY to get the correct solutions.

After all, they're not so hard if you are a real film fan. They contain the names of well known stars, terms used in producing pictures and just plain little ordinary words that every school child knows. There may be a few that you wouldn't have heard about before finishing the eighth grammar grade but not any more than that.

All of the names of the stars used in the puzzles can be found in March PHOTOPLAY. They include some of the best known satellites in the cinema world. Other puzzles will be run in subsequent issues of PHOTOPLAY. Save this issue because next month's puzzles will be based upon it.

Five hundred dollars in cash will be given as prizes for the correct solutions of the puzzles, AND the best sentence containing words used in the puzzles. The first prize will be $200, the second $100, the third $50, then five prizes of ten dollars each and twenty of five dollars each—twenty-eight prizes in all. Rules governing the contest will be found on opposite page.

Any or all members of the family can send in solutions.

Remember that you have to write only one sentence besides solving both puzzles. That sentence must be made up of words that will appear in both puzzles after you have solved them. Of course if you don't solve the puzzles correctly and use words in the sentence that don't appear in the solutions you will be out of luck. First solve the puzzles correctly. Then write the niftiest, snappiest sentence you can out of the words in the puzzles. The answers will be published in the May issue. The awards will be announced in the June issue.

Get busy at once. The time is limited. Be sure you read the rules, then follow them.

Viola Dana holds the cross word puzzle championship of the screen

The Screen Idol of America

Signor Rodolpho Alfonzo Raffaelo Pierre Filibert Guglielmi di Valentina d'Antonguolla

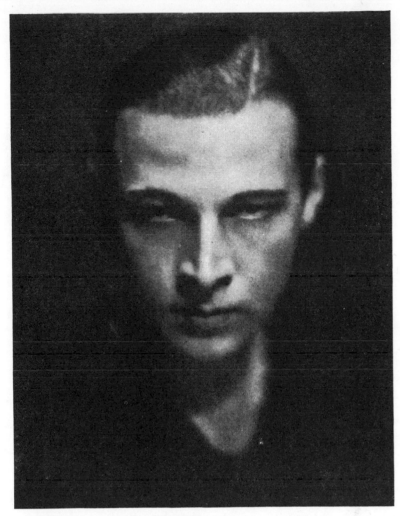

Rudy's last photograph, made specially for PHOTOPLAY MAGAZINE. He brought it to New York with him and it was received too late to use it in the rotogravure section of this magazine. In the next issue it will appear in the rotogravure section.

In Memoriam

By Margaret Sangster

His feet had carried him so very swiftly,
    Into the lands of wonder and romance;
And yet, although they travelled far, they never
    Forgot to dance.

His lips had learned to speak a stranger language,
    His smile had warmed the wistful, lonely earth—
Yet fame had never taken, from his spirit,
    The gift of mirth!

Although his eyes glimpsed bitterness and sadness,
    They saw a dream that few folk ever see—
God grant the dream may tinge, with lovely color,
    Death's Mystery!

YOUTH

New stars. New ideas. There's a new and youth

Charles Rogers

Dolores del Rio

Charles Farrell

Louise Brooks, Lasky's leading subdeb

Janet Gaynor

YOUTH!
It's the new battle cry of filmdom.
Youth! Paramount has been doing most of the shouting about it—but then Paramount always does shout vigorously. Paramount screams over Clara Bow, rushes forward Gary Cooper, advertises five junior stars, its Paramount school graduates, its fledgling favorites.

Youth!
Metro-Goldwyn-Mayer goes Paramount one better and electrics not only flip William Haines and saucy Sally O'Neill, but young executives like the dynamic Irving Thalberg, young directors like Monta Bell and George Hill, young writers, young exhibitors, young advertisers.

Youth!
Fox outmarathons them all, for quietly and without bombast it has created two genuine girl stars, Janet Gaynor and Olive Borden, signed Lois Moran, has in the grooming Charles Farrell, Barry Norton, Richard Walling, Charles Morton and Nick Stuart.

Youth!
Cecil B. De Mille, hampered by intense and old loyalties, frees himself enough to signature Frank Marion, Virginia Brad-

The youth movement is not restricted to any one lot in Hollywood. This season it is dominating the whole screen world. It pertains not only to actors but to executives, writers, directors, technicians, salesmen. *Passé* personalities have given way. Youth, cry the studios and the fans. This year marks the complete downfall of the older dynasty in favor of one joyous in quality and bright with promise.

names. New faces. New spirit abroad in Hollywood is its slogan

By
Ruth Waterbury

Gary Cooper

Josephine Dunn

Richard Arlen

ford, Junior Coughlan, Jeanette Loff, Joseph Striker, Sally Rand.

Universal, pushing aside a couple of Germans, highlights Barbara Kent, Arthur Lake, George Lewis, Raymond Keane, and a real boy cowboy, Newton House.

First National close-ups on Alice White, Yola d'Avril, Maria Corda, Gilbert Roland, John Westwood, Loretta Young, Donald Reed. Warner's have Dolores Costello.

Even United Artists, where good stars go when they die, has among its tired profiles that vibrant daughter of the Dons, Dolores del Rio. This, however, is largely accident, for it is not quite polite to be young at United Artists.

Dolores is under contract to Edwin Carewe and her success has been achieved all over Hollywood, at First National, Fox, Inspiration, Metro, wherever Eddie farmed her out. Now Eddie belongs to United Artists and when Dolores makes "Ramona," United Artists will release it.

Consider the miracle of it, names unknown two years ago, world famous today, names world famous yesterday shunned tomorrow. The motion picture industry deals essentially in commodities and its greatest commodity today is youth. Youth is the common dream of all mankind. Childhood looks forward to it, age looks back at it, but

Paramount's Hall boy, James, the sheba slayer

Comes the second dawn in the movies, heralded by whole constellations of new stars in the movie sky. The older stars, overshadowed by the glow of the newly discovered, have become as pale sparks, twinkling feebly. Already many of them have set in the uncharted ocean of movie oblivion, their frescoed charms and starring vehicles worthless compared to the unstudied splendor of the young lights now holding the world's attention.

Thelma Todd

the great and beautiful appeal of it never dies.

Yet, though the industry has known for years that this infusion was necessary if it was to be kept alive, it hasn't until the past season done anything particularly intelligent about securing it. This year, however, marks the complete overthrow of the older generation, the complete mastery of the new.

With the single exception of Lon Chaney, every star of the older group has waned, every ascendant star has risen higher.

While the racial monarchies of the world have been crumpling, the dynasties of the screen have been following them. Old-stars can no longer be bolstered into box office babies through massive sets, costumes, trick lighting, tremendous advertising.

Even the producers are trembling slightly. New young men are entering their ranks.

Says Jesse Lasky: "The most hopeful thing of the past season is that we producers are realizing there is no such thing any more as a sure-fire picture. 'Sparrows' was sure-fire. 'The Fire Brigade' was sure-fire. 'Old Ironsides' was sure-fire. All were failures. Opposed to them comes 'The Way of All Flesh.' We expected it to be an artistic failure. We had Jannings under contract and he refused to make a commercial picture. We gave in to him because we had to. 'The Way of All Flesh' is one of our box-office hits.

"AS for the youngsters we are training for stardom, we have come to regard our lot as a movie university. We are very hopeful for Dick Arlen, Charles Rogers, Louise Brooks and James Hall, our junior stars. Our Paramount school people, whom I admit did not look too interesting at commencement, are developing rapidly in Hollywood. Certainly Thelma Todd, Josephine Dunn and Walter Goss are changed personalities.

"As in any other university, the majority will fail and one or two will make good. The seniors, stars in this case, look at the freshmen and think they never beheld such an impossible group. Those freshmen, advanced to seniors, will feel similarly regarding new entrants. Our most valuable acquisition of 1927 is that each studio recognizes the hit-or-miss method is past. Paramount now has Authors' Councils in the East and West looking for new, young writers. We have scouts everywhere looking for young actors. And we are frankly experimenting in all lines."

CECIL DE MILLE disagrees with Mr. Lasky. De Mille still believes in proceeding slowly. "A young player needs approximately seven years' training before he is ready for stardom," he asserts.

"William Boyd worked with me that long before I gave him 'The Volga Boatman.' Vera Reynolds served as protracted a novitiate. I have been watching Virginia Bradford's work for more than four years before I put her under contract. Frank Marion is really a child of the theater.

"But beginners like Lena Malena and Jeannette Loff cannot expect to be skyrocketed under my management.

"A player made overnight dies overnight."

At which Irving Thalberg, pointing to the glamorous Garbo, made in a single picture, laughs lightly.

"THE motion picture public itself is young," argues Mr. Thalberg. "Its age range is between eighteen and twenty-four. A player who waits seven years to reach them will be too old. At Metro we are giving Ralph Forbes, Marceline Day, Dorothy Sebastian, Joan Crawford, and such beginners, education, leads and publicity simultaneously.

"Players reign only so long as the whims of their fans dictate and rise and fall according to how well they are managed according to the caprice of the public.

"The producers' only hope is an untiring search for talent that can constantly be brought forward in the place of those who have reached the fade-out."

With all due respect to Mr. De Mille, I feel that Mr. Thalberg wins the hand-knitted lawnmower for superior argument.

The battle cry of filmdom is really Hail and Farewell.

THEY pass in review, those great favorites now retiring, some with grace and some with bitterness, the old survivors of Biograph, the last survivors of Triangle, Fine Arts, Vitagraph, the old Goldwyn organization. There is a quickened, more intelligent spirit abroad in the new organizations. When one sees stars today, one sees not starring vehicles for a Pola Negri or a Corinne Griffith, but of the flesh, vibrant emotionalism of a del Rio or a Gaynor. Into the widened horizons there rises Gilbert and Garbo, Banky and Colman, Moran and Forbes, Bow and Cooper, Gaynor and Farrell, Borden and Rogers, a distinguished group, certainly, talented, handsome, ambitious, earnest.

The fans are young and the new stars are young. Youth calls to youth and the hand that cranks the camera rules the world.

Stagg

MAKING pictures is play for "Our Gang," but this is real work. Here they are—Mary Kornman, Freckles, Farina, Sunshine Sammy— who has a private tutor (at right) and the rest, all at school on the Hal Roach lot

Vandamm

*Y*OU'RE going to admire and envy, simultaneously, this extremely blonde and atrociously pretty newcomer to pictures. First, she's really a raving beauty. Second, she's zat fascinating Maurice Chevalier's leading woman in his second American picture, "The Love Parade." Jeanette MacDonald is her name, and she came to the studios from a line of Broadway musical comedy successes, including "Yes, Yes, Yvette" and "Sunny Days"

Richee

WHAT a year for Gary Cooper! He's jumped to feature rôles, been reported engaged to Clara Bow and been assigned a leading part in "Beau Sabreur." What more could any young fellow possibly want?

Ball

YOU are going to see a lot of this girl. She is Claudette Colbert who made a hit in the stage play, "The Barker." She has been signed for the movies and she will play opposite Ben Lyon in "French Dressing," when Ben gets back from Europe.

That Stockholm Venus

By Myrtle West

Greta Garbo has jumped from Sweden to stardom in a single film

GRETA was very worried. A frown corrugated her brow. Blonde hair swept back and curled, in Byronic style, about the collar of her bright red jacket.

She was more worried than she had been when she attempted, with disastrous results, to use her first English word.

The word had been "Hell!" Final and unrelenting. It could not be disguised.

But how was Greta to know that the cheerful sounding English word —spoken brashly by a shipboard companion — was taboo even in polite Hollywood poker circles?

How was she to know the effect of her word upon Ricardo Cortez when he gallantly questioned:

"And what do you think of Hollywood?"

Said Greta, tossing her head in her quaint foreign way:

"Ah, he-ll!" And the double "l" lurched, song-like, up the scale in the manner of Swedish-born people. Like Anna Q. when she is agitated. And Greta Nissen.

Today Greta Garbo was very much worried indeed. Worried over a problem that assumed monumental importance.

"Vhat vill all the peoples do vhen Culver City, Los Angeles and Hollyvood are all one beeg city? It vill be verry nice to have such a beeg city. But vhere vill they all poot their motor cars?"

It was an overwhelming question.

Would double-decked boulevards solve the problem? Perhaps.

"Ja? Maybe! Thanks God!"

Greta Garbo has been in America three months. Three amazing, flurried, bewildering months. Haste to do this. Haste to do that. Greta cannot understand the relentless hurry to do things. In her Stockholm—where there are several brothers and sisters—one does not rush. One has plenty of time. But, of course, this is America. This is Hollywood of which one has heard so much.

Hollywood of which returning travelers have glowed and gloated over. Such fine restaurants in which to eat! Such beeg ballrooms in which to dance. Such beeg hotels in which one can live forever, almost, without stepping out once. Eating, sleeping, dancing. All under one roof.

Ja, they have beeg hotels in Europe, but the hotels there do not seem like American hotels.

Hollywood is not quite as Greta expected. She had visioned a combination Valhalla and Paradise. It is lovely, however, and she is glad she is living in . . . Santa Monica. Santa

The lovely Garbo startled Hollywood by using her only English word, "hell," to express all things. But the Metro officials didn't reprove her. They had seen her in "Torrent" and were too busy shouting "Halleluiah"

Monica where the broad blue Pacific crashes against the palisades like her own northern seas against the mainland, filling fjords with salty water.

Greta has no desire to join the vacuous circle of teas, dinners and dances into which the favored newcomer is invited. Besides, she has no time for men . . . or love. This, by her own admission.

Instead of a Hollywood bungalow she lives at a Santa Monica hotel in a little colony of her fellow countrymen who consist of the so-called "Swedish invasion." There is Maurice Stiller, the director whose Swedish-made pictures attracted the attention of Louis B. Mayer to both director and star. There is Lars Hansen, known as the John Barrymore of Sweden, and his wife, who was formerly in pictures in Europe. There is Benjamin Christianson and there is an art director from her own country, in addition to several others of equal importance.

A "little Sweden" on the banks of the Pacific. Quite inviolable from the attacks of Hollywood's social set. Quite happy in their enjoyment of the new land.

"Are you not foreign? Ja?" queried Greta, her fascinating mouth laboring over the unfamiliar words.

"No. But half English."

"So-o-o! Vhat is the other half?"

"French and Irish and Scotch."

"Scotch?" quoted Greta. "Ja. I have heard of Scotch here. It is what you say pro . . . pro . . . pro-hee-bee-shun!"

And now Greta is learning to ride horseback. She is learning the Argentina tango so she may dance it with Spanish Antonio Moreno in also-Spanish Senor Ibanez' novel, "The Temptress," which she hopes will be directed by Swedish Mr. Maurice Stiller.

"Da—da—dum—de—de," chanted Fanchon of ballet fame as Greta and Tony dipped and swirled about the floor in the intricacies of the dance.

"Now dip! Now turn!" called Fanchon, and Greta stopped, puzzled.

"I do not know the vord 'deep.' Vill you tell me please?"

She is a tall girl. Long-limbed like so many Scandinavian women, but with slender grace that is not always seen in that race. Blue eyes, a lengthy blonde bob, a fascinating mouth. A face that you would remember long after the body had crumbled away.

The Evolution of a Kiss

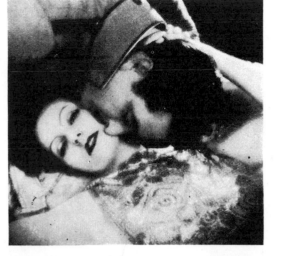

Here is what happens to Jack Gilbert when he demonstrates the technique of a kiss to Greta Garbo in "Flesh and the Devil." Guess what rôle Marc MacDermott plays. Her husband? Right the first time. Draw your own moral

The BIG BOY tells

This is the House that Gary Built—a beautiful Spanish bungalow in the Beverly Hills district that is studded with bright stars. And there is Big Boy himself, standing on the veranda, and looking very much monarch of all he surveys!

The tale of how Gary Cooper, six feet, four of Montana Boy, comes to Hollywood, the city of dreams —goes hungry, loses, and wins!

In the first installment of Gary Cooper's life story, printed last month, he told of his birth twenty-seven years ago in Helena, Montana—of his father, a distinguished jurist, and his gentle Anglo-French mother.

Of the hardships of a ranch that turned out to be a white elephant, of schooldays in England, of the homesickness for Montana's plains and mountains that never leaves him, even during the hours of his film fame.

Now, in the second chapter, we find him on the brink of manhood, ranch days and his Hollywood career still beyond the horizon.

PART II

MY latter teens were full of happenings. I spun up from a kid into a spindling, lean boy of six feet, four. In less than a year I grew ten inches, and then stopped. By the time I was sixteen I was as tall as I am now. And conscious of it.

My brother left for France at the beginning of the struggle, when America went into the war, and left a kid brother. Arthur returned to find me towering well over him.

Those years were not uneventful. Two of them were taken bodily from my school life by an automobile accident that forced me to the ranch to recover.

I didn't mind that. I did not crave to go to school, but something within me wanted the amber and red sunsets, the clear bright days with a buzzard planing through the sky, not moving a wing for thousands of feet, and, as I turned my head, a bald eagle circling, ominously, above a hidden prey.

There are things one remembers as if yesterday. Wallops that life has handed you. I remember, now, the sock in the ego that I got when I was told that I had flopped in my first dramatic part, and that I was out of the cast.

Gary Cooper and his mother at the door of the Montana lad's home in the hills above Hollywood. Mamma Cooper and her husband were dead set against a film career for their big boy, but now that success has come, they are happy

His Story

As told by

Gary Cooper

to

Dorothy Spensley

I remember, as yesterday, the automobile accident that knocked me out of active life for many months and sent me to Sunnyside. I can recall the big touring car I was driving as it whizzed along. The sudden impact. How it rolled over. How I got up and walked to the curb, not dizzy, nor weak, my senses sharpened to a super-human degree. And then how my left side failed me. It hung like a heavy dead thing. And everything went blue. I guess that is the way you feel when you faint.

I awakened in a hospital. They said I had a broken leg, and other complications too numerous to mention.

Richee

A vivid close-up of Gary Cooper, tousled hair, frank eyes, and all. Among all the stars that shine in the firmament of film-land, Gary typifies what we like to think of as the best of young American manhood

I recall, distinctly, that I thought of mother and dad. I didn't have any regrets about the car, or myself. I thought of the dirty trick life had played on us, just as things were beginning to clear a bit, and the ranch was showing signs of living up to its name.

CONVALESCENCE on the ranch was easy. There were always cow-hands around to tell stories, play cards or to whang away at a two-stringed mandolin. Some of the fellows that drifted in and out again as soon as they had earned a couple of months' pay, had harmonicas, and we listened to "Pretty Baby" interpolated with some old buckaroo bar room ditties picked up along the Borders, North and South.

I had great admiration for one taciturn old ranger. His name was Ashburton Carter and his fame among the sweating, two-fisted punchers was that one winter he had been snowbound for six months in Colorado and had not spoken a word to a human being all that time.

A rare old print of Gary, at the age of 16, playing Indian. The picture was taken during his ranch days. No doubt he is wearing the tribal feathers of old Chief Don't-Hog-the-Camera

It was my fun, when I was well enough to permit it, to tag after Ash, begging him to tell me his experiences, and to tell me again how, desperate to hear the sound of a voice again, he held long conversations with his horse. And how startled, at first, he would be at the strange grating sound of his voice in his desolate throat. He thought he was going mad.

We had about five hundred head of cattle then and when I was stronger, I helped to ride the range.

It was a good chance to think and plan and dream. Pleasant, too, to slouch down in your saddle, your firm-legged pony taking the rough spots like so much

The Big Boy Tells His Story

lightning. Gave you a chance to think of what life meant to you. Whether it meant sliding along from day to day like this—happy, free, getting no place, materially, but with a spiritual contentment moistening your very roots—or going into Helena or some big city and being smothered by musty books and stifled by rows of adding machines.

The best thing, though, was to imagine you were a heroic cowboy, like those in the wild western films, and to stick your heels into your pony's slats and go like hell-bent-for-salvation after Indians. Ride for miles like the devil incarnate, wind shrieking past your ears, head bent low over the pony's. Speed! Speed! The Indians are coming and the girl must be rescued. Speed! The rabbits scurry out of the way. A wise hoot owl blinks amazedly down at you. The grass bows before you. You stop. The horse's sides are heaving like bellows.

WHERE are the Indians? That's a bunch of mesquite. Where is the girl? That's only a clump of greasewood. The girl is incidental. She represents no ideal. She is there because the plot demands that somebody be rescued. It couldn't be "the papers." They are too inanimate.

The pony is panting. Its mane is flecked with foam. You pat it and fish out a piece of sugar stolen from the breakfast table. Or an apple. It nibbles it, upper lip thrust derisively back, and quivers. You pat it again. Good horse!

What would a man do if he were harnessed to a desk from nine until five every day except Sundays?

In the Spring and Fall the cattle were driven to the railroad siding, noisy, frightened, stamping, to be herded into the cattle train that took them to St. Paul, Chicago or another stock marketing center. With the cattle went the more experienced punchers, who had taken cattle to market before. With them, as I grew older, I also went.

Travelling was no particular thrill to me. The biggest thrill was in getting home. In watching for the first range of mountains—I think it is the Bear Paw range—and feeling that at last I was back where I could take a deep breath. It had been that way when I returned from England as a kid. It was always that way.

I LIKED to go to market, though, with the men. I liked to see them dicker with the city men and watch them get their money and stick it inside their flannel shirts or in the little front pockets of their tight-fitting pants.

At night they went in for hell-raising, to which I was usually an interested onlooker, unless I went to a theater, and later, literally picked them up and got them onto the night train that would take us back to Montana.

The liquor they got on their cattle-selling expeditions was a lot more potent than the white mule they imported, secretly, to Sunnyside.

In the summer months, when the High School at Bozeman was closed, I worked as guide at Yellowstone National Park. I wanted to do something that brought in money, and the family agreed to it. I couldn't imagine myself in an office job. I was too restless. I am still that way.

Vacation days in Montana. The dashing figure on the left of the quartet is Gary Cooper. Note the rakish slant to the sombrero, the wicked holster and the cartridge belt. Gary was about 14, and so were the other blades, here shown ready to set out to hunt varmints in them thar hills

I can seldom finish a book. It takes too many sedentary hours to sit, motionless, and read. Hours that could be spent in riding or walking or doing something vital. I think that is one reason why I did not become a cartoonist.

I liked drawing, had a flair for it, so I was told, but the tedium of sitting for hours, sketching, to get one little thing flawless was too great a demand on a restless spirit.

So for three or four summers I took "dude cowboys" from the East through Yellowstone and kept white-collared campers in creased khaki from throwing bits of soap into Old Faithful Geyser to see it spout; and elderly ladies from fainting by assuring them that the cinnamon bears were harmless unless you pulled their ears or kicked them.

That was work to my liking. I could sneak out of my bunk before the "dudes" were stirring, and steal out into the open to the tune of their snores. I could watch the sun come up from where the North Fork of the Shoshone flowed. I could see an osprey come swooping down for his morning meal, grab up a struggling fish, only to drop it when a huge eagle swerved down on him, and see the eagle catch the glistening morsel in mid-air.

Even when I left high school and entered Grinnell College the summer vacation found me back at the Park.

Women always have much to do with molding a man's life. I don't mean the sentimental attachments that make you tramp on clouds. And I don't mean marriage. Something beside the biological urge. I mean the women who are our mothers. And the mothering souls who have to do with forming ideals and aspirations. School teachers, for instance. In their constructive hands, kids are so much human clay. Everyone can look back in his life and recall a school teacher who stands out as a sort of beacon light to kids who were groping and grasping at life.

Miss Davis was that sort of person. Through her I decided to enter Grinnell College in Iowa. She was my English teacher. Slight, a grey-haired woman that a big wind from the prairie could easily have blown away, she was of the type that is born to mother somebody else's sons. I liked her, and listened to her, because she had the same fundamentally sound ideas that my mother had.

I WENT to Grinnell for two and a half years, during which time I absorbed all the adult experiences I could. I studied commercial art intensively. I fell in love. I became engaged. I was going into the advertising business and make a success, either as an artist or as an executive. I was going to marry and have a home and family.

I was twenty. After two and a half years I left college. Our engagement was broken. Perhaps it was well.

At twenty life has a different hue than it has at twenty-seven, or thirty-seven. Dad was assisting Joseph Dixon in his campaign for Governor of Montana and I tried my hand at cartooning on one of the Helena papers. I could have stayed in Helena and done cartooning.

I felt that my choice of occupation bound me to a city.

WHY not to a bigger city where the possibilities of advancement would be greater? Why not go to New York or Los Angeles? I could not get myself to go to New York. I knew I could not love its canyons of big buildings and the rugged crags of its skyscrapers. They could never take the place of the West. Los Angeles, on the other hand, was a Western city, sprawled over desert and mountains.

I arrived in Hollywood on Thanksgiving Day four years ago. It was the first big shove-off from home. The family didn't like to see me go. Summers at Yellowstone were all right, and so was school at Bozeman and Grinnell, and that job as timekeeper in an Iowa corn canning factory that I held a part of one summer.

They felt in closer contact with me. Now we were separated by the Rockies.

Once in Los Angeles, it was the usual story of trying to get work in a new town. There were no horses to break or cattle to herd. I

The Big Boy Tells His Story

tried all the local papers to get on as an artist. No use. The advertising agencies were full, too. And I was told that all the big advertising accounts were handled in New York City of Chicago. I did the only thing I could.

I got work by the day or the hour. Anything to eat. I sold photograph coupons from door to door. I tried to sell real estate. The papers were full of ads for suckers to come and invest money.

IT wasn't so much fun living in a dinky, smelly room and eating sinkers and coffee. But I wouldn't write home for money. It was when I was flatter than a beaver's tail that I discovered motion pictures. Extras were getting five a day and I thought I'd try my luck. That, at least, was better than having angry housewives slam the door in my face when I asked them to buy photographic coupons.

I got my first day's extra work at Fox. It was in a Tom Mix picture. He was using two hundred extras in some sort of legendary flash-back taking place in Sherwood Forest in Robin Hood's heyday. I crawled into a pair of green tights, slipped on a leather jerkin, put a funny little cap with a feather in it on my head, and someone shoved a bow and arrow at me. I was an archer. My picture career had begun. In the distance I saw Mix's leading woman, Billie Dove. I thought she was beautiful. I decided Hollywood was interesting.

I was bowled over by studio life. I was drunk on what, at first glimpse, appeared to be its utter freedom and lack of restraint, and what I learned later is the most delusive thing about it. There is no real freedom in Hollywood. It's a mirage. Every movement, no matter how slight, is commented on, and a motive, often erroneous, is given to it. I thought this freedom matched that which I had always craved. And so I stayed.

My first part of any importance was secured by hiring an agent who placed me in the part of *Abe Lee* in "The Winning of Barbara Worth." I got an agent after playing Westerns and going hungry and playing extra and going hungry. It wasn't hard to play *Lee*. He was a lean, lanky cowboy. I knew him as I knew myself.

IT was after the picture was released that Mr. Schulberg signed me to a Paramount contract, and gave me a bit in "Wings." After that I played with Clara Bow in "It."

It wasn't hard to do the stuff I did in those pictures. The part in "Wings" was minor, and William Wellman, the director, was a regular fellow. In "It" Clara was helpful. She is that kind of a girl, generous with her friendship and praise.

I had never before known an actress. She was a new type of girl, glamorous, full of fun, devoid of jealousy. I was grateful to her and admired her.

We went around together.

It looked as if I was going to make a success of pictures. But something was incomplete. I knew, well, what it was. I was homesick for Montana.

I'd try to compensate my desire by driving up into the desert for a few days, between pictures.

But it wasn't like chucking a slab of bacon, some flour, baking powder, coffee and sugar into a roll, tying it on a horse and disappearing into the mountains for a span of days.

I sighted an eagle's nest one day when I was fishing off Catalina Island and scrambled along a narrow path, high over the sea, bedded with crushed rock where wild mountain goats sleep, to look down into it.

But it wasn't like Montana. I missed our family life, too.

The inevitable happened. I never laid claim to being an actor. To this day I do not consider myself one. I don't think I have any divine talent. I am disappointed, many times, in seeing myself on the screen. I fall so short of what I think I should be as an actor. Only on rare occasions have I seen traces of what I am striving for.

IN "The Shopworn Angel" I saw a faint glimmering of the sort of characterization I would like to give.

The inevitable was that I failed in my first dramatic part. It was drawing room drama and I was unqualified. We worked on one scene for "Children of Divorce" for a full day, making shot after shot. By the time we had photographed it seven times, my nerves got the better of me. My mind refused to govern my body.

My limbs wouldn't function properly. I went hay-wire.

Frank Lloyd was directing. The next morning he called me into his office. I knew what was up. A sleepless night hadn't been for nothing. It was hard for Lloyd to tell me, but I knew I was out of the picture. It looked like the upset of everything; that my career was ended.

I jumped into my car and beat it for the Mojave, driving like the devil. I stayed all night on the desert, in a ramshackle hotel. It was quiet, like a balm.

The next day I came back down the coast road, through Malibu, with the mountains rising on one side, the ocean beating on the other.

I didn't know just what I was going to do, but I knew I could think straighter.

It was about noon and I was hungry. I went straight to Henry's. As I entered the door a man stood up and grabbed me, "By God, Gary! We've been looking all over town for you.

"Even had the police on the search. Thought you might have jumped off a cliff.

"You're back in the picture." It was Lloyd. The rushes on the third day's work had shown improvement and I was back in the cast.

Experiences are valued by their effect. Because I went back to the picture after failing, I helped to overcome a natural reticence—a self-consciousness.

It is that reticence which prohibits me from going into detail about a few feminine friendships that I value.

Privacy seems to be a thing that is denied a motion picture person. It is a thing that constitutionally, I crave. It happens that I have made friendships with women who have aided me in my work and that have been happy contacts.

It was that way with Clara. In Evelyn Brent I found the companionship of a woman who was wise and brilliant.

I was first attracted to her as a woman who had her feet on the ground and was not riding the clouds.

IN Lupe Velez I find a girl who takes the same joy out of primitive, elemental things that I do. In each friendship I have found that the most casual linking of our names caused dynamite.

I am going to marry. I want, like almost every man, a home and a family. I want a permanent union, not one of these week-end impermanencies.

I want, eventually, to convert Sunnyside into a "dude ranch," but on the lower ridge that slopes up into the higher mountains I want to build a chalet, clinging to its side, where I can go when my Hollywood days are over.

I want, before my life is over, to go back to Montana.

The Microphone-*The Terror Of The Studios*

By Harry Lang

Mike, the demon, who sends the vocally unfit screaming or lisping from the lots

THIS is a story of Terrible Mike, the capricious genie of Hollywood, who is a Pain in the Larynx to half of filmdom, and a Tin Santa Claus to the other half!—who gives a Yoo-Hoo-There Leading Man a Voice like a Bull, and makes a Cauliflower-Eared Heavy talk like Elfin Elbert, the Library Lizard!—and who has raised more hell in movieland than a clara bow in a theological seminary.

Why, you can't even begin to write the half of the story of Terrible Mike and what he's done. You can only take a heap of ha-ha's here, and boo-hoo's there—laughs and sobs, heart-leaps and heart-aches, sudden wealth and sudden ruin, funny things and tragic things and howcum things—and try to string 'em together into some semblance of yarn.

And even then, every Hector and Hectorine that struts the streets of Hollywood will read it and say: "This guy ain't said NAW-thin' yet. . . ." And they'll be right—but here goes.

* * *

IN the first place—or is it? but let's put it there—young John W. Microphone, to give Terrible Mike his family name, has made the leading lady of the screen a LADY in fact as well as in name. Not that she wasn't ALWAYS a lady—no one'd EVER go so far as to say that. But look—

Before Mike crashed the studio gate and brought in his lady friends, what was little Miss Starlet like? You know. Ya-da-da-DA-poo-POO;—let's GO!!!—THAT'S what she was.

Little and hot, like a red pepper—and the Mexes were the hottest. She thought poise was just the label they put on imported canned peas, and *savoir faire*, she'd guess, was just the French name for a chocolate cruller, huh? She was a cute kid or a jumping bean from over the border, and Sex-Appeal and "It"—whatever THAT was—were her everything.

AND so Clara Bow says she's planning to take a year's trip abroad when her present contract with Paramount ends, and Ruth Chatterton is knocking 'em dead in the talkies. Mona Rico, for whom they had to fireproof the films, is God-knows-where, and Pauline Frederick flares into first-magnitude stardom.

Alice White is thanking Allah that she can sing, besides being cute, while Winifred Mrs. Bill-Hart Westover comes out of obscurity and wows it in "Lummox"!

Terrible Mike has cooled down the incandescent flapper—he's giving her an awful kick, and is putting Poor Old Lady Has-Been back on the throne.

> Miss Humpty-Dumpty sat on a wall;
> Miss Humpty-Dumpty had a great fall—
> For all of her "S. A." and all of her "It"
> Just couldn't make her in talkies a hit!
> —from "Mother Goose in Hollywood"

Consider Bebe Daniels and Clara Bow. Envision for yourselves a see-saw. One end goes up; the other end goes down. Bebe is on the end that's going up, and Clara is—well, er, let's confine ourselves to her own admission that she's going to take a European trip by and by because she's tired.

"I've been working hard for years," she told a Hollywood friend the other day, "and I need a rest. So I'm figuring on going to Europe for a year or more, when my contract expires." It expires in about thirteen or fourteen months, and not a soul at Paramount has said it'll be renewed.

And at the same time, Mr. Paramount is kicking himself all over the lot because of Bebe Daniels. Bebe, you see, bought up her own contract with Paramount not so long ago because they didn't think she was worth two toots in talkies. They were paying her a fat salary, and using her in ordinary pictures. They couldn't afford to spend much on her productions, was the excuse, because her salary under contract was so big that they had to skimp on her pictures to make money. When they wouldn't give her a talkie chance, Bebe slapped down $175,000 and bought back the contract that called for her to make three more pictures.

And now what?

WHY, just this: Bebe Daniels, as this is written, has just finished the lead in "Rio Rita" for Radio Pictures. And there isn't a doubt in the world, say the wiseacres of Hollywood, that that talkie will be one of The Big Shots of the talkie year. Bebe's work is one of the biggest sensations of the millions of sensations Terrible Mike has pulled.

Strange, too. Bebe has a voice that you wouldn't think twice about, ordinarily. Nice voice, and all that, but no power—no force. Now that's just where Mike does his stuff. He took all the nice things in Bebe's voice—and there were plenty of 'em—and added the thing she didn't have—POWER. And boy, what a voice it gives her on the screen!—you'd even fall in love with a strabismic wart-hog if it had a voice like that.

On the other hand, Clara Bow's voice certainly didn't lack power. Her first all-talkie—"The Wild Party"—proved that. Her first scene called for her to dash into a dormitory full of girls and greet them with, "Hello, everybody. . . .!" Well, the sound-mixing gentleman in the monitor-room above the stage, not being familiar with the—ah—er—vibrations of Clara's voice, didn't properly tune down his dials for Clara's words.

She burst in, told them "HELLO, EVERYBODY!!!"—and every light valve in the recording room was broken!

> Little Miss Starlet, in ermine and scarlet,
> Getting a thousand a day,
> Along came the talkies, revealing her squawkies—
> And put poor Miss Starlet away!
> —from "Mother Goose in Hollywood"

How'd you like another contrast—even more startling than the case of Clara and Bebe?

125

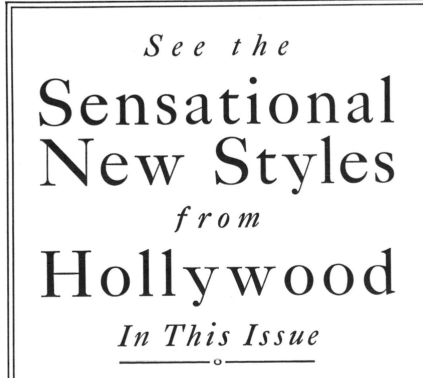

Well, then, here are Mona Rico and Joan Bennett—

Joan, you know, is one of the three daughters of the interesting Richard, which really doesn't matter.

Anyway, she, like thousands of others, sought fame in pictures—and sought and sought and sought, also like thousands of others. She got a bit here, and a bit there, but she never burned them up. She just looked sweet and pretty and nice and mary-ann-ish and so on.

And then she married herself out of the pictures, and that seemed the end of Joan. Married a chap named Fox, whose father had a lot of timberland.

ONE day a reporter called on her and chronicled the birth of a Foxlet. He found Joan and her hubby and baby living in a walkup flat in the south-of-the-tracks part of Beverly Hills, which is you know. Joan was just a nice little *hausfrau* who didn't look any happier than any other little *hausfrau*. And it turned out she wasn't even that happy—for she soon got a divorce.

And everybody in filmdom that cared said "Poor Joan" and "Life is like that," and forgot her.

But along came Terrible Mike, and Ronald Colman needed a leading lady for "Bulldog Drummond." Star after star was tested for the part—and somehow, poor Joan Bennett got a test. Maybe somebody felt sorry for her.

And Terrible Mike did his stuff—the stuff for which everybody that tried out, except Joan, calls him "Terrible." He set Joan out so far ahead of every other tryer-out that they gave her the part. And "Poor Joan" was such a success in the part that she's on her way to the top—she's played opposite George Arliss in "Disraeli," opposite Harry Richman in "Playboy," is signed for the lead with Joseph Schildkraut in "The Mississippi Gambler."

And from her walkup flat south of the tracks in Beverly, she's moved into one of those lemme-see-your-bankbook apartments in a house called the *Chateau Elysée*.

That's the story of Joan. Turn the picture, and see Mona Rico and what Terrible Mike has done to her—

Once upon a time, a little Mexican extra girl was standing around the United Artists lot, waiting to be called for the next scene so she could earn her day's $7.50. Director Ernst Lubitsch was giving a man a screen test. He needed somebody to work the test scene with the fellow.

"Hey, you!" he yelled at the first girl he saw. "Come over here and do so-and-so. . . .!"

The girl who called herself Mona Rico did. And when they ran off the "rush" of the test footage, Lubitsch forgot all about the man in the take and dashed wildly out to find Mona. She had stolen the scene.

It was one of those things that little extra girls dream about. And before she knew it, Mona Rico was playing lead opposite John Barrymore.

She put on all the stuff that went with it—apartment, maids, autos, chauffeurs, clothes. Lupe Velez must have lain awake worrying o' nights.

BUT Terrible Mike has a Nordic superiority complex or something. He stepped right into Mona Rico's life, planted himself before her, and said:

"You!—how do you speak English? . . ."

Poor Mona Rico! Gone is the dream. . . .

And gone or going with it are that swarm of duco-haired Don Tabascos who were cluttering up Hollywood.

> O, Don Ro-dreek was a movie Sheik,
> Knocking down a grand a week;
> He gave the frails an awful kick—
> But now he's OUT? He "no can spik. . . .!"
> —from "Mother Goose in Hollywood"

The superheated senoritas and their male companions in arson aren't the only ones to suffer from Terrible Mike's linguistic demands. It's tough on other outlanders—even, as the passports say, "including the Scandinavian!" There are, for instance, Nils Asther and Greta Garbo.

A year ago, Nils was getting enough fan mail from heaving-bosomed damsels in the midlands to paper a ballroom with. And even yet.

But Nils, he bane got Swedish accent, and Terrible Mike is laying for him.

Ditto goes for the Garbo. So far, they've dodged Mike by sticking to the silents—they just made a valiant stand together in that picture ballyhooed by the billboard showing Greta in that bathing suit with Nils bending over her—quick, boys, the pyrene ! ! ! "Actions speak louder than words" is their motto—and their hope.

And a German beauty, as lovely a *fraulein* as ever was "Made in Germany," ran afoul of Terrible Mike in Hollywood and has returned to Deutschland to do her klang-filming.

TRUE, some of the importations have so far survived the terror of the mike. But only by a sort of artificial respiration—they've confined themselves to stories that call for an accent!

They can't talk English straight.

They can talk it, though, with a twist here and a twist there. And so they play the rôles of foreign princesses and things like that—leetle Fr-r-r-ranch *m'mselles, hein?* And manage to live.

Interesting, here, is the fact that Sessue Hayakawa, the Japanese star of how-long-ago, crashed back into celluloid BECAUSE of—not in spite of—the mike! As this is written, Hayakawa has just finished a short talkie back east for Warners, called "The Man Who Laughed Last."

It's Hayakawa's vaudeville skit, done for the silver screen—and probably ninety per cent of the people who see and hear him will be amazed to find out how well he speaks English!

Hayakawa died in the silent pictures many years ago because he could only do ONE kind of story—the Japanese prince or something who married the white girl and paid for it.

Or didn't, and paid anyway!

And so it's a funny thing, isn't it?—how Terrible Mike makes 'em or breaks 'em. . . . Old-timers come back through his ministrations, and the big shots go boom. . . .

> Eenie, Meenie, Minie, Mo—
> Stars, they face the mike with woe;
> If they holler, watch 'em go. . . .!
> Eenie, Meenie, Minie, Mo!!!
> —from "Mother Goose in Hollywood"

The demon mike didn't frighten Gloria Swanson. Coached in speaking lines by the famous Laura Hope Crews, and with a high-priced singing teacher putting her through the eighth-notes, Gloria gave the performance of her life in "The Trespasser," and will undoubtedly find the greatest and most productive period of her long career in talking pictures.

But there's Vilma Banky. She had her Hungarian accent to lick.

Jane Manner, the New York voice coach, had Vilma in hand for six months, and now Sam Goldwyn is paying the Hungarian Rhapsody her $2,000 a week while the camera crank isn't turning, until the girl can clip her "dar-links" and speak better English into the ear of the choosy microphone.

THERE'S Lila "Cuddles" Lee, who has miked a comeback.

Starred by Paramount at fifteen, she grew up—and out of it.

Then she married James Kirkwood, disap-peared from the screen, and finally, when he went abroad, she managed to get by, doing quickies here and there.

And now, suddenly, she's found the pot of gold hidden in the microphone.

No big smash, you know—just a good actress with a lovely mike voice. Maybe she'll never be a star, but with what she's got, she'll always be in the money.

And there's H. B. Warner. Of H. B., they used to say:

"Oh, yes, he's the fellow that played *Jesus* in that DeMille thing. What's he doing now?"

The answer is that he's got a great talkie voice and a First National contract.

Look at Louise Fazenda—good old Louise. She was always a good actress. But Terrible Mike has made her better. He's taken that fazendish giggle of hers and let the citizenry hear it.

Results?—Louise played in "No, No, Nanette," "Loose Ankles," "The Desert Song" and plenty more to come.

TERRIBLE MIKE has boosted Betty Compson to the top—for the third time in her career.

Young Douglas Fairbanks, Jr., who had the misfortune to be only his papa's son for a long time in the stillies, has been going fine in the talkies since Terrible Mike was good to him in "The Barker."

These are some that have been given a helping hand by Mike the Erratic. But look what happened to Dolores Costello, the sex-quisite.

Magnificent thing that she is, this Mrs. Jack Barrymore, she's got something in her voice that Terrible Mike simply snarls out loud about.

Headed for the heights she was, until she played in "Glorious Betsy."

Poor Dolores—there are two opinions in Hollywood as to what her mike voice sounded like.

One clique says it sounded like the barkings of a lonesome puppy; the others claim it reminded them of the time they sang "In the Shade of the Old Apple Tree" through tissue paper folded over a comb.

It's not Dolores' fault; it's just one of the Terrible Mike's dirty tricks.

And anyway, Dolores should worry—she and hubby Jack have gone back East to prepare for a new addition to the Barrymore family.

If it's a boy, it's certain they won't name him Michael.

But what Terrible Mike did to Dolores in "Glorious Betsy," he did just the opposite in the same opus for Conrad Nagel.

Conrad was just a nice blond leading man before that.

But suddenly the world discovered he had a marvelous voice.

And now the name of Conrad Nagel in Hollywood is as the name of Abou ben Adhem in that thing you had to learn when you were a kid.

And now we'll move on to the peculiar situation of Dick Barthelmess! . . . Dick, who has been helped and hurt at one and the same time because of Terrible Mike.

Dick has always turned out darned good pictures.

More than that, he has turned out a good talkie.

The word is used advisedly— for while Dick talks well, Dick is *not* a singer. And yet, in his talkie, Dick is seen to sing! . . .

And as he is seen to sing, there emerges from the screen a lovely voice. It synchronizes perfectly with Dick's mouthings on the screen—and if you didn't know better you'd say: Ah, how he can sing! . . .

But you know better. From East coast to West, and from border to border, there was printed in the public prints the news that a "voice double" had sung the song while Dick Barthelmess made his mouth go.

LIKE the golden idol with the clay feet, Dick Barthelmess was not perfection—his feet were all right, but his vocal cords needed tuning!

And it didn't help a bit when the 24-sheet billboards tried to kid the public with:

"See AND HEAR Richard Barthelmess in So-and-So. . . ."

The public, being a number of years older and wiser than in the days of Phineas T. Barnum, read the billboards, made a sound like a moribund raspberry and wanted to know how they got that way.

But see and hear him in "The Drag." He's our old Barthelmess again.

But don't draw the conclusion from that that voice-doubling is rare. Ah—no—Terrible Mike has brought a bag of money to a group of people who have heretofore had no chance whatever in the movies . . . people who can sing.

You who see and hear these talkie extravaganzas with the dazzling chorus girls, and wonder how they could find so many beautiful girls who could sing, too—cease your wondering. They DON'T SING! It's like this—

THE cameras are trained on the beautiful chorus girls, who dance and move their lips just like Dick Barthelmess did. But they are as silent as a bill collector isn't. And down below the camera-range, or at one side, are the microphones—in front of a dozen or so lovely-voiced creatures whose loveliness often ends there.

"Yes, dearie; I've got a job in the pictures."

"You! With that pan?"

"No, dearie—do-re-mi-fa-sol! . . . With this VOICE!"

And in just the same way as these chorus songs are "doubled," so, with a little rehearsing, can individual songs be doubled for such stars as can act and talk for Terrible Mike but who sing like a $198 piano six months after you have it paid for. But voice doubling will soon go out of style.

The one sad Barthelmess experience taught the movie makers a valuable lesson. In the future, the stars who can't sing will dance, or tell riddles.

One could go on and on and on about the big-timers to whom Terrible Mike has done so-and-so and this-and-that—Norma Shearer, who has been definitely located, thanks to her success in "The Trial of Mary Dugan" and "The Last of Mrs. Cheyney"; Bessie Love, who was just drifting and had gotten down to ukuleleing it in personal appearance stuff with a Fanchon-Marco road show, and who suddenly jumped through the microphone back into the starry realms in "Broadway Melody"; the Duncan Sisters, who left Hollywood rapidly after making a silent "Topsy and Eva" for United Artists, and whom Terrible Mike beckoned back because they CAN sing, to make "Cotton and Silk."

And so on, and on, and on.

But let's forget, for a bit, the actors and actresses.

Terrible Mike's machinations have had effect elsewhere.

HE has brought coffers full of golden shekels —or aren't shekels gold?—to others than these.

He has fattened the exchequers of the Building Trades unionists, since every studio has begun building sound stages on the subdivision plan.

He has made clinky the pockets of all sorts of ham-and-eggers who got on his band-wagon by opening schools of dramatic expression and elocution, even though they themselves talked of "erl" wells and "moiders."

He gave rise to a lot of funny stories about the people who didn't know the mike was turned on, and expressed their opinion of the director or supervisor as a bad ancestored person of amazing habits.

He gave the studio press agents a lot of things to write that never got into the papers or magazines.

And he's—he's—well, one more excerpt from "Mother Goose in Hollywood"—

Hey, diddle, diddle
  Mike is a riddle,
He makes 'em both poor and rich!
  The joke may be good,
  But to Hollywood,
He's a—
    gosh-darned mean old thing!

A Rare Old "Still"

THE picture was "The Pullman Bride." The lot was Sennett's. The cast, reading from good to better, was Tom Kennedy, Mack Swain, Polly Moran, Gloria Swanson and Chester Conklin, the latter two playing the leads, and Phyllis Haver furnishing the big-eyed background behind Mack Swain's shoulder. Happy days, those. Their aggregate salaries were $250 a week. Now they're a hundred times that, $25,000

HAVE YOU HEARD THE NEWS?

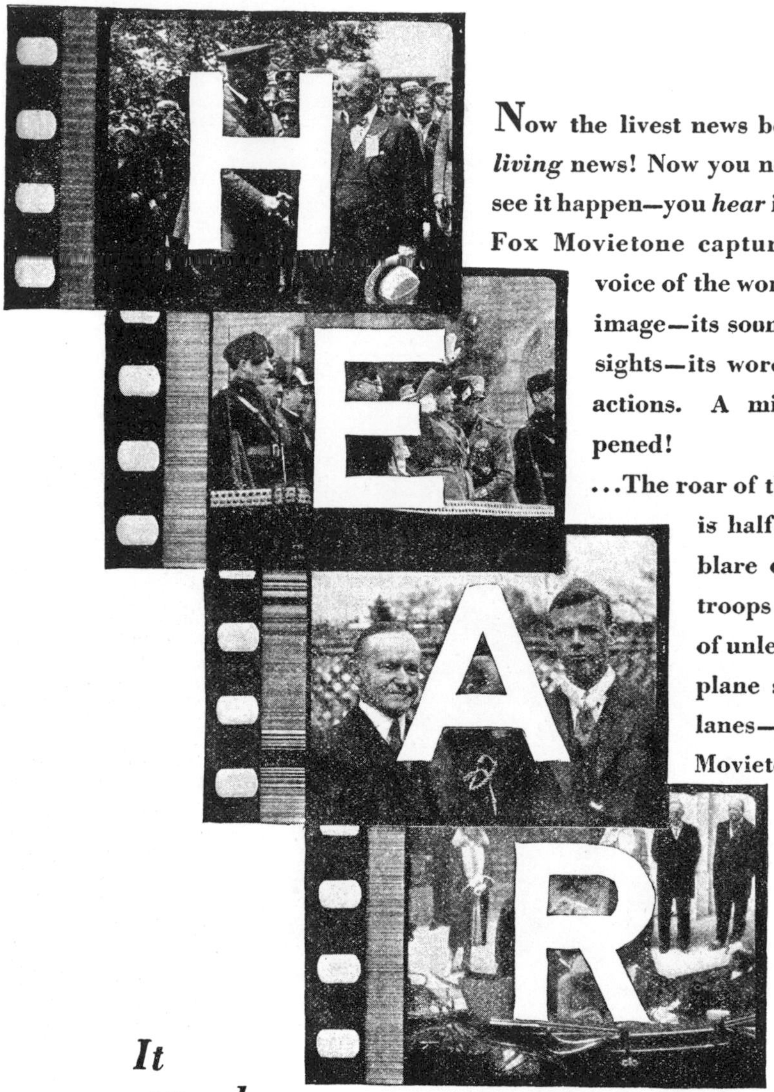

128

H E A R

Now the livest news becomes *living* news! Now you not only see it happen—you *hear* it! Now Fox Movietone captures the voice of the world as well as its image—its sounds as well as its sights—its words as well as its actions. A miracle has happened!

...The roar of the crowd which is half of football's thrill—the blare of martial music as the troops wheel past—the thunder of unleashed horsepower as the plane speeds through the airlanes—all these come to you in Movietone! They make you an ear-witness as well as an eyewitness! *They really take you there!*

...Have you heard the news? ...If not, go today to the theatre showing Fox Movietone News, and prepare for the thrill of a lifetime!

It speaks for itself!

FOX MOVIETONE NEWS

—*developed and presented by* WILLIAM FOX

What Next for Gloria?

Her future is in your hands

By
Katherine Albert

Gloria Swanson's first dramatic picture was called "Smoke." In it she wore this outfit, described as "the first aviation bathing suit ever designed"

A GOOD many years ago a little, snub-nosed girl in a cheap, silk dress stood before a second-rate director and tried to look as if she had never worked in Keystone Comedies.

It was useless, for the remains of custard clung to her symbolically. There was an over-developed muscle in the right arm. It got there from slinging pies.

She could conceal her Keystone past no better than she could hide a vivid personality. In spite of the frouzy dress and the "very chick hat, dearie," Gloria Swanson had what it takes.

She was given her first dramatic rôle. It was a decided departure and Gloria got it by a fluke. Up to that time screen actresses had been divided into two divisions. They were either nasty nice or dirty bad. The word "flapper" had not yet been coined. But Triangle had bought a story, the protagonist of which was a hoyden who, in spite of a gay exterior, was a nice girl after all. Executives, fearful of trusting the rôle with one of their stock players, who could be nothing but good—oh, terribly good—or bad—just rotten bad—had called in an outsider.

The outsider was the snub-nosed Gloria who tried to look as if her only acquaintance with pies was at the dinner table.

And with the big dramatic part she was given unheard of riches. She found that her weekly envelope contained, instead of the $35 Keystone had paid her, a neat $150.

Gloria became, at that very moment, a motion picture star. Someone told her of the installment plan. She wanted a car and a home and clothes—for which she had no taste at all—and luxurious furniture. And she had them, as she has had whatever material things she wanted. She bought them simply by writing her name to little pieces of paper. It was as easy as acting. But when she was through she found that she had contracted to pay $165 a week on a $150 salary.

Thus Gloria Swanson—who has always spent $165 for every $150 earned.

She married the Marquis de la Falaise de la Coudray. It was a romantic marriage and, for a time, a happy one. Henry now spends much of his time in Paris, away from Gloria and Hollywood. For Gloria, men can only be a side issue

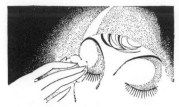
What Next for Gloria?

Thus Gloria Swanson—four years ago the most sought-after star in America, who is now working her way back to the top from a precarious position on the screen.

Thus Gloria Swanson—who came from nothing to a position at the very top. And who is now awaiting the effect of her newest picture, "Queen Kelly," upon the genus-public to see if she is still popular. That is, if "Queen Kelly" is ever released.

AN amazing woman, who has had everything and lost it and had it again. Over and over. A cynical woman in the early days. A cynical woman still. One of the unhappiest actresses on the screen, who is still envied by thousands of girls.

Envied—and she doesn't know when she may have to leave her luxurious home in Beverly Hills to move into a small apartment.

Envied—and she cannot bear to be alone for a moment. She is afraid of her thoughts. Introspection is impossible for her.

Envied—and her whole future (for there is still a Swanson future as there always has been) rests upon the public's reception of "Queen Kelly." She has not been seen on the screen

Her past is one of the Amazing Stories of an Amazing Town.

THERE have been many people in her life who affected her deeply, who left an indelible mark upon her future. Elinor Glyn was one of these. Madame Glyn, I firmly believe, taught her how to clothe herself. For the woman who was to become the synonym for *chic* the world over knew less about her dressing than the Thanksgiving turkey. She had been swathed in De Mille atrocities. She had never worn clothes.

Luckily for her, her first starring picture away from De Mille was Madame Glyn's "The Great Moment."

The writer of novels of purple passion is noted for her frankness. Upon meeting a world famous male star she said, even before the conventional gestures had been made, "You must change your barber. Your hair cut is frightful."

Nor was she any the less tactful with Gloria. She attempted to make a lady, and a well dressed lady at that, of the Keystone comedy girl. And she succeeded. For this white flame that is Swanson is pliable when she is properly approached. Otherwise,

in nearly two years. There is no reason to envy the unhappy, melancholy Gloria.

But something may happen, as it always has happened to Gloria. Years ago it was the financial failure of a studio that saved her from ruin. Shortly after she was given her Triangle contract the company went into bankruptcy. But Cecil B. De Mille had seen her in her first dramatic rôle (the picture was released, if it was released, under the title of "Smoke") and liked her so much that he gave her a contract that more than doubled her salary. The creditors were quiet for awhile.

WHAT has happened to her lavish apartment on top of a Manhattan building where a cohort of carpenters and painters worked for weeks so that it would be ready for her? What has happened to her Westchester property, where she and Henry, her husband, and the children were going to live for the rest of their lives?

And what will happen to her Beverly Hills palace that she bought from Gillette, the safety razor king? Once she gave it up to move into a small apartment. Rumor began. One of the Gillette officials was questioned about it. He refused to admit that the place had been taken from Swanson. He also refused to deny it. And this significant fact constituted a newspaperman's confirmation.

She is living back at the old home. But how long will she continue there? It all depends on you and "Queen Kelly." We, who know her, hope it will be the beginning of a happier era. And yet Gloria remains a personality. She is still a significant and startling figure in the intricate design of Hollywood.

she is as forceful as a night nurse. Paramount found that out when they attempted to keep her.

WHEN Gloria was a star she wanted to leave the home studio. She had done as she pleased there for all her quarrel with Pola Negri, when the two ruling geniuses of the lot vied with each other for best dressing room, best pictures, best exploitation and best money. Paramount was prone to favor Gloria in these squabbles.

Shortly after her return from Paris, following her marriage, Maurice Cleary persuaded her to hold out for a fabulous sum from Paramount. They wanted to keep her. But not that badly. Their final offer was $20,000 a week for two years. She left and, after a year's absence from the screen, signed a contract with United Artists to produce her own pictures.

"To produce her own pictures"—that has hurt more than one star. Gloria had the final word on story, direction, photography, clothes, casting. It isn't practical. Neither is Gloria.

What has happened to Gloria as a person during those fitful, restless years, those years of misery and ecstasy, of bottom to top and back again? Has she changed?

Her marriage to Henry brought her something, for he is a sweet, gentle soul of unusual kindliness; too gentle, I'm afraid, too sweet for Gloria. He is now in Paris as a foreign contact man for Pathe. And the word is out that they are separated.

Men cannot fill Gloria's life. They can only be a side issue, for she is too full of energy and vitality and activity to give herself completely to a husband.

Help John McCormack Select His Movietone Songs

Vote for your ten favorites on the ballot below

WHAT songs do you want to hear John McCormack sing in his Fox Movietone production?

That is a question uppermost in the minds of Fox Films executives. The beloved Irish tenor has become so thoroughly established as an American institution that all music lovers are familiar with his repertoire.

McCormack will sing ten songs in the Movietone production about to begin shooting and microphoning in Ireland, with Frank Borzage directing.

In the ballot below, you will find a list of McCormack's best loved songs. Check your ten favorites. In the blank spaces you may write in any of McCormack's songs which may have been omitted from the list.

Mail your ballot to John McCormack Picture Director, Fox Studio, Los Angeles, Calif.

John McCormack

To John McCormack Picture Director
Fox Studio
Los Angeles, Calif.

I suggest that John McCormack sing the ten songs designated:

☐ Believe Me If All Those Endearing Young Charms	☐ At Dawning	☐ Beneath the Moon of Lombardy
☐ The Harp That Once Through Tara's Halls	☐ Macushla	☐ Little Mother of Mine
☐ Silver Threads Among the Gold	☐ The Rosary	☐ Wearing of the Green
☐ When Irish Eyes Are Smiling	☐ Ave Maria	☐ Kathleen Mavourneen
☐ When You and I Were Young, Maggie	☐ Mother Machree	☐ Dear Love, Remember Me
☐ That Tumble-down Shack in Athlone	☐ Roses of Picardy	☐ I Hear You Calling Me
☐ Somewhere a Voice Is Calling	☐ Moonlight and Roses	☐ My Wild Irish Rose
☐ Serenade (Softly Through the Night)	☐ Dear Old Pal of Mine	☐ A Little Bit of Heaven
☐	☐	☐

Name_____

Street Address_____ Town and State_____

Motoring *Beauty Hints*

By Lois Shirley

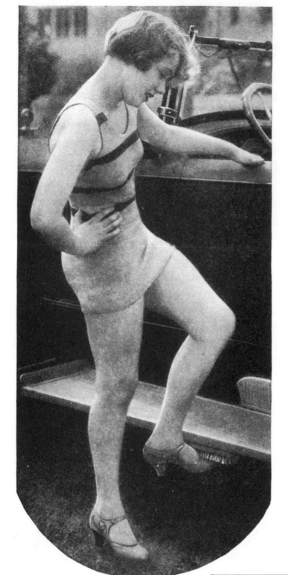

P ITY the poor motion picture stars — they must always be beautiful and smart!

It is only in the sanctum-sanctorum of their inner boudoirs that the screen favorites may rest and smear their faces with cold cream. At the beach, on the tennis courts, during shopping tours, they must always look their best.

Those of us less endowed make an attempt at beauty, but it is not a vital necessity. Yet strenuous as it is, the example set by the stars is an excellent one. Every daughter of Eve cherishes the hope of being beautiful, well groomed and charming at all times. Therefore, take a lesson from the stars and learn their secrets.

Motoring is devastating to beauty. An open car—or even a closed one, for that matter—is hard on the complexion, the hair and the hands. Most of us know the proper creams and lotions to counteract the bad effects, but the stars have introduced some new tricks of looking well in an automobile that are worthy of attention.

Anita Page drove her car home from the beach and the sand on her shoes got in the gears. The repair charge was twenty-five dollars. For twenty-five cents, she bought this shoe brush and attached it to the running-board. Just the old door-mat brought up-to-date

How to step, all dripping wet, from the ocean and show up for luncheon a few minutes later looking smart and calm. Dorothy Sebastian has a hair-dryer attached to the battery of her car. Her hair is naturally curly so she doesn't have to worry about how to get a wave

Some interesting suggestions from the stars on how to look your best before the traffic cop

There's Norma Shearer, for instance, and her ubiquitous curling iron. It was not ubiquitous at first until a nice eye to economy inspired Mr. Thalberg's wife. On location Norma dispenses with the hair dresser and carries her own curling iron along. An electrician at the studio rigged up a contrivance whereby the necessary implement of beauty could be attached to the automobile battery, and this worked so efficiently that Norma uses it when she plays tennis or golf or when she swims.

LOOKING beautiful just after a swim is always a problem, but you can't beat these girls from Alabama. Another neat car contrivance for the beach is Dorothy Sebastian's hair dryer, that works in the same way as the curling iron. This plugs into the socket and runs to the battery of the car. It is a boon to a girl as busy as Dorothy, for it means that she may have her swim, change from her bathing suit into her dress, dry her hair and be ready for a smart luncheon party without having to go home and waste a lot of valuable time that could be devoted to bridge.

Now don't get the impression that the stars are all extravagant young women! Anita Page didn't like it a bit when her car was laid up in a garage

A powder box, not to be used in heavy traffic, is concealed in the steering wheel of Barbara Kent's car. When the box is closed the horn will honk. While there may be time for fixing the make-up when the traffic lights go red, Safety First Societies should look into this

The battery that starts Norma Shearer's motor also curls Norma's hair. This curling iron saves the trouble and expense of sending a hair-dresser on location trips. Norma also finds it convenient after a game of golf or tennis. When not in use, it hooks on the dash-board, but, while still hot, should not be confused with the brake

134

Gifts
of Leather

*that indelibly
distinguish the giver*

HERE are gifts that will last and improve with the lasting. Let Meeker Made leather accessories of imported Steerhide solve your gift problems. In them you find the utmost in utility combined with the utmost in rare beauty. That's why they make gifts that are always cherished.

Any Meeker Made ladies' handbag—under arm or vanity—may be selected with certainty of its appropriateness. For each item in the Meeker line embodies the most modern, exclusive design—the smartest shape and style—and unusual, up-to-the-minute fittings.

AND for the men, Meeker offers exclusive designs in individual bill folds, key cases, attractive novelties or Boxed Gift Sets . . . two piece or three.

Meeker Made finest quality leather goods are tooled, hand-colored, hand-laced and fashioned out of genuine, imported Steerhide. Displayed by better dealers everywhere.

MEEKER MADE
smart leather gifts
from the shops of
The MEEKER COMPANY, Inc.
Joplin, Missouri

Largest Manufacturers of Steerhide Leather Goods in the U. S. A.

and the bill came to $25. It happened one day after she had come from a swim. The sand from her shoes got into the gears. Well, Anita is as clever as she is pretty, so she conceived the idea of having a shoe brush attached to the running board of the car.

She uses it not only after a swim, but finds it serviceable when she is all dressed up and wants a quick shine. The brush cost just 25 cents.

This business of having nice looking shoes when you step out of a car confronts every feminine motorist. There are various heel guards on the market, but Doris Dawson pre-

Great invention of Jean Arthur for solving the problem of how to wear a floppy hat in an open roadster. Prevents accidents, traffic jams and bad language. Jean catches up the brim with rhinestone pins that are also used as ornaments when the hat is worn picture style

fers an entirely different method. She carries an extra pair of nicely polished, well heeled slippers on an elastic band stretched across the inside of the door. The slippers are placed in shoe trees and keep their shape perfectly. Then she can wear her oldest slippers and not care a prop-boy's damn how much she has to manipulate the brakes.

Correct from head to foot while motoring—that seems to be the motto of the stars. Jean Arthur has solved the picture hat and the top-down roadster problem with an idea as unique as it is chic. All of us who drive have cursed loudly or silently, according to our standards of being a lady, when that big floppy hat lashed its brim across our face just when we were making a tricky left-hand turn. So give a cheer for Jean.

Two rhinestone and pearl pins do the trick. When she starts for the smart tea party she takes the twin pins from the crown of her hat, rolls back the floppy brim into dashing lines and pins brim to crown at the sides. When the drive is finished, she takes down the brim and repins the ornaments in a V shape on the crown of her hat.

This not only serves the goddess of chic but it may prevent accidents as well. However, Barbara Kent, with her auto contrivance, won't be a favorite with the officers. Over the

horn on the wheel of her car is attached a small vanity box. When the box is closed the horn works. Barbara has promised that she'll use the powder puff only when the car is standing still.

Mary Brian's cape for driving is quite decorative, but its real purpose is utilitarian. It protects her dainty frocks from the dust that is bound to collect on the seat of a car. Smart little Mary—it saves her many a cleaner's bill. Made of dark silk, it is large enough to cover the entire costume and when she arrives at her destination it may be folded into a small pack-

age and put into the pocket of the car, so that it is always handy and ready for service.

According to Lina Basquette and Dorothy Dwan, half the battle for beauty is won when one is comfortable. But Lina, being a fastidious young woman, won't have your plain, ordinary driving pillows for her back. No sir, she insists upon using a dainty one of silk, lace trimmed.

However, the cover is detachable and may be replaced by others when necessary.

The back seat of Dorothy Dwan's car is made pleasant in summer time by an electric fan, which Dorothy declares is an absolute necessity for a closed machine.

Of course, the stars take the greatest precautions from the wind and sun when they drive.

Those who want a coat of tan—so fashionable this year—cover their faces and arms with a bit of olive oil and those who insist upon being fair and old-fashioned use a light layer of cold cream under the powder.

The strange part about it is that most of the girls keep chauffeurs, whose sole duty seems to be to cart their friends about.

For the most part, these modern Hollywood damsels drive their own gas buggies.

The Big Parade

ONE of the most remarkable pictures to be released in the next few months is "The Big Parade," with John Gilbert, directed by King Vidor. Coming immediately after his great success in "The Merry Widow," it will establish John Gilbert as one of the greatest stars of the screen.

It's a story of an American doughboy and contains some of the most accurate and dramatic picturizations of the American army in the World War. One scene especially is one of the greatest scenes ever shown in a picture. It shows, with gruesome faithfulness, a regiment advancing on the German trenches. Below is a scene in the American trenches in which the doughboys are awaiting the onrushing Germans, and another of Jack Gilbert, who, pain crazed, is escaping the American hospital to join his sweetheart, only to find her home destroyed and *Melisande* (Renee Adoree) gone.

The BUTTERFLY Man

The sad love story of two gay and gallant stars

The man who loved life

THE man who loved life.

And the girl who loved laughter.

Surely, surely, a romance between those two should have spelled happiness.

Yet Mabel Normand lies seriously ill at her home in Hollywood, and out on the desert, Lew Cody is fighting a desperate battle for strength to go to her.

They called him the butterfly man on the twenty-four sheets that acclaimed his witty, worldly pictures.

And we who knew her called her the beautiful clown.

They met and laughed together. Laughter ripened into friendship, and friendship ripened into love and love suggested marriage—at three o'clock upon a September morning almost three years ago.

Their wedding march was a dance tune and in gay, golden bubbles they drank their marriage toast.

We read about it in the morning paper. We were a little surprised. After all, we hadn't realized that Lew and Mabel were in love. They had seemed almost too good friends to be

in love. Then, when the surprise had passed, we were delighted. It seemed such a natural, right thing. Lew would take care of Mabel and Mabel would take care of Lew. Their home would be full of life and laughter—a splendid place to drop in for wit and gaiety and good fellowship.

But sometimes two and two don't make four.

That is why some folks call life a game.

The love story of Mabel Normand and Lew Cody has not, so far, had the happy ending which we had written for it.

No one—least of all Lew and Mabel—knows what lies beyond. Somehow they seem now to stand hand in hand against a slowly darkening sky.

There is confetti yet in Mabel's dark curls—bright, silly stuff.

Her tiny feet are bound fast with yards and yards of the colored paper ribbons that clutter dance floors after a party.

HER eyes are twin graves of laughter. And nothing is so sad as dead laughter.

Under the elegant motley he has always worn, Lew's shoulders seem to sag with despair. For life doesn't come to you. You have to go out and meet it and Lew can no longer do that. He has always gone forth gallantly to meet life—the good and the bad, the successes and the failures, the lean days and the fat ones.

Looking at Lew in the game of life you could never tell whether he was winning or losing. Only being denied a seat at the table has brought him to despair. But the candle he burned so brightly—"my candle burns at both ends, it will not last the night, but oh, my friends, and ah, my foes, it gives a lovely light"—is very, very low.

Only a miracle, the doctors say, can bring Mabel back to health.

But, where Mabel is concerned, I want to believe in miracles. I want to believe in some kind hand that will reach down and lift up that tragic, helpless little figure—the most tragic of all Hollywood's broken idols—and put it back at the start of things again. Surely somewhere—if not here, somewhere else—a kindly God can turn back the hands of the clock just a few brief years and let Mabel start all over again. It doesn't seem much to ask for the girl who never did harm to anyone in all her life.

IT seems that whatever power planned things in the beginning owes Mabel something for giving her that divine gift of laughter and then sending her through life without any protection from the ruthless parasites, the selfish sycophants, the birds of prey that hover over the gay, the talented, the generous.

Mabel Normand was the greatest comedienne the screen ever knew. I would not dare to make that statement upon my own opinion alone. I heard it said first by Charlie Chaplin. No one, I think, would dispute his authority. I have heard it said often since by those who should know.

and the Little Clown

By Adela Rogers St. Johns

Yet today when she lies so desperately ill we remember that it is years since we saw her on the screen, since "Mickey" delighted us past measure. She has been out of pictures for years, when her great talent should have been keeping pace with the development of the motion picture art. Today she should occupy the place among the women of the screen that Chaplin holds among the men.

But Mabel is proof positive that women are not able to meet the world as men meet it. Physically and professionally she broke under the things piled up against her. We are the losers, for we, too, have lost Mabel's gift of laughter.

Perhaps there will be a miracle.

I KNOW. Who better? I am proud to say that I have been her friend since first she came to the land of motion pictures from some factory in Brooklyn, a mingling of youth and beauty and laughter that fairly took our breath away.

I know what is chalked up against her.

A lot of hot-headed, wild, young foolishness such as most of the flaming youth of today has to grow out of.

But bad luck rode beside her on the highway.

She got herself into messes that made great headlines. Her friends got her into things. Mabel has always been the fall guy. She never got away with anything in her life. There are plenty of girls in the world who have done in fact the things Mabel was only suspected of, and they have righted themselves and gone on. But Mabel had no balance, no perspective, no cold streak through her warm emotionalism to teach her how to handle life.

More brains and less sense than any woman I ever knew—that is what I would say of Mabel.

You don't hear about that brilliant, fascinating, cultured brain of Mabel's. Mention any of the great books of the past ten years, either in French or English. She has read them and she has thoughts about them almost as interesting as the books themselves.

You don't know that, even in these last years when Mabel has been far from herself, there are a dozen of the cleverest men and women in Hollywood who delighted to spend a quiet evening before her fireside, talking books and music, men and world affairs.

YOU don't know that all Hollywood, from the topmost rung of the ladder to the depths of the lowest gutter, is spangled with Mabel's enormous charity. Real charity—for it came from a purse that was often empty, from a heart that was near breaking, from a mind that always managed to find some good in everyone, even those who found no good in her.

You don't hear how, in the old days, Mabel brought her divine gift of laughter into our dark days—and how she could, in some way, make laughter synonymous with courage.

The girl who loved laughter

The world doesn't know those things and even in Hollywood, they have been too easily forgotten.

But the world knows, and Hollywood, which has become very self-protective and a little smug with success, remembers a lot of other things and that remembrance has weighed upon Mabel and broken her.

William Desmond Taylor and his murder!

How that thing did cling to Mabel's skirts for years because she was the last person known to have seen him alive.

If she told me herself that she knew who shot Bill Taylor, I wouldn't believe her. And let me tell you that there were two nights, one on the long distance telephone to Chicago, one in a house in Altadena soon after the tragedy, when I believe that if Mabel had known who shot him, she *would* have told me.

When you come right down to it, what was there about Mabel's connection with the Taylor murder that should have been held against her? She had dropped in to see her friend, Bill Taylor. Mabel had many men friends. Later, that same night, someone killed him.

Then that thing about the young clubman from Denver—was his name Courtland Dines?

A crazy kid chauffeur who idolized Mabel, as does everyone who ever worked for her, shot Dines. In his stupid fashion, he thought he was protecting Mabel. Instead, he involved her in another mess. But Mabel understood the motive back of his silly interference and she stood by him at some cost to herself.

The worst indictment against Mabel is that she has been foolish, that she wasted and allowed others to waste her great spirit. But on the other side are those things of which Paul speaks in the greatest passage in the Bible—the 13th chapter in his Epistle to the Corinthians. That should be Mabel's "swan song."

Do you remember it—"Faith, hope and love. And the greatest of these is love. Love suffereth long and is kind. Seeketh not her own, is not easily provoked, thinketh no evil."

Mabel came to us a young, uneducated girl. She became a great personality, a star and an unusually brilliant woman. Then she faded into oblivion and we lost her bright image.

Scandal and tragedy haunt those years, but not a single accusation of unkindness, ill temper, meanness, selfishness, envy or betrayal. The craft and the malice and the trickery of life. They were too much for the little clown who never understood nor expected them.

THEY won't let anyone see Mabel now, in her Beverly Hills home where she lies so ill and wasted.

Do you know why?

Because she is so touched and grateful that anyone remembers her, that the wasting fever climbs up and up to a danger point. Even flowers bring tears of joy and appreciation to the laughter-loving eyes—and Mabel has no tears left except those that come from her very heart and her poor heart has all it can do these days to keep pace with life.

It is cowardly, but I am glad that I cannot see her. Because it hurts so to think of Mabel in that pitiful state, with all the great things that her life should have meant, undone. I know how brave her eyes would be, and how the ghost of laughter would rise in them, and how that haunting little voice would remember to speak only of her joy in my happiness.

Perhaps Lew in his struggle to win back enough health to leave his desert, feels something like that. Understanding life as he does, he understands Mabel. I think he married her to protect her—in one of those gallant gestures of his. But he wasn't strong enough.

So the romance of the butterfly man and the beautiful clown has come to its unhappy ending. The screen lacks, and will lack for some time, perhaps forever, two people who gave much happiness and who, so far as their work was concerned, always gave their best.

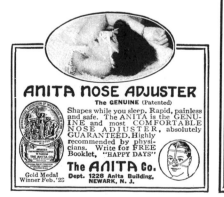

Kornman

BECAUSE, unlike some California producers, he doesn't believe eucalyptus trees grow on Broadway, Harold Lloyd will actually make a New York comedy in the big town itself, thereby shattering an old movie tradition.

Does Rudy Speak

By Frederick James Smith

Natacha Rambova, in an unusual camera study suggesting the psychic. Miss Rambova recently returned from Paris and announced a series of spirit messages from Valentino

(PHOTOPLAY *wishes to make clear its position in presenting the so-called spirit messages of Rudolph Valentino. These messages are presented as a matter of news. The many questions of spiritualism, theosophy and reincarnation cannot be discussed here. It must be noted, however, that many scientists and men of world wide prominence, including Sir Arthur Conan Doyle, William James and others, believe in the possibility of receiving authentic spirit messages.*

On the other hand Houdini, who devoted his life to exposing spiritualistic fakes and who died recently, never has communicated with his wife, although a series of signals had been arranged. Other spiritualists have claimed to receive communication from Houdini but they fail to reveal the secret code the magician had given his wife).

ested in something supernatural," he writes. "Just what it was I did not know. Afterwards it turned out to be automatic writing and a form of the psychic. Before making any move, they consulted this power."

Miss Rambova explains that the so-called messages from Valentino came to her with the aid of George B. Wehner, a trance medium. These messages began to come three days after Rudy's death, she says, while she was in South Europe, completing the work of illustrating a special edition.

PHOTOPLAY submitted a set of questions to Miss Rambova. These, with Miss Rambova's answers, are presented in this article. She explains that they are summarized from a series of messages, which will appear in their complete form in a book Miss Rambova is now completing. This book, at present titled "Rudolph Valentino Intime," will consist of two parts. The first will be devoted to Miss Rambova's personal recollections of Rudy, presenting hitherto untold stories of the actor in the Hollywood days when he was striving for success. The second portion will be given over to the so-called spirit messages.

Here are PHOTOPLAY's questions and Miss Rambova's replies:

Is Valentino happy?

"At first he was anything from happy. That was immediately after his passing. Three days after his passing I received his first message. Incoherent as it was, it showed Rudy as resentful and bitter at his taking at the height of his career. The spirit of his mother spoke, too, protesting at Rudy's terrible unhappiness. Then the tone of Rudy's message changed. Not, however, until after his final burial service in Hollywood. Concentrated public thought had held him earthbound. The prolonged cross-country funeral had held him in the agonies of the spirit in passing.

"Rudy, of course, saw his funeral. He was torn with unhap-

WHEN Natacha Rambova, the former wife of Rudolph Valentino, arrived in America recently she won a place on the front pages of the newspapers of the country by declaring that she had been and was receiving spirit messages from the famous film star.

Most of the nation's newspapers dismissed the statement lightly. But, among Rudolph Valentino's intimate friends, the statement aroused much comment. It is a matter of record that both Rudolph and Natacha were interested in the psychic during their marriage. S. George Ullman, Valentino's manager, refers to the fact in his book, "Valentino as I Knew Him":

"I had observed that both Rudy and Natacha were inter-

From the Beyond?

Natacha Rambova tells of the Spirit Messages she claims to have received from Valentino

piness as New York mobs fought for a view of his body. He realized his great popularity as he had never realized it and knew what he had lost by being taken. To him it was wonderful but cruel.

"He was lonely, too. He could not reach his friends. He could not touch their sorrow. He tried to talk to them but they could not hear.

"Of course, he felt the loss of adulation. Soon, however, the interests of the astral world began to hold him. Now he is radiantly happy, anxious to begin his work there."

Whom has he met?

"He has named Wallie Reid, Barbara La Marr and little Olive Thomas. He has been most interested in meeting and talking with Enrico Caruso. Caruso, of course, was the idol of all young Italians. When Valentino first came to America, to make his living as best he could, Caruso was at the apex of his operatic career. To Rudy he represented all success and all greatness. You can imagine, then, his joy at meeting the great tenor over there. Caruso has taken Rudy to the opera and to hear astral concerts. Rudy, too, has met the personal friends with whom we used to communicate by means of automatic writing."

What have they said?

"They have explained the astral world to him. He is slowly coming to comprehend the sublime qualities of the new life about him."

Does Valentino know of the sorrow that swept the world at his death?

"Naturally, he was conscious of the world's sorrow. It was visible all about him. It tortured him in those earthbound days."

Valentino has referred to the opera and the spoken drama on the other side. Can he tell more of this?

"Opera and drama, sublime things of radiating tones, moods and colors, he says, are presented in massive theaters built of thought-substance."

Valentino has said there are no movies. Why?

"Because the films are a mechanical perversion of the drama. In the astral world there is nothing mechanical. There is a point here I want to make clear. All inventions are created first in the astral plane. As earth-people perfect themselves and achieve the point where they can reach across, they snatch these inventions from the astral. Everything earthly is a materialization of something conceived in the astral plane. Motion pictures, on the other hand, require mechanism for presentation. Mechanism is material and consequently not of a part of the astral scheme of things."

What earthly successes does Valentino remember now?

"He remembered all, at first. Rudy wandered the film theaters where his last film was being shown to sorrowing

One of the last portraits of Rudolph Valentino. Natacha Rambova, his former wife, claims to be in receipt of a number of spirit messages from Rudy via a trance medium

audiences. He walked his old haunts on Broadway, particularly around 47th street, where he used to spend many hours of his old penniless dancing days. He suffered because his old friends used to pass him by, unknowing. Yes, he tried to speak to them, without avail. He shouted 'I am Rudolph Valentino' but they did not hear. It was hard for him to understand. He was just as alive, but in a different vibration. As Rudy has grown in astral knowledge, however, these earthly recollections have lost their appeal. The old glamour of the earth-people is passing. Our world is growing fainter."

Has Valentino any message for his old host of worshippers?

"Yes. He has a message for

142

Beautify your skin intelligently

Science declares the value of soap

"YOU cannot be clean without a good soap. The ideal soap is one which aids the secretions, removing just enough to take away the dirt and yet leaving enough of the oil to make the skin soft and flexible."

This quotation from a recent article by a prominent physician and health commissioner well describes the action of Resinol Soap, and it is the Resinol ingredients which make this result possible. Any soap will *clean* the skin, but Resinol Soap goes a step further—it soothes as it cleanses.

To an exquisitely pure, scientifically balanced, toilet soap, have been added the Resinol properties which to thousands of people are synonymous with clearness, softness and beauty of skin. In the lather of Resinol Soap, these properties are carried deep into the pores. That is why skins bathed with Resinol Soap are thoroughly cleansed—yet seldom troubled with dryness, smarting, stinging and redness.

Buy a cake from your druggist or toilet goods dealer today. Its distinctive, refreshing fragrance, and rich color will reveal at once the presence of the Resinol ingredients, and a week's use will prove their beneficial effect.

RESINOL OINTMENT is a ready aid to Resinol Soap. In addition to being widely used for eczema, rashes, chafing, etc., thousands of women find it indispensable for clearing away blackheads, blotches and similar blemishes.

A Free trial awaits your request—Mail this coupon today

RESINOL, Dept. 15-A, Baltimore, Md.

Please send me free trial of Resinol Soap and Ointment.

Name..

Street..

City............................State............

Does Rudy Speak From the Beyond?

everybody. He wants earth-people to know and realize that there is no death and no separation. He wants earth-people to miss his heartrending experience. He wants them to realize and believe in the beauty and perfection of this after-life."

If Valentino were to live again, would he try motion pictures?

"He would try whatever circumstances permit. He would have to meet the problems of the earth-life."

Miss Rambova, after giving her answers, elaborated upon them. She says that she believes firmly that the messages come from Rudy. "When we receive a telephone message from another city," she countered, "how do we know who is speaking? From mannerisms, from thoughts, from the topics of conversation. Every message from Rudy undeniably has carried authentic earmarks."

I ASKED Miss Rambova what relation marriage had to the astral. "Marriage is physical and of the earth," she answered. "If, however, this union is sincere and real, the spiritual contacts remain the same after one's passing." To her spiritual closeness to Rudy, Miss Rambova attributes her messages.

I asked Miss Rambova regarding her use of mechanical writing during her marriage with Valentino. "Rudy was really psychic. We used to do mechanical writing a great deal," she said. "One of our principal spirit contacts was an old Egyptian who calls himself Meselope. He gave us psychic lessons and prayers but never spoke of material things. Just once he spoke of the earth to me. That was the Friday before Rudy's death. I had received that day a cablegram from Mr. Ullman, stating that the physicians believed Rudy out of danger. Meselope told me that night that Rudy would not recover."

Miss Rambova believes in reincarnation. "We come back without memory to see if our lessons have been thoroughly learned," she says. "Now and then we have faint, dim catches of previous existences. I believe that I lived in previous ages, as did Rudy. Undoubtedly we met. The memories and lessons of those existences are not clear, of course. If they were we would be at a point of psychic perfection."

Emil Jannings' Last Laugh. Just before Jannings sailed for Europe his friends gave a party. And they served plenty of the sort of drinks that are forbidden in America but not *verboten* in Germany

Hommel

OR do you prefer the strictly American team of Fay Wray and Gary Cooper? In "The Legion of the Condemned," Fay and Gary worked together so sympathetically that Paramount has decided to co-star them in a series of light romances of the younger generation.

Tragic

Falcon's Lair, the home of Rudolph Valentino, has never been occupied since his death. Superstitious and foolish stories are told about this house, all typical of the countless legends that have grown up around the memory of Valentino

Hollywood houses of sorrow. They stand back in well-kept gardens. Their walls gleam in the bright sunshine of Southern California. Red tile roofs are a blaze of color. People pass by unthinking and forgetful. But the walls could tell stories of romances ended, careers shattered and death.

A ROMANTIC but foolish legend says that Falcon's Lair is haunted. Irresponsible stories have been told of a caretaker who fled screaming down the hill, never to return.

This is the house that Valentino bought and rebuilt for Natacha Rambova. It was furnished magnificently with treasures gathered from all over the world. At Valentino's death household and personal effects were sold at public auction. Shop girls bought his scarf pins, struggling clerks purchased articles from his wardrobe. At last Falcon's Lair stood barren of its furnishings. Then the weird stories of the place began, just as they circulate about any house that isn't occupied.

HAUNTED houses, to look the part, should be gray, grim castles with a surrounding moat, and at least a somber bat or two circling about the turrets. Houses which shelter poignant memories should be vine-covered cottages with old rose gardens. Tragedy houses can be anything from hovels to mansions, for tragedy is as old as the world and as new as next season's hat—and no respecter of persons.

Hollywood has its dwellings of tragedy. There they stand, the heartbreak houses of heartbreak town.

High up on the ledge of a mountain is Falcon's Lair, the home left by Valentino when he went to New York, never to return. There is Fred Thomson's beautiful hillside home, and Joseph Schenck's great mansion on Hollywood Boulevard. Then there are the houses of Barbara La Marr, William Desmond Taylor, Roscoe Arbuckle, Charles Ray, Mary Miles Minter and Harry Langdon. Sheltering their memories, outliving the fame and sometimes the lives of those who passed through their rooms, those who have laughed and loved and have gone from the screen.

They do not look like the harboring places of tragedy, these

There's a road that wanders about a hill in Hollywood, and along this strange little road are picturesque cottages. Among these cottages is a small brown house, nestling in the shade of giant eucalyptus trees. You have to climb down from the road to get in the upstairs of the house. It is a different sort of a dwelling and it is cursed with beauty. Barbara La Marr built it, and here she lived during the last tragic year of her life.

IT was here that she undertook one of the strictest of diet regimes. She lost her health and was dying when she made her last picture. She died before it was completed. And now, strangely enough, the house that once belonged to the too beautiful girl is occupied by the too beautiful boy, Philippe de Lacy, the war orphan who so many times was close to death during his babyhood in shell-torn France.

Farther down-town, on Alvarado Street in Los Angeles, there is the house that could tell a tale of the strangest murder mystery in the annals of crime. S. S. Van Dine has never evolved a more baffling plot, and this plot has never had a solution. Perhaps it never will.

Mansions

Some fine dwellings that stand as monuments of shattered careers

By
Cal York

In 1922 William Desmond Taylor was murdered in this imposing building, and his death signified the writing on the wall for Mabel Normand and Mary Miles Minter.

Both stars, the greatest of that day, were brought into the case. There was an avalanche of publicity from which they never quite escaped.

Curiously enough, Miss Normand and Miss Minter were living within two blocks of each other at the time. Mabel's house has been transformed into a flat building, with business structures creeping upon it. Mary Miles Minter's beautiful residence, in which she never found the semblance of happiness, is a club. Now Mabel is very ill and Mary Miles Minter is living in Paris.

The year 1922 is one Hollywood will never forget. For the first time the actor realized that he could not dance without paying the piper's

This placid bungalow court apartment saw the murder of William Desmond Taylor, one of the most baffling mysteries in the annals of crime. The murderer was never caught but innocent persons suffered an unjust stigma

price. Fame before had seemed a safe, assured thing.

Never again could it be "the public be damned." At the same time as the William Desmond Taylor murder, Roscoe Arbuckle was on trial for his life in San Francisco, the aftermath of a gay holiday party.

The fat fellow who had made millions laugh would never be a favorite on the screen again. He, too, was paying the piper. The trial cost him his place among the stars, and his wealth. His big cars, specially made, were sold. He lost his great

Here, in the hillside home of Frances Marion and Fred Thomson, dwelt youth and wealth and romance. After Thomson's death it was sold to an Eastern capitalist

In the heart of the most conservative section of Los Angeles lived Roscoe Arbuckle. The sedate English home was sold to foot the expenses of his trial

hacienda of Fred Thomson. Here was youth and romance and wealth. Thomson, the athletic star, was the idol of Young America. His wife, Frances Marion, was one of the most successful of scenarists. Their romance read like a story book.

Frances Marion had been introduced to Fred Thomson during the war, when the tall, curly-haired boy was a chaplain of the Fortieth Division. She had journeyed down to San Diego with Mary Pickford, the honorary colonel of the regiment, to see a service football game. Fred had made a forty-yard run, and then was tackled by four husky sailors. His leg was broken in three places.

MARY and Frances visited him in the hospital. That was the beginning of the romance. They were later married in France. When he returned from the war he became Mary Pickford's leading man. Fame came easily to him.

Fred seemed the last person to die in youth. He had such a splendid physique and lived such an exemplary life. Yet he did not survive an operation.

The Thomson hacienda has since been sold, at a sacrifice, to an Eastern capitalist. The place held too many poignant associations for any member of the motion picture colony to desire it. Fred and Frances were a marvelous host and hostess.

Now Frances Marion is living in Charles Ray's former residence in

house, and since that time not many people have cared to live in it.

Just this year there have been the inevitable stories that the place is haunted. That there have been lights and sounds of revelry when such things did not exist in reality.

Arbuckle's formal English house stands on West Adams Street, Los Angeles' most aristocratic residence boulevard. From the back of the place the windows overlook Chester Place, the holy of holies of the city's smart set. Across the street is the Huntington Minor home, in days gone by the mansion that ruled the destiny of Southern California society.

The Arbuckle gardens join the wide lawns of E. L. Doheny in Chester Place. On the other side is a parish house. A strange environment for the dwelling place of the film comedian who loved reckless parties.

There were many stories of these parties long before Arbuckle had to sell his house on 400 row to pay lawyer's fees.

It didn't seem that tragedy could ever find shelter in the beautiful hillside

Charles Ray sank a small fortune in his Beverly Hills residence, one of the first of the luxurious homes of the movie stars

Five families knew tragedy in this handsome residence. Douglas Fairbanks, Norma Talmadge and Emil Jannings lived here at unhappy moments in their careers

Beverly Hills—from one house of sorrow to another. Charles put a fortune in the building of this graceful mansion. It was to this place that he brought his bride, a cultured society girl.

When Charlie lost his fortune, the house in Beverly Hills was sold, but the bride and groom rented it from month to month, loath to leave the house where they had been happy.

At last they had to give it up. But it may be that Frances Marion will here find happiness again.

THEN there is Harry Langdon's towering Spanish castle on the Argyle hilltop, in which he spent so many unhappy days, beset with domestic trouble and the worries of a career which had promised so much and yet did not last. He signed over the house to his wife and went back to vaudeville. Now he is back in Hollywood, beginning again, but he is not living in the Spanish home.

One of Hollywood's most imposing mansions, known to everyone in the film colony, has had its two decades of sorrows. Five families, at different times, have failed to find happiness back of its white stucco walls and have left for new surroundings.

Douglas Fairbanks lived there, so did Norma Talmadge, and most recently Emil Jannings. Now it stands vacant again as it has from time to time in the past.

The big dwelling on one of the world's most publicized thoroughfares, Hollywood Boulevard, was built by the late Albert Ralphs, a Los Angeles grocer. He had started business humbly, waiting on all customers from the first families to Mexican day laborers.

Thrift and faith in the future of the city built the great Ralphs fortune. The mansion was a monument to his success, but it did not bring the happiness expected. Soon after taking possession of the place he was struck by a falling boulder and never recovered from the accident.

The family did not live long in the house after his death.

Douglas Fairbanks lived there during his early picture career in Hollywood. The film colony in 1918 and 1919 was agog over the fact that he paid $500 a month rent. That is quite a figure for rental now. In those days of wartime frugality it was considered enormous.

It was a trying period for Fairbanks. He had just been divorced by the first Mrs. Fairbanks, the mother of Douglas, Jr., then a youngster of nine.

Later, when Mary Pickford became Mrs. Douglas Fairbanks, "Pickfair," the beautiful home in Beverly Hills, was purchased. Doug was glad to leave the expensive showplace in Hollywood.

John P. Cudahy, a son of the late Michael Cudahy, one of the great packer barons of the nation, next took possession of the residence. His tenancy was one of the gayest, and yet the most tragic. There were many parties at the Cudahy house, music and dancing, plenty to eat and drink. Restraint was not one of Jack Cudahy's virtues. His name had been blazoned in headlines many times. His life was one continuous law suit. There was talk at the time that his wife was about to divorce him.

Although the Cudahy fortune was of many millions the estate could not be divided for seven years. Payments came at stated intervals.

When there was money there was gayety, when there was not, there were bills and threats from tradesmen.

At one of the critical periods of penury Cudahy tried to negotiate a loan for $10,000, his only security the golden flood of money in the future. No one would take the risk.

ONE spring morning in 1921, in one of the beautiful upstairs bedrooms, Jack Cudahy took the suicide's way out of life. Mrs. Cudahy, in an adjoining dressing room, heard the shot. Their two children were playing downstairs.

During the past few years, Michael Cudahy, Jack's son, has figured often in newspaper stories. Recently he married a film player, Muriel Evans. He was once a suitor of Joan Crawford.

Now Douglas Fairbanks, Jr., has wedded Joan, so by a strange twist of fate there is a link between the two families who occupied this house of sorrows.

Joseph Schenck, multimillionaire executive of United Artists studios, and husband of Norma Talmadge, purchased the mansion for her. For a time it seemed that the tragic spell exerted by this apparently cheerful house had lifted. Outwardly the producer and his wife

were the happiest of couples. Through the spacious, luxurious rooms moved the most famous people of the screen world. Norma was at the very peak of her popularity.

Then the old spell came back to the house. Rumors began to circulate that Norma was not happy.

In time the house was closed again. Joseph Schenck moved to a Hollywood hotel, and Norma went abroad.

When Emil Jannings came to America, fresh from triumphs in the studios of Germany, he leased the mansion from Schenck. Fairbanks had paid $500 a month rental. With the passing years values had increased. Jannings paid $1,250.

HERE was an all-conquering star, and surely the old spell could not influence his career. His first American pictures were hailed as triumphs by the critics. He was the screen's greatest actor.

There were many parties for the foreign colony in the rooms which had seen so many parties and so many social sets.

Then came talking pictures. Jannings, in spite of his God-given ability to play upon the emotions, could not learn to speak even fair English during his years in the United States. The conquering hero returned this year to his homeland, defeated. He cried when he left.

Now the place is vacant again. It is as beautiful as ever with its fresh, white walls, beautiful lawns and great trees.

Who will be the next to live in the house of sorrows?

They say that Joseph Schenck intends to live there alone. The bride's bower will become bachelor quarters.

Perhaps the now rather old-fashioned mansion has run through its cycle of tragedies. It may bring good luck to future tenants. The coming years will tell the rest of the story.

Domestic worries and business tribulations disturbed Harry Langdon when he lived in this Spanish castle. It was here that his high hopes of a brilliant career went glimmering

Photomontage By Cushing-Klepser

They have the *esprit de corps* of our overseas doughboys—that great army of the motion picture personnel—from script girl to star and director they march on, undismayed, certain of victory. That is their challenge to "Depression"

Introduction to the Thirties

Out on the breadlines, they were singing "Brother, Can You Spare a Dime?" In the movie places, it was
"Keep Your Sunny Side Up." The homeless slept on park benches, or inside theatres if they were lucky.
Up on the screen, the girls belted out "We're in the Money."

Unreal, an opiate? No sir! This was Hollywood's war on the Depression, and their weapons were unique
to say the least. "Spend! Spend! Spend!" Joan Crawford advised her *Photoplay* readers as they gazed at
the opulence of Marion Davies's home. Better yet was the physical opulence of Mae West, who was
giving the Hays Office a run for its money. The run was short, but legend-making.

A new hero was emerging—Clark Gable—unlike any leading man the fans had seen before. Tough-
tender, an unromantic romantic, he seemed the one man capable of coping with both the Depression and
the new sex symbol it was giving birth to.

Jean Harlow—hardfaced, looking totally and newly manufactured, an expensive golddigger exuding
raw sex. A tough sexpot for tough times—that's what the fans saw and loved. But to *Photoplay,* she was
something else. They called her Baby, sensed her vulnerability, and Jean knew it. A special friendship
developed, and when Jean died *Photoplay* published a fiction story she wanted to do. Amidst the sex-
filled, sensational hullabaloo, *Photoplay* wanted to show the Jean they knew.

Jean was a star for the thirties, but it was now that the ladies for all time were beginning to emerge.
Garbo, surviving the Talkies with her famous "Gimme a visky," was already a legend, a cult, a mania.
But there were two new actresses, *Photoplay* noted, who might give her competition—Marlene Dietrich
and Katharine Hepburn—ladies who would become legends and develop cults of their own.

But the movies' biggest weapon against the Depression—its surefire cure for money problems in Hollywood if nowhere else—was the musical. Indeed, if the new President, Franklin Delano Roosevelt, could
try singing them out of it with "Happy Days Are Here Again," why not the movies?

Forty-second Street was the first shot fired, and the "singies and the dancies" were born. This was the
Golden Age of the movie musical, and its stars the most popular in the nation. Dick Powell, Ruby
Keeler, Jeanette MacDonald and Nelson Eddy, Irene Dunne, Alice Faye, Joan Blondell—they all
helped us forget. Busby Berkeley would become a name immortal—as would Ginger Rogers and Fred
Astaire. And a radio singer named Bing Crosby wouldn't fare too badly, either. But the biggest phenom-
enon was a three-foot-tall singing, dancing moppet named Shirley Temple. She dominated the box office
in the mid-thirties, holding top place over everyone—including Gable. Rival studios soon retaliated with
some young folks of their own—Deanna Durbin, who never got a bad review, and told her girlish
secrets to *Photoplay;* wistful Judy Garland, a little sad even then; Mickey Rooney, Judy's screen beau,
and the nation's Andy Hardy.

By mid-decade, the Depression was definitely over in Hollywood, and they were beginning to wonder
if it wasn't the greatest thing that ever happened to southern California. The new stars—the new
movies—were grossing more than ever.

But *Photoplay* hadn't forgotten their old friends. They repeated their cry of injustice for Fatty Arbuckle and published his plea for work. But the Depression had been around a lot longer for Fatty than anyone else, and soon he would be dead.

Dead also was the forgotten idol of the last decade Jack Gilbert. But *Photoplay* didn't forget. The same year that Greta Garbo made *Camille* with a new leading man, Robert Taylor, Charles Farrell and Janet Gaynor became Hollywood's new love team.

And that wasn't all that was new. Hollywood romances were coming thicker and faster and wilder than ever before. Mexican spitfire Lupe Velez and Gary Cooper were driving them out of the Hollywood hills with their fights. The noise did not subside when she fell in love with Johnny Weissmuller, the new Tarzan. And newlyweds Lili Damita and Errol Flynn described their mad tussles to *Photoplay* in detail. Poor Loretta Young couldn't seem to stay married or in love with anyone.

The only ones not in trouble were a group *Photoplay* called "Hollywood's Unmarried Couples," Barbara Stanwyck and Robert Taylor and Clark Gable and Carole Lombard among them. The story title was unfortunate and nearly started a scandal in the press. But *Photoplay* quickly explained that they were only clarifying the reasons these people weren't married—and were suggesting no other thing.

Well, soon they'd all be married anyway, and *Photoplay* would be left to wonder, prophetically, if Clark and Carole would find lasting happiness.

But other things were starting to happen now—and quickly. There was a fairly new girl around who hadn't been heard from much until recently. Her name was Bette Davis, and it looked as if she was going to be the biggest thing in pictures. By the end of the decade she would be.

And there was an Austrian girl who'd made a wild picture in Europe called *Ecstasy*. It was notorious, and Hedy Lamarr was the most exquisite thing since Greta Garbo.

Sonja Henie, the petite Olympic skating champion, was the latest on the musical front.

Tyrone Power, eclipsing the beauty of all of his leading ladies, promised to be the next decade's most handsome idol. Cary Grant was as mysterious about his private life as Garbo—but so charming and so funny. Boyer's accent would become a symbol of Continental and sophisticated romance.

Cocky little Jimmy Cagney, Robert Young, Jimmy Stewart, Edward G. Robinson had all started making film history of their own. And that plug-ugly but beautiful Spencer Tracy was already making the fans wonder why he always lost the girl to Clark Gable. Sure, they still loved Clark—always would. But they loved Tracy, too, and they wanted him to be the hero as well.

The talents, the triumphs were coming almost too quickly. And right in the midst of them, Hollywood and *Photoplay* lost a dear friend—Will Rogers. But before the decade's end, they would both also receive their most fantastic triumphs.

Photoplay would find themselves with a brand-new writer—Mrs. Eleanor Roosevelt, the First Lady. Could anyone doubt they were the bible of Hollywood now? The movies were about to embark on *the event* of their history—filming the fantastically successful novel *Gone with the Wind*.

Photoplay, with the rest of the nation, successfully campaigned for Gable as Rhett. The casting of Scarlett was less simple, and every actress in Hollywood would have sold her soul to do it. *Photoplay* kept tabs on the stories, the heartbreaks—and the final casting. Relatively unknown Vivien Leigh, creating scandalous gossip with Laurence Olivier, whom she would shortly marry, was it. The most talked-about movie in the annals of films was made, and it disappointed no one.

If it hadn't been for a war threatening over in Europe again, the decade which had begun so badly would have ended perfectly.

'TIS "Bolero," the dance made famous after adapters had jazzed the music of Maurice Ravel's famous composition. And how Carole Lombard and George Raft can turn their toes to its exciting, sensuous rhythm, in the picture of the same name! George plays the rôle of *Raoul*, the gay night club dancer who makes love to his floor partners

The New Ambitions *of* Joan Crawford

"THE time is so short—and there's so much to do—"

I had just asked Joan Crawford about her plans for the future.

I hadn't talked with her for any length of time since twelve years ago, when she was an unhappy, work-weary student at a Missouri college. From the future then, she wanted desperately freedom, recognition, a chance for expression, and some security — things she had never known then.

The woman who now sat across from me beneath the white pergola in the garden of her Brentwood Heights home had all of those things.

She had carved a monumental career out of nothing. She had satisfied a consuming inner demand to be somebody. She was a star, one of the greatest stars in the movie heavens — high, shining brilliantly.

From where we sat we could see the perfectly appointed, substantial house, which painters and decorators were then remodeling to meet her whims. The expansive swimming pool flanked by her newly erected little theater and a bath house spoke eloquently of the comfort and stability she had achieved.

The woman who sat across from me in a white lawn chair, looked, in the pergola-filtered sunshine, very much like the college girl I had known.

Joan Crawford turned in my direction the same clean carved, faintly freckled face with its wide, intense blue eyes. She smiled with the same generous mouth; shook the same auburn tinted locks over her shoulder.

But all her security, her fame, triumphs, possessions — somehow I forgot them.

For beneath the mobile masque of the actress was also that same restless, harried look, which had made you look twice at that vital college girl and wonder what it was she *wanted* out of life!

That shadowed crevice between her brows. That tense tug at her under lip.

Eager, insistent, seeking—for something more—struggling against restraining bonds—

"The time is so short." Short? For Joan Crawford, still in her middle twenties?

"My contract calls for three pictures a year," she told me, "with an option for a 'special' picture. So it may mean four. I never know how long they'll take. 'Dancing Lady' took five months. I never know when the next one will start. I can't plan on any definite free time between pictures.

"And when I'm working, all of my energy, all of my time, goes to the picture. I can't do—I can't even think—of anything else. Everything has to be so perfect."

I know what she means. Joan Crawford doesn't have one costume fitting—she has five and six for each gown. One make-up doesn't last her through the day. Each noon she spends her lunch hour changing to fresh make-up—eats in ten minutes.

Sundays are her only days off. She spends them learning new lines or a new dance routine. Nights, spare minutes, meals—she never relaxes during a picture. Her nervous

Above, Joan Crawford and Clark Gable in a scene from "Chained." Left, Joan on her way to work. For her now there are no holidays or vacations. Every minute's time is taken: work, study rehearsals, more work. Yet she says, restlessly, "I can't just sit back and be a star"

Today she is one of the brightest stars shining in the cinema heavens, yet she sets new goals for herself to attain

By Kirtley Baskette

energy is taxed to exhaustion. She worries until her stomach sickens—she's made that way. A picture takes everything—everything—from her, leaving nothing with which to accomplish the things that she feels must be done.

I asked her if she didn't think maintaining a movie star's career was enough.

"But I can't just sit back and be a star," she said. "I've got to justify my life. I have to develop. I need so many things—so *many* things. I need the experience of the stage. Not only for my work but for *me*.

"I haven't enough self confidence. I haven't enough poise. It makes me miserable."

In the middle of a scene of "Forsaking All Others," Joan was working with her back to the door of the sound stage. Suddenly she stopped, taut. She hadn't seen anything. She hadn't heard anything. But she knew that someone had

Crawford seven years ago, Joan of "Rose Marie." She has learned so much since then, and gone so far, it seems entirely possible that her present plans and ambitions for the future will be attained

Crawford of today—beautiful and gloriously successful. Yet she is finding no satisfaction in fame, and Hollywood, once so important, means nothing to her today

come into the place who was criticizing her, mentally. Someone had entered, who, unlike the crew and the cast, *wasn't with her*. She turned around. Another star had slipped in to watch her work. Joan had sensed the measuring mind. She couldn't go go on until the visitor had left.

"That isn't poise, certainly," she declared. "Even previews are torture for me. I can't eat for hours before. I'm a wreck when they're over.

"That's what I've got to conquer. And the only thing that can do it is the stage. I don't want the fame of the stage, I want the *experience*.

"It isn't the money, either. If I could have the time off, the studio could take any extra profits. But I haven't the time. I'd need six months. But when have I ever had six months? When will I?"

The crevice between her brows deepened. Then her tense, earnest face relaxed with a smile.

"Of course," she admitted, "the very thought of it scares me to death. I would be petrified, I know. But I must do it. That's one reason I built the theater here."

We walked over to the famous and somewhat mysterious

little theater. Mysterious because few have seen it. "You're one of the first," Joan said.

It's white, with natural wood paneling. Simple, but tastefully attractive, Joan and Bill Haines designed it.

"Between pictures we're going to put on one-act plays," she said. "The more literary plays. You see it's a hobby, an experiment, and an education all at once. You know how pitifully little education I really have—"

I didn't. I knew she had gone to three girls' schools.

"Where I learned mostly how to work, and where I thought mostly of getting away," said Joan. "The things I've studied since I came to Hollywood have been the things I had to learn for the screen—diction, screen technique. But now I want something more, something of the things I've missed. Every minute that I'm alone I read aloud. And I have a dictionary handy. I used to have a professor from the university come up and tutor me every week. But I had to stop that. I was so busy."

I ASKED her who would act the plays— she and her intimate group of friends?

Joan nodded. She read my thoughts. "I've heard about my going high-hat," she volunteered, "and restricting myself to an 'intimate group.' I'm not high-hat. But I have so little time that I can't waste it on people to whom I can't give something. I used to think I had lots of friends. Then, when Douglas and I separated, I found I had two—just two real friends. Now I have five. I know they're my friends, because they have come back. I can give them something, and they have much to give me. But Hollywood—

"Hollywood doesn't mean anything to me. It's just a name to me now. I'm completely apart from it. My studio is in Culver City, and my home is here. Hollywood used to mean so much to me. It was my life.

"When I first came out I sat around for months with nothing to do. They wouldn't even let me touch greasepaint. I had to let my energy out somehow, so I went dancing. I loved to dance, then, so I became," Joan grinned wryly, "the 'hey-hey' girl.

"But I'm not sorry. I think it helped me very early in pictures, although I've never yet been able to get away from the 'modern American girl' classification.

"But Hollywood was capable of hurting me so much. The things about Hollywood that could hurt me then, can't touch me now. I suddenly decided that they *shouldn't* hurt me— that was all.

"I have a memory like an elephant," she smiled.

As we left the little theater, Joan assured me that her ambitions for the future were still definitely with the screen, in spite of all this stage talk.

"I wish I could do one stage play a year, because I need the training. But I'm just as anxious to do a costume play on the screen. I'd like to do," she hesitated, "Joan of Arc!"

I said she had the right name.

"It would thrill me a great deal," she sighed, "to do one costume play a year. I've never done one. When I was doing all of those flaming youth parts I wanted badly to be a dramatic actress. Now I've done several dramatic parts, but you can't just go on forever being sad and making people cry.

"The picture I just finished is a comedy. They wanted comedy and I tried to give it to them. I did everything, fell on my face even. And I liked it. In the future, I'd love to do one very heavy picture, one costume play and one

comedy a year—and a stage play if I could squeeze it in."

"And that would be enough?"

"Oh, no," Joan's face tightened. Her eyes glistened. "I want to sing."

"On the screen, Joan?"

"Yes," said Joan, "until I'm ready."

"Ready? For what? Grand Opera?"

She nodded eagerly, almost mischievously. "Oh, it's a wild dream," she admitted, "but you never can tell. It would thrill me to pieces."

It all came out. She has been taking voice lessons an hour every day when she isn't working. She has discovered that she possesses a voice with a range of three octaves—which is quite low and at the same time quite high. She even started Franchot Tone singing, thereby uncovering a very impressive basso-profundo voice.

And it seems, he likes it so well that he practices at six o'clock in the morning and during lunch hours!

"I'm going to sing in my next picture," she told me, "for the first time. Popular songs," she added. "So, I'm going to give them strictly a crooning voice."

I wondered if I could hear the voice, and Joan said she had some records in the house. We played them. Some were the "crooning voice" and some were what "my teacher said I had courage to even try," smiled Joan.

I'M no vocal critic, but I thought her voice was lovely—a low, rich mezzo-soprano, not fully trained, but clear and promising. I wouldn't be a bit surprised if, some day, she made that wild dream of opera come true.

In fact, I wasn't surprised when she told me that besides wanting from the future a screen star's continued glory, a stage star's self-confident poise, and an opera singer's career, she also wanted to dance, really dance. Classically. Ballet.

You can tell by her eager, restless face that she still wants many things.

I wondered if she wanted marriage again.

"What about marriage?" I asked her.

"What a shame," Joan said, pointing to the back of my coat. "All white. It's off the lawn chairs I'm so sorry."

It was disconcerting, because the suit was new and also dark. I dusted furiously, but rallied.

"What a—"

"What a pity," said Joan, "that you have to leave. I'll get your hat."

I waited grimly at the door.

She returned, smiling sweetly.

"What about marriage?" I repeated, "I've got to say *something* about it."

"Why don't you say," suggested Joan, handing me my hat, "that you asked me about marriage and I changed the subject."

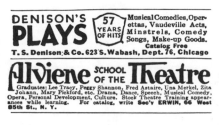

WHAT the well-dressed lady will wear—model by Miss Temple, borrowed from her mother's wardrobe. Shirley was eager to show folks the newest addition to the family, too. The child, she says, will in no way interfere with her career. And her career is doing nicely, thank you. She crashed to stardom in her latest film success, "Bright Eyes"

Marion Davies' Beach

MARION DAVIES has for many years been queen of Hollywood's society. And, as befits a queen, she lives in a palace and here friends are royally entertained

THE marine room is one of the more informal rooms of the house —where small parties are held and games are played. It is entirely panelled in genuine English walnut and furnished with fine period pieces. Note the massive beauty of the big library desk

THIS is the main dining room, used for formal dinner parties. The paintings are all original old masters. These and the beautiful Oriental rug give the room a rare richness of color. The dazzling array of silver is old English sterling serving pieces

House *at* Santa Monica

THE lovely lady of the house, Miss Davies, divides her time these days between social life at home and work at the studio. She recently finished work on "Going Hollywood"

Photos by
Clarence Sinclair Bull

THE music room, one of the smaller rooms, is brightly decorated, with patterned draperies, a lovely white mantelpiece, and a marble-top table. Ceiling is painted with murals. This room, like the others pictured here, commands a splendid view of the ocean front

THE gold room is the most elaborate room in the house. The walls are decorated in gold-leaf against a gold background. The draperies are gold brocade and the chairs are upholstered in the same material. It is the room used for very formal social functions

If the ostrich whose feathers grace the hat of Mae West in "Klondike Lou" could recognize his former finery, he'd never hide his head in the sands again!

Richee

Mae West, that luring Lorelei, may start out as a Salvation Army lassie in her latest, "Klondike Lou," but she still symbolizes to us—"Dangerous Curves Ahead"

160

clark

Clark Gable goes back to his down-to-earth he-manner in his next, "San Francisco." Also, he will have gorgeous Jeanette MacDonald to sing to him. (There's no mention of whether Clark will sing. But he has been known to warble — informally. No serious complaints from any of his friends—as yet)

CLARENCE SINCLAIR BULL

The girl of the allure plus, Jean Harlow, is now in "Riff Raff," with Spencer Tracy. "China Seas" mixed Miss Harlow up with a pretty tough crowd, and her latest M-G-M film has her in just as hard a life, and again on the water front. Actually, Jean loves her mother, white lounging pajamas, swimming, barbecued hamburgers

jean

*G*ARBO, is strange fascination, unique in filmdom, leaves the screen to smite men and women with equal force. Almost nothing is known about her, but she has millions of devoted followers who take her part against the world, the press and the devil. The slightest criticism, however kindly, stirs a storm of protest. There are a million raging Garbo-Maniacs!

One of Them Screams to the High Heavens Garbo Can Do No Wrong—The Slightest Criticism in PHOTOPLAY and the Post-office Works Overtime

By LEONARD HALL

HOLLYWOOD puts its hand where its heart should be and swears that its Heaven is full of film stars.

Billboards scream it—press agents toot it on their E-flat cornets and boom it on their big bass drums. Electric lights spatter stellar names across the night, and starry voices squawk out upon the evening air.

But I am in the trenches, and I wink a roguish eye. I know better. There are only a few great stars left in the skies of filmland, and of the whole kit there is one outstander—Greta Garbo, Scandinavia's gift to the world. Explorers, scientists and practitioners of other arts are dim figures when set against this astonishing woman with the pale face and yellow hair.

There are those who say that the star system is on its death-bed and rattling its last. In any event, it is a safe generalization to say that the smartest, craftiest talking pictures that have so far squeaked into the public fancy have been the product of what we used to call "all-star casts," or of troupes with no stars at all. In other words, pictures are bigger than the stars.

AND out in Los Angeles a funny thing happened. In the heart of the sound-maddened movie world, an old-time silent picture came slinking across a screen. When the smoke had cleared away and the casualties had been counted, the head men found that the picture had broken all existing records for the theater, sound or silent.

And need I add that the star of the voiceless opera was Greta Garbo, the Stockholm storm?

True, there are plenty of so-called stars shining their little hour. But there is only one queen, aloof and majestic on a lonely mountain top, who can do no wrong. That's La Belle Garbo, the woman who makes honest, home-loving American burghers look dubiously at their faithful, lawful wives.

It didn't use to be so.

In the noble days every star was fought for by her own group of maddened maniacs. To hint that Mary Pickford wasn't all she should be was to court a kick in the face. He who suggested that Fairbanks had his flaws was in jeopardy of a stinging left jab to the jaw. The Gishes, Pearl White, Jack Kerrigan, Wally Reid, Valentino—all were swallowed hook, line and wiggling worm by their bands of devotees, who made the nights hideous with brawls over the merits of their favorites.

Those maudlin days are long gone. They ended with the era of debunking, which hit motion pictures at the same time it struck the other lively arts.

Mary Pickford has been under fire for some years for various alleged professional mis-demeanors, and no critic has been hanged or shot at. Fans and critics have been announcing the end of her long reign for years. Even now she is everlastingly sniped at from various quarters, as she sits on the lonely throne her husband erected for her at Pickfair.

Formerly she was the adored idol of millions—now she is courted by stray nobility touring Hollywood to look at the animals.

Fairbanks is in no better case. Nor is Clara Bow, Joan Crawford, Dick Barthelmess, Billie Dove, Jack Gilbert or any other of the newer crop of stars. Let them speak out of turn, and around their ears rattles a barrage of epistolary criticism—not from enemies, but from their own gang of fair-weather fans.

The modern kings and queens can do plenty wrong. Their thrones are built of raspberry jello. One false squirm, and away they go!

ALL but Garbo! That weird and wonderful woman from the far north never seems to fumble a grounder, no matter how hard hit. She could ride around Hollywood on a howling hyena and leading a stuffed duck, and it would be all right with the Garbo-maniacs. Greta gets away with personal idiosyncrasies that would send other stars' fans shrieking away in droves.

But everything's all right. It's Garbo. And Garbo can do no wrong.

The Greta's position, in this respect, is unique.

Drolly enough, the more writers play truth about Greta, the more bitterly they are attacked and the more fiercely her fans rally round the standard, to fight and die for God, for Sweden and for Garbo.

Queen Garbo in the plain old coat and slouch hat that seem to comprise her pet outdoor costume. Right, one of the quaint, unfashionable gowns she wears on the screen. But let us hint that they are in any way odd or out of order and, swish! Off go our editorial heads!

Garbo-Maniacs

Not long ago our Miss Lois Shirley wrote a simple, kindly story in PHOTOPLAY about Greta and her double, one Miss De Vorak. Lois' article was friendly in the extreme. She simply retailed what nearly everybody knows—namely, that the star is remote, retiring, unsocial, unfashionable in dress—and she said it all in no carping spirit.

And what happened? PHOTOPLAY was buried alive under a terrific avalanche of denunciatory mail. Not even my long nose stuck out of the mountain of missives which denounced Miss Shirley, Editor Quirk, the magazine, its hired hands and anyone who even hinted that Garbo lacked one attribute of utter and complete perfection.

I'LL quote from some. This is from a man in Oakland, Calif.:

"I like Greta Garbo for her simplicity and old-fashioned ways. . . . Keep up the good work, Miss Garbo. Lead your simple life, and remember—there will always be a critic."

From a young lady in Ruleville, Miss.:

"If Greta is cold, aloof and mysterious, this is entirely a Garbo trait. . . . I love to think of her as being mysterious. The public loves Greta Garbo with all her faults—and there can be no substitute."

From a gentleman in Berkeley, Calif.:

"You certainly slammed Greta Garbo in the August issue of PHOTOPLAY for not dressing up and going around showing off like the rest of the so-called stars. Garbo is far too clever for that. She is a genius, and does not have to dress to attract attention. . . . How happy her mother would be if she knew how good her girl was, out here all by herself. I wonder how many young girls in Hollywood are as respectable in private life as this great star, Greta Garbo?"

From a miss in Louisville, Ky., heart of the Blue Grass:

"Of all the stupid people I ever heard of, Lois Shirley takes the cake. I never had a favorite until I saw Greta Garbo. She is my ideal—she is wonderful. The thing that bores half these so-called writers is the fact that Greta Garbo minds her own business and doesn't let everyone in on her affairs. My own opinion is that Jack Gilbert married Ina Claire because he couldn't get Greta Garbo—meaning no disrespect to Miss Claire. Three cheers for Greta Garbo!"

And, most astonishing of all, this—from the wife of a druggist in Kansas City:

"I suppose all of us have a foolish wish that can never come true. Mine is to shake the hand of Garbo the Great. Have we not many Claras, Crawfords and Pages? We have one God—also one Garbo!"

WELL, there you are. Those, and a hundred like them, were stirred up by a simple little story containing nothing that hadn't been printed before a score of times about the Stockholm siren.

And what about Garbo?

The facts are just the same, but nobody cares. She can dress as she darn pleases, and does. If she wants to wear twenty yards of opaque cheese cloth to a formal gathering, it's quite all right with us. In the greatest scene Garbo ever played—the renunciation sequence in "A Woman of Affairs"—she wore a slouchy old tweed suit and a squashy felt hat. She never looked more mysterious, more alluring, and she never acted with greater authority or arrogant power.

It is probable that in the whole history of the world no artist ever grew to such great glory on utter heedlessness of what anybody thinks, says or writes.

After hours of speculation on her reactions to her life and art and the funny world around her, I have come to the conclusion that Greta Garbo simply does not care one single hoot in a Nebraska twister.

She has her job, her maid, her comfortable slippers, her windows looking out upon the sea.

She is the one great queen of the screen who not only has never courted public favor, but has actually fought to a standstill all attempts to haul her into the limelight.

Where others scrabble and squall for notice, submitting to photographers and the pawing

This eight-year-old youngster may soon be as famous as her name. She's called Mitzi and she was headlining in vaudeville when Paramount signed her for talkies. The first kid so contracted for

of the herd, Garbo crawls into a hole and pulls the hole in after her.

Whether it is a trick or whether it is the nature of the lady, it is absolute perfection. Where others leave off, she begins.

More, Garbo is the one great star who has attained unique power and public interest without one lovable screen trait.

Far from being emotionally appealing in any way, she is cinematically heedless, cold, arrogant.

I have even watched some of her magnificent scenes which seemed almost insulting to her fellow actors and to her enormous audiences.

And from her, we take it, bat an eye, gape and love it. For she is Garbo.

Garbo and her work, in addition to being tremendous rousers of men, have more women adorers than any male star of the screen. Women flock to her pictures, to wonder, admire, gasp and copy. In every hamlet of the country slink and posture a score of incipient Garbos.

For every girl child who kicks up like a Velez, a dozen whiten their faces and gaze through half-closed eyes upon a tiresome, boresome world.

And I, a calloused old picture reviewer filled with scars and aches, scuttle to her pictures

as fast as they come and sit in a daze as that astonishing figure goes about its cinematic business.

For Garbo, in her own quaint way, is an undoubted genius—one of the three or four surviving in American motion pictures. She conquers as much by what she leaves undone as by what she does, and her odd beauty has that weird, intangible quality that fascinates the beholder and makes dreamless men dream dreams.

Pardon a little personality, it adorns the tale.

I know a girl who is a calm, cool New Yorker, a trifle blasé around the edges. She meets the great and the near-great and never throws even a mild fit. Yet this Garbo girl puts her in a spasm. She snoozes through talkie after talkie, no matter how loudly the actors bellow, but she dragged me twice to see "A Woman of Affairs" and is still pursuing that Garbo opera into obscure neighborhood theaters, up blind alleys.

IN Hollywood she went Garbo-wild. Metro-Goldwyn put a huge, fire-snorting motor at her service, like a fire truck, and whenever this girl heard that Garbo was on location she jumped into the car and lit out in pursuit, cut-out open and siren screaming. The day she jimmied her way onto the Garbo set in Culver City went down in her history along with the day she got her first proposal and the day she got a bad break and met me.

She has a better collection of Garbo photographs than M-G-M, and I am under daily orders to steal more—from bent old ladies if necessary.

I drag this in to show what the Greta can do to a sophisticated New York gal who knows her Menckens and Nathans. Garbo is no respecter of persons.

The cream of the jest is, of course, that nobody knows exactly what Garbo is all about.

Reporters are poison to her, and though they chase her up hill and down canyon, they seldom get close enough to her to see more than a hank of yellow hair scooting down the cellar stairs.

Naturally, Hollywood is always alive with talk about her, but much of it is probably wild shooting from the hip.

Stories that appear about her in magazines and newspapers are, with few exceptions, pipe dreams or a dreary and sentimental rehashing of all the old tales. During the trying times of the Gilbert marriage to Claire, Garbo used excellent taste and strategy. To all the reporters who came within gunshot while she was on location at Catalina she said absolutely nothing, with her usual bland eloquence. One young sprout, it is said, broke her down momentarily—but that story has never been printed and probably never will.

GARBO, in spite of gabble and gossip, is always largely conjecture.

My hat is off to her. Not only is she a sizable artist—I have a feeling that she must be, in a sense, a great woman. She has licked the Hollywood racket to a pale frazzle. She has made almost no mistakes, personally or professionally.

She is one of the few people in the world who do exactly as they please. But—she makes millions like it.

She slouches along her own sweet way, and even her slouch is a regal gait to those who idolize her.

I smile skeptically at the odd spectacle of Greta Garbo, and yet I genuflect in admiration. As the race of queens dies out and is replaced by ordinary erring, faulty, frail men and women, she alone remains—the greatest and loneliest of a mighty line.

DON ENGLISH

Marlene Dietrich, sultry, yet mysterious. She's striving for a new screen personality. Notice those tantalizing curls—in her latest, "Caprice Espagnol." It's the last picture in her stormy association of five years with Director Josef Von Sternberg

Her uncounted thousands of fans have risen as one mighty army and shouted "One Mickey Mouse, one Shakespeare, one Joe Doakes, one Garbo!" Frenzied by the thought that anyone dares, even by act of Providence, to resemble Greta Garbo, they are bombarding this editorial trench with heavy shells filled with short, sharp little words that bite and sting.

Garbo vs. Dietrich

By Leonard Hall

IS that thunder, mother, that is shaking the plaster down into my bean soup?

No, my child, it is the guns!

The battle of Greta Garbo and Marlene Dietrich—one of the most ferocious in the history of the screen—is now raging.

And nobody started it!

Heaven knows Garbo didn't. She's been toiling on the sets and retreating to her guarded castle in the Santa Monica hills. As far as we know, the gorgeous Dietrich, to her, is still an unconfirmed rumor.

Dietrich didn't. She's a jolly German girl, even more beautiful than sin, who was lured to this country, trained and groomed, and pushed before the camera. Paramount didn't fire the first gun—on the contrary, it fought for peace by demanding that their Miss Dietrich and Metro's Miss Garbo never be mentioned in the same ten breaths. Metro, of course, merely sat out in Culver City, smiling the smile of the Sphinx.

Yet the battle that no one started screams and thunders across this fair republic.

There is an old and toothless gag to the effect that it takes two sides to make a fight. This is strictly the old hooey, or, in the original Latin, the *phonus bollonus*.

IN the case of any argument, bickering or brannigan in which the name of Greta Garbo appears, only one side is sufficient to make a battle of major proportions. That, of course, is the side of the Garbo-maniacs, to whom the Beautiful Swede is only one hop, skip and jump from downright divinity—and sometimes not even that.

The history of the first skirmishes of the Garbo-Dietrich battle is brief and pointed.

Director Josef Von Sternberg "discovered,"—for the American screen—and brought to this country, a very beautiful German musical comedy and screen actress named Marlene Dietrich. The moment her first pictures appeared in the American press, there was a flurry. She bore a distinct resemblance, from some angles, to the current queen, Greta Garbo. She also resembled, in profile, the late Jeanne Eagles.

The Garbo-maniacs, raving mad in their idolatry, issued from their caves and began growling.

In due time Miss Dietrich's first American-made talkie appeared. "Morocco" was a labor of love and justification on the part of Director

The battle is on! Into the dugouts! A verbal barrage thunders over the charms and talents of Paramount's rising star and the goddess of M-G-M's studio

And here's the unwitting, or innocent, cause of the great Garbo-Dietrich war now raging— the beautiful Marlene herself. Do you think she looks like Garbo—that she's *trying* to resemble Garbo the Great? True, she's blonde, beautiful, mysterious and alluring. But so are several others. We vote that Marlene Dietrich is Marlene Dietrich, and no copy of anyone!

Von Sternberg. With infinite pains he had trained, rehearsed and projected his German find.

No question about it—Miss Dietrich showed definite Garboesque symptoms, at least in the minds of the Garbo fans. The critics remarked on it. The low growls of the Garbo devotees became shrieks, then roars.

THE beautiful German girl, new to the madnesses of Hollywood, lonely for her husband and little daughter in the Fatherland, just trying to make good for God, for country, for Von Sternberg, and for Marlene, became the focal point of a vocal and epistolary storm that is wrecking bridge games, tea fights, family gatherings and erstwhile happy American homes all over the nation.

A couple of months ago PHOTOPLAY stepped into a hornets' nest.

We printed an informative story about Miss Dietrich. It was entitled "She Threatens Garbo's Throne." It described the Prussian Peacherino, and definitely hinted that a potential rival to the solitary Swede was now on deck— another beauty, bursting with a similar allure, possessing more than a dash of screen mystery, and with a talent both wide and deep.

Bang! Sumter was fired on! The Maine had been sunk! The fatal shot was heard again at Sarajevo! Sheridan was at least thirty miles away! And the author, Katherine Albert, ran for her private cyclone cellar.

The Garbo-maniacs, to whom any mention of an actress in the same wheeze is sheer blasphemy, seized their pens, and clattered their typewriters like so many machine guns.

HEAR some shots from the barrage that has fallen on this trembling editorial dugout in the past month:

From M. L. K., of Detroit, Mich.:

"The woman to compete with Greta Garbo will not be born! Garbo to us is not a woman— she is a goddess. There will be one Garbo. Down with the imitators! *Vive la* Garbo!"

From Miss J. D. W., of Chicago, Ill.:

"Garbo's subjects are legion. If she ever descends from the throne, that throne, like Valentino's, will remain vacant! Long live the queen, Miss Greta Garbo!"

"A Garbo-Maniac," situate in Meridian, Miss., takes her fiery pen in hand:

"This Marlene

168

GRAYING HAIR?

*Why surrender to gray hair?
This famous approved way
means radiant color again.
We send demonstration FREE.*

ALL AROUND you, you see them, these modern women who stay young. Their secret—known to millions—is one that every woman with graying hair should know—the famous clear, colorless liquid called Mary T. Goldman's. By this time-tested way women are safely bringing youthful color to faded strands—so evenly that you would think nature herself had put it there.

You Need No Experience

Mary T. Goldman's method can be done at home. Merely comb colorless liquid through the hair. Any type of hair matched —black, brown, auburn or blonde. Color blends evenly. Hair becomes lustrous, live-looking—easy to curl or wave. No "artificial" look. Nor will color wash or rub off on linens or hat linings.

Entirely SAFE to Use

Mary T. Goldman's has been used by discriminating women for over 30 years. Medical school authorities have pronounced it harmless to hair and scalp.

Test It FREE!

Try it first on a single lock snipped from your hair. See results this way. Why hesitate to make this *safe* test? We have sent it to more than 3,000,000 women. If you prefer, you can obtain full-sized bottle from your druggist on money-back guarantee. Or just mail the coupon. We'll send FREE TEST PACKAGE.

[**FREE**
This Famous
Single Lock
Test Package
Use Coupon]

MARY T. GOLDMAN

OVER TEN MILLION BOTTLES SOLD

Garbo vs. Dietrich

Dietrich may be a good actress, a beautiful woman and all that, but please understand right now that no one can be compared with Greta Garbo. Anything she does is all right with me—and fifty million others. She is the greatest and most wonderful woman of all time!" You can gather, from this tiny assortment from a great batch, the divine madness that grips the true worshipper of that amazing Swedish girl. Let us turn to the less perturbed section of the populace—the milder spirits whose judgment is settled and whose souls are more serene.

MR. J. V. K., of Cumberland, Ky., pours some oil on the roiled and stormy waters: "How could anyone get mixed up on this Garbo-Dietrich situation? Both Dietrich and Garbo can speak the same language, have the same likes and mysteries. Why not let them alone and let them become friends? Garbo is so much like Marlene Dietrich, and Dietrich so much like Greta that I am sure they would become fast friends."

A hopeful note is struck by Miss E. B., of Henderson, Tex.:

"I believe all the Garbo fans will like Miss Dietrich. She isn't trying to take Garbo's throne. She merely wants another one beside it."

And Mr. J. B., of River Forest, Ill., is a little bored with it all:

"Why this everlasting bringing-up of the 'new menace to Garbo's throne' idea? But since another 'new menace' has again come up, let's give the new girl a break. I am, of course, also a Garbo fan. But I'm not a narrow-minded maniac. Let there be (and here Mr. B. grows ironical) one God, one Caesar, one Lincoln, one Napoleon, one Mickey Mouse, *one Garbo.* But why not also *one Marlene Dietrich?*"

And Mr. J. B. strikes the keynote! He points the way to peace! Why not one Dietrich, indeed?

After all, can Marlene help it if she looks something like the Queen of Culver City?

Is Hollywood only large enough for one beautiful girl who employs restraint and whose screen personality is alive with the glamor that gives certain actresses of stage and screen their true greatness as public magnets?

I answer my own question. Certainly not.

And may I point out that the tricks, attitudes and methods of *la* Dietrich are less Garboesque than they are European? Let us, in this moment of armistice, remember that Garbo is the only European trouper to attain great Hollywood eminence since Negri's time, and that's long ago, as *tempus fugits.*

But there's no need of getting deep-dish about this war. We should get the boys and girls out of the trenches by Lincoln's birthday —nay, they should be out now, cooling off their fevered typewriters and turning to the productive arts of peace.

Miss Dietrich's "Morocco" was a hit. The country's fans and critics gave her a nice send-off. They welcomed her as a distinct personality—a fresh gift to the American screen. Great Caesar's perambulating ghost, isn't the American motion picture big enough to support two foreign ladies who drip personality, even though one is a tweedish Swedish divinity named Garbo?

As soon as Marlene had finished "Morocco," she was set at "Dishonored" by the ardent Von Sternberg, this time with big Vic McLaglen opposite. This done, she set off for Germany to see her little daughter, for whom she had been pining. She left behind her the dawn of a first-rate American reputation, born amid the thunders and alarms of a one-sided war.

God willing, she'll be back—back, I hope, in peace. She's a fine actress, this lush Teuton with the slumbrous eyes. We need her. Even the Garbo-maniacs need her, as they'll realize as soon as they cool off and discover that Marlene is no copy-cat trying to steal thrones at night. Garbo's Garbo and Dietrich's Dietrich, and thank Heaven for both. That's the attitude, and that is what will happen.

You are cordially invited to attend a big shenanigan I am promoting for the spring drinking season.

It is to be held at Madison Square Garden, New York City—a banquet seating as many as can be herded in. At one end of the table will be a throne for Greta Garbo—at the other a throne for Marlene Dietrich. Each will be exactly the same size, and contain as many diamonds, rubies, emeralds and sapphires.

A HUNDRED flappers, dressed in white and carrying olive branches and autographed photographs, will attend each monarch. In between will be Mr. and Mrs. John H. Fan and the little Fans. Each will have one eye on Marlene and one on Greta, who will both be smiling, whatever the cost.

Paramount will furnish a band to play at one end of the hall—Metro-Goldwyn-Mayer will hire one to tootle at the other.

At the proper moment, I shall rise with a glass of pop in each hand. Bowing simultaneously to both thrones (a very good trick if I can do it) I shall propose the toast, "The Queens, God bless them!" and will then drink from both tumblers at once. (Another good trick. I learned it in India from a Swami.)

And you all will drink it too—even the wildest of you Garbo-maniacs.

Hush now—nobody's trying to steal your baby's throne!

Plains, Mont.

When you are only eighteen—eighteen with its dreams and its belief in happy endings—and you are so hideously deformed and scarred that people shudder when they pass you by on the street—is life a dreary prison, a cruel trap from which you cannot escape?

Ah, no, for there are the movies! You slip into a theater and there in the friendly darkness you forget your ugly face and twisted body and through the art of Mary Pickford, Ruth Chatterton and all the lovely army of exquisite, gifted women, you find love and laughter and adventure.

Peggy Baker

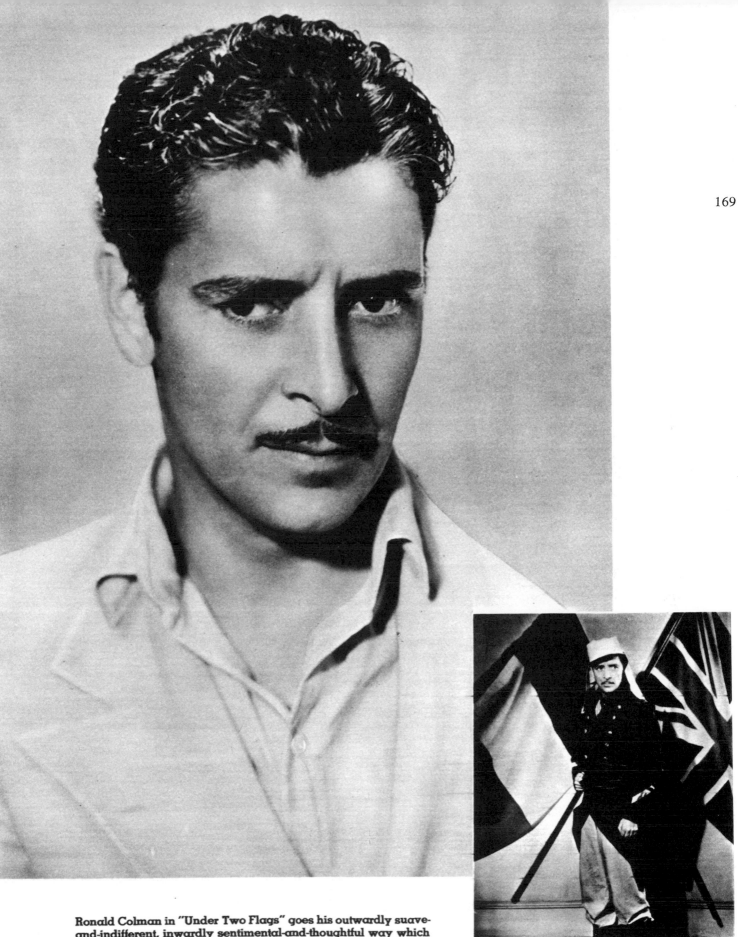

Ronald Colman in "Under Two Flags" goes his outwardly suave-and-indifferent, inwardly sentimental-and-thoughtful way which he has held to for twelve years without a disturbing challenge

The Lure of New York Stage

HERE is something that, it is said, has never appeared upon the screen before. It will be shown in Warner Brothers' production of back stage theatrical life—"42nd Street."

The new feature you will see in this picture is a series of three revolving stages, each of which is really a large disc, turning in opposite directions. The cameras are mounted on the outer disc and, of course, travel with it.

As the dancers go through their movements, the effect is dizzying and breath-taking—one finds himself gripping the seat ahead for support.

Above we see one of the big dance numbers of the show.

Life Set to Music and Drama

Photo by Stagg

Those two cute girls with the lights turned full upon them are Ginger Rogers and Una Merkel, whose parts call for a place in the chorus.

This is one of those scenes in the production for which highly technical knowledge is necessary.

So directors stand back while a dance expert—the man with out-pointed finger—puts the hoofers through special dance steps.

And looming over all are the figures of Dick Powell, Warner Baxter, Ginger Rogers, Bebe Daniels and George Brent—the major characters in the rhythm, the laughter, the music and the heartaches of "42nd Street."

The Big Broadcast

More stars in this picture than there are in heaven! And more fun than you'll find anywhere else on earth!

Bing looks skyward to croon, "I Wished on the Moon." Come back down, Bing! That's far too far away! The girls won't like it!

Right. You might not believe it to look at her, but Ethel Merman's hit song in "The Big Broadcast" is entitled, "It's the Animal in Me"

Lyda Roberti says two men are twice as good as one. Jack Oakie's in the luck. But Henry Wadsworth's turn comes next. It's Lyda's cue to sing "Double Trouble"

Mary Boland is about to make a thermometer hit a new high, taking Charlie Ruggles' temperature!

Left. A bigger and better chorus. Easier to train than girls, too, 'cause elephants never forget

# of 1936

Just a little knit-wit, our Gracie. George is trying to tell his wife that sweater won't fit. But Mr. Burns will have to wear it anyhow

Andy is head of the A & A grocery chain, and it looks like he's in a pickle. Business must be just a sack of sugar for Amos at the moment

That sweet soprano of the air, Jessica Dragonette, who'll hypnotize you with her singing of "Alice Blue Gown"

Sweet music and plenty of hot-cha are supplied by Ray Noble and his lads. He wrote, for the Paramount film, a new hit song, "Why Stars Come Out at Night"

Bill Robinson does some of his most spectacular tapping in "The Big Broadcast." He struts his stuff to the rhythm of a little ditty, "Miss Brown to You"

174

Senorita

Hmm-mm, howsa about this, folks? The petite blonde Alice Faye, in the Fox film "Music and Magic." Alice has certainly risen to high rating since her advent into the movies less than two years ago. And now she goes senorita, which should prove very interesting

JEAN HARLOW is representative of an extreme, exotic type of beauty. Her platinum hair set a world-wide vogue. Her half-moon brows accent her pastel coloring. Make-up is concentrated at eyes and mouth. She depends upon good health, fresh air, exercise, cream, soap and water, followed by an ice water rinse, for her perfect skin. Note her lashes. They are naturally long.

Beauty Shop

Conducted By
Carolyn
Van Wyck

All the beauty tricks of all the stars brought to you each month

HIGH, narrow and very arched are Jean's eyebrows. She uses a finely pointed eyebrow pencil. The high brow enlarges the eye, gives clarity, an appealing quality.

JEAN uses a true red cream rouge for her lips, blending the line perfectly and carrying the color well inside to prevent a break in tone. Those very long lashes are black.

SKIN-TONE powder is then puffed lightly but thoroughly over Jean's face and neck, with special attention to nostrils, eye corners and chin. And, always brush from brows.

JEAN'S platinum halo has probably aroused more comment and curiosity than any one feature of any star. Naturally blonde, Jean encourages whiteness by weekly shampoos with white soap and a final rinse containing a few drops of French bluing. She brushes for softness, sets her wave with water and vinegar.

MAE WEST TALKS

"I'm a single gal with a single track mind, and it doesn't run to matrimony," Mae says, emphatically

Mae West is not only an ardent fight fan (seen here at a bout), but a scrapper in her own right, as eight men who phoned and called her "wife" know to their own sorrow

"Every time the postman rings," says Mae, "I get a dozen proposals. I ought to sue 'husbands' for alienation of propositions." She's with Paul Cavanagh, "Goin' to Town"

"MARRIAGE," said Mae West, "is wonderful!"

"Of course," she added, "I'm just guessing, but it must be wonderful. Already I've got for a husband a dozen guys I've never met. Peggy Hopkins Joyce can't tie that."

Hollywood's Number One bachelor girl, grass widow or spouse (you name it) flashed her famous upper row of ivory and then curtained it quickly with serious lips. Her arched brows lowered.

"Look here," she said, "you say you want to know the truth about my 'marriage.' Well, if you want to know the truth, the whole truth and nothing but the truth, I'm beginning to get just a little burned up about this whole marriage business. It was funny for a while—even to me. Then I got a little annoyed. Now I'm getting just plain sore. I didn't mind it so much when it was just one marriage—but now it's practically bigamy!"

We were talking, of course, about the completely crazy-quilt pattern of mixed dates, double identities, confusing coincidences and controversial claims which have made the marital (or unmarital) status of La Belle West on a puzzling par with the eternal hen-egg-egg-hen dispute. Did she or didn't she? Is she or isn't she? Newspapers have even printed editorials congratulating Mae on pushing Hitler's jingoistic jitters and the Veterans' Bonus off the front page.

It was the first time Mae had unbosomed herself on the subject which she had just confessed, was giving her fits. Up until now she had contented herself with a rapid fire volley of telephonic "no's" to all questions, ranging from the laughing, amused "No" to the dangerous, now-you-lay-off-of-me "NO!"

"There's a saying," she reminded, "that when a woman says 'maybe' she means 'yes' and when she says 'no' she means 'maybe.' But not me. When I said 'no'—I didn't mean maybe!"

Just picture a penthouse—or anyway an apartment—'way up in the sky. All in white and gold and satin and silk. With a couple of polar bear skins spread out on the floor to lend their cooling effect to the heated lady of the house in a mood to slam the door on the Fuller brush man's foot. And all because a scattered crop of Mae Wests and Frank Wallaces had apparently put the Marrying Mdivanis to shame—and put all the answers up to Mae.

"Since the first of the year," Mae revealed, "eight different guys have called me up to tell me I married 'em. In Oshkosh or Oscaloosa, in Tulsa or Toledo. Now it's Milwaukee and points East. They've been traveling men, singing waiters dance men, reporters—but not a single millionaire—darn it!

"Which makes it bigamy—and big o'me, too, if you'll stand for a punk pun. The point is," pointed Mae, "I like a laugh, like anyone else. I've got an elastic sense of humor—but if you stretch it too far, it snaps. A gag is a gag—and if this one gave the guy a chance for a job, then it's all right, with me. But the gag has gone too far."

The determined jaw of Battling Jack West's daughter settled back into place. She smiled.

"It's all right to have a man around the house," she explained, "but when you wake up every morning to find a new husband with your grapefruit—say, I'm beginning to feel like the Dionne quintuplets. When you come up to see me now you have to look cross-eyed—or use mirrors."

"Getting down to one particular lord and master," I said "what about this Frank Wallace in New York?"

Mae dropped a stitch with her eyebrows. "Well—what about him?" she repeated. "I'm like Will Rogers—all I know is what I read in the papers, and I've quit reading about Wallace. I never went much for the comics, anyway."

"He says you married him in Milwaukee."

ABOUT HER "MARRIAGE"

To
KIRTLEY BASKETTE

"It was funny for a while— even to me," says Mae. "It wasn't so bad when it was just one marriage, but now it's practically bigamy!"

Frank Wallace of New York might have paraphrased the title of one of Mae's pictures, "She Done Him Wrong." He claims that Mae's denial has made him suffer

Genial Jim Timony, Mae's manager, has not escaped the "husband" touch. They labeled him such last year

Mae's "Belle of the Nineties" (with Roger Pryor) could apply to the number of males who are yelping that she deserted them

"The only thing I know about Milwaukee," said Mae, "is that they make beer there. It's pretty good beer—but it never was good enough to make me get married and then forget about it."

"Then," I rallied, "he says you played Omaha."

"Wrong again," said Mae, "I picked Nellie Flag. Us girls have got to stick together," she explained. "I wish I had played Omaha," she sighed wistfully, "on the nose."

"Pardon me," I said, "but I mean the town."

"Oh," said Mae, "I thought you meant the horse. Well, either way, it's a horse on me. I never played either one."

"This Wallace quotes certain figures," I began.

"I've heard some favorable quotes on mine," interrupted Mae.

"Let's take a look at his figures—" I began again.

"You wouldn't be interested in taking a look at mine, would you?" queried Mae. "I think it speaks for itself. What do you think?"

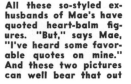

All these so-styled ex-husbands of Mae's have quoted heart-balm figures. "But," says Mae, "I've heard some favorable quotes on mine." And these two pictures can well bear that out

"I'm not thinking," I assured her. "Do you mind if I open a window?"

"Not at all," said Mae, "but don't fall out—and don't shout for help."

"Hardly," I replied gallantly. "Now about these husbands—"

"Husbands," said Mae airily, "are all right in their place."

"But you never placed one?"

"Listen—" said Mae, poking the polar bear rug with a determined French heel, "let's get this settled once and for all. *I'm not married. I never have been married.* Not to Frank Wallace. Not to Jim Timony, my manager—they used that one last year. Not to that fellow in Texas—what was his name—Burmeister? Nor to the guy in Illinois, nor to anybody else. Shall I draw a diagram? I'm a single gal with a single-track mind—and it doesn't run to matrimony."

"Well—that seems to be that," I gasped. "You wouldn't be kidding me?"

Mae's glance missed me and killed a fly on the wall.

"And another thing," she proceeded in the same tone of voice, "if I ever do get married, nobody is going to have to dig around into a lot of records to find out about it. After a girl has put a lot of time and effort into getting her man, she's got a right to brag about it. Believe me, I'll brag plenty."

"I can say then," said I, "that you consider marriage a commendable condition?"

"Marriage," quoted Mae, "is a great institution. As I've always said, no family should be without it. What's the matter don't you feel well?"

"I was just wondering," I ventured, to explain that vacant look, "how come with your-uh-appeal, you've managed to stay in that well known state of single blessedness as long as you—uh—say you have?"

"Stop wondering," said Mae. Her eyes became serious, "In the first place, I've never felt up until just recently that I could get married, if I'd wanted to. My folks made a lot of sacrifices for me when I was a kid. We were a family that was close together. I had obligations as long as my mother and dad were alive. My life hasn't been any bed of roses. I never felt anything like secure until just recently. I've never felt free to get married."

I knew the story of Mae's devotion to her parents. It was a pretty fine thing, as anyone in Hollywood knows.

She shook off the serious mood with a grin.

"Besides," she said, "maybe I've never met the right guy—one that I liked well enough to tie up with for life."

"No chances?"

"What do you mean, 'no chances'?" Mae bridled, "say, every time the postman rings twice I get a dozen proposals from guys who must have gone to school at a mail order college. Not bad, either. Of course, there was the widower who said he'd let me mother his six kids, but then there was another from a gent in some foreign country who wanted to make me a duchess, or a maharanee—maybe it was a queen. And that reminds me—since the papers have been full of this marriage stuff, I don't get as many offers

Mae West Talks About Her "Marriage"

as I used to. They're all holding off to find out whether I'm in the market or not. I ought to sue some of my 'husbands,'" she laughed, "for alienation of propositions."

"That might be a job," I suggested. "It looks like everyone whoever proposed to you is now claiming to be an ex-husband."

"And then some," Mae agreed, "they're coming as often as a chain letter. Maybe if I'd send 'em a dime, they'd stop. But they'd probably expect a diamond instead of a dime. A bunch of sour grapes would be more appropriate."

"From your recent and other experiences," I wondered, "what do you think of men now?"

"Often," confessed Mae. "Didn't you say 'when'?"

"No," I told her, "I said 'what'."

"That's different," she qualified, "I like 'em. In fact, I'd say they're nature's greatest gift to women. I like some men for class and distinction, some for brains, some for looks, and some for an understanding nature. I like 'em to come up and see me," she insisted, "but this guy and the rest of my 'husbands' must have misunderstood me. They thought I said 'come up and *sue* me sometime.'"

THE New York Frank Wallace, still insisting in the face of Mae's denials that he was the head man, has tried to put Mae on the spot by asking for a declaratory judgment from the courts stating whether she is or is not his past or present wife. He claims that Mae's denial of their former wedded state has "caused him untold suffering, held him up to the ignominy of his companions, injured his standing in the community and damaged his professional rating." I reminded her.

"Is that all?" said Mae. "Well, that's one way to court a girl. I'll take the old fashioned way. But say," she declared, "I'm getting tired of talking about it. I'm not married. I'm still a bachelor girl—and that's all there is to it. Who brought all this up in the first place?"

"Not me," I said. I told her I thought it was a government "boon doggler" in Milwaukee who unearthed the marriage registration of a Mae West and a Frank Wallace. Then the newspapers hunted up Frank Wallace in New York.

"AREN'T 'boon dogglers' these New Deal relief guys who spend their time making something out of nothing?" asked Mae.

"Then this one," added Mae, "can go right to the head of the class."

HOLLYWOOD FASHIONS

PHOTOPLAY is the undisputed leader in revealing what the stars wear and What They Are Going to Wear

Readers of PHOTOPLAY ARE STYLE LEADERS

Mabel Normand Says

Mabel Normand and Charlie Chaplin played together in the early Keystone Comedy hits—the golden age of slapstick. Left, Mack Sennett, the great comedy director who discovered and developed Mabel. Right, Lew Cody, the devoted husband she married in 1926

BATTERED and beaten by life, little Mabel Normand has gone home to the Great Heart who understands all.

I am sure that voices have whispered love and encouragement and devotion to her on her long, frightened journey across the Dark River—voices of crooning old Irish women whose last days were made comfortable by Mabel's generosity—voices of pitiful little extra girls who had turned to her for help and sympathy—voices of hunger that was fed—of tears that were dried.

There would be one voice whispering in a proud, strange tongue; and this would be the voice of old Minnie, the Sioux Indian who was sheltered by Mabel's bounty and who loved her with a wild devotion.

Mabel Normand was the most extraordinary character I have ever known. Certainly, the most interesting and unusual personality the screen has ever known.

There will never be another Mabel Normand. Few such vivid individualities have appeared in the world in any *metier*. Beyond that, the screen world has become too standardized to offer scope and right-of-way for another such character.

Generous, impulsive, self-effacing, impudent, untamed, misunderstood and not resentful of the cruelty of that misunderstanding. Daring in spirit, tender, brilliant, and with the eager curiosity of a child.

It was not without significance that Mabel's lips were always slightly apart—like a child drinking in a fairy story. That was the keynote of her

Mabel Normand

By MARGARET E. SANGSTER

BENEATH the gallant sparkle of her laughter,
  There always lay the hint of wistfulness,
As if she knew that storm must follow after
  The brightest day . . . Perhaps her soul could guess
That tragedy was waiting, eager handed,
  To block her path, to stay her dancing feet,
To leave her lonely, pitiful, and stranded . . .
  Yet who shall say her life was incomplete?

For, oh, she brought swift smiles to sorry faces
  She taught a weary-hearted world to sing;
Her presence lent new grace to lonely places,
  She had the radiance of waking spring.
Behind her mask of comedy, she waited
  For every hurt the future held in store;
She gave herself to all, nor hesitated . . .
  And died when she, at last, could give no more!

life. Her avid eagerness for all that life held. It was as though she realized in some dim way that she had not long to live and wanted to take a bite out of each cookie.

She was the best listener I have ever known. She listened to tramps and great authors; to soldiers who talked to her of the intricacies of military strategy and to jail birds who told her of fights with policemen.

Mabel will always be pictured in my mind as the little Irish tad with a sable coat, as the little girl who ate peanuts all over the back seat of a gorgeous imported limousine.

I suppose that no woman ever lived who has been showered with more fame and more attention; and no woman who has known so cruelly the voice of unmerited scandal. She took the brickbats without bitterness and the bouquets with a giggle.

Mabel was without vanity. She has a quality rare in creative artists of being a spectator looking at life.

When I first knew Mabel, she was the star comedienne of the old Mack Sennett Comedy Company. That was the time when the Keystone Kops were in their heyday.

MACK SENNETT was one of the greatest figures of the screen world and Mabel was recognized as being without a peer.

In those golden Keystone days, with Mack Sennett driving and inspiring her, Mabel's great talent for comedy was in full flower. Her fellow artists were quick to recognize it.

Once PHOTOPLAY asked Mary Pickford who her favorite actress was.

Mary, at that time the fans'

Goodbye

By
James R. Quirk

Mabel's Message

"MABEL NORMAND'S two great comforts, as she lay dying, were the devotion of Lew Cody and the letters from her fans. They enabled her to meet death bravely. She asked me to tell the public, through PHOTOPLAY Magazine, of her love and appreciation. 'They have been dear to me, and sweet and kind,' she said."

greatest pet, answered quickly, "Mabel Normand!"

She was just the same then as when misfortunes overtook her later on. There was not one pretentious thing about her. The electricians on the set all adored the ground she walked on; and the cameramen would die in their tracks for her.

SHE was famous at that time for the fact that she scattered money around like a sailor on a spree; but I only found out little by little and always by accident, the places where her dollars rolled away. The operations she had paid for; the impoverished families she was supporting; the orphans and the widows she was helping.

I remember one incident—a gesture that no one but a natural aristocrat could have achieved.

A very old Irish woman—a relative of one of the studio help—had one ambition. She wanted to meet Mabel Normand. By request, Mabel went to have dinner with her—dressed in her most elegant party clothes.

Once in the presence of her divinity, the poor old woman was simply paralyzed. She was straight from the bogs of Ireland. Her table manners were something to send goose flesh down one's spine.

But so sweet were the manners of Mabel Normand that she promptly hung a napkin under her own chin as the old lady did. When the chops came on, she picked up the meat and gnawed it off the bone.

And when the old lady timidly took out her pipe, Mabel found a pipe, too, and they whiffed together. That will remain, to my mind, one of the most delicate acts of chivalry it has ever been my lot to know.

Mabel had a peculiar relationship to Mack Sennett. She loved him; fought with him; feared him and respected him with something like awe. Mack Sennett was, in fact, her *Svengali*. She resented the awe she had for him; but she never could rise to artistic heights without him.

Away from Sennett, she ceased to be the great artist of the screen and became commonplace. Mostly I think it was a matter of understanding. Sennett, as Irish himself as the banshees, alone knew how to get the best from Mabel's wayward, rebellious Irish heart.

HER relationship to Charlie Chaplin also was one of the odd chapters of the screen. When he first came to the studio, Mabel liked to torture him with taunts in the mischievous way a child might have made fun of a queer-looking stranger. But she was one of the first to recognize his genius. Much of Chaplin's success in those earliest days was due to Mabel's untiring tutoring. Chaplin was a great artist from the day he was born, but he did not know screen technique.

No one grieved more sincerely over her death than he. "She was one of the truest friends I have ever known and one of the most remarkable, brilliant

The Mabel Normand who entered pictures so long ago—gay and pretty, with a great talent for screen comedy soon to make her famous

Mabel at the height of her beauty and the peak of her career—graduated from Keystone, with the great success, "Mickey," already achieved

Mabel Normand Says Good-Bye

and self-sacrificing women any one has ever known. She was a great woman and a great character."

MABEL'S illness was of long standing. When I first knew her fifteen years ago, she was suffering from tuberculosis; but so brave was her spirit that she tossed off the threat with a gay indifference.

In later years, this malady was aggravated by grave troubles and worries. Mabel was the *Patsy* who got the blame for what other people did. She suffered humiliation and disgrace in silence when she could have set herself right—by "telling on" some one else.

There was the case of the chauffeur who adored Mabel so devotedly, that he shot a man whom Mabel knew but slightly, but whom the half-crazed boy thought was bringing bad company to her harem-scarem, topsy-turvey house.

There was the William Desmond Taylor case of which Mabel honestly knew nothing; but which brought down odium and club lady resolutions upon her.

As usual in such cases, Mabel's bitterest critics were often those who owed her most of money and kindness and tolerant charity.

She realized that she had to die and met the issue bravely and without whimpering. One of her last messages was to me; when she asked me to tell the public through PHOTOPLAY Magazine of her love and appreciation. "They have been dear to me, and sweet and kind," she said.

The affection between Lew Cody and Mabel Normand that resulted in their early morning marriage has never been understood. But to one who knew them both intimately, it was a sweet story.

They had been devoted friends for years. Theirs was a comradeship of laughter—laughing at life, laughing at and with each other, laughing off troubles.

LEW loved Mabel, and Mabel adored Lew. No woman could have helped loving a man who brought such happiness and sunshine into a life over which death was even then trying to cast a shadow.

Even at the last, she did not lose her thirst for life.

So weak she could scarcely talk, she took up the telephone to ask eager questions of a war correspondent friend of mine who had just come back from a Mexican revolution. What the air raids were like; tell her about the Mexican girl who fought in the trenches; and what became of the dog who ran up and down on the top of a fire-swept trench?

He told her about a tramp aviator who had a steel extension in his leg which he used to loosen and tighten up with a screw driver he carried for the purpose. Mabel laughed. "You are a liar," her voice came gasping over the 'phone. Impudent to the last.

Mabel has gone from us, but like Chevalier Bayard—without fear and without reproach, she goes boldly forward.

Mabel Normand in her early days at Keystone. At the left, Ford Sterling is inspecting the slipper, while the Old Master, Mack Sennett, does one of his Dutch scowls. Few pictures remain of Sennett in character in his acting days

184

It isn't the jolly "Fatty" Arbuckle of his great Paramount starring days of a decade ago. There's somberness in that big moon face that made millions laugh in the good old days

Under another name, Roscoe Arbuckle directs short comedies for a Hollywood producer. And still he cherishes a faint hope that some day he can stage a come-back before his own camera

"Just Let Me Work"

Illusions lost and hope fading, Roscoe Arbuckle just jogs along directing other people's comedies

THIS is a story about "Fatty" Arbuckle. And it's *not* a "sob story."

It's not a sob story for the simple reason that Arbuckle isn't sobbing. There's nothing to sob about!

But neither is it the "head-high-facing-life-courageously" sort of thing. For Roscoe Arbuckle wouldn't fit into that classification any more than the whiner category. "Fatty's" not fighting very hard any more. A decade of battle has knocked most of the fight out of him. But he isn't bawling, either.

This story, in short, is merely a presentation of the case of "Fatty" as he stands today.

It was nearly ten years ago, now, that headline ink was smeared thick and ugly across the gay-hued Arbuckle shield. The jovial clown that had rolled 'em in the aisles with his elephantine antics became overnight a sinister figure whose name might not even be mentioned in polite company.

Journalistic sensationalism had its customary Roman holiday—and the fact that a jury acquitted Roscoe Arbuckle of the charges against him made no difference in the fact that he was a ruined man.

Well, all that's an old story by this time. You've read it time and again, and you've read interminable arguments for and against Arbuckle. You know, too, that with his friends in movieland solidly behind him, "Fatty" tried to fight back to the place he had lost.

He fought strenuously. He made speeches. He toured the country, in personal appearances and in vaudeville. He sought backers to put him again on the screen. He fought, courageously, against the organized campaign to keep him off the screen—the campaign that has ever been waged by the extremists to prevent him from coming back.

For years, his name and the news of his fight were good copy. But then, inevitably, came the indifference that is worse, in "Fatty's" profession, than the most rabid condemnation. "Fatty" was left to be forgotten.

By Tom Ellis

And that was the break that did for him. "Fatty" stopped fighting, then—and whatever he has done since, to tell the truth, has been half-hearted at best.

And that brings us to today—when "Fatty" Arbuckle isn't even a name any more! Literally, that is. Because Arbuckle, smashed at last by the futility of ever trying to live down the shadow of that name in headline ink, has changed it. Today he works in Hollywood, but not under the name of Roscoe Arbuckle. He has adopted an entirely different name.

That new name has been printed, here and there. We won't print it, because to do so would mean merely another hardship for the man. Under that new name, he has achieved a certain measure of success—certainly not great, but enough to earn a living—at directing comedies. To divulge the name of the company that is making his pictures would mean only the probability of unfair prejudice against his work. And that would be tragic—for some of the two-reelers Arbuckle is turning out are superior to many feature pictures! He knows his stuff!

TODAY then, "Fatty" Arbuckle, the hilarious comedian, is gone. Instead, there is a big fat fellow behind a director's desk in a Hollywood office, the door of which bears a name that doesn't even remotely resemble Roscoe Arbuckle.

There's no grin on his face. It's almost always serious. There are lines there that weren't on that cherubically asinine countenance that beamed from the screen in the old "Fatty" comedies.

He works hard. When he's casting his comedies, he makes a point of picking the names of old-timers he used to know. He's particularly happy when he can give a few days' work to some fellow who's had the breaks against him.

He doesn't court publicity. Now and then, a writer or an editor will say: "What can we do for you to help you, Roscoe?"

Arbuckle will half-smile and say, usually: "Aw, never mind me; I'm doing all right. But you might give a story to So-and-So"—naming either an old-timer who's heading for the rocks, or a newcomer who needs a boost.

He has learned that his field is motion pictures, and it is in that field alone that he must seek whatever the future holds for him. He tried, disastrously, restauranting. His friends backed him—first with the Plantation Club, a night resort near Hollywood. It went well enough, in a way, but "Fatty" got nothing out of it to speak of. His name was blazoned there in electric lights, and it was called "his" place.

But all he really was was entertainer there. And it didn't last.

THEN some friends promoted another place for him, in Hollywood. But it was off the beaten track.

Friends are few—real friends, that is. Not many people came to Arbuckle's café. And that flopped, too.

"It's pictures for me," he realized. He had been brought up in pictures, and pictures was all he knew.

He hasn't many resources. So he turned back to pictures.

Producers were afraid of his name. They knew that to mark their product with the name of Arbuckle was to invite disaster.

It was Mack Sennett who took the first chance. He gave "Fatty" a job directing and gagging. But even Sennett had Arbuckle use another name. Four months, "Fatty" stayed there.

Then he went to Radio Pictures. Radio kept it very, very dark. If "Fatty" happened to get into a photograph taken on the set he was working on, while acting as gag-man, the negative was destroyed. The studio adopted a rigid hush-hush policy on Arbuckle's presence while he worked there as comedy adviser on two pictures.

From there, "Fatty" went to another producing organization that specializes in two-reel comedies.

For the past several months, he has been successfully directing there under his new name. He is reasonably happy.

When we say that, we mean that "Fatty" is resigned. He has lost his fight; he has lost his illusions. And of hope, he retains only a vestige.

That hope is the one thing he has never given up. It is the hope that some day, somehow, he may once again return to the screen—on the screen! And it's not because he thinks he can make more money—because he's making a good living now. It's because he can never forget the place he once held in the hearts and affections of movie-goers. He wants that place back.

"ALL I want to do is to be allowed to work in my field," is the way he puts it. There's no longer any enthusiasm behind his saying it, though.

"It isn't for money. I'm not broke. I never have been broke. I don't want anybody sobbing or whining over me.

"I've no resentment against anybody for what has happened. My conscience is clear, my heart is clean. I refuse to worry. I feel that I have atoned for everything.

"You know, people can be wrong. I don't say I'm all right. I don't believe the other side is all right. And anyway, so much worse has happened in history to people vastly more important that I am that my little worries don't matter, in comparison. So why should I kick?

"People have the right to their opinions. The people who oppose me have the right to theirs. I have the right to mine—which is, that I've suffered enough, and been humiliated enough.

"I want to go back to the screen. I think I can entertain and gladden the people that see me. All I want is that. If I do get back, it will be grand.

"If I don't—well, okay."

Double the enjoyment of the evening

try this marvelous Beauty Bath

IF you're compelled to come dashing home from the office or a shopping tour, and the event of the evening requires a quick "tub"—swish half a package or more of Linit in your bath, bathe as usual, using your favorite soap, and when dry, feel the exquisite smoothness of your skin.

One outstanding feature of the Linit Beauty Bath is that the results are immediate—no waiting.

Nor will you waste precious minutes "dusting" with powder, because after the Linit Beauty Bath there is a light, exceedingly fine "coating" of Linit left on the skin which eliminates "shine" from arms and neck and which harmlessly absorbs perspiration.

Pure starch from corn is the basic ingredient of Linit and being a vegetable product, it contains no mineral properties to irritate the skin. In fact, doctors who specialize in the treatment of the skin, regard the purity of starch from corn so highly that they generally recommend it for the tender skin of young babies.

Linit is sold by your Grocer

LINIT FOR THE BATH — Makes Your Skin Feel Soft and Smooth

The bathway to a soft, smooth skin

The Tragic Truth about

He will be remembered as the boy of "The Big Parade" and for those tender love scenes with Renee Adoree

If John Gilbert had known what it was to lose Garbo, he later discovered, he would have made any sacrifice to continue this great love of his life. Why did they part?

THE boy of "The Big Parade" has gone West.

And in your heart, and mine, we sound taps for Jack Gilbert, because we loved that boy, and because he brought glamour and romance and adventure into our lives.

Thirty-eight is young to die.

Thirty-eight is so very young to lay down the glory and the burden of living.

But into those thirty-eight years Jack Gilbert had packed more living and loving and fighting and working than most people ever know in three score years and ten. And I think he rests quietly and if, somewhere, he hears an echo of the taps we sound for him, the music of it will be pleasant to his soul, for life without the woman he loved and without the work he loved, had ceased to be worth living.

It is hard to write of Jack Gilbert as dead. There is an emptiness in the very words. He was my friend. To him, the word

was vital, and beautiful, and not to be used lightly. He was one of those friends that are always there in the background of your life, an anchor to windward, a port in a storm. Maybe you didn't see him for months, or think of him for weeks. But you knew he was there. If you were in trouble, Jack would be in your corner—and he was a great guy to have in your corner. If you needed something and Jack had it, you could have it. Whatever you did, he'd understand.

That kind of a guy, part of your life, something to be counted upon.

It is hard, in this little crowded difficult life, to sound taps over a friend like that.

I am poorer today than I was yesterday, because Jack Gilbert is dead, dead in his prime, and maybe glad to be dead.

Doesn't matter much to you or to me where he was born or where he went to school or how he happened to get into pictures. He used to say he was born in a theater dressing room somewhere in Utah and cradled in a wardrobe trunk and that he made his first stage appearance at the age of one year. He was married four times and he was one of the really great stars of the screen and one of the three or four great screen lovers—Wally Reid, Valentino, Jack Gilbert, Clark Gable.

But those things aren't the measure of the man.

It's cold outside today. There's snow piled

Slim young Virginia Bruce tried her best to make the moody artist happy the few years they had together

John Gilbert's Death

One of his dear-
est friends tells
you the heart-
breaking facts

By Adela
Rogers St. Johns

JOHN GILBERT

JAMES MONTGOMERY FLAGG

"He was one of those friends that are always there
in the background of your life, a port in the storm"

In the last days, John Gilbert was seen everywhere with Marlene Dietrich. What did it mean
to him? Was it an echo of the one great love?

up and the trees are black against it. I would
like to keep my own little memorial service for
Jack here beside my fire—he so loved an open
fire—and I think he would want me to, talking about him to you who loved him for his
triumphs and his failures, his strength and his
weakness, the boy and the man who came
through to you on the screen.

Times I've cried over him.

Times I've cheered for him.

Times I've wanted to break his neck.

"There is only one code I have, only one
creed I know," he said to me once. We were
walking along beside the ocean, and the wind
was strong with salt from the sea, and he flung
his head back as though he challenged it.

At twenty-one, he played the
juvenile lead opposite Mary
Pickford on the old Ince lot

"Honesty. What good is anything
if it isn't honest? My faults, my
frailties, my virtues——if I've got
any——they've got to be honest or
don't exist at all." And once he
himself wrote——he loved to write
he was always full of plots and ideas
for stories, bubbling over with
them, he loved the company of
writers——with somewhere, latent
perhaps, but ever present, a determination to struggle onward, and
upward toward honesty.

Well, he did. It landed him in
jail a couple of times. It got him
into jams at his studio—for speak
his honest mind to the powers-that-
be he would!——it cost him friends
and got him in the headlines——
but he was honest.

And right or wrong he lived to the
top of his bent; loved hotly, drank
deep, suffered more than he needed
to suffer. And died young, as such
men often do.

190

Gilbert gave up a good job as a director to elope to Mexico in 1922 with Leatrice Joy. They had one daughter

He married Olive Burwell from Mississippi in 1917 when he was making eighteen dollars a week as an extra

He had only known the witty Belasco star, Ina Claire, three weeks when they were married, in 1929

Blonde Virginia Bruce was twenty-one when she married him in 1932. She bore him a child, Susan Ann

When his love of life died, that was the end of Jack Gilbert. For that was all of him, the thing we loved him for. That began to fade when he lost Garbo.

How can you write or think or speak of Jack without Garbo?

I cannot. Nor would he wish it. For she was all of life and love and work to him from the day he first saw her on the Metro-Goldwyn-Mayer lot to the day his heart stopped beating. He told me this less than a year ago!

"There may be many women in a man's life," he said. "I have cared for—many women. But a man loves but once, with all of himself and to the top of everything in him. Just once. It's worth any price you have to pay to have known that one great love. Lots of people live and die without knowing it. Thank whatever gods there be—I didn't. But there's never been a day since Fleka" (that was his pet name for Garbo, the name he always used, the name he must have used when they were together) "and I parted that I haven't been lonely for her. And I think she has always been lonely for me."

As you go through life, you wonder about love. Is there such a thing, as the poets sang it?

The greatest love I ever knew a man to have for a woman was Jack Gilbert's for Garbo.

The heart that stopped beating the other day broke long ago. For that's the kind of a man Jack Gilbert was.

Not a happy love. But a magnificent one. Heartbreak at the end of it. But that was Jack Gilbert. There were no safe and sane middle grounds for him. Crash if you must, but fly toward the moon and the stars while you can.

One night when Greta and Jack were very much in love, when they expected to marry, they had been on a cruise aboard his yacht. They had quarreled and when they came back Jack came right up to my house—and we sat before just such a fire as this—rather I sat and he paced up and down, for he was restless always, he could never sit still, I never saw his face in repose. That is why I cannot think of him now as still and dead and his face only a quiet, white mask.

He talked about Greta, and his love for her, and the terrible differences of thought and desire and character that divided them.

"Why couldn't I have fallen in love with someone who'd be a good wife to me, make me a home, bear my children, give me peace and contentment and——?"

"And bring your carpet slippers?" I said, watching his face very intently.

He turned on me swiftly and then that shout of laughter that I can still hear, above the taps sounding in my heart, rang through the room.

"You're right," he said. "I'd rather have one hour with Fleka than a lifetime with any other woman."

It was Garbo he loved. The glamour of her, the strangeness of her, the very things he couldn't possess nor understand The mystery of her that he could never solve. Yet there was nothing between them but love——and in time they parted. I asked Jack once if he really knew why, since they had loved each other so much, since they were both free, since there was nothing outside themselves to separate them.

He told me. It took him all

The Real Truth About John Gilbert's Death

one long afternoon, in a New York hotel, where he was reading plays with the idea that since he was finished in pictures he might go on the stage. And he had just made what he didn't know was the fatal mistake of turning down "Men in White."

But I can only tell you that it was because if they married, he said, she wanted to retire from the screen, give up her career, buy a big ranch way away from everything, and have many children. And Jack still wanted the glamourous Garbo, and he didn't want to retire from a world which he loved so very much, nor from the life and work that fascinated him so deeply.

"If I had known——" he said, and stared out at the gray afternoon.

If he had known what it was like to lose her, perhaps no price would have been too high. But, you see, he didn't really believe that he would lose her. He thought that in the end she would come his way. She told him, when they parted forever, on the night of her birthday, "You are being a very very foolish boy, Yacky," she said. "You quarrel with me for nothing. I must do my way—as I see. But we need not part."

HE left her, sitting in her car. Without kissing her good-bye. He thought she would come back. But she didn't. And he was too proud and then—it was somehow too late. That is the way things happen sometimes.

The tragedy of Jack Gilbert is a Hollywood tragedy.

Things moved so fast. They grew so big. They came at him from all sides. And the boy never had any balance. People who give you and me what Jack Gilbert gave us don't always have balance; they aren't steady and sane and systematic. I think Hollywood never knew anyone who had so much and so little as Jack, who had so many glorious chances and so many bad breaks.

For it was just when he had lost Greta that his work, which he loved with a burning sort of passion, folded up on him, too. The talkies came and Jack got caught in them while they were incomplete.

"I was the first man ever to say 'I love you' out loud on the screen," he said moodily one night. "It ruined me. They laughed. It was something new. And the so and so and so and so machine squeaked and my voice jumped around like a so and so tenor—and you know you can survive anything but ridicule."

He fought to come back and somehow I always thought he would. We wanted him, didn't we? The boy of "the Big Parade." The dashing lover of "Flesh and the Devil." Of course we wanted him. But——things went all crosswise and Jack was partly to blame. He behaved like a temperamental idiot part of the time. Couldn't be handled. Got his feelings hurt. Fought and insulted the bosses——and all because he was so bitterly, deeply hurt inside himself. The very throbbing emotion of him, that made him what he was on the screen, defeated him because——in the end, he was just too much trouble. And when his chances came, he'd let himself go too far nervously to take them.

Funny. I can't believe he won't come back. I always thought he would. The waste of it! He had so much. But genius and that wonderful emotional charm——they don't amount to much if you can't harness them and drive them, and somewhere——after he lost Garbo ——Jack lost control of the gifts God had given him.

You see, Jack had one great curse.

He knew it, because we had talked about it, often. Tried to thrash it out.

He was desperately afraid of injustice——he expected it——he was always on the look out for it.

AND that, he told me, was because he thought his mother had been unjust to him when he was a little boy.

I don't know anything about Jack's mother. I do know, that as sometimes happens, Jack loved her——and bitterly resented things that she had done to him. He carried into manhood a strange mark from his little-boy days. He never quite trusted love nor life. He was always afraid of what it might do to him. When I first knew him——I think he was about eighteen ——he was all fire and defiance outside, and all sensitive shyness inside. We were kids twenty years ago, working on the old Ince lot, and he used to come and talk to me. Afire with ambition, trembling with desire for life——and more life——but wary as a young colt. And through twenty years of friendship, I watched him grow and triumph and fail——and always I saw underneath it all that sensitiveness, that so-easily-hurt quality of him, that all his laughter——and he loved to laugh——all his acting and belligerence——he loved to fight, too—— could never hide. Poor darling—he never quite grew up. And he never found in the women he loved, the mother he was always seeking.

And injustice, somehow or another, pursued him, as though the thing he greatly feared had come upon him.

He had love. He had friendship, too.

Once upon a time he was one of Hollywood's Three Musketeers. They were all young and handsome and they had decided that women gummed up a man's life and that they would not be bothered with women anymore. They lived upon a hilltop, or upon three hilltops, but in those days they were always together. One for all and all for one. That was the age-old motto of Ronny Colman and Dick Barthelmess and Jack Gilbert. They were exceedingly pleased with themselves. They gathered about them such wits and kindred spirits as Laurence Stallings (who wrote "The Big Parade") and Donald Ogden Stewart, and they had a devil of a time, doing a bit of masculine drinking, playing tennis——and talking. How Jack loved to talk. And how they loved each other, those three. As Athos, Porthos and Aramis did once upon a time.

That was a happy time.

But unfortunately they were wrong about being able to do without women.

I think it was just about then that Jack met Ina Claire——and that was a great tragedy.

I think, in many ways, that was the greatest tragedy, the worst break, of Jack's career. For had he met another kind of a woman, a woman

with more of the maternal in her——maybe not. Maybe it wouldn't have mattered.

Ina Claire, in my opinion, is the best actress on the American stage. She is also, with the exception of Dorothy Parker, the most brilliant woman conversationalist I have ever heard. She is also a most fascinating person and a charming companion.

Perhaps it wasn't her fault, perhaps it was just the way the cards were stacked. But, you see, it was like this: Jack was trying to fight his way back in the talkies. Trying to learn a new medium of expression. I remember just before they were married going on the set with him one day when he was making that terrible failure "Resurrection." And he was as nervous and as unsure of himself as a man could well be. He had his chin out a yard, he had his left up, he was fighting to keep his self-confidence, or to get it back, to find some support for the natural self-assurance and pride a man must have if he is to succeed at all. He was afraid of his lines, afraid his voice would break——it was pretty ghastly.

And Ina Claire——well, you see, Ina probably knows more about speaking lines, more about how to get shades of feeling and emotion into the voice, more about the very medium Jack was trying to master than any other woman in America. The first time Jack told me about her, and that he was in love with her, was at a luncheon in Frances Marion's hilltop home. And he called her "the most charming adult human being I ever met." But——Ina came of the New York school. She was glittering, she was brilliant. But she didn't know how to get over to Jack what she knew without reducing him to pulp. Without forcing him to defend his masculine pride. I saw it happen with my own eyes when I was with them. Everyone saw it.

Trying her best, she just didn't understand about the little boy in Jack that needed to be babied and comforted and told how good he was. She was—too adult, perhaps.

It robbed Jack of his last remnants of belief in himself—and he never got it back. Without it, he didn't amount to a damn. And that's the truth.

Virginia Bruce, his last wife, was a lovely girl, and she understood. A lot of it she understood. But it was too late, and she was too young. He told me once that he had a fondness for Virginia and an affection for her such as he had never had for any woman. But that slim, young, lovely thing, bearing his child, absorbed almost at once in motherhood—— what could she do against the deep, dark depression of Jack's soul, the loneliness for his great love that grew upon him, his bitterness against life, his self-indulgence that weakened him and drove him half-mad, his idleness that lay upon him like a medieval torture?

IT was too late——and she knew it, soon. He sought peace and contentment and thought he had found it in her fair, serene loveliness, her young devotion. But the furies of the past wouldn't let him go.

It was too late when M-G-M gave him that last chance to make a picture. There wasn't strength behind that broken heart, that mortally wounded pride, to drive through. There

191

192

wasn't enough fire left in the fading fires of his love of life to blaze again. The engine was worn out.

His first marriage to Olivia Burwell had been a kid marriage. "Didn't mean anything," he said.

He had been happy with Leatrice Joy. Terribly happy. But he was young and wild with success as it came and——do you remember that Leatrice separated from him just before the baby was born and wouldn't let him see his daughter? That, I said then and I still say, was hitting below the belt——and I think in time Leatrice came to know it. It marked him again, with that sense of injustice.

Jack was the godfather of my youngest son, who is now seven.

I was sitting on the beach at Malibu, watching Dicky swim one day when Jack came striding along, followed by his dogs. He sat down on the sands and we watched together, while the two-year-old battled the waves.

"I don't know that I'll ever be any good to him as a godfather," Jack said. "But, darling, don't let him be hurt while he's little. Don't ever let him think he isn't loved. Don't ever let him know what it is to be without somebody's arms to go into when things seem strange. Let him always be sure of you——and your love. Discipline isn't so important. Teaching 'em things isn't. But letting them be sure——sure——that you love them and will always be there and stand by, that's the important thing. Will you remember that?"

Yes, Jack, I'll always remember that.

And, my dear, I'll always remember the day you comforted me, when the best friend I had in the world had——gone where you've gone now. I'll always remember that you said, "You've lost her, but you can't ever ever lose what she meant to you. The glory of that isn't ever going to die out of your life. You had it, and nothing can take it away from you."

And I'll remember you once, a long time ago, when we were kids and I was sick and you came to the hospital and threw your week's salary envelope on the bed, in case I needed it, and in those days nobody had eating dough beyond that week's salary.

AND we'll all remember you——not as the great lover, not as the great screen star, not as the man who was hammered down by life, not even as the man who loved Garbo and whom she loved——but as the boy of "The Big Parade." The symbol of every doughboy that ever went to France and wore a tin hat.

Maybe you'll find little Renee Adoree, somewhere, in that place where you have gone, and you can sit together once more under the trees, as you did in that never-to-be-forgotten picture, and smile at each other.

And maybe faintly you'll hear the taps we're sounding in our hearts for you——bon voyage, Jacky. We're going to miss you desperately!

Harvey White

J OHNNY WEISSMULLER rose to fame on the strength of his handsome physique, and lovely ladies, the world over, have gambled with each other ever since for a permanent mortgage on the brawny, tawny *Tarzan*.   First, 'twas Bobbe Arnst, who held claim, then Lupe Velez, and now who shall it be?

Prof. Albert Einstein and his host, Charlie Chaplin, at the Los Angeles opening of Charlie's "City Lights." Chaplin was the one man in Hollywood Einstein wanted to meet. Well, he met him—and about 50,000 others, too

Einstein *In* Hollywood

THEY say Professor Einstein was trying to explain his theory to a big studio executive.

". . . for instance, consider Betelgeuse," Einstein was explaining. "Betelgeuse, one of the greatest stars in the whole system, can be photographed merely by means of one ray of light . . ."

"Uh-huh," uh-huhed the executive. Later Einstein went home.

At once, the executive grabbed a telephone and called his casting director.

"Say, you," he shouted, "I want you should go out and sign up this feller Betelgeuse. And I want you should sign him up quick. Einstein, who knows everything, says he's one of the greatest stars in the business.

"And economy!—hah, lissen—we can shoot him with only one light, Einstein says!!"

At the Warner Studio the Einsteins were coaxed into this bouncing car. Cameras cranked, tricksters worked. Two hours later the guests received a film of themselves flivving 'round the world!

He can comprehend the Universe, but the picture business left him dazed

The celebration of Carl Laemmle's twenty-fifth anniversary in pictures was on, and Einstein unwittingly helped the party. "*You* tell *me* about relativity?" is what Hollywood thinks Mr. Laemmle is saying, referring to his relatives on the Universal lot

195

That is just one of the dozens that are being told—true and otherwise—about Einstein's visit to the moving picture capital. Queen Victoria in a tap-dancing school wouldn't have been half as out of place as Einstein was in Hollywood.

Now, of course, Einstein has about as much in common with Hollywood as maple sugar has with canned salmon. But Einstein, being human, naturally wanted to get a look at Hollywood while in California. And Hollywood, being Hollywood, naturally wanted to grab off the lion's share of the unprecedented publicity Einstein was getting.

AND so it all began—this amazing business of Einstein-in-Hollywood, as soon as he arrived in Pasadena. The purpose of his trip of course, was to visit the famous scientific laboratories at the California Institute of Technology in Pasadena, twenty miles from Hollywood. He was provided with a bungalow, where, it was assumed, he would go into retirement to ponder on the vastnesses of the universe.

But Hollywood wouldn't go for things like that! To let Einstein hide away, and thereby overlook a headline like "EINSTEIN VISITS COLOSSUS STUDIOS" was not in any Hollywood press-agent's book of rules. And so the race began.

Universal won.

It seems that "Uncle Carl" Laemmle, bland potentate of Universal City, was having a twenty-fifth anniversary of making movies. It would be nice to have a lot of big people there. So huddles were huddled and plans were planned, and what eventuated?—

An invitation was sent to Professor Einstein in Pasadena. Would he care to see the famous film "All Quiet on the

By Harry Lang

Western Front"? Einstein's a famous pacifist, by the way. And having heard much about "All Quiet" and its force for peace, Einstein innocently said yes.

Fine, said Universal right back at him, we'll have a showing for you on such-and-such a day. Well, such-and-such a day was the day of the anniversary celebration. And then, invitations were sent broadcast through filmland to come on over to Universal on such-and-such a day—Laemmle's twenty-fifth Anniversary and Einstein as attractions.

Did it work?

Well, even Queen Mary was there—Mary Pickford. So was Gary Cooper, in his eye-paining yellow-and-green open car, even though it rained that day. Will Rogers came. Executives from all the other studios were there. Filmland turned out *en masse* to see Einstein. And the most surprised person of all was Einstein! He expected to see a moving picture. Instead, he saw countless scores of movie celebrities he didn't know, plus countless Laemmle relatives. "There were so many relatives," said one person there, "that you couldn't get to the buffet luncheon table!" And that's the beginning of the famous crack about what Laemmle might have said to Einstein:

"What! You're telling *me* about relativity?"

It was at the Einstein visit to Universal that the famous Mary Pickford episode happened. Celebrity after celebrity was introduced to Einstein.

Among

Einstein in Hollywood

those who tripped down the line to meet him was Mary.

"I'm so very glad to know you, Professor Einstein," she purred. Einstein bowed gallantly but with the usual bewildered expression.

Immediately afterward, he turned to an interpreter.

"Wer ist dass?" he whispered.

He was told it was Mary Pickford. Einstein's face was still blank as he turned to Frau Einstein.

Frau Einstein came to the rescue. She beamed on Mary.

"Oh, yes," she said, "we came to America in the same stateroom on the *Belgenland* in which your husband traveled."

A FEW of the Hollywoodites never could get the distinction between Einstein and Serge Eisenstein, the Russian director who had left Hollywood just a short while before the German scientist arrived.

Eisenstein it was who left after he and Paramount had failed to come to terms for the Russian to direct Dreiser's "American Tragedy."

And it was at the Universal affair, too, that another beautiful actress—spare the name!—cooed to Einstein:

"Oh, Professor! I can't begin to tell you how sorry I am that you're not going to direct the 'American Tragedy.'"

Naturally, photographers in hordes were about the Universal lot.

News cameramen—nine of them in a row, each with microphones poised—started grinding off footage as Einstein and Laemmle stood talking in German.

Einstein speaks little English. Uncle Carl and he chatted earnestly, while cameras and sound tracks reeled on.

It wasn't until the films were being developed for national distribution that it was learned that the conversation went about like this, in German:

EINSTEIN—But I wish that you would see to it that these pictures are not broadcast.

LAEMMLE—I assure you that they shall not be.

And Universal, frantic that the newsreels in every picture house in America would show Uncle Carl promising Einstein the newsreels wouldn't be shown, had to get the Hays office to help recall the negatives—just in the nick of time!

Innumerable promoters in Hollywood tried to sign Einstein up to a movie contract. They hadn't the slightest idea what he would do in front of a camera—"illustrate your Einstein theory," one of them suggested—but they tried to sign him anyway. To all these, Einstein turned a deaf ear.

But the greatest shock he gave was not his refusal of the movie money, but his refusal to meet all the stars!

IT was funny to see the greatest names in moviedom, hanging about Einstein's heels exactly like a crowd of fans hang around the heels of a film star, waiting for an introduction.

And Einstein, embarrassedly explaining that he couldn't speak English and didn't know much about movies, begging not to have to meet them.

Of course, all this was a vast puzzle to Einstein.

He understood theories about time and space beyond most other mortals' ken, but he didn't understand Hollywood.

While he was being escorted about the Universal lot, for instance, he'd turn now and then to Frau Einstein and whisper:

"Jetzt gehen wir zum nachsten ring!"—

(Now we're going to the next ring!)—just like a kid at a three-ring circus.

At Warner Bros.-First National lot, Einstein and his wife got into the circus performance themselves, though.

The Warner lot was visited by the Einstein party on the same day they visited the Metro-Goldwyn-Mayer studios, several days after the Universal affair.

At Warners the publicity lads asked the Professor and his wife to step into a flivver, mounted on a wooden scaffold before a big blue screen.

Einstein, taking off his hat and exposing that fright-wig head of hair, did. So did Frau Einstein.

Then lights were turned on, the car was jiggled madly from beneath, and cameras whirred.

And two hours later, before he left the studio, Professor and Frau Einstein saw themselves on the screen, driving around the streets of Hollywood, Paris and Berlin, in the ancient flivver! Warner technicians had set a record with a trick-process double-exposure shot.

It was on the Warner visit that the battle of Einstein-vs.-Barrymore was staged!

Barrymore, in his frowsy long-whiskered make-up for *Svengali*, was told that Einstein was to be the guest of Jack Warner and studio officials at lunch, and would Barrymore join the party.

Barrymore replied that in view of his make-up and shooting conditions, he was not sure whether he could attend or not. And he sent over to the luncheon room a picture for Einstein to please autograph to him.

IN the meantime, Einstein had arrived and explained that, because of lack of time, he was afraid he could not visit all the stages, and would Mr. Barrymore please come to the luncheon and meet him there?

The message was taken to Barrymore.

Barrymore, famous for his temper and his language, rose to great heights. He said a lot of words about Einstein, to the effect that if Einstein couldn't come to the Barrymore stage, Barrymore would be so-and-so if he'd go to the Einstein lunch.

Then Einstein declined to autograph the Barrymore picture!

Barrymore said more things. Einstein stood pat.

At this juncture, a technician on the Barrymore set hastened over to the lunch room and when Einstein and officials came out, presented his autograph book.

Einstein took it.

Frau Einstein took it out of the professor's hands.

"Nein! Genug heute!" she said—(No! Enough today!)—and handed the book, unautographed, back to the lad. Crestfallen, the boy went back and Barrymore overheard his tale.

Then the Barrymore rage knew no bounds.

"Why, the——! ! !" he shouted. "Lock the doors. Lock *all* the doors. Don't let that—— on this set!"

And the doors were locked. And Barrymore didn't meet Einstein and said he didn't give a tinker's, and Einstein didn't meet Barrymore and didn't seem to care, either. And Barrymore, who up to then had been an Einstein enthusiast, isn't interested in Einstein theories any more.

EINSTEIN was lured to the M-G-M lot by virtue of the fact that two of his countrymen, working in a picture there, had known him in Germany. He didn't want to turn down their invitation. They were Heinrich George and Paul Morgan, known as the "Will Rogers of Germany."

As a matter of fact, Einstein visited longer on the stage where they were making the German version of "The Big House" than on any other lot in Hollywood. He could speak German at last—and he was always annoyed at the other lots through having to be bothered with interpreters. He swapped German with Morgan and George and the other Germans for several hours. But he didn't understand Director Fejos.

Fejos, "taking it big," was the ultra-director while Einstein watched. He had one scene taken three times over. Afterward Einstein shook his head.

"It looked," he said, "that the first scene was perfect. The second was grand. But he insisted on another one being made. H'm—he's too hard to please, I think!"

AS a matter of fact, throughout all his studioing, Einstein looked bewildered. He plainly was.

Look at his photographs. He seemed to breathe sighs of relief when he finally left each studio.

He had said, even before reaching California, that the only man he wanted to meet was Charlie Chaplin.

He did.

He met Charlie and went with him to that terrific Los Angeles opening of Chaplin's picture, "City Lights."

The mob of 25,000 spectators that night broke all police control, and celebrities were manhandled by the star-worshippers as they entered the theater.

It was all Chaplin and Einstein and their party could do to get into the theater. Through it all, Einstein never said a word.

He just stared in utter amazement at it all. But later, he sighed a bit and confessed to Charlie:

"I have visited the world's famous laboratories. I have looked through the greatest telescopes. I have seen science's wonders. But never have I seen anything like that. And never, I hope, shall I again."

And most startling of all, Einstein was shown something science does not admit—that one body may be in two places at the same instant.

One night, while Einstein was in his Pasadena bungalow, he appeared at a Hollywood party. All the guests met him and he talked a few words to them in German. He left early.

IT wasn't until the next day that it was learned that the host—a moving picture official—had hired a clever make-up artist and a German actor, and that the "Einstein" at the party was only a double for the scientist!

Poor Professor Einstein!

He can understand the most profound things —relativity, the Unified Field theory, mathematical equations that take two years to work out—But he admits, in so many words, that he can't understand Hollywood!

Shooting Stars

WITH
HYMAN FINK

Hyman gets snapped snapping Jean Harlow and Bill Powell. The news of the Cary Grant-Mary Brian romance is—they're together again. Check it! Valiant is the word for Bob Taylor in that dressing gown, his pride and joy. With him is Dave Gould, M-G-M dance director

Hyman surprises that inseparable about-to-be-married couple, Loretta Young and Eddie Sutherland. Left, Madeleine Carroll created a sensation at the Cafe Lamaze both with her bandeau and her beau, Tyrone Power, Jr.

The Most Romantic Love

1

2

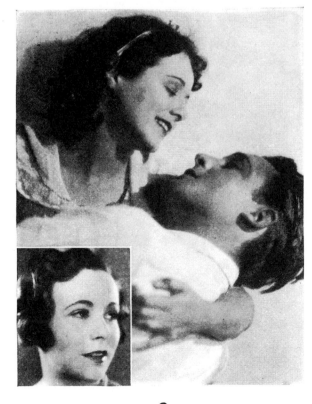

3

1 They met on the set where they were making "7th Heaven," that tender love story that was to touch the hearts of millions—and make the boy and girl great stars. He was tall, handsome, and twenty-two—she was little, winsome, and twenty. Making one of the loveliest of love stories, Janet Gaynor and Charles Farrell fell in love. They became *Diane* and *Chico* to the world, and to each other. Janet broke her engagement to Herbert Moulton, the Los Angeles newspaper man who had helped her on the hard road upward.

2 Rumors of the engagement of Janet and Charlie flew faster when they played opposite each other in "Street Angel." How happy they were! Their boy-and-girl romance was in full flower—this picture shows them in their happiest sweetheart days. But no announcement was forthcoming. Why, asked the world? For here was a romance the fans actually wanted to see consummated. Thousands of letters poured in approving the romance the picture world had seen begin in "7th Heaven" and flower in "Street Angel." But the youngsters were just happy in their work and affection for each other.

3 The answer to the question of "Why don't Janet and Charlie get married?" was undoubtedly Virginia Valli. She and Farrell had been pals since his earliest days in pictures. She always loved him in a thoroughly unselfish way and was friend, advisor and critic. Charlie's nature is something like Virginia's. She had devoted weeks to helping him plan his home at Toluca Lake. During this period of home-making, Charlie saw more of Virginia than of Janet. Two girls in love with the same boy—that was Hollywood's verdict.

Story *in* Film History

4

5

6

4 "Lucky Star" gave *Chico* back to *Diane* in pictures. Word circulated that Janet and Charlie were to be married any day. Charlie was to tell Virginia. Hollywood prepared congratulations. Then, without warning, Janet rushed to Oakland and married Lydell Peck, rich young San Francisco society man. What had happened? The story was that Charlie had gone to call on Virginia, that Janet, piqued, had wired Peck her acceptance of his proposal. They were married September 11, 1929. Hollywood was amazed.

5 "Sunny Side Up" brought them together again in pictures —but Janet was Mrs. Lydell Peck now. Then came "High Society Blues," and Janet's flight from the Fox lot. There was the episode of her trip to Honolulu, with Charlie accidentally boarding the same boat, and beating a hasty retreat. Janet cried! Ten heart-breaking months away from the studio. And then a glamorous return in "The Man Who Came Back." Who, seeing Charlie and Janet together in that picture, could doubt that the youngsters were still the best of friends? Again the world wondered about Janet and Charlie!

6 Then came the sudden death of Charlie's mother. It hit him pretty hard. PHOTOPLAY announced that Virginia and he were to be married, and sure enough, when Charlie got a vacation and time for a honeymoon they sailed for the Mediterranean, man and wife. They were married in New York a few days before sailing. And a happier pair of kids never leaned over a ship's rail and waved farewell. If you believe in astrology, ask the stars. Janet was born October 6, under the sign of Libra. The romance of Janet and Charlie—not to be!

The High Price of Screen Love-Making

Those torrid kisses you pay to see at your local theater often leave lingering memories with the players as well as with you

"HOLLYWOOD men too often forget that screen love-making is just a part of the script!"

Bette Davis made this remark immediately after she had married a boyhood sweetheart who knew absolutely nothing about screen love-making.

Bette was unwilling to risk married life with a man whose very work called for him to make love to other women.

Many Hollywood women seem to have preferred husbands who were not actors. Gloria Swanson's first husband (Wallace Beery) was from the screen, but her last three have been non-professionals.

Marian Nixon, Constance Talmadge, Connie Bennett, Joan Bennett, Janet Gaynor and a host of others have chosen men who are not actors for husbands.

Likewise, Clark Gable, Neil Hamilton, Robert Montgomery and Richard Dix have non-acting wives.

On the other hand, Lilyan Tashman and Edmund Lowe, Joan Crawford and Douglas Fairbanks, Jr., Mary Pickford and Doug, Sr., Clara Bow and Rex Bell, Vilma Banky and Rod LaRocque, and a long list of others are professional, as well as personal, partners.

WHICH is the wiser choice? No one can make definite answer. The problem is as relatively old to Hollywood as the "egg or the chicken first" is to the world. There are dangers in either direction. But then, any matrimonial boat faces rough seas, whether launched in Hollywood or Des Moines, Iowa. And screen actors and actresses are just as faithful and loyal, as a class, as any other group of people.

Love always seems to anticipate that marriage will change human nature. Human nature is not so easily changed. If it were—we would already have a Utopian civilization and a divorceless Hollywood.

But a Hollywood marriage faces exceptional dangers. If an actress chooses an actor she has, immediately, two possibilities. Screen love-making and professional jealousy.

The same is true, of course, if an actor chooses an actress.

If the partner is non-professional—the danger is in the opposition of interests. Bette Davis may be faced today with the

Smart girl—Bette Davis! When she married she wanted her husband for keeps. "It's safest to marry a non-professional," she reasoned, and so Harmon O. Nelson was elected to be the lucky man

thought; "Will he be known as Mr. Bette Davis?" and more deadly still, "Will he become content to be known as Mr. Bette Davis?"

She preferred that risk to the one of having him an actor who would spend his days making love to other women.

I have said — you can't change human nature by marriage. Let us take this jealousy between an actress wife and an actor husband as an illustration.

ALL actors must be jealous to reach the pinnacle of fame. It is the great "I am" within them which pushes and propels from one rung of the ladder to another. They must feel that they are better than the other fellows. And they must feel jealous of the one who seems to be succeeding more rapidly. Jealousy is an absolutely normal part of their egotistically ambitious natures.

Joan Crawford and Douglas, Jr., for example, swore in the first heat of that mad passion which swirled them away from life's normal channels that they would never be jealous. They swore they would change their normal actors' natures. I can remember Joan sitting on her kitchen sink in the old Beverly Hills house and saying, "I will always want Dodo's success ahead of mine." He retaliated in like manner. Brave words —but each is still zealously furthering his own career.

Mary and Doug, Sr., are just now proving that marriage has not, through all these years, changed their natures. Doug is ready to retire and live upon the wealth and the laurels which pictures have already brought him. Mary is not. Marriage has never been able to kill the intense ambition within her.

Actors are more highly tuned, more emotional than the average person. Also a necessity of the profession. And if an actor is making love all day long to a beautiful girl as part of his profession, can you expect him to forget the moment the last scene for the day is completed?

Be reasonable. If you spent a day in Ronald Colman's arms, could you forget it? Or, if you are a man, and you had spent eight hours clasping and unclasping, kissing and un-kissing Marlene Dietrich—would you forget it?

Could you go home to your sweet, thoughtful,

By Evaline Lieber

The High Price of Screen Love-Making

kind, loving mate and swear to yourself that such days had made no impression on you!

Certain actors have reputations for falling in love with each of their leading ladies. PHOTOPLAY has already told you how many of Greta Garbo's leading men fell under her spell. You know the allure Garbo inspires from the screen.

What must she do in person? Ask almost any one of her leading men and watch their eyes as their lips frame some quick but unconvincing answer to you!

We all knew, in Hollywood, that the home of Ruth Chatterton and Ralph Forbes was not quite the love-nest that young couples dream of.

AND then George Brent was cast as Ruth's leading man. Have you ever seen George Brent in person? I don't blame Ruth. He radiates, as a man, what Garbo does as a woman.

I remember I had luncheon with George soon after he commenced that picture. He had been through one matrimonial experience and was afraid of marriage. "The next woman must be intelligent. She must have lived enough to have wisdom; be kind; understand—"

When he had finished a lengthy description, I said, "Look out, George. You are describing Ruth Chatterton."

He looked startled. I do not believe he had realized of whom he was talking until I jolted him into realization. But he had been making love to Ruth Chatterton on the screen and had unconsciously described her as his dream woman.

Although directors are not so closely in contact with the women they direct, even they have been known to fall under the spell of some highly fascinating star.

There's a star in Hollywood, right now, who is recovering from the effect of too much director-propinquity. The director's wife hurried him to Europe. She's a wise woman. She understood.

She knew she could not change the natural results of the propinquity but she could remove the propinquity.

Jack Gilbert got Greta Garbo as far as the Santa Ana courthouse. They were in the midst of their screen love-making. But as love-inspiring and inspired as Garbo can become, she never entirely loses the natural shrewdness of her Nordic nature.

She had sense enough to know that marriage or love could not change that nature within her and that it would never completely melt with Jack's volatile, erratic one.

The man who paid the price for the results of this screen romance was, I believe, Mauritz Stiller. It may have helped to break his heart.

But could Garbo and Gilbert help it because they found their hearts attuned in their necessary screen love-making?

DO you remember the days when Beverly Bayne and Francis X. Bushman startled the then more prudish world by their marriage? Beverly and Francis were doing screen love-making. They liked it. They made the mistake of trying to perpetrate what could not be perpetrated.

How well I remember the night Lupe Velez heard a rumor that Gary Cooper and his leading lady were interested in each other. Lupe went to location. And Lupe can hold her man against any competition when she is among those present.

Gary didn't have another chance to remember whether the lips he was kissing for the screen were those of a live girl or a mummy.

He was thinking of Lupe.

BUT how few wives can go on the set with their husbands? Lupe wasn't a wife. If she had been, well— "Afraid to trust her husband, eh? Follows him everywhere like a pet poodle."

How many times I have heard remarks like that made of a woman who drops in only casually to see her actor husband.

There were rumors that some one was "interested" in Clark Gable. Mrs. Gable proved what a wise little woman she is. She went to New York and remained until those rumors had subsided. Perhaps they had no basis in fact, but she was not taking any chances. And these rumors were all started because of screen love-making.

The price is high. No husband or wife of an actress or actor can rest assured of a mate's continued loyalty.

Being a Hollywood mate requires infinite patience and almost super-human understanding.

Which explains why there are so many Hollywood divorces. Just old-fashioned human nature, the kind which cannot be written in or out of a script.

Answers by Sylvia

REDUCE

Dear Sylvia:

I've always been inclined to be fat but I didn't care much. Now I'm engaged to be married and am going to have a big wedding and want to look pretty in my wedding dress. Do you think I can lose twenty pounds in a month?

M. T. R., Los Angeles, Calif.

I know you can. I don't advise people taking off more than fifteen pounds in one month—but this is a special case and deserves drastic measures. This month I told you how I helped Connie Cummings to reduce her bust by going on a three day buttermilk diet, but you can reduce your entire figure by another buttermilk diet. Here it is: For three days drink nothing but buttermilk, six ounces every two hours. Then for three days eat three meals a day, but light ones, avoiding creamy soups, creamed vegetables, rich foods, pies, pastries, etc. Don't drink water with your meals and don't eat between meals. Then, after three days, go back to buttermilk. Do this until you have lost the twenty pounds. I hope it's a beautiful wedding and that you look grand in your white satin dress.

My dear Madame Sylvia:

I've been on the diet which you recommended in PHOTOPLAY, for several months with great success. Now my sixteen-year-old daughter wants to lose a little weight. Do you think it would be harmful for her?

Mrs. J. J. C., Baton Rouge, La.

If she is a healthy girl, not at all. On my diet you get plenty of good nourishing food. You haven't felt weak on it, have you?

INSOMNIA

Dear Sylvia:

I'm coming to you as a last resort. I used to be nice and plump, but lately I've lost a lot of weight and I know it's because I've gotten so I can't sleep at night. Please help me.

L. W., Birmingham, Ala.

I don't like being a last resort, but I can tell you how to sleep. In bed at night, lie on your stomach and with your fingers work up and down your spine. Then turn over on your back, lie straight in bed and relax and with your fingers gently massage the outer corners of your eyes with a rotary movement. Press slightly as you do this. Then with your hands work the back of your neck and the back of your shoulders to get those muscles loosened up.

Before going to bed drink a glass of grapefruit juice. Relax during the day whenever you can, and whenever you feel yourself tightening up, massage the muscles at the back of your shoulders and neck with your hands. If you wake up in the wee small hours of the morning and have trouble going back to sleep, don't just lie in bed and toss—get right up, dress and read or walk around the house or take a shower. Do anything, but don't lie in bed awake. The next night you'll fall right off to sleep. Don't *try* too hard to go to sleep. Let it come naturally.

PRETTY FINGERS

Dear Sylvia:

My fingers have been made blunt by constant use of the typewriter. I play bridge a good deal and would like to have pretty hands.

D. D., Billings, Mont.

You can mold the flesh on your fingers exactly as you can any other part of your body. With the thumb and forefinger of one hand press the stubby fingertip tight, and pull until the hand with which you are massaging slips off the end of your finger. Press hard—simply squeeze the flesh off to make your finger ends pointed. This can be done.

Give each finger about ten minutes of this treatment a day. And it won't hurt to massage the whole hand with lots of hand lotion on it. Work at your fingers as if you were pulling on a tight glove. It's grand for molding the hands.

RICH FOODS

Dear Sylvia:

My husband likes fried meat and rich pastries. So do I, but I've been trying to go on your diet and it is certainly hard to do it when I have to cook the things I like for my husband but can't eat any myself.

Please tell me how to reduce the upper part of my arms, particularly.

Mrs. J. T., Los Angeles, Calif.

Certainly, it's hard to see foods you like and not be able to eat them but that's what I've been trying to tell you. You've got to have courage and grit to be beautiful. And you've got to stop whining. I suppose you think it wasn't difficult for Connie Bennett to leave a party at which she was having a good time to get home at nine o'clock! But she did it—and even a professional pastry cook can keep on a diet if she really wants to. Snap out of it and stop complaining.

To reduce the upper part of your arms stand with your face to the wall and reach up along the wall with your hands. Stand on tip-toe. Do this in your stocking feet. Then, slowly, trying to keep your finger tips in their original place on the wall, sort of wiggle and jerk down to your heels, concentrating on keeping your fingers high. Of course, your hands will move slightly, but try keeping them up. You can feel the muscles in your upper arm pulling and you will know you are doing the exercise correctly.

201

"*I'll Be at Doc Law's*"

Revealing where Will Rogers spends his evenings, and why

By Kirtley Baskette

"YEP," declared Doc Law, diverting his gaze from the artistic luster he was applying to an ice-cream soda glass for a squint at the door, "I wouldn't be a bit surprised to see Bill happen in any minute now. About time he's showing up."

When Doc Law speaks of "*Bill*," he means his crony, Will Rogers, who lives a ways up the canyon from Doc's drug-store and refreshment parlor, just off the Coast Highway at the mouth of Santa Monica Canyon, out of Hollywood.

Each day, past the inconspicuous little beach corner where Doc's drug-store, a barbecue counter, souvenir stand and sundry other establishments invite ocean bathers, flash the shining automobiles of Hollywood's stars, en route to Malibu, up the coast. Few, in passing, even notice the sign around the corner which reads, "Burton C. Law, Drugs."

Yet Burton C. Law, erstwhile motion picture character actor, now Doc Law, pharmacist, corner drug-store proprietor and buddy of Will Rogers, was making pictures before most of them had ever seen a camera, when Director Frank Borzage was getting from two to five dollars a day doing stunts, when Robert Leonard and Frank Lloyd were blood-and-thunder flicker heroes, when Harold Lloyd was an ambitious pest of studio lots.

But all that was almost twenty years ago. And Doc Law has been running his drug-store now for about eleven years. In fact, Doc had sort of forgotten about his days as a screen actor, until Bill Rogers moved into "the neighborhood," up the canyon a stretch, some six years ago, and started dropping in of evenings just to talk over old times, sit a spell and discuss politics, maybe, watching the people who are continually flowing in and out of the store, remarking about this and observing that, while Doc handled the desultory evening trade.

In those six years, it has kind of gotten to be a habit for Will, when he feels "on the loose," to mosey down the canyon to Doc's drug-store, where he doesn't have to dress or put on any airs, where he can sit unnoticed back in the prescription room, among the paregoric and pills, the laudanum and elixirs, and peek through the curtains at a plain world he finds every bit as absorbing as Hollywood's dizzy sphere of which he is somewhat reluctantly a part.

"I guess it must have been about fifteen years ago that I worked with Bill in a picture called 'Honest Hutch,'" reminisced Doc Law. "I recall I played an Italian character, but Bill was the whole show.

"He always has been just naturally funny—still is. Why, it seems like just the way he says things makes them funny. I don't think he ever thinks much about what he says before he says it, either. Just spontaneous. Don't believe he ever particularly planned to be funny in his life. That stuff he writes

These two cronies have a gay time reminiscing. Will Rogers and Doc Law, old-time character actor, now proprietor of a drug-store in Santa Monica Canyon

for the newspapers—he just sits down and writes it right off, you can bet, as easy as he talks.

"*How* does he talk? Why, just like he does in his pictures. Maybe not so much emphasis on that Oklahoma drawl, but pretty near the same.

"The other night," remembered Doc, "Bill came in with Mrs. Rogers. Wasn't anyone in the store except myself and Mrs. Law.

"'Hello, everybody!' he said. 'Well, we got the kids all put away in their stalls, and me and the wife are on the loose. Can't tell where we'll end up, might end up anywhere—maybe in jail!'

"It's real amusing sometimes the plain way Bill talks to people he meets. I remember not long ago, I was alone here one night when an Irish priest came in. While I was fixing him up, he mentioned that he understood Will Rogers lived around here. Right up the canyon, I told him.

"Well, at that he got excited. It seems that Bill had been in Ireland when they had a bad fire over there somewhere, and he had flown right over to the place,

"I'll Be at Doc Law's"

put on a benefit performance and raised about six hundred dollars for the homeless people. This Catholic father came from there, and he said he'd give anything to meet Will Rogers.

"Right at that minute, believe it or not, in Bill walked! Of course, I introduced the priest, who grabbed him, and I thought he was going to wrestle him right there. He was pumping Bill's arm and telling him what a great fellow he thought he was. That sincere enthusiasm warmed my heart.

"The funny part of it is that before he left, Bill was talking to him just as if he was a cowboy pal of his."

DOC drew a large beaker of foaming three-point-two from the suds-dripping nozzle of his new drug-store department, and raised it above his close-clipped Buffalo Bill goatee.

"The night beer came back," he related, "I had a hunch. Bill would be dropping in. You know he doesn't touch tobacco in any form or any kind of hard liquor, but he does enjoy a good glass of beer every now and then. Of course, I knew that there wasn't any use of having any beer at the store, because you couldn't get enough then to last a minute, so I kept what I could get hold of up at the house.

"Sure enough, Bill wandered in a little later and said he would kind of like to sample the new stuff so he'd know what everybody was talking about.

"'Come on up to the house, then,' I told him, 'and we'll see what it's like.'

"'Okay, Doc,' said Bill.

"So we tried out the brew in the kitchen of my house, which, of course, isn't anything like the place Bill's got up there on the hill. But that never made any difference to him. He's happiest, I think, when he's comfortable in his overalls, boots and an old slouch hat, and when he's in plain surroundings—so I didn't worry about serving the refreshments in the kitchen.

"Speaking about houses, I remember one time I told Bill if I ever got enough money, I was going to build me a house high up on a hill, all by itself.

"'I already got one,' said Bill, 'but that doesn't mean a thing. Why, I never know what I'll meet on that trail leadin' down the hill from my place. You ought to see the critters that gather along that stretch.'

"THEN Bill grinned and told me about the time not long ago when he was leaving in a hurry for the East. His wife rushed around the house packing his suitcases and getting him ready to leave in double time so he could make the train which left in a few minutes.

"Bill rushed out of the house and on down the driveway to the gate, and there was a whole crowd of people waiting for him. Salesmen, solicitors, autograph hunters and people that had always wanted to meet him, waiting for him to come out. He was in an awful hurry, but he couldn't just pass right on by all those people waiting there to see him. It wouldn't have been nice, he said. So he stopped and talked to all of them.

"'When I got through,' Bill said, 'doggone if I hadn't missed the train!'

"What's that?" queried Doc Law. "Why doesn't he keep his gate locked? Oh, he does. It's locked all the time—tighter 'n a drum. But that doesn't keep anybody out.

"No, because the key is hanging right around the back of the gate-post; it's easy to reach around there and get it. Everybody knows that. *How* do they know it? Why, he *tells* them, of course!"

Doc Law grinned and shook his head expressively as he hurried away up the counter to assist a customer.

"That's Bill Rogers," he chuckled over his shoulder.

"Just friends" to the world at large—yet nowhere has domesticity taken on so unique a character as in this unconventional fold

BY KIRTLEY BASKETTE

The romance of Clark Gable and Carole Lombard is an interesting manifestation of how famous untied twosomes take to one another's hobbies. But calling the case of Paulette Goddard and Charlie Chaplin (top) is something else again. Did they take the vows on Charlie's yacht? Even Hollywood wonders

EVERY afternoon, for the past three years, a little meat market on Larchmont Avenue, near Paramount studios in Hollywood, has received a telephone call from a woman ordering a choice New York cut steak.

Sometimes she orders it sent to the Brown Derby, sometimes to an apartment penthouse on Rossmore Street, sometimes to the studio.

Wherever George Raft happens to be dining. The woman who sees that George Raft has his favorite evening meal, no matter where he may be, is Virginia Pine. She is not George's wife, although there's little doubt that she would be if George's long-estranged wife would give him a divorce.

Carole Lombard is not Clark Gable's wife, either. Still she has remodeled her whole Hollywood life for him. She calls him "Pappy," goes hunting with him, copies his hobbies, makes his interests dominate hers.

Barbara Stanwyck is not Mrs. Robert Taylor. But she and Bob have built ranch homes next to each other. Regularly, once a week, they visit Bob's mother, Mrs. Brugh, for dinner. Regularly, once a week, too, Barbara freezes homemade ice cream for Bob from a recipe his mother gave her.

Nowhere has domesticity, outside the marital state, reached such a full flower as in Hollywood. Nowhere are there so many famous unmarried husbands and wives.

To the outside world Clark Gable and Carole Lombard might as well be married. So might Bob Taylor and Barbara. Or George Raft and Virginia Pine, Charlie Chaplin and Paulette Goddard. Unwed couples they might be termed. But they go everywhere together; do everything in pairs. No hostess would think of inviting them separately, or pairing them with another. They solve one another's problems, handle each other's business affairs.

They build houses near each other, buy land in bunches, take up each other's hobbies, father or mother each other's children—even correct each other's clothes—each other's personalities! Yet, to the world, their official status is "just friends." No more.

Yet George Raft, a one-woman man if there ever was one, is as true to Virginia Pine as a model husband would be. He has been, for three years. He has just bought her an expensive home in Beverly Hills. Recently, when they had a slight tiff, George took out some other girls, but was plainly so torch-burdened he could hardly stand it. He has never seriously looked at anyone else. Nor has Virginia.

Consider the results—strictly out of wedlock.

Before they met and fell in love, George was the easiest "touch" in Hollywood. He made big and easy money and just so easily did it slip through his fingers and into the outstretched palms of his myriad down-and-out friends. George, who came up the hard way, still has a heart as big as a casaba melon and as soft inside. But he is more careful with his money now. He invests it—and well.

Before he met Virginia, George's civic interests ventured little further than Hollywood and Vine, the fights, and a few of the hotter night spots. Now George Raft has his finger in a dozen Los Angeles business ventures and community interests. He is a solid citizen.

Before George and Virginia teamed up as a tight little twosome, George gloried in flashy, extremely-cut clothes. His suits, always immaculately knife-edge creased, had trousers with the highest waistlines in town. His coats were tight across the shoulders, narrowed extremely at the waist. His shoes were narrow, pointed and Cuban-heeled. He was Mister Broadway.

Virginia talked him into seeing Watson, one of Hollywood's most exclusive tailors. What's more, she talked him out of the theatrical clothes and into a more conservative taste.

All this is called "settling down." It usually happens to people after they've been married. Only George and Virginia still aren't married. He lives at the El Royale Apartments and Virginia lives in another building up the street. They just go together. But she orders his meals. And he spoils her little girl to death.

Gilbert Roland (top) has been Connie Bennett's devoted slave for years, while Connie's titled husband remains in Europe. Just "going together" are Virginia Pine and George Raft—but she orders his meals and he fathers her little daughter, Joan

Another "almost perfect" domestic picture—Barbara Stanwyck (top, with her son Dion) and Robert Taylor. Interests—deep, expensive, permanent—merged when Bob bought the knoll adjoining Barbara's Northridge ranch. Marriage couldn't have worked more of a change

No real father could be more infatuated than George with Virginia's five-year-old daughter, Joan. Nor would you call George the perfect picture of a family man, either. He has already paid up an insurance policy that will guarantee Joan a nice little stake when she is ready for college. He seems to lie awake nights planning something new and delightful to surprise her with whenever he sees Virginia, and that's usually all the time.

One of the stories the salesgirls still tell down at Bullock's-Wilshire, Los Angeles' swankiest store, is about the day Virginia Pine and little Joan came into the shop. Joan spied something she wanted right then. But Virginia, wishing to impress upon her daughter that a person isn't always able to have what he or she likes in this world, said, "But, Joan, you can't have that. You haven't the money to pay for it."

"Oh, that's all right," stated Joan in a loud, clear voice. "Just charge it to George Raft!"

When Bob Taylor docked in New York from England and "A Yank At Oxford," he waited around a couple of hours for a load of stuff he had bought over there to clear customs. Most of it was for—not Bob—but Barbara Stanwyck and her little son, Dion.

They've been practically a family since Bob bought his ranch estate in Northridge and built a house there.

Northridge, itself, is an interesting manifestation of how Hollywood's untied twosomes buy and build together. It lies in a far corner of the San Fernando Valley, fairly remote from Hollywood, all of fifteen miles from Bob's studio, Metro-Goldwyn-Mayer. No coincidence can possibly explain his choosing that site, pleasant and open though it is, right beside Barbara Stanwyck's place.

Barbara was there first. With the Zeppo Marxes, she established Marwyck Ranch to breed thoroughbred horses. She built a handsome ranch house and moved out. Bob Taylor had never been especially interested in either ranch life or horses until he started going with Barbara. But witness how quickly their interests—deep and expensive, *permanent* interests

—merged after they slipped into the unique Hollywood habit. Marriage couldn't have worked more of a change.

Bob bought the acres next to Barbara's ranch. He started putting up a ranch house within a good stone's throw of hers. He bought horses. He spent every minute of his spare time working on the place. Overnight, he turned into a country squire. When, in the middle of it all, he was called to England, the work never stopped. Barbara supervised it. While Bob was away she ordered the things she knew he wanted. She oversaw the decoration and furnishing of the place. It was all ready when Bob came home.

Bob's house and Barbara's house stand now on adjoining knolls. The occupants ride together and work together and play there together in their time off. Bob trained and worked out for "The Crowd Roars" on Barbara's ranch. Almost every evening, after work at the studio or on the ranch, he runs over for a plunge in her pool.

If it isn't fight night—they've long had permanent seats together at the Hollywood Legion Stadium—or if they're not asked to a party—they're always invited together, just like man and wife—they spend a quiet evening together at either one or the other's place.

Or if Bob has a preview of his picture, Barbara goes with him to tell him what she thinks of it, and vice versa. Bob saw "Stella Dallas" four times. Once he caught it in London and bawled so copiously that when he came out and a kid asked him for his autograph he couldn't see to sign it! But he was a long way away from Barbara then.

When he's home, he's a little more critical. But never of Barbara's ice cream. Bob has never forgotten his Nebraska boyhood ecstasy licking the dasher of an ice cream freezer. That's why Barbara whips him up a bucketful every week, before they roll off to see the folks.

All in all, it's an almost perfect domestic picture. But no wedding rings in sight!

Even gifts and expressions of sentiment take on the practical, utilitarian aspect of old married folks' remembrances when these Hollywood single couples come across. Just as Dad gives Mother an electric icebox for Christmas and she retaliates with a radio, Bob Taylor presents Barbara Stanwyck with a tennis court on her birthday, with Barbara giving Bob a two-horse auto trailer for his!

THE gifts Carole Lombard and Clark Gable have exchanged are even more unorthodox. Whoever heard of a woman in love with a man giving him a gun for Christmas! Or a man, crazy about one of the most glamorous, sophisticated and clever women in the land, hanging a gasoline scooter on her Christmas tree!

For Clark, Carole stopped, almost overnight, being a Hollywood playgirl. People are expected to change when they get married. The necessary adaptation to a new life and another personality shows up in every bride and groom. All Clark and Carole did was strike up a Hollywood twosome. Nobody said "I do!"

Clark Gable doesn't like night spots, or parties, social chit-chat, or the frothy pretensions of society. He has endured plenty of it, but it makes him fidget.

Carole, quite frankly, used to eat it up. She hosted the most charming and clever parties in town. She knew every-

body, went everywhere. When the ultra exclusive and late lamented Mayfair Club held its annual ball, Carole was picked to run things. It was Carole who decreed the now famous "White Mayfair" that Norma Shearer crossed up so wickedly by coming in flaming scarlet—an idea you later saw dramatized by Bette Davis in "Jezebel."

These things were the caviar and cocktails of Carole Lombard's life—before she started going with Gable. But look what happened—

Clark didn't like it, Carole found out—quickly. What did he like? Well, outside of hunting in wild country white men seldom entered, and white women never, he like to shoot skeet. Shooting skeet, of course, is an intricate scoring game worked out on the principle of trapshooting. It involves banging away at crazily projected clay pigeons with a shotgun.

Carole learned to shoot skeet—not only learned it but, with the intense proficiency with which she attacks anything, rapidly became one of the best women skeet shooters in the country!

Gable liked to ride, so Carole got herself a horse and unpacked her riding things.

He liked tennis, so she resurrected her always good court game, taking lessons from Alice Marble, her good friend and the present national women's champion. Playing with a man, Carole had to get good and she did—so good that now Clark can't win a set!

It goes on like that. Clark, tiring of hotel life, moved out to a ranch in the San Fernando Valley. What did Lombard do? She bought a Valley ranch!

Carole has practically abandoned all her Hollywood social contacts. She doesn't keep up with the girls in gossip as she used to. She doesn't throw parties that hit the headlines and the picture magazines. She and Clark are all wrapped up in each other's interests. While Gable did all the night work in "Too Hot To Handle," Carole, though working, too, was on his set every night. She caught the sneak preview with him

and told him with all the candor of the little woman, "It's hokum, Pappy—but the *most excellent* hokum!"

Like any good spouse might do, Carole has ways and means of chastening Clark, too. When she's mad at him she wears a hat he particularly despises. Carole calls it her "hate hat."

Their fun now, around town, is almost entirely trips, football games, fights and shows. Their stepping-out nights usually end up at the home of Director Walter Lang and his new wife, Madalynne Fields, "Fieldsie," Carole's bosom pal and long-time secretary. They sit and play games!

Yes, Carole Lombard is a changed woman since she tied up with Clark Gable.

But her name is still Carole Lombard.

THE altar record, in fact, among Hollywood's popular twosomes is suprisingly slim.

Usually something formidable stands in the way of a marriage certificate when Hollywood stars pair up minus a preacher.

In Clark and Carole's case, of course, there is a very sound legal barrier. Clark is still officially a married man. Every now and then negotiations for a divorce are started, but, until something happens in court, Ria Gable is still the only wife the law of this land allows Clark Gable.

George Raft can't marry Virginia Pine for the very same good reason; he has a wife. Every effort he has made for his freedom has failed.

Some of them, like Constance Bennett and Gilbert Roland, go in a perfect design for living, apparently headed for perpetual fun with each other. Connie maintains one of the most luxurious setups of them all, with a titled husband in Europe and Gilbert Roland her devoted slave in Hollywood. Years have passed and the arrangement seems to please everybody as much now as it did at the start. Why should it ever break up?

On the other hand, the unmarried partners sometimes get a divorce—or at least a separation, a recess, a moratorium—whatever you care to call it. Calling the case of Charlie Chaplin and Paulette Goddard requires more than a bunch of handy nouns.

No one has ever been able yet to say definitely whether or not the gray-haired Charlie and his young, vivacious Paulette were ever married. Such things as public records exist for just such purposes, of course, but in spite of the fact that none can be unearthed, a strong belief hovers around Hollywood that Charlie and Paulette did actually take the vows, some say on his yacht out at sea.

But when, a few months back, Charlie was seen more and more in the company of other young ladies and Paulette began stepping out with other men, an unusually awkward contretemps was brewed. What was it? The breaking up of a love affair? Or the separation of a marriage? If a divorce was to be had, there had to have been a marriage. But was there? Charlie wouldn't talk; neither would Paulette. Hollywood relapsed into a quandary. It's still there as concerns the Chaplin-Goddard unmarried marriage. Meanwhile, both Charlie and Paulette seem to be having a good time with whomever they fancy. But the interesting thing is that Paulette still entertains her guests, when she wishes, on Charlie Chaplin's yacht. So maybe she has an interest in it that a mere separation couldn't efface.

THE most tragic, as well as perhaps the most tender match of them all gave way to an irresistible rival wooer, Death. At the time of Jean Harlow's untimely passing, she and William Powell had reached an understanding that excluded any one else from either's thoughts. Both had fought for happiness in Hollywood without finding it, until they found each other. Then Death stole Jean away and Bill has never recovered from the effect of that stunning blow.

There was only Jean Harlow's family, her doctor and William Powell in her hospital room the night she lost her fight for life. Jean died in Bill's arms.

In every way since, he has acted as a son-in-law to Jean's mother. He bought the crypt where Jean lies today and arranged for perpetual flowers. This year, on the anniversary of her passing, Bill Powell and Mrs. Bello, Jean's mother, went alone to visit Jean's resting place. He sent Mrs. Bello on a trip to Bermuda last winter to recover from the severe grief she has suffered since Jean's death. She visited Bill regularly during his recent spell in the hospital. Both have one regret—that Bill and Jean never got to be man and wife.

And that, it seems, would point a lesson to the unique coterie of Hollywood's unwed couples—Bob Taylor and Barbara Stanwyck, who could get married if they really wanted to; George Raft and Virginia Pine, Carole Lombard and Clark Gable and the other steady company couples who might swing it if they tried a little harder. You can't take your happiness with you.

For nobody, not even Hollywood's miracle men, has ever improved on the good old-fashioned, satisfying institution of holy matrimony. And, until something better comes along, the best way to hunt happiness when you're in love in Hollywood or anywhere else—is with a preacher, a marriage license and a bagful of rice.

M-G-M's reputation for smart showmanship advances another notch with their release during the holidays of Charles Dickens' "A Christmas Carol." Reginald Owen takes the rôle of crusty Scrooge; Terry Kilburn, as Tiny Tim (in doorway) will give the traditional happy blessing, "Merry Xmas to you all—God bless us every one"

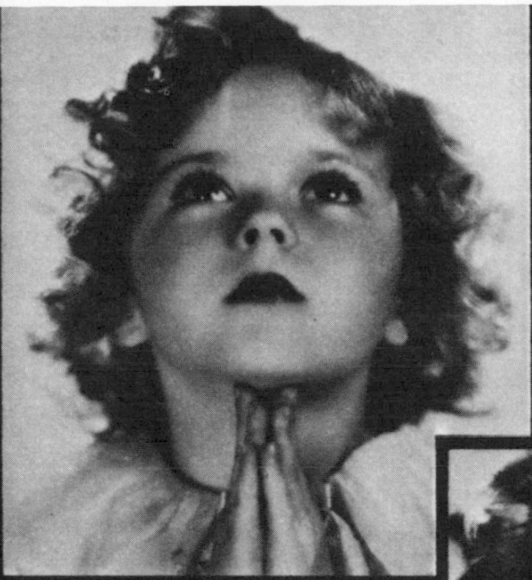

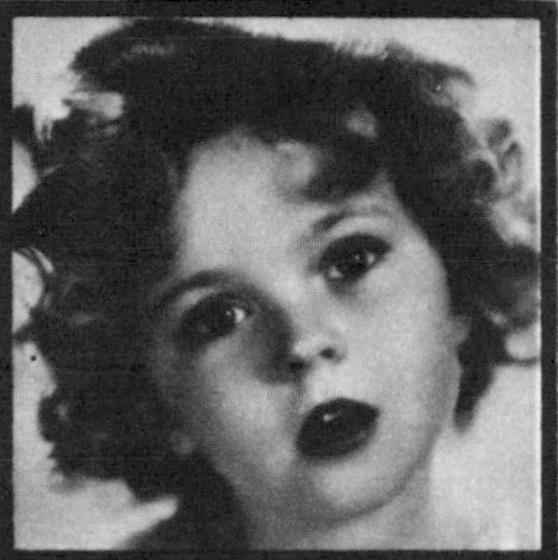

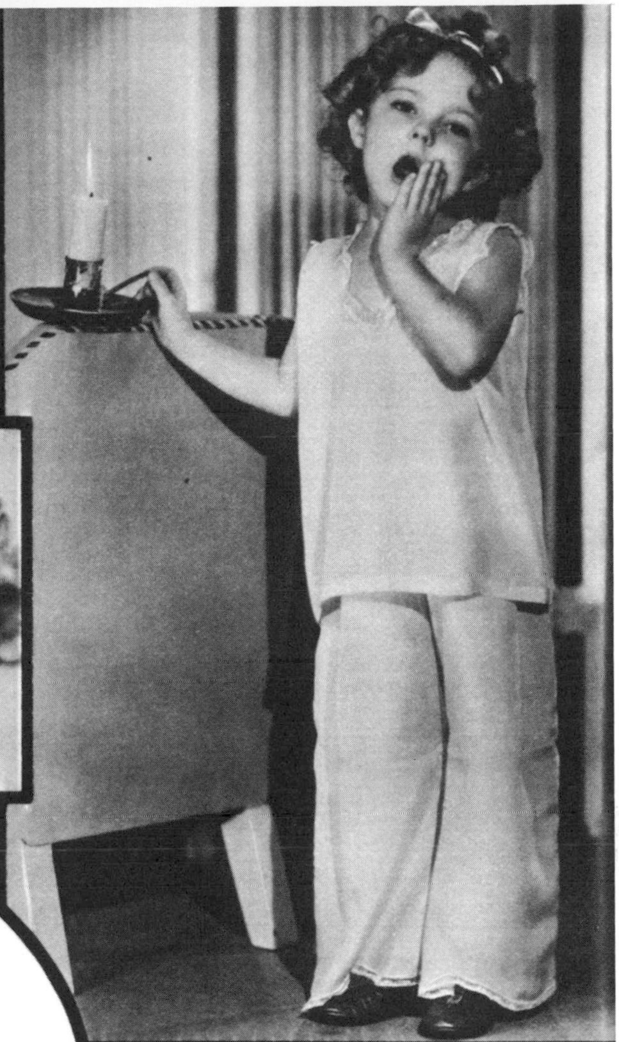

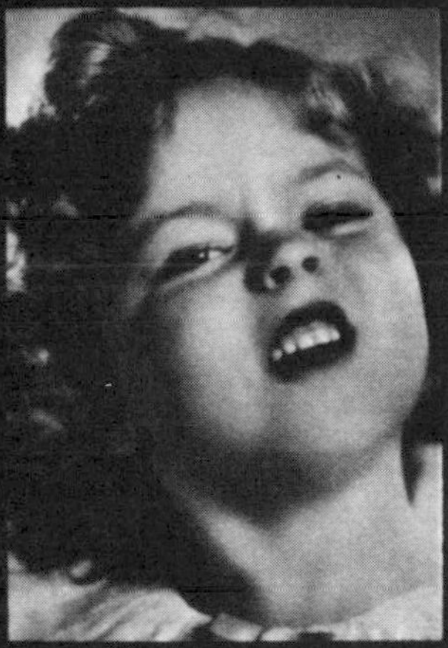

207

SHIRLEY TEMPLE is cute any way you take her. The photographer told her to be a good little girl, so she looked angelic. But she can, just as delightfully, pout or play at the art of the coquette (they're never too young!). Shirley willingly posed at the studio, but when the cameraman came into her garden, interrupting her romp—*that* wasn't so nice. As for having pictures taken at bedtime, Shirley just yawned at that

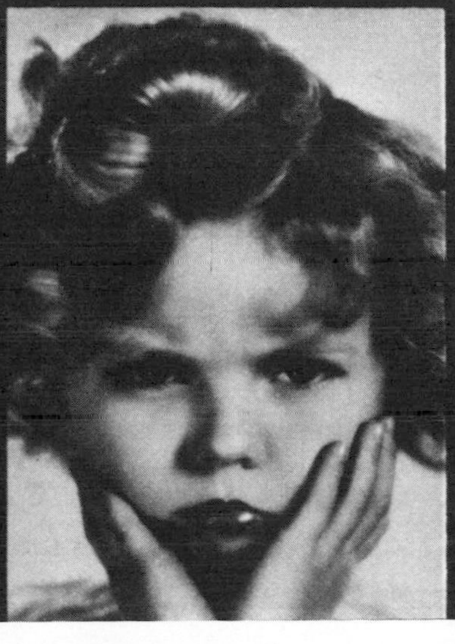

MICKEY

THE McCOY

Rough and tough and hard to bluff is

Mickey Rooney, the one kid in Holly-

wood who has all the answers ready

BY KIRTLEY BASKETTE

WHEN the scene was over, Gladys George turned to the little, impudent, yellow-headed guy who had stolen it. With a quizzical frown she said,

"You're starting that a little early in life, aren't you?"

Mickey Rooney grinned as politely as he could. If he had followed his natural inclinations and stuck strictly to facts he might have answered like this: "Shake yourself loose there, Toots. Whaddaya mean, starting early? This is old stuff for me. After five hundred pictures, pinchin' scenes comes natural. Now less gab on the set and let's get this in the can. I'm a busy man."

From a brief spot as a midget with Colleen Moore in "Orchids and Ermine" to star billing in "Love Finds Andy Hardy" spans Mickey Rooney's amazing Hollywood career. He was four then; he's seventeen now. He's never stopped making pictures; he's never stopped making money; he's never stopped making everybody with him step lively to keep in the picture. He's never stopped being Mickey Rooney, either, which means he's never stopped being boy, and plenty of it.

THE first time I saw the spunky little mug was at a big benefit performance one night in the Shrine Auditorium in Los Angeles. Nobody knew much about him then, although he'd already starred in almost three hundred kid comedy movies. On the other hand, everybody was bowing to the talent of a popular boy star. Both were on the bill. The kid star came out first, in his best precious child manner, prancing and smirking. He was delicious—and he was a flop.

Then Mickey, about as big as a cigarette butt and every bit as unpretentious, shot out of the wings. He didn't fool around; he was as direct as a kick in the pants. With the same little croaking, husky voice he has today—it's never changed—he launched into his patter; he sang, he danced, he jawed with the audience—he wowed 'em. He made the kid star look like a cream puff somebody had stepped on.

Mickey Rooney has been doing the same devastating thing to the precocity parade, on the set and off, ever since. Because, in the first place, he's one of the most genuine little artists in Hollywood, because he's a veteran, because he knows the answers, all of them, and because he's no mama's boy trailing apron strings daintily behind him.

He's Mickey (Himself) McGuire, rough and tough and hard to bluff, which isn't so strange

Even back in 1932 he dared to pull the famous Rooney trick on Tom Mix

Seven or seventeen, Mickey can still give such stars as Gladys George (top) a bad headache in the movie-making job

when you realize seven years of his childhood were spent bringing Fontaine Fox's tough little neighborhood terror cartoon character to the screen. When most current kiddie screen wonders were building blocks or playing paper dolls, Mickey was swaggering around in oversize button shoes under a massive derby hat, a cigar tilted in his tiny trap, slapping the stuffings out of the rest of the kids in Larry Darmour's kid comedies. In fact, Mickey's name was once officially Mickey McGuire, until the cartoonist Fox objected legally to having his thunder stolen. Then they changed it to Rooney.

His name is really Yule, Joe Yule, Jr.— "Sonny" Yule, as the vaudeville and burlesque folks used to know it.

Mickey's folks were vaudeville people. His mother, Nell Brown, danced; his dad, Joe Yule, was a funny man. He still is, often performing in Los Angeles burlesque shows on Main Street, only a few miles from his famous kid in Culver City. Mickey now lives with his mother, who runs a restaurant on Wilshire Boulevard.

Mickey has stuck up for himself ever since the day he crawled onto the stage, where his folks were cavorting, and sneezed. The tank-town audience yowled with glee, so his dad stuck a French harp in his little paws and Mickey was in show business. He's never been out of it since.

But a lot of film has spun over the reels since they drafted the swaddling Mickey from Will Morrisey's Revue to play a grown-up midget in pictures. So many thousands of feet of it have registered Mickey's snub-nosed pan in a half a thousand movies that you'd need an adding machine to count it up.

I CAN remember the little snipe stealing a picture called "My Pal the King," right in the face of Tom Mix's two six-shooters. Maybe it discouraged Tom. It was one of the last pictures he tried. And I could see half-pint Mickey, whip in hand, strutting around the rank-smelling set of Clyde Beatty's "The Big Cage," baiting lions and tigers roaring helplessly in their cages. And training a lion cub, the same cub, "Tarzan," who later grew up and bit Charles Bickford in the neck, just to get even with the human race.

And then Max Reinhardt and his raves, calling Mickey Rooney the perfect *Puck* for Shakespeare's "A Midsummer Night's Dream." And Mickey, forthwith, scooting a toboggan down the mountain slopes at Big Pines in the middle of production and cracking his thigh in two. They said it was tough for the kid to give up that great part to little George Breakstone who substituted. But nobody has ever heard of George since; and Mickey is still very much around.

Forty pictures he has made in the last year and a half. Fighting Freddie Bartholomew pretty even in "Little Lord Fauntleroy," "The Devil Is a Sissy," "Captains Courageous" and "Lord Jeff." Going to town to the tune of nation-wide approval in "Love Finds Andy Hardy." Everywhere drawing the professional praise of directors, other stars, critics. But what had happened to Mickey Rooney personally, I didn't know. He must have grown up by now, I thought. Good Heavens! He might have even turned into a young gentleman!

MICKEY said, sure, come on out for lunch.

Maybe you, like me, have been under the impression Metro-Goldwyn-Mayer was owned by the Schencks, Louis B. Mayer and a few thousand scattered stockholders. Let me correct you: Mickey Rooney owns the joint. He strode ahead to the commissary, all the five feet, one inch of him, solid as mahogany, tough as hickory; cocky and strutting. If you have ever watched kid stars mince self-consciously about studio lots hand-in-hand with loving parents or doting relatives you'll realize what a welcome relief is Mickey Rooney's assertive get-along.

People passed, front office big shots, directors, stars, grips, props, gaffers, mugs. "Hi, Butch!" signalled Mickey. "Nutsy, boy!" "Yah, Fred—how'djuh come out on that third race?"

"A great gang around this lot," confided Mickey. "Regular Jo's."

In the commissary we brushed by Clark Gable and Spencer Tracy, at a table. "Hi, boys," said Mickey. Then to me, "A couple of pretty good actors."

Above the clatter of plates and dishes and excited hum which is a studio beanery at noon, Mickey Rooney, seventeen, held forth on the really important goings-on of life as he found them.

"Women," stated Mickey flatly, "are the bunk. Nuts to 'em."

I thought of Tarkington's tortured "Seventeen" and sighed. But, of course, Hollywood's no small town.

"Yeah," croaked the Mick, "a lotta janes did me wrong—so nuts to 'em. The boys and me decided to give 'em the atmosphere. We play poker and pal around, you know, just the boys."

The waitress came up. Mickey slipped her a loving pat. "I'll have the salad, dear," said Mickey, seventeen.

"Okay, honey," said the waitress, thirty-five.

"I'm in training," offered Mickey, explaining the salad. "It's awful — no fancy foods, no dissipation—can't even shave."

The training to which he referred was for the Big Game, Sunday. It was a sell-out, he said; he'd been peddling tickets all over the lot for weeks, and training like an acrobat. His team, Mickey Rooney's M-G-M Lions, stacked up against the Sequoia Panthers, another kid outfit. Wayne Morris was to be head linesman, Gene Autry, field judge and Jackie Coogan, umpire; it was all set to be the battle of the Century. The newsboys got the gate receipts.

M-G-M had forked out six hundred frogskins for uniforms and Clark Gable had promised to show up and lead a cheer or something. Mickey, of course, was the quarterback.

"Then it's true," I ventured, "that Freddie Bartholomew's going to play a blocking back as advertised?"

"Haw, haw," chortled Mickey. "Him? Say, this is a *real* game. That," he confided, sotto voce, "is just publicity." He winked. I winked.

Mickey has always been unusually active in extra-studio shebangs. He used to have a peewee football team, three or four years ago, that ran out on the field between the Los Angeles professional gridiron games. He had a twelve-piece jazz band once. He was junior Ping-pong champ of something or other the last time I heard. He used to dodge around the L. A. Tennis Club cooking up this and that. It was a sight to see him batting balls against six-foot Lester Stoefen.

"Yeah," said Mickey, and his tone was slightly wistful. "You see, if I didn't do those things, I'd miss the fun the rest of the kids get. I never got to go to public school. I was always making pictures, studying on the lot. I had to stir things up—or, well, I guess I'd have been pretty lonesome."

He's always got what he wanted though, even if it took some stirring. When Mickey was just a little squirt around eleven he had ambitions for an

A Queen of the Screen rode pickaback on a Queen of the Stage when Shirley Temple was guest of honor at a tea given by Gertrude Lawrence on her recent holiday in Bermuda

automobile. His mother thought he was much too young, which he was, and that he'd surely kill himself in a car. So, instead, she handed him fifteen dollars for a bicycle. In a few days, Mickey showed up, not with a bike, but a car. He'd scoured the old car lots and found one—for fifteen bucks!

Mickey speared a sheaf of lettuce. "I've always been a little guy," he said. "I guess I'll never be much bigger; my folks were little. But," he brightened, "maybe I'm lucky at that. I've never been shoved out of the money like a lot of kids when they got awkward. I got the nicest flock of annuities you ever saw."

One, continued Mickey, pays him $750 a month when he's twenty-one and $1000 a month when he's thirty, which ain't exactly hay.

"Sure," said Mickey, slightly piqued when I put the question, "I handle my own dough—what you think I am—a baby? Listen, I've always worn long pants. Never had a pair of bloomers on in my life!"

Another nice thing about being a perpetual peewee, said Mickey, was that you could get away with murder with the dames. He made hot love to Patricia Ellis without any kicks when he was only thirteen — on the screen of course.

"But girls are out now," reaffirmed Mickey. "I'm through with 'em."

A lovely little dream with caramel hair and big round eyes sat down at the next table. The M-G-M commissary is always crammed with startling unknown bit-and-extra beauties. Mickey halted his fork halfway to the hopper.

"U-m-m-m-m," he said. "Would I like her for Christmas!"

HIS pals, Mickey informed me, were assorted—Frankie Darro; a bunch of boys' names I didn't know, Woody Van Dyke, the director, and Spencer Tracy. No gals. Judy Garland? "Just the old build-up," assured Mickey. "Don't you believe it. I haven't got any time for kids. Listen, I work."

He figured it out. He averaged a picture and a half a month or more. But, at that, it was a cinch, Mickey said.

"I never study any scripts at home," he scoffed. "A lot of guys do, but that's a lot of spinach."

A studio scenarist passed by our table. Mickey collared him. "Say," he said, "about that script. I read it over the other day and my part looks a little weak. Now here's what I thought—"

They argued it earnestly for five minutes.

"The trouble with living, though," said Mickey, returning to me, "is the twists. Too many dames hanging around."

"Dessert?" said the waitress.

"Well now, dear," replied Mickey, staring boldly across the hall, "if you could bring me that cutie over there with the streamlined gams and that come-hither look for dessert, I might talk business."

The waitress giggled. She said the cutie wasn't on the menu—only chocolate, strawberry and vanilla ice cream and the pudding.

"No dice," croaked Mickey. He rose. "Well," he informed me, "I've gotta go. Think I'll drop some money with the bookies this afternoon. You got the dope on me, haven't you?"

"Sure," I said.

"Swell," approved Mickey. "Just say I'm a regular guy with a regular gang, that's all. Say I can take care of myself all right. And—say that as far as I'm concerned—dames are the bunk!"

"Oh, sure," I agreed. "The bunk—absolutely."

Mickey shook hands. "Well, so long," he said.

He whirled and shot through the broken field of tablecloths; waitresses dodged nimbly to one side. Two little blonde extras at one table inched their chairs over nervously as Mickey passed. In their eyes were looks of mild terror.

And in mine, I'm sure, was a happy reassured gleam. Neither the years nor the movies had softened up the one genuine tough little nut in Hollywood. Seventeen or seven, he was still Mickey (himself) McGuire, rough and tough and hard to bluff. Mickey Rooney is still Mickey the McCoy. And nobody knows it better than himself.

A Garland

Judy with her earliest accompanist—her mother

The son they had hoped for turned out to be a third little daughter— but few men achieve more laurels

BY DIXIE WILLSON

"Francis Gumm Jr." at the age of six months

FOR JUDY

THE evening issue of the Grand Rapids, Minnesota *Independent* for June 10, 1922, announces the birth of Francis Gumm, Jr., describing the event as presenting young Mr. Francis Gumm, owner and manager of the local New Grand Theater, with his third . . . daughter.

Just a superfluous young lady for a close-planning little family wanting nothing if not a boy. Besides which the new baby was red-headed, pug-nosed and even her mother admitted she was homely. Rather a secondhand setup for the third little Gumm girl. But witness June 10, 1940. Francis Gumm, Jr., in Hollywood, walking straight into stardom, possessing a home in exclusive Bel Air, her own swimming pool, badminton court and cream-colored roadster. The third little Gumm girl, doing all right for herself after all! And here, if you will, is the story:

Way back in 1913, Frank and Ethel Gumm, an old married couple of two anniversaries, contributed to vaudeville, an act billed, atmospherically, as Jack and Virginia Lee, Sweet Southern Singers. But time came when the pending arrival of a son and heir (who would of course be named Francis Jr.) called for the cancellation of bookings, whereupon the young Gumms acquired the New Grand Theater in pleasant little Grand Rapids, Minnesota, and took up just plain old-fashioned domestic life.

The cradle was filled quite as per schedule, excepting that the name decided upon was Mary Jane. Which was all right too. Every family wants a girl sooner or later. But it was a glad day five years later when the nursery was trimmed in new blue ribbons. For now Francis Gumm, Jr., was unmistakably on his way.

Little Brother, however, pulled a fast one this time too. In his stead arrived Virginia. Okay, said Frank and Ethel. But twenty-two months later, when the stork rang up a girl for the third time, they named her Francis, Jr., anyway . . . and called it a day.

A dozen and one years before, young Frank Gumm, just graduated from Sewanee University, had left a Southern home to spend a summer vacation in Superior, Wisconsin where, quite to his surprise he got a job singing in a movie. And found pretty Miss Ethel Milne playing the theater piano. Not long afterward, he married her. And billing themselves as Jack and Virginia Lee just because that sounded the way they thought it ought to, they made their debut in vaudeville.

It appears, however, that in Gumm family history, the debut of real importance happened some eleven years later, when, in Grand Rapids, Minnesota, their third daughter, at the age of thirty months, sang "Jingle Bells" on her father's Christmas theater program. After the "Jingle Bells" episode, it was plain to be seen that, behind the footlights, the baby certainly knew her stuff. And when that same baby was five, Virginia seven, Mary Jane twelve, Mama and Daddy Gumm found themselves parents to a singing dancing trio which could stop *anybody's* show!

Now the Gumms had always wanted to live in California. So one fine day they sold the New Grand, packed up their two-seated Ford, took Granny Milne along, and soon found themselves snugly settled in Los Angeles on one of those endless little streets of California bungalows as like as cupcakes on a shelf. The plan was to buy a theater in some propinquant town. But when six months became twelve and Frank Gumm was still looking for a deal, the dwindling bank account made it less and less possible. And so Mrs. Gumm, having felt strongly all along that she owed it to the children to do something about their talent, had this added reason to try and find out if they could really turn "professional."

She made them costumes and routined a program; three little stairsteps, with Mother at the piano. They did the act for an agent. He was

"The Glum Sisters" (Mary Jane, Francis and Virginia) before they became "The Three Garlands" (Suzanne, Judy, Jinny). Left, five-year-old Judy in the costume she wore that day at Chicago's Oriental

enthusiastic; could book them without any trouble, he was sure. He'd call soon.

They went home in breathless excitement, practiced hard, made new more professional wardrobes . . . and waited for the phone to ring. A week passed. And six. And ten. And then finally came the call! A dinner was to be given at the Biltmore Hotel and would require entertainment. It was a "civic affair," said the potential hostess, so the entertainers wouldn't be paid a lot . . . but something.

Eagerly excited, the three little Gumms were washed, ironed, curled and rehearsed. The act went over like a million and when the weary little troupe went home at midnight, Big Sister Mary Jane carried their first pay envelope!

They saved the exciting moment of opening it, however, to share with Dad. Gathering around their own dining-room table, at last, three flushed and thrilled little girls, and proud Mr. and Mrs. Gumm, prepared for the surprise . . . and got it. The check was for $1.50 for an entire evening's entertainment!

BUT from that night on, the girls didn't give their mother a moment's peace. They wanted to be singing and dancing, and that was that . . . and then suddenly and unexpectedly Frank Gumm began to fail in health. Suddenly the dancing feet of his three little girls became the most important asset the Gumm family possessed.

Week after week they tried for work without success. Then at last came a chance in Denver. Ethel Gumm and the girls unhesitatingly boarded a bus . . . traveled two days and two

nights . . . and stole the show. And were told that if they could but land a booking in Chicago's Oriental, they would really be on their way.

They went on to Chicago. Mrs. Gumm, sending the girls out to find a flat, promptly called at the office of an important agent and asked, as she had been advised to do, for booking in some small suburban house where he could "catch" the act. Denver press notices turned the trick. He booked them then and there for a week at the Belmont, four shows daily with five on Saturday and Sunday.

It was an unimportant house, but since they had staked all they had on this Chicago agent's impression, they went the whole way and counted out enough dollars from Denver to rent for the week a set of real stage costumes and a special curtain. After that . . . not knowing at which show of the week the agent might be in the house, they went out for every performance with their hearts in their throats, their pulses pounding.

The week over, they sat tightly in their little rented flat counting hours until he would call. When he didn't, after four days waiting, Mrs. Gumm called *him*.

He hedged a bit . . . avoided an opinion . . . and said something about her calling in a day or two. However, said he, he couldn't *promise* anything. Dreams faded of crashing the Oriental. Then Mama Gumm tumbled to something. "Now wait a minute," said she to herself. "He doesn't want the girls at all!"

The truth was clear. Chicago just hadn't

bought the act.

Next morning, discouraged, hurt and disappointed they were packing their bags for the long trip home when the telephone rang. It was a gentleman who had seen the act backstage at the Belmont but who hadn't told them, until now, that he was none other than the drummer at the Oriental!

Now he was calling to say that an act which had been sour in the morning rehearsal had just been fired. If they could get there fast enough, the manager would hear them sing . . . .

That afternoon the trio faced the Oriental audience and took it hook, line and sinker! That night they stayed awake fairly all night long to dream about morning, for their name was to be in lights! They went downtown very early to see it. Sure enough there it was. No mistake about it . . . no mistake, excepting that what the lights spelled was . . . "The Glum Sisters."

Mr. George Jessel was the week's m.c.

"That's bad," he said to Mrs. Gumm. "These girls are going places. They'll be called the Dumb sisters and the Bum sisters and the Rum sisters and you better pick a new name right now." He looked up from his morning paper. "Now here's the columnist Robert Garland," he said. "What's the matter with that for a name?"

There was nothing the matter with it at all. The girls loved it. And so the Gumms became the Garlands . . . just like that.

"Well, if we're fixing our names over," said Mary Jane, "why don't we fix our first ones too? Why can't I be Suzanne?"

"And I could be Jinny," said the middle-sized Miss Gumm.

"And I could be Judy," put in Francis.

So lights which that morning had spelled "The Glum Sisters," that afternoon spelled "The Three Garlands," who were no longer Francis, Virginia and Mary Jane, but Judy, Jinny and Suzanne.

THE girls worked the next week in Detroit, then in Indianapolis, then in Kansas City. And everybody loved them. And now, their talent proven, their mother wanted to go home to Dad and California. Surely *now* the girls would find engagements there.

So back home they went. And they *did* find engagements.

"I don't know anything about numerology," Mrs. Gumm says, in telling the story, "but after we changed their names they never stopped."

The following summer brought them a season's contract at Lake Tahoe. Judy, who was now thirteen, was the star of the troupe, her singing voice poignant and unforgettable.

The season closed. The last day came. The Garlands piled everything into their car and started home. Then discovered that Jinny had left her hatbox. Of course it was little sister Judy who went back. The Lodge was deserted excepting for the manager and a young composer who had dropped in to telephone. A third gentleman was there too, an agent. In the huge empty room the voices of the three echoed across the open grand piano, the composer running his fingers over the keys.

Judy trudged across the porch, her arms encircling a scarlet hatbox.

"Now there's a kid you ought to get hold of," remarked the manager to the agent. "She can sing and I don't mean maybe."

He called her in and asked her to do a number. She was very willing but didn't see how she could do it since Mother was out in the car and couldn't play for her.

"Maybe I'll do," offered the composer. "Maybe you can sing a number *I* know."

"My favorite is 'Dinah,'" said Judy. "Would that be all right?"

"Quite all right," said the man at the piano, and the accompaniment he gave her was supercolossal!

Though Judy didn't know it until weeks later, he was Mr. Harry Axt, "Dinah" his own hit song.

The agent went along with Judy to speak to her mother; wanted to know why a little singer like this wasn't in pictures.

"I've never thought she was pretty enough," said Judy's mother frankly.

"Well you never can tell," remarked the agent. "Better come in and see me in Los Angeles tomorrow."

But the Garlands didn't go. Somehow they hadn't too much confidence in agents.

Three days later Mrs. Gumm, returning home late in the afternoon from shopping, found Judy in rumpled gray slacks, a dirt-smudged face, a gingham shirt with the tail outside, in which make-up she was energetically raking the lawn.

Her mother asked about supper . . . had there been any phone calls . . . and how was Daddy feeling.

"He's feeling pretty happy," grinned Judy. "He took me out to M-G-M today. The agent came after us."

"You didn't go looking like *this*!" interrupted Mrs. Gumm.

"Yes, Mother," said Judy, "and I got a contract for seven years."

(The only contract ever given on the M-G-M lot with neither screen nor sound tests.)

That was October. In November Frank Gumm died, taking with him the joy of remembering that he and his little namesake had together taken the first step toward what was certain to be a real career.

AN M-G-M contract. But even now, success was a weary day away. There were months of waiting, of doubt and concern. After a long while she was given a small picture role. Then a part of a little more importance . . . the sincerity, the genius of her work were unmistakable. And at last "The Wizard of Oz," one of the most expensive Hollywood pictures ever made, was bought and planned as a vehicle in which to present her as a star!

Judy Garland had arrived!

* * *

She works harder than most eighteen-year-olds; has to go to bed early to be fresh for work and on the lot for make-up at six a. m., but Judy is so happy she can't believe it. She is keen about working with Mickey Rooney. They know each other so well, she explains, that each of them always knows exactly what the other is going to do.

"Last year was wonderful," she said. "This one will be even better because I'm older. It's grand to be getting older," she said with real feeling.

The family is still together . . . or very *near* together. Jinny, married to Bandleader Bob Sherwood, is his singer, and the mother of two-year-old Judith Gail. Suzanne, turning out to be the domestic member of the family, designs the family clothes, sews, gardens, knits . . . and loves it. The trio of sisters is still devoted and still quite likely to go into a song and dance when you least expect it.

But best of all Judy, now deluged with success, still finds her thrills in just simple, pleasant things. As we visited, the maid brought long tall glasses of orange juice with bright napkins and straws. There is plenty of orange juice in California. Judy is constantly showered with attentions. But this little unsolicited thoughtfulness brought spontaneous appreciation into her eyes.

"Oh boy," she said. "Thanks, Leola."

It was nearly four. She had a radio rehearsal at four-thirty. Presently she excused herself, planted a green beret on her auburn hair, and bade us goodby.

"Mama," she said, "could I have some money?"

"Take two dollars out of my purse," her mother said. "That will be all you'll need the rest of the week."

"Okay, Mom," said the third little Gumm girl, planting a kiss on her mother's chin.

Striding down 1940 she is definitely a star. It has cost her work, hope, discouragement, effort and determination. It isn't easy to keep on trying to convince the world you have talent when nobody really cares whether you have or not. And then, if you break the barrier . . . if, at sixteen, you know the thrill of your name in lights the world around, at seventeen your arrival in New York brings out police to referee your fans, at eighteen your days are a succession of photographs, interviews and press raves . . . it takes plenty of balance not to feel called upon to change the angle of your nose or the height of your bonnet.

And so for Judy who stuck to the ship till the tide came in, worked hard enough to tuck under her arm an Academy award for last year's best juvenile performance, and with it all is still just a natural likeable kid . . . for the third little Gumm girl of Minnesota and Hollywood, we recommend, but definitely, orchids.

The heroine of "A Garland for Judy" at a Cocoanut Grove dinner with the chap she's so keen about working with—Mickey Rooney

HEARTACHES IN T

Great stars, famous socialites and

unknowns — behind these Scarlett

aspirants run tales of broken dreams

BY ADELHEID KAUFMANN

Most likely applicant at present is Paulette Goddard

Now it can be told why Shearer is no longer a candidate

THE greatest woman hunt in all movie history has been going on for more than a year now, and many the heart that has been broken and many the thousands that have been spent.

They are searching for Scarlett O'Hara in "Gone with the Wind" and as yet she is nowhere in sight.

The newspapers have frequently printed headlines over all these months about the signing of this star or that. But those statements were simply dreamed up, usually by the actress' agent, and had no basis in fact.

You have heard stories about Tallulah Bankhead and Margaret Sullavan, of Miriam Hopkins and Bette Davis, of Paulette Goddard, Norma Shearer and Margaret Tallichet, and you have probably read that each of them in turn has been signed for the Selznick production of Margaret Mitchell's novel. Fine reading, but none of it is true.

David Selznick, the producer, wishes it were true that he had his Scarlett. George Cukor, the director, would be delighted to know that the cast question was settled. For everything is set to go. The script is all finished. The costumes have all been designed.

The settings are all ready. Rhett Butler—and more of him later—is close at hand. But Scarlett, that minx, still remains as elusive as she was in the original story.

Behind all this, however, run tales of true heroism, the stories of the girls who have tried for the rôle and failed.

First of all, you must understand that Selznick has had more than a hundred talent scouts searching every part of the country for the right girl. They combed the South, invading every school, every dramatic society, every little club below the Mason-Dixon line.

Added to the professional scouts, there have been the wistful amateur ones, the proud Aunt Nellies and Uncle Zeds of Small-town, who see in their niece, Lilybelle, just the girl to play the rôle. When these amateur scouts reported they had the ideal heroine right in their own homes, or towns, or country, the real talent scouts checked up. Several village debs were put under contract by just this method.

Other youngsters, who weathered the tests of the field talent man, then an interview with Director Cukor, and finally Producer Selznick, were even brought to Hollywood for a while. Besides this, orders were given that any woman, regardless of age or appearance, who either called in person, or even wrote a letter saying she believed she could play Scarlett, should be given an interview.

And out of all this just one girl has emerged with a permanent contract. But it isn't a contract to play Scarlett. Her name is Bebe Anderson and her history is typical. She is the daughter of a real-estate broker in Birmingham, Alabama, where a talent scout discovered her. Bebe, who is in her teens, is five feet two and weighs one hundred pounds. She is not only very pretty but really cute. She is accustomed to admiration, having been voted the prettiest girl in her high-school class, the cutest girl in her freshman class at college, the cutest girl in her sorority, and just this year, her sophomore one, the most glamorous.

Which is just the kind of nice going that gets a girl to Hollywood and makes her stick, if you ask us.

Contrast to the lucky Bebe the tragic bravery of a young Southern girl who continues to haunt the Selznick studio. She came to California with the few pennies she'd managed to save from her small job back home and a stack of clippings from her local paper to the effect that "Gone with the Wind" read like her own life story.

"It would be unfair to cast anyone else as Scarlett when the story was written about me," she will tell you. "Why, everybody down South knows that I'm the real Scarlett O'Hara and that Miss Mitchell got the plot for her book from the facts of my life as told to her by one of my girl friends.

"Of course," she adds magnanimously, "many incidents have been added in the book and the part about the Civil War was put in simply as background. 'Tara' with its avenue of cedars was my grandfather's place."

Her eyes fill with tears whenever she talks of her youngest child, who was killed going over a jump with her Shetland pony, just as Scarlett's child met her death in the book.

"The studio might find an actress with more acting experience for the part but she wouldn't be the real Scarlett," she declares.

The studio has firmly told this deluded girl she isn't right for the rôle, but she hangs around, hoping.

Among the stock qualities found in almost all these aspirants who have Scarlett ambitions are, first, that they have read the book and consider themselves to be "exactly like her." Second, they have a Southern accent and come from Georgia. Third, they are excellent horsewomen, let them tell it, and almost without exceptions, their grandfathers were Southern colonels.

One girl came all the way by bus from Minneapolis to Hollywood to see Director Cukor. She was down to her last penny, but she was more fortunate than the other moneyless girls (and most of them are absolutely broke), in that she had a round-trip ticket in her purse.

"I realize I'm not the Scarlett type," one tall, raw-boned matron from Kentucky offered, when she was ushered into the casting office, "but I would be very valuable as her stand-in, knowing the story as I do."

Or there's the girl who painstakingly studied every character in the book because she felt the studio might hire her as an understudy if they realized she could be dropped into any rôle.

A young girl visitor at the studio, who with a group of others had come out from the East, encountered Director Cukor interviewing a group who wanted various assisting rôles. She confided that she knew she could play Melanie, if not the high-spirited Scarlett. She wanted to give him a reading on the spot.

"I'll tell you what I'll do," the director protested kindly. "I'm going to make a test of another girl, not for Scarlett, but for a small part. I'll throw you in on the other girl's tests background." Later, Leslie Howard happened to see the test and voiced his enthusiasm for the figure in the background. On the strength of this recommendation, an agent immediately called upon the girl to see if she couldn't stay in Hollywood and study in stock. But now the poor girl has no money left.

Many of these inspired arrivals have novel qualifications. Take, for example, the determined girl who had memorized two-thirds of the book. Although it had taken her

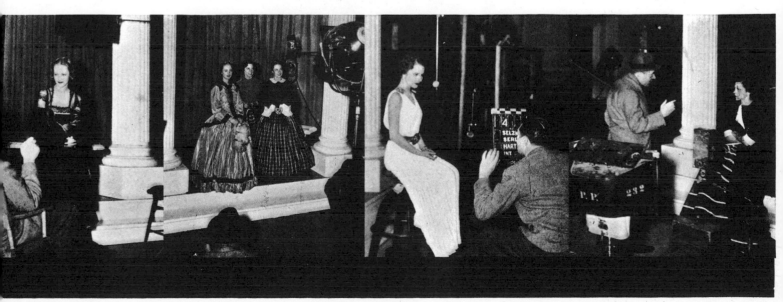

nearly eight months, she knew by heart every direct quote from Scarlett through "Gone with the Wind"'s 1037 pages!

Many couples appear at the studio, too, the man to play Rhett and the wife to play Scarlett. Amusing, too, is the number of social register personages who turn up, debs and matrons alike, wanting a fling at Scarlett's rôle, "Just for a lark," as they embarrassedly explain.

Few seem more eager than the mother of a three-year-old child from Atlanta, who wants her child to play Bonnie. The tiny tot arrived at the studio with petitions signed by State Senators from Georgia and the Governor of Georgia, not to mention the Mayor of Atlanta.

She and her mother have finally returned to their home in the South, but the studio has almost daily reminders of them in the form of the clippings and interviews about their Hollywood experiences and ultimate hopes that they have given out to their home-town papers. One such clipping stated that the child had just received a wire from another leading studio urging her to return to the film city to play a part in a Southern picture. According to these stories "Bonnie" won't consider the offer because she still has hopes of playing Scarlett's daughter and of having Clark Gable for her picture father.

Four hundred school girls came to Los Angeles in a motor caravan from Georgia recently and parked their busses near Director Cukor's offices. He went outside to see what all the racket was about, and remained to pick out eight of the loveliest to whom he gave photographic tests.

Meanwhile, four little girls from the South and two important Hollywood personalities were under direct consideration. The four Southerners were Susan Falligant, Louisa Robert, Alicia Rhett and Adele Longmire. They were all young and very pretty. Miss Falligant is a student at the University of Georgia; Miss Robert, an Atlanta debutante; Miss Rhett, a socialite from Charleston, S. C.; and Miss Longmire, a New Orleans stenographer. Those lucky four emerged triumphant from initial tests in their own home towns, through interviews with George Cukor when he returned from a trip to Europe, on to Hollywood and the eye of the impersonal camera. Nice girls, they were, pretty girls, but after their first little contracts with the studio were up, they were not renewed.

As for the Tallulah Bankhead legend, here is the truth of that, for the first time. Tallulah is a friend of the whole Selznick studio. They all adore her, and when she flew out from New York all on her own and asked for a test they gave it to her. The only thing against Tallulah for the rôle was that brutal fact of age. She could have acted Scarlett magnificently. But no longer did she look the part.

That Norma Shearer was in the running for a while can now be told. Selznick at no time has wanted a star who was under contract to anyone else. But he did consider Norma Shearer in that little interval that existed between the death of Irving Thalberg and Norma's eventual decision to resign with M-G-M. When she did sign up again, the thought of her playing Scarlett was dropped.

Paulette Goddard is now under definite consideration. She looks the rôle, but as yet no contracts have been signed with her. And the search is still going on. At the studio the letters suggesting candidates for the part have long since passed the half million mark —and every one of them, incidentally, has been answered, and each one that came from a hopeful aspirant has been investigated. Photographs flood in, too, tragic ones, funny ones, beautiful ones. They mean potential heartbreak for someone every time they are returned.

And if, after all this about Scarlett, you wonder why there has been so little mention of the search for Rhett, here is the reason.

There are three possible Rhetts, all

Although she's one of those "dam' Yankees," Bette Davis, too, was tested for Scarlett

in Hollywood, and undoubtedly one of the three will play the rôle.

First and foremost, both in popular voting and in the producer's opinion, comes Clark Gable, who is most certainly PHOTOPLAY'S choice, as we've announced. If Gable can be borrowed for the rôle, Selznick will look no further.

If, however, Metro won't let him have Gable, then Gary Cooper or Ronald Colman will be secured.

But there is one little story typical of this whole search that you should know.

A nice-looking young man, and you will understand why we can't reveal his name when you've read this story, sold his interest in a small business back in Tennessee to come to California to play Rhett.

So sure was he that he would be pounced upon for the rôle that he planned to send for his wife and their two tiny children when the good news was announced.

He appeared at the Selznick studios one dog day in midsummer, exhausted and penniless, to claim the rôle of the dashing young Southerner. No, he'd never been on the stage, he admitted to the studio casting office, but deep in his heart he knew he could play the handsome renegade from Charleston better than any actor alive.

It wasn't the customary thing to do but the lad was so touching and had such real personality that they gave him a job in the studio, taking inventory in the stock room.

He accepted the job willingly but lost none of his hopefulness at getting the expected "chance."

His little family soon joined him in Hollywood. They were rather happy about it all, too, until that heartbreaking day when the pretty young mother was bathing their tiny baby, while their little boy played near by.

It all happened in an instant. The two-year-old toddled over to the window, the screen fell out, he plunged downward several stories and was killed instantly.

Hollywood stepped in then and took charge.

The studio took up a collection that covered the funeral expenses. At the young father's request one of the studio's cameramen took a picture of the baby, waxen white in the tiny coffin.

Then they went to another studio where they knew a baby was needed and got the other child under contract at what seemed to the stricken parents as a very big sum indeed. So he's a coming movie-star, even if his father's dreams of playing Rhett Butler have faded.

GABLE AS RHETT

Drawings by Vincentini

PHOTOPLAY THROWS ITS HAT IN THE RING

Herewith we enter the Great Casting Battle of "Gone with the Wind," because to our mind there is but one Rhett—Clark Gable. So sure were we of our choice that we had Vincentini paint this portrait of Clark as we see him in the rôle: cool, impertinent, utterly charming. We like all the other handsome actors mentioned as Rhett—only we don't want them as Rhett. We want Gable and we're going to stick to that regardless

What!

ANOTHE

—perhaps. In any event, here is

an amazing disclosure of Hepburn's

secret fight for this coveted rôle

BY ADELHEID KAUFMANN

In spite of Katie's boyish, brusque attitude, she has proved more than once that she is a poignantly feminine creature. She proved it as the beloved *Jo* in Louisa M. Alcott's "Little Women"; again, in her exquisite portrayal of *Phoebe Throssel* in "Quality Street."

It is the spirit, the soul of a character, which must be portrayed, and Hepburn has the rare gift of thinking, breathing, living the part she plays.

When Katie first read "Gone with the Wind"

Scarlett O'Hara, as artist Vincentini portrayed her in a recent issue of this magazine

she was wildly enthusiastic. She tore into Pan Berman's office at RKO and begged him to buy the book for her. But, before producer Berman could say "Jack Robinson," David Selznick had beaten him to the finish by reading this successful best-seller in galley-proof form at the publisher's; thus triumphantly scooping Hollywood on the distinguished novel of the year.

Naturally, this was a bitter disappointment to Katie but, characteristically, she didn't give up hope. From that day to this she has never relinquished her dream to play the part of *Scarlett.*

IT has been said many times that the indomitable Hepburn invariably gets the thing she wants. As I checked back into her colorful young life, I realized this was no fallacy.

Hepburn always manages to hang on to the right side of the wishbone. It isn't luck or fate; it's a power greater than these two things. It is Hepburn's determination plus faith in her own

It has been said that Hepburn invariably gets what she wants. She wants to play Scarlett—and she has already started a strange campaign to that end

"WHAT'S happened to Katharine Hepburn?" is the question all Hollywood is asking. "When a leopard changes its spots, what can it mean?"

During the last week or two of the shooting of "Holiday" everyone noticed that Hepburn—the hellion of Hollywood—had become a tame little lamb.

No longer did she object when a few chosen visitors were allowed to visit her set. This was, of course, an unheard-of thing!

Apparently welcoming such opportunity as a great personal pleasure, she consented to pose for dozens of tiresome fashion photographs.

When the "Holiday" company went on loca-

tion in the North, Hepburn got up at dawn every morning, sneaked off by herself and came back with mountain trout for the crew's breakfast. Needless to say the crew became momentarily speechless from admiration and a new wonder.

After this picture was finished, there was a big party given at the fashionable Victor Hugo in Hollywood for the entire company.

To everyone's surprise the unsociable Hepburn stayed until the last gun was fired. She stayed to applaud, in hilarious amusement, Cary Grant doing the Big Apple.

Hepburn was completely charming and natural. Gone was all trace of the *enfant terrible* of former days.

capabilities as a superior dramatic actress. She studies and works day and night to achieve her ultimate goal. Innumerable obstacles, which seem undefeatable to Hollywood, disappear like thistledown before her tumultuous attack.

If she does play *Scarlett O'Hara,* which at this writing seems inevitable, it will be a triumphant *tour de force.* For it is amazing to watch the Hepburn strategy. With the dexterity of a polished diplomatist, Hepburn has achieved an abrupt right-about-face in the Hollywood acting world.

Katie can whip up an unholy scare in a new leading man if the impulse comes over her to do so. She's proud and haughty and gets a kick out of putting people in an uncomfortable spot. As far as she's concerned, everybody is a sissy if he doesn't pay back her way. In other words, the gal may be a "debil" but she is dynamite enough to get away with it all.

In view of all this, her capricious about-face caused people to grow suspicious, for Hepburn is not the sort of person to turn into a temporary angel for nothing.

Your guess is as good as mine as to why all this is happening. I can only report on her behavior and draw my own conclusions. Ever since the rumor started that Hepburn had signed a new contract with David Selznick, she has been constantly with her favorite director, George Cukor, who directed her in "Holiday" and who will direct "Gone with the Wind" in the autumn.

The two have had one conference after another in the seclusion of Cukor's famously beautiful house, hidden behind ivy-covered walls. If she isn't in a verbal huddle with him she is in his marble swimming pool.

It was Cukor, if you remember, who was responsible for bringing Hepburn to Hollywood in the first place. She was his discovery and when she made a hit in "A Bill of Divorcement," he behaved like a man who had just won the Kentucky Derby.

She followed this first triumph with "Morning Glory" and with a later triumph directed by Cukor, "Little Women."

So, it would seem like a born natural for Cukor again to direct Hepburn's destiny, should she get the lead rôle, *Scarlett,* in "Gone with the Wind."

MEANWHILE, Constance Collier goes right on coaching Paulette Goddard for the *Scarlett* rôle.

There are rumors whispered around that Paulette's tests were not so hot. That's one rumor. There are many others, such as the report that Charlie Chaplin doesn't want Paulette to make the picture.

Paulette told me with tears in her eyes, "My real story is a crazy one. I want to work more than anything else in the world but I'm never allowed to—"

She twisted a new two-inch cabochon diamond and ruby bracelet around her slim brown wrist, while she looked wistful about no job.

Those who think Hepburn too boyish for the rôle of *Scarlett* must remember "Little Women" and "Quality Street." If they think she is too thin, perhaps not voluptuous enough for the off-the-shoulder dresses, they must remember that the world's greatest designers can create almost any illusion of perfection. But don't forget that Hepburn is a great actress! She can throw herself so completely into a characterization, she *is* the person she portrays.

Hepburn is *Scarlett O'Hara* at heart. George Cukor said in a recent interview: "*Scarlett* is typically Southern. That kind of woman couldn't have happened anywhere else. She is very female and like the average woman has no abstract sense of proportion. She hasn't much of a mind and she has no nobility. Yet she has a lot of character.

"I know at least five women in Hollywood and on the stage not as stupid as *Scarlett,* but who have her kind of temperament. They all came from the South and they have cut a wide swath," Cukor laughed.

Much later, we talked about the dress problem in "Gone with the Wind." An amusing person on the left of George Cukor at the luncheon table said, "*Scarlett's* clothes reflected the bad taste she displayed in picking her friends—she chose them because she thought they were fun."

Hepburn used to work on commission and got a percentage of box-office receipts when she insisted on doing arty costume productions. She made a great many unnecessary financial sacrifices for her art. Now that there is a possibility that she is to do the biggest rôle of her entire career, this becomes a vindication of Cukor's faith, and, in a way, it becomes a vindication of all those years in which Hepburn sacrificed her salary for her art.

Doesn't a modern quote like this from Hepburn's own lips sound a little as though *Scarlett O'Hara* might have spoken had she been a young star in Hollywood?

"I have moods," said Miss Hepburn. "Well, they're mine. Why should I change? If I don't feel like having my picture taken at a tennis match, why should I? If I feel like putting my hands over my face, why shouldn't I? Posing for pictures takes time. You know that I will not be anything but myself for anybody. Why don't you leave me alone?"

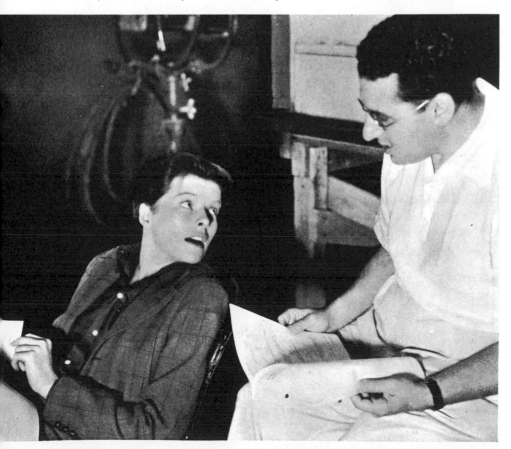

George Cukor, below, who is set to direct "Gone with the Wind," first brought Hepburn to Hollywood. It was he who directed her most successful films. Now, today, Cukor and Hepburn are constantly in conference. One more proof?

Don't forget Hepburn is a great actress. The difficult rôle of the Southern vixen needs one

Adored by men the world over, is it Lili's fault she expects the same of Errol?

HOLLYWOOD is a moonstruck town, where love runs amuck, and its citizens view the usual amorous didoes of the movie people without so much as batting a fake eyelash. And so it is a glowing tribute to the mad unpredictability of the rambunctious romance of Errol Flynn and Lili Damita that it has the film world in a highly nervous and jumpy state, and that throngs stand before newspaper offices watching the fever chart that records its ups and its downs.

For the "off ag'in, on ag'in, gone ag'in, Errol Flynn" union of this extraordinarily handsome pair is as colorful and exciting as any Hollywood has ever known. To the mere beholder in the cheap seats it is more thrilling than a cage of Nubian lions in an earthquake. They love each other like crazy and they hate each other like mad. They part forever—and the next day hurl themselves into each other's arms, swearing deathless devotion. Sour-faced realists on the sidelines say these two beautiful, willful people should never have dared the married state, and they are probably right, from the standpoint of sanity. But sanity plays no part in such love as that which grips the Flynn and the Damita. Apart, they would have missed glories and agonies such as few know—and the rest of us would have missed a thumping good show.

The fact is that I do not see how I can keep this

story from dating. I had no sooner started to strew rose petals on the grave of this romance than I learned that Lili and Errol, after ending it all, were once more closer than a three-cent stamp on a gas bill, and were about to set off on a European post-honeymoon. Before I reach the end of the chronicle of this passionate adventure I am fully prepared for the news that the couple battled and divided in Budapest, and that Flynn is in Tahiti, Damita in Cannes and Cupid is dead and buried. They can't get along with, they are miserable without, and if the Flynn kept a diary (which God forfend) it would read something like this—

Jan. 3—Lili is a selfish, silly butterfly. Drives me mad.

Jan. 4—I adore her, the darling!

Jan. 5—Going stark wacky with this routine. Packed and moved out.

Jan. 6—Moved in again.

Why is this thus? Why do these mag-

The
MADCAP LOVE
of the ERROL FLYNNS

nificent young people hate and worship each other with alternate breaths? Once they are under the microscope it is easy to understand.

Hollywood, ultra-conventional and strictly patterned for all its external goofiness, has never seen precisely the likes of this Flynn boy.

His own master since boyhood, relentlessly following the main chance, in spite of the buffetings of Fate, Errol Flynn is his own man. He is a Hard Guy, a clear-eyed realist and a thorough individualist. The Gene Tunney of the leaping tintypes, he approached the movies as the handsome boxer did the gentle art of mangling noses. It offered big money quickly, and everything indicates that the big boy proposes to get his, make a snoot at the studios, and step into the sort of life dearest to the heart of Errol Flynn. He is a movie career man if there ever was one, and to date he has not made a single professional mistake. His business dealings with Warner Brothers have been both keen and successful, proving once more that personal beauty is no handicap to smartness.

Flynn can write, too, and he will not perform for buttons. The kid has an eye for a pay check with a lot of nice figures on it, and if such is not forthcoming he simply covers the typewriter, picks up his marbles and goes away. Toughened by his boyhood struggles and thoroughly hep to the chicanery of his present profession, Errol Flynn will get what he wants in

large, juicy gobs. Nothing, probably not even his Damita-madness, will ever stand in his way.

And what of lovely Lili, a heart-demolisher of worldwide reputation?

In the first place, she is one of the most beautiful women I have ever seen, and my professional life has forced me to eye hundreds of them in envy and despair. She had been off the boat but a few days in 1928 when I lunched with her and her mother at a great Fifth Avenue hotel, and so blinding was the beauty of la Lili that I dropped the cutlery, knocked over two illegal cocktails and got Hollandaise sauce in my ears.

All her adult life, men, here and abroad, have been reduced to this sad, gelatinous state by her loveliness. They have trotted about in her wake, yelping wistfully for bones. She has been courted, petted, deferred to and spoiled by a long procession of pop-eyed, incoherent admirers, and they, not she, are to blame if she wants what she wants when she wants it, and then gets it instantly on a silver tray, trimmed with parsley and uncut emeralds!

How in the universe could this professional Dream Girl, secure in the knowledge of her beauty and accustomed to abject adoration from men, hope to cope with the unyielding, realistic individualism of such a Man's Man as the Flynn? She probably never even gave a thought to such insoluble problems She only knew she wanted him!

Speaking by the book, these two glamorous people should never have come within 10,000 miles of each other. But it is in just such cases that life plays its most comical

They love each other like crazy—they hate each other like mad. The amorous didoes of these two beautiful, willful people have all Hollywood guessing

By LEONARD HALL

If ever a man was not the husband type it's this headstrong young Irishman

The Madcap Love of the Errol Flynns

tricks—and of course they met, on a luxury liner America-bound!

The golden legend of the Love of Lili and Errol paints us the picture. We can see Lili in the grand saloon of the ship, surrounded by gaping males in claw-hammer coats. The big Irishman notices her and feels his collar catching fire. Elbowing through the throng, he asks her to dance.

Pulling Trick No. 1 out of her coquette bag, she says, "Come back in five minutes." Flynn didn't like this, but he did. Damita, following her plan of campaign, not new but forever good, probably said, "Oh, I'll see you around!" The old gag worked, as it always does, and Flynn said to himself, "I want that." Lili, still besieged by the hopeful horde, said the same internally. Obviously, it couldn't be long—and of course it wasn't!

ONCE in Hollywood, things began to hot up. Damita, then still raking in the blue chips from the studios, took up her film commitments, while Big Boy reported at Warners under a modest salary agreement. And all this time the terrifying type of forest fire love raged with redoubled violence.

Flynn moved helplessly toward matrimony, fighting every step of the way.

"I'm not the sort of chap who ever should marry," he told his friends—and a few days later the beautiful couple was off, helter-skelter, to Yuma, and the halter which now hitches them in the holy bonds.

It was inevitable that they should scuffle, and they did—almost from the take-off. In fact, war correspondents were regularly assigned to cover the Flynn-Damita front, and while ducking strong adjectives they wired their papers of bitter word-battles in which nothing was hurt but the feelings. During the filming of "The Green Light," Flynn packed his elegant English luggage and beat a strategic retreat, only to come back with his arms open and declarations of devotion on his lips.

His big break came when Robert Donat, the British Wonder Man, defaulted on playing the leading rôle in "Captain Blood," cut and tailored to his measure after "Monte Cristo," and the big red apple fell into the lap of Errol. He swashed and buckled through this showy part while women moaned and swooned all over the Republic, and within a week he was a big shot in pictures. Fame and adulation didn't take Big Stuff's clear eyes off the main chance. He merely told Jack Warner, with a convincing ring, that he now sported a very costly wife, and another figure or two was added to the proper end of his pay-check!

Kismet, all this time, was delivering its usual kicks in the derrière. As Flynn rode high, Damita was chuting the chutes out of the cinema picture. The time arrived when no one called her but the grocer. Hollywood experts opine that this shift of fortunes had nothing to do with the subsequent shindies, tears, rages and partings, but to this notion I significantly touch my long nose and wink sourly. Nobody can tell me that a famed and beauteous film star is going to be cut down to an occasional quickie, while her recently unknown spouse zooms to fortune, without suffering severe lacerations of her proud spirit. Within a month, Flynn was a hot shot and lovely Lili was practically nothing but his

wife. I needn't say that these things are very tough indeed to take—especially for a girl who has received the back-scratching and goose-greasing that fell to the lush lot of Damita for so many years.

But Flynn stayed strictly in character. Rich or poor, dim or famous, he was the same husky Irishman, heading in a straight line for what he wanted. He began building a house on an inaccessible mountain-top, surrounded by wild beasts and birds of the forest. The lock-step

Miriam Hopkins and Director Rouben Mamoulian are a new nightly combine about town since the fair Miriam returned from England

of married life began to grow as unbearable to him as a tight collar on a dance floor.

He hated the routine. He loathed having his days and evenings reduced to a social chart. Scheduled teas, dinners and the usual Hollywood round of free-for-all parties grew to be rank poison. He was nearly always late for dinner, simply because he hated being told that at eight he was doomed to sit down and attack the soup. If ever a man was distinctly not the marrying kind, it was this tall, handsome come-hither from Ulster.

Lili likes the hot spots, the lights, the music, the bubbles in the thin-stemmed glass, the adoring glances. Errol would probably rather be playing dominoes with Capone in Alcatraz than face a constant course of Hollywood night life. And there the poor things are!

Strictly on the record, these two spectacular people don't belong anywhere within dish-hurling distance of each other. They are oil and water. And yet, when you see them together, so glorious to look at, you can't help feeling that there is something almost miracu-

lously right about this mad, embattled teaming. They are a truly thrilling sight to see, in all their youth and beauty. As a vision of what two human beings can be when the Creator really bears down, they are nothing short of superb. As a married pair they are undoubtedly the leading example of marital madness.

Delectable Damita became what she is at present by a long course of private and semi-public worship. For years she was kept busy clambering from under mountains of costly flowers and saying yes, no and perhaps to a long and glittering line of love-struck swains. Flynn became the independent, non-conforming realist the hard way.

The son of a professor at Queen's University in Belfast, Errol didn't do much with book-learning, and in practically no time the kid was in Tasmania, at the other end of the world. He had the true stout heart and eager spirit of the adventurer. He was all jumbled up with gold and head-hunters in fabulous New Guinea, and took a good, sound rooking from high-pressure finance wolves. He was in the pearl trade in Tahiti, and appears to have been a member of the British Olympic boxing team at Amsterdam in '28. He touched all the bases, and loved it—and if, in a few weeks, he is reported as chasing the wall-eyed oophus in the Gobi Desert, hardly an eyebrow will be lifted. Flynn's like that.

He is probably the most surprised man in the world, even yet, to find himself married to a petted beauty to whom socializing and mass mauling are the very breath of life.

But there it is—the unfathomable chemical reaction commonly called love has this badly-matched, ill-mated couple in a death grip, and it shows no signs of letting go, scream and struggle though they may and do.

What can their future hold but incessant battles and passionate embraces, and perhaps a final, irreparable explosion for a grand finale? I frankly don't know—your guess, and theirs, is as good or better than mine.

IT is too much to expect that Lili, the caressed kitten, and Flynn, the clear-eyed adventurer and opportunist, will change so radically that their schemes of life will ultimately meet and blend. How can we hope for that? No—I fear they will continue to be what they are—beautiful, tigerish, proud lovers and haters tossed into each other's arms by snickering Fate. The Great Parting of Nov. 15, 1936, was followed by the Great Reconciliation of Nov. 26—and these things can go on and on, and will.

I only know that here, in the mad mismating of Lili Damita and Errol Flynn, we find a rare and perfect example of love in the grand manner. No timorous, half-hearted union based on a common liking for badminton, but a full-blooded, ardent love affair, heedless of consequences, in which anything can happen and invariably does.

I dare swear that no good will come of it, at long last. But I also say that we can be very grateful for the Flynn-Damita melange as a spectacle and as a reminder that the race is not yet dying of pernicious anemia. And we can also be thankful, perhaps, noting this weird mingling of hell and heaven, that we take our own romances with a spoonful of salt. Or are you?

Hurrell

THEY were talking about this Robert Young the other day in Hollywood. "That boy has everything—pep, poise and real screen warmth," was the consensus of opinion. And lots of movie-goers wrote to PHOTOPLAY protesting because his name wasn't in electric lights over "The Wet Parade." It'll be there soon or we don't know star stuff!

BY RUTH WATERBURY

IF I had an atom of sense I wouldn't try to write about Tyrone Power.

For what every writer learns the very instant after purchasing his first batch of pencils and wad of paper is that one writes really well only about people one hates. After all, writing is just gossiping to the world at large instead of to three or four friends in your own parlor, and you know yourself how the conversation sickens and dies when you get around to talking about one of those people about whom you have to say, "Well, I've never heard anyone say a word against her." You really have to be able to pick flaws to get the conversation going really hot, or reveal some deadly secrets.

And so it is with writing, too; yet here I am, sticking my neck out, trying to write a piece about Tyrone Power, against whom I can't say a word.

Despite this almost rabid admiration I have, I can explain him to you. For this I know—and no two ways about it—more misconceptions, more nonsense, more downright lies have been

Ty has a remembrance of things past which serves as his best protection

Alice Faye was a "friend in need"

RIENDS DON'T KNOW HIM

Have you heard that Tyrone Power is ungrateful, a poseur, a flirt? Then it's time someone who really has his number sets you right about this lad who's wilier than a politician but still young enough to have ideals

published about this young star than almost any other in Hollywood. He has been painted in some quarters as being ungrateful to the people who "knew him when," in others as being a poseur, in still others as being a heartless flirt entirely concerned with breaking lovely women's hearts. All of which stories are nonsense, but which have arisen, I think, from that sort of destructive jealousy people get for personalities they do not easily understand.

Tyrone is no Gable, who is able to make everyone like him instantly. He is no Robert Taylor, with a boyish, ingratiating quality about him. He is, instead, at once subtle and shy, at once realistic and romantic and in him there is a sardonic strain of bitter humor that rarely goes with acting talent.

Take, for example, the reason for "Sing, Baby, Sing," being his favorite tune. When you know the reason for this, you will understand much of the fellow himself. It will, I think, show you why he is now the triumphant success that he is. It will give you the basis for his deep friendship with Alice Faye, and to me, at least, it is the reason for believing that five years from now he will be an even greater star than today, and ten years from now an even greater star than in five years.

Not that I wish to give the impression that Ty bounds out of bed every morning and joyously lilts away on "Sing, Baby, Sing."

One reason he doesn't is because he is much too moody a soul not to have mornings when he feels like a wet February and wouldn't sing if a

gun were held to his head. The other is that he can't carry a tune even for the short distance between a bed and a bathtub.

But he does encourage his friends to "Sing, Baby, Sing" at him and it gives him a fine glow when he enters a restaurant, preferably an expensive one, and hears the orchestra giving out with it.

Yet the reason for his liking this tune is as bitter a little pill as anyone was ever asked to swallow. That song was the big hit of the picture of the same name and that picture was the first one that Ty was cast in under his Twentieth Century-Fox contract.

THE story has been told so often that you undoubtedly remember how he got that contract, so right here I'll only repeat that the contract came to Ty only after weary years of job hunting—when, due to his father's swift and sudden death, if he was to eat at all he had to find work. He was just as talented and handsome a boy then as he is now. He had had acting experience, ever since he had, at the age of seventeen, graduated from Purcell High School in his native city of Cincinnati and had taken a job in a stock company.

After his father's death he went around to all the managers and agencies where the name of Tyrone Power was respected. His father had been Tyrone Power, the 2nd and he was Tyrone Power, the 3rd, so everyone was very polite in that utterly charming and completely defeating way that is possible only to people in the theatrical profession. In Hollywood they have a word for those ultracourteous profitless meetings. They call them "the brush off," meaning you're in and out of some big shot's office before you know what's happened. Ty went through nearly two years of "the brush off," getting thinner and hungrier and learning more and more about the economic facts of life the while. But finally he did get the tiniest bit in a Broadway show.

A talent scout saw him and the Twentieth Century contract resulted. That was, of course, all that he had dreamed of. He was only twenty-two then and his optimism bubbled over. Here was life being served to him with a platinum spoon off a silver platter.

IT was, that is, until he was cast in "Sing, Baby, Sing." He appeared on the set early, anxious to show everyone that the great Darryl Zanuck's faith in him was justified.

He had studied his rôle valiantly and had worked out a couple of bits of business that he believed were distinctive. He couldn't possibly have been more eager or more happy than he was that first day.

Two days later, he was kicked out of the cast —not only kicked out, but told that he might be Tyrone Power, the 3rd or the 9th, but he certainly was no actor and never would be.

Now Ty at that time didn't know Alice Faye at all. She was the star of "Sing, Baby, Sing," you remember. But Alice, alone and unasked, sought out the humiliated, beaten boy, made him come to dinner with her, took him along to a simple restaurant in Beverly Hills that is called "The Tropics" and spent the whole evening talking to him, telling him that he could act, that he would get his chance, that he did have personality, and that, what-the-heck, his life was still before him, wasn't it?

Today, star of Hollywood's biggest pictures, sought after, lionized, Tyrone still eats, night after night, at "The Tropics." The place is

His is a complex personality, at once realistic and romantic, but there's reason for his sardonic strain of bitter humor

quiet and secluded, not the giddiest Hollywood rendezvous, but it gives Tyrone satisfaction to go there. And when he speaks of Alice, his voice is charged with emotion. He feels that without her encouragement that black night he would have lost his nerve completely, and if an actor ever does once lose his nerve he's through.

There is, too, the contrasting incident of Tyrone and a Hollywood Glamour Girl. Around three years ago, Tyrone was in Hollywood, but he had no work. Nonetheless, he knew a pretty girl when he saw one and he knew how to get an introduction too, and the very moment he did meet the girl he tried to get a date with her. But she was a Glamour Girl and he was a nobody, so she couldn't be bothered. However, when Tyrone clicked, the girl sought him and insinuated that a date with her would be very much in order. But this time Mr. Power was busy, very busy.

You see, he has a remembrance of things past.

I T is right here that I believe Tyrone is deeply fortunate. For all his talent, for all his handsomeness, there runs through his life a strain of bad luck that is the best protection he has. The devastating loss of his father forced him into a quick maturity. The fact that he couldn't get work easily has shown him the awful value of money and the vast need of true friends. Getting his ears slapped down by a director at the very instant when he first clicked in Hollywood undoubtedly kept him from getting the big head. And the fact that several lovely ladies of Hollywood looked at him with eyes like frozen glass before he was a hit protects him from those same ladies who now melt beneath his cynical glance. For one of the biggest distortions that has been printed about this star is that he is a "perfectly normal young man." He is as un-normal—and don't get me wrong: I said un-normal, not abnormal—as they come.

For he is distinctly wiser than his years and wilier than an Irish politician (he's Irish, anyhow, so that's probably where he comes by the instinct). If, on his arrival in stardom, he did the natural thing and took out attractive girls like Sonja Henie, Loretta Young, Janet Gaynor and numerous others, he now is retreating just as quietly from the traps that are laid for his handsome feet. And, believe you me, those traps are laid. In other towns, a beautiful girl is pursued wherever she goes, but in Hollywood the reverse is devastatingly true. A handsome young man in Hollywood may be able to call his soul his own, but that is usually all that escapes. But, at the moment, Ty is quite fancy-free and I'd bet my bottom dollar that he has been heart-whole all the time. For, while he is undoubtedly romantic and will talk on and on about his "ideal girl" (keeping her description so generalized that she sounds like no one on earth), the thing he really loves is acting.

A FEW months ago I happened to be in Kansas City waiting for a plane out for New York. By pleasant happen-chance, Tyrone was there at the same time, waiting for the same plane. So we went to see a movie together. Unfortunately, however (that typical Power bad luck), we got in on the "B" feature of the program and had to sit through the performance of one of the most ghastly actors on the screen. I asked Ty, "What makes him so bad?" "Well, he was acting," said Ty and he gave the word

"acting" a great emphasis. "You don't have to act."

"What is it you do then?"

"You have to feel," Ty said. "You've got to know what the emotion is like to put it across, but you've also got to keep yourself out of it, stay cold and listen to yourself and stop yourself the moment you hear yourself getting phony." He paused for a moment, his sun-tanned face concentrated. "Look," he said, "that's why actors aren't really great lovers. That's why so few of us have satisfactory marriages. What have you got to give, at home, when you return from a whole day of doing love scenes? All day long you've had a beautiful girl in your arms, and you have said the most beautiful speeches to her, speeches that some other man has written for you. She has answered you, too, in lines that have been written for her. Yet her lines and your lines are almost the words you must say in a real love scene at home. That girl, waiting for you outside the studio, wants you to say them to her. But you can't repeat them. You can't go on saying those things over again, those things that have been work to you all day. So there you are. You have nothing to give. But you can't expect your girl to understand that, unless she, too, is an actress, and not always then."

Now you must admit that is no normal young man speaking. A normal young man would just go ahead and get married, as Don Ameche did. Tyrone thinks that perfect Ameche marriage is one of the loveliest things on earth and in the moments when he is lonely, and those

Tyrone Power and his mother at the dedication of a plaque in honor of Tyrone's father, who played the rôle of Brutus in "Julius Caesar" in May, 1916, in Beechwood Canyon. It was the first play to be given on the site of what is now the famous Hollywood Bowl

moments are numerous, he wishes he had gone and done likewise. He watches with almost equal envy Richard Greene carrying on, quite unmolested by the press, his romantic courtship of Arleen Whelan. He doesn't realize that neither of these handsome men has about him that electric spark that automatically attracts attention to everything he does.

The reason for his loneliness actually is the most romantic thing about him. For try to hide it as he will, try as much as he can to play the sophisticated man of the world, actually the boy is a romanticist. Today, with his great rush of fame, with his sudden new and exciting wealth, he still has, buried deep within him, a set of ideals that he is trying to work out. One of these ideals concerns itself with friendship. Being the politician he is, he goes dutifully to the parties that he should go to and smiles at all the proper ladies; but, when

it comes to real friendships, he has about him a very few but trusted and loyal acquaintances. Except for the very mild gatherings he has with this little clan, he is much alone. For he is, as I've said, a moody guy who likes solitude in which to read and think and listen to music. His favorite composer is Johann Strauss, and certainly no one has ever written more romantic music.

WHAT is actually happening, of course, is that behind his fame, he is trying to discover himself and find out what manner of man he wants to be. He is so grateful to his public that he feels a sense of responsibility toward it. He is glad that he has been cast in romantic rôles, feeling that since there is almost no romance in modern life perhaps he can be the medium that will bring it into lives that might otherwise be utterly colorless. For this reason, he likes costume rôles, reflecting as they do the glories of gentler days than ours.

He is still young enough that he believes that life can have significance, young enough to believe that there is beauty to be had, and friendship and loyalty. But he admits these things only to the people who are close enough to him to understand him. To casual acquaintances, to the world at large, he can be just a young fellow who—in the Hollywood phrase—"has a lot of laughs." Actually, his humor is devastating and his descriptions of people have a hilarious but biting edge to them. But he has learned to hide this side of himself, too, having watched the destructive quality sharp wit has when it gets on paper in the form of a quote from a popular actor.

Pinned down to a formal interview, he gives out select, careful phrases which could come from any one of a dozen of Hollywood's younger generation of stars. But catch him alone and he will talk on and on for hours, on every subject under the sun, till your whole mind will take fire from his enthusiasm and you will finally see him for what he is—a brilliant, highly wrought, sensitive artist whose head rules his heart and whose heart rules his face.

If this doesn't make for simple happiness, of this you may be sure—he will live whatever it is to the final drop, living it with every sense he has and with that alert mind of his savoring its special flavor, always expecting disillusion, yet always dreaming of perfection.

226

Ferenc

HE'S back—rebellious Jimmy, who for a few mad months wanted to play a doctor rôle for life. He's come up smiling, glad he's starring in a new Warner picture, first called "Bad Boy" (the obvious title for a Cagney film!) but probably subject to the usual title changes. Anyhow, he promises to be a good boy now, except in picture rôles

WE WILL NEVER UNDERSTAND
Cary Grant in Hollywood

This charming person has built around his inner self a dam of isolation that is impenetrable!

Possibly "Wings in the Dark," which he did with Myrna Loy, is a fitting title for Cary

This was once a triangle without a rift—Cary, his wife Virginia Cherrill, and Randolph Scott—but then Virginia sued for divorce

THIS is my first and last story on Cary Grant.

For I know our friendship will never survive a second pen and ink vivisection of his soul. And not, mind you, because there are any secret corners in this tall Englishman's past that would flare up painfully under a thorough biographical probing.

Cary suffers from the strangest of Hollywood phobias.

At the risk of sounding hopelessly trite, I must somehow make you believe that honestly and sincerely, he cannot bear to see his name in print.

This malaise, naturally, is not stirred up by good or bad reviews of his pictures, art in magazines or routine news items concerning his picture work. But I have seen Cary look appalled and liverish for days following the publication of what most players would consider an innocuous enough interview.

A misquotation or a misstatement of fact in a newspaper, which is considered all in the day's work by the average Hollywood celebrity, can make him actively ill.

Call it what you will, an act, a fetish, a Garbo pose. But I know that Cary carries this burden honestly, and what is really admirable, he keeps taking it on the chin in absolute silence. Only a handful of his closest friends have discovered this superfastidious streak that makes him cringe from any public revealment with a self-consciousness that is torture.

I experienced repeated head-on collisions with Cary's peculiar aversion dating from the day he signed his Paramount contract in 1931.

Because I was, at that time, in charge of magazine publicity for the same studio, I received must-go orders to get a story on Grant published in every motion picture publication. A large order, but I considered the job a cinch with a new personality to present, especially a personality that was six feet, two inches tall, handsome and undeniably charming.

But the Cary Grant publicity campaign proved to be the greatest flop of my press agent career. I worked like a fiend for months. I dragged scribes in droves to his dressing-room onto the set, into his home.

My efforts were rewarded with a mere dribble of stories concerning the facts of his birth, education and stage career and then things came to a complete and dismaying standstill.

I did not know then that Cary was running a campaign of his own, and directing it more skilfully than mine. His graciousness to the press was as flawless as it was disarming. He showered reporters with sincere hospitality. There was always lunch, tea or cocktails awaiting them as well as an avalanche of talk that never quite got around to Mr. Grant's opinions on anything less abstract than the Versailles Treaty And the adjective jerkers never failed to leave him smiling broad smiles that vanished abruptly enough when they sat down at their typewriters to turn out a Cary Grant yarn.

And because Hollywood publicists die very, very hard, I stooped to pumping his few close friends, even his cook and John, the negro house boy. And I garnished the few ill-gotten crumbs with appetizing bait and fed it to a press hungry for intimate news on Cary. But when the first of those distinctly personal items flared into print, my studio-toughened conscience felt its only painful tweak in a full decade.

I saw, for the first time, Cary's eyes lacerated with a soundless writhing.

I thought then that time and Hollywood would teach Cary as it had other reticent Britishers before him, to ignore filmland's peep-show publicity. I recalled my lively jousts with Clive Brook and Herbert Marshall and felt assured that Cary's complete cure was just around the corner. But I was wrong.

Cary Grant will never know peace as long as his name spells

Not even Randy Scott, his closest pal, has the key to Grant's nature. This is in happier days: Vivienne Gaye, Randy, Virginia, Cary

By JULIE LANG HUNT

news. His fixation, or complex or mania (it is difficult to find the exact words for Cary's hyper-sensitivity) was planted during his childhood, and it was unwittingly nurtured during a strangely solitary youth.

He was only ten the winter he was called home from school because his mother had died suddenly. At that age a boy is very close to his mother.

He found himself unexpectedly bereft of a single outlet for all his boyish confidences. There was no one in his small world to listen with sympathy and patience to his imaginative secrets and immature philosophies.

The average hobble-de-hoy of ten would rapidly fill such a breech with boon companions, but Cary unfortunately (or was it really fortunate) was never the robust, commonplace, game-loving English schoolboy.

He recalls but a single chum during his entire term at school, a Horace Phillips. And the tie between them has never been broken although many years and endless miles have separated them since they were twelve.

During his final years at school, Cary remembers that he spent most of his game and play hours studying because he had to win scholarships to pay his tuition. There was no time left to join the rowdy cliques that gathered nightly in the dormitories for the natural adolescent recreation of snickering confessions and boastful bullyragging.

You see, he missed all the elementary lessons in the art of expressing to outsiders his hopes, his dreams and his despairs. Next to Horace, his closest companion was silence.

Perhaps all this explains the few women who have played any serious part in his life. Recently Cary told me that in spite of all his splendid

Locked up in his own past, present, and future, Cary Grant is somewhat of an enigma—no one can get over the outside barriers into what he thinks

training in poise and fluency for the stage, he becomes grotesquely tongue-tied, absurdly flustered and unbelievably awkward when he plays the rôle of Romeo in real life.

"When I go a-courting it's a very sad performance," he said. "I guess it's the deadly combination of intensity and a struggle to translate deep feeling into words."

And because he was stubbornly uncommunicative even at the age of twelve, he was expelled from school for the misdemeanor of another student. It wasn't so much a matter of not squealing on a schoolmate as it was an instinctive recoil from the humiliation of pleading for his rights.

A few months later the mistake was discovered, and Cary was reinstated, but his first encounter with the adult code of justice and fair play had left his childhood a shattered, dead thing.

He ran away, but was found quickly by his father and summarily returned to the academy. He remained a few months and ran away again, this time to join the famous Bob Pender Troupe of Pantomimists and Acrobats.

NOW ten years of Hollywood press agenting has inured me to bizarre and fantastic biography, but the next phase of Cary's life will always remain the most singular real life incident in my lengthy list of human phenomena.

First, you must understand the mechanics of that amazing organization known on the Continent and even as far as New York City as the great Pender Troupe. There is nothing in the American tableau to serve as a likely comparison or illustration.

In a large house at Brighton, Bob Pender kept a group of not less than thirty-five boys in constant training for his spectacular acrobatic and pantomime acts that filled engagements in the music halls of Europe.

The boys were bivouacked like a regiment of soldiers, working, playing, rehearsing and eating with bugle-call regularity. During the theatrical season the troupe made the circle from London to Budapest and back, but at such times the methodical routine of Brighton was relaxed only long enough for the daily performance on some glittering stage.

At thirteen, following his second and finally successful French leave from school, Cary joined these theatrical recruits. Strangely enough, he loved the rigid discipline, and the unflexible sameness of the days. He liked the blessed privacy of his tiny room in the Brighton house far better than the crowded dormitories. He liked the exhausting morning hours in the chilly rehearsal halls where he was taught back bends, nip ups, tumbles and acrobatic dancing. He liked even better the afternoon sessions when he was instructed in the delicate art of miming. For this he possessed a large talent and within a few months of his enrollment, he was selected for important work in all the pantomime numbers for the music hall tours.

For five years Cary lived in this placid monastic seclusion, barely touching or being touched by the world that surged beyond the footlights and the Brighton house. And during those years his only fraternal tie was Bob Pender, but this large-hearted man was too occupied with the direction of his theatrical battalions to offer consistent companionship.

During lulls between scenes with Greta Garbo in "Anna Karenina," Maureen O'Sullivan became a devout nature lover, dashing off to lake and mountains for a few days

The boys in the troupe were amiable enough, but Cary would not find a Horace Phillips among them. And so he grew to manhood with all his beliefs and credos, his reveries and his very emotions crowded behind a firm dam of isolation.

When he was eighteen, the Pender platoon crossed the Atlantic to fill its first engagement in America, and during a lengthy run at the Hippodrome Theater, Cary's tranquil orbit was obliterated quite suddenly by the restless, savage rhythm of New York City.

Almost at once he knew that he must stay in America, that he must conquer the mad tempo of this new country with his vast knowledge of miming, dancing and singing, and if necessary his deft acrobatic flips.

THE rest of his story merely repeats the familiar and dreary details of the Broadway saga.

There was the usual procession of hall bedrooms, nights spent on Central Park benches, handouts, backwoods strandings and life-saving jobs in Coney Island concessions.

There was eight years of this sort of thing for Cary, and only once did he share his luckless struggles to fall in step with the mad pace of Manhattan.

During the winter of 1927, he met Orry-Kelly, now costume designer for Warner Brothers studios. Here was another stranger in an indifferent country, recently arrived from Australia to search Forty-Second Street for a set designer's job.

The pair decided to share a crowded Greenwich Village room as a means of solving the rent riddle.

Strangely enough the lowest ebb in the careers of both these famous Hollywood men was touched during the fateful year they bunked together.

At one time they met the threat of certain eviction by painting neckties by hand and forcing them upon unwilling shopkeepers in the Village. The process was one Orry-Kelly discovered years before, and it must have been a good one, for the hand tinted neckwear became a sudden rage, and the pair felt crisp greenbacks in their pockets for the first time in months.

THOSE flamboyant ties were the starting flags for Cary's final sprint to success, but he traveled those last miles alone.

It is true that in Hollywood, Cary finally found a candidate for Horace Phillips' place in Randolph Scott.

Their friendship has endured the stormy passage of Cary's recent courtship, marriage and divorce.

And yet, the other day when I asked Randy if he could explain Cary's frenzied hankering for an impossible privacy, he shook his head.

"I can't tell you why," he told me, "but I've seen him actually lose sleep and weight after reading certain items that touched upon his personal life and thoughts.

"Why, he will probably do the same thing when he reads your story."

And so I wonder, will these words I have written make him writhe and grimace? Will our friendship survive my first and certainly my last article on Cary Grant?

I wonder?

■ Charles Boyer, the most Latin sex-appeal since Valentino!
The world and its girl-friend, mainly the girl-friend, excitedly await his return from England to do another film

Pat O'Brien was responsible for Spencer's joining the Navy during the War—Here's Spencer as a gob

232

THIRTY-SEVEN years ago, when this present century crashed into being to the accompaniment of a gleeful world banging on tin pans and blowing whistles, it brought with it many things:

A commercial answer to wiseacres who protested that the motor car was only a toy for millionaires; the conviction that there would never be any more wars; the sharp vision of flight by mechanical contrivance; the discovery of a new star; three front page murders. . . .

And, in its first year, a Peck's Bad Boy, born in Milwaukee on April 5th in a swank apartment house facing Prospect Avenue. His parents—the John Tracys—all unknowing named him merely Spencer.

He was truculent even at the beginning, causing as much trouble as possible and frightening everybody, even the doctors, out of their-wits. Upon his eventual arrival he was unduly noisy. But he was a husky baby born with sturdy arms and a crop of brown hair and his own ideas, and a large hunk of wanderlust.

JOHN TRACY was general sales manager of the Sterling Truck Company, a position that carried with it the need for intelligence, and a salary large enough so that a little time after the break of the century he was able to move himself and his wife and his two small sons out of the apartment on Prospect Avenue and into a house.

You must know the sort of house it was—solidly American, on a solidly respectable street, presenting a clean face behind the hydrangea bushes and under the slate roof. If you remember, the furniture of the period was a hideous revival of ponderous walnut, curving mahogany, plush; well, there could be none of that in the rooms over which Carrie Tracy presided. She was a Colonial lady in every delicate sense, stately in mien, gentle of eye, controlled of voice—and the chairs and tables and cabinets of her house had the dignified grace of the Colonial period.

They weren't stylish, but smart; which is a different thing.

You would have loved Mrs. Tracy—everyone did, and does now in this modern-day Hollywood where she lives with her sons and is still a great lady.

But you would have adored her husband.

Behind him generations of fighting Irish, with their shades of banshees and flailing shillalahs and the sod; with him the reserved, meticulous influence of Carrie; before him a new,

He has always lived dangerously. Beginning the absorbing biography of the

THE ADVENTUROUS LIFE of Spencer Tracy

By HOWARD SHARPE

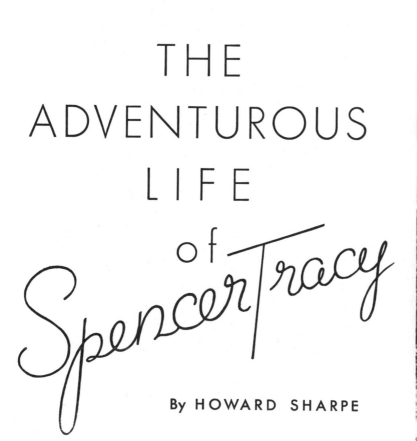

briskly antagonistic century—he represented the first, reflected the second, met unhesitatingly the problems of the third.

Of which the worst was Spencer. Family, teachers, counselors could only, in their exasperation, mutter "That *boy!*"—and reach for the hickory.

He was a little brat, and admits it cheerfully. His saving graces were an inherent honesty, sympathy for animals (later, after he'd been hurt enough times himself), and a flaring temper which burned itself out quickly. He was not sullen. He did not lie, because he had courage.

Spencer will tell you these things, as he told them to me, if you ask him. And there's no sentimentality in the telling. He does not excuse the things he did with the alibi of environment, since his environment was ideal, you will get no anecdotes relating how he beat up the neighborhood bully and untied cans from the stray mongrel's tail.

The thing was that the boy had enormous energy. He had imagination. His mother tried to understand this, and seldom did, and thus wept often. His father understood, to the extent of having a twinkle in his eye as he trounced his son for escapade after escapade. Spencer knew about the twinkle and felt the weight of his father's hand without any special consideration of its meaning.

It was his mother, with her quiet air of I-am-puzzled-and-hurt-but-I-love-you-still, who had the most impressive effect. She had only to look at him with sorrowful eyes brimming, and he would burst into an orgy of wailing repentance, self-recriminations and promises about regeneracy—all of which he meant at the time.

His first recollection (at the age of seven) is an amusing one. He awoke one bright summer morning in his own bed, blinked in the sunlight that slanted through the windows, noticed that he had kicked off all the covers during the hot night, and

Today — a fighter still. His magnificent acting in hard-boiled rôles is often a reflection of what his life has been

233

sat up. Simmering at the back of his mind was an unpleasant thing in connection with this day.

Then he remembered. School. Good-by to habitual freedom, fast-moving days spent playing in the sun, other little boys, older than he, had told him about the teacher with the mole on her chin, a fearsome creature with a ferrule and a gimlet eye. She made you sit, with your hands folded, while she talked to you. She made you add up sums and read out of silly books. She stood you in a corner if you socked anybody. Also she tattled to the folks, and they licked you when you got home.

fighting Irishman who battled his way through poverty and tragedy—and won

Young Spence sighed dolefully. Resignation slowed his movements as he crawled out of bed and began to dress.

But not for long. The Tracys were never a clan to surrender easily. One leg encased in trousers, one foot poised, Spencer thought—sniffed twice—and acted. So they were going to do this to him, when *he* hadn't ever done anything to *them!* Tears of fury and melodramatic outrage slid down his cheeks as he yanked on his shoes.

Outside the window of his room the roof slanted down; only a foot or so below the eaves was a screen porch, and then an arbor. With the extra precaution of the guilty, he raised the window, inch by inch. His pants tore with an angry sound as he bumped softly down the first stretch of slate, and for a moment he wasn't sure whether the porch roof would hold him or not. The lattice on the side of the arbor gave way as he clung precariously to it, but a soft flower bed was beneath.

He clambered up, took one last, misty look at his old home, and departed hurriedly.

When, gasping, he finally stopped running, nine blocks were between him and the danger of capture. He had never been so far away—alone—before, and he had never been up and out so early in the morning, either. The parkways and the trees had a freshness not yet eaten away by the hot sun, the air hung moist and still cool above the quiet streets. Beside the curb a horse, left waiting with its wagon, stood in utter depression, its bones arranged in geometric patterns under the tight skin. Spencer thoughtfully pulled up a clump of drying grass and proffered it, clod of earth and all. The horse ate first the grass, then the earth, and hung its head again.

S PENCER walked thoughtfully on.

He had headed South, and if you knew Milwaukee in 1907 you remember that South Side; narrow streets and towering, dirty buildings; saloons on every corner and, in between, houses with shuttered windows, alleys. Squalor.

The section was awake and humming when the young runaway reached it. He was fascinated. The gutters were intriguing, running with things that smelled. Fish and garbage, cooking food (and he was getting hungry), alcohol and beer and "Free Lunch" from under the swinging doors, the odor peculiar to streets over which horses habitually trod.

He met Mousie and Rattie, sons of the most successful saloonkeeper in the neighborhood, on a corner. They surveyed him belligerently from under their dirty caps (being of the South Side aristocracy they had caps, and also shoes) and Spencer did not flinch. He put up his small fists.

"Wanna fight?" he said.

Mousie and Rattie consulted. "Aw," Mousie said finally, "we could tear yer backbone out and roll ya up if we wanted to."

White-faced Spencer stood. "I'll fightcha—both at once. I'll send ya runnin' home to mama." His lower lip was an insult.

There was a long silence. "I know where there's a swell barrel to make a fort out of," Rattie said casually. "Back in Donovan's alley."

Spencer put his hands in his pockets. "I'll be the captain," he said.

Hours later the frantic Tracys found him there, in Donovan's alley—grimy, sweaty, indomitable captain of the barrel fort. He was perfectly happy.

They brought him home howling, home to tears and loud discussion and bed-without-supper. He began school the next morning.

But Mousie and Rattie were his friends from that day, unto eternity.

He saw them often. On increasingly periodic afternoons Milwaukee's truant officer—one Mr. Fischer—came to the Tracy door and inquired skeptically of the maid if Master

Lottie Pickford died at her home in Beverly Hills on December 10th of a heart attack. Born in Toronto, Canada, on June 9, 1895, Lottie appeared in vaudeville with Mary in Canada, and later was on the screen in many pictures through the early 1920's. A striking brunette, she was married four times. Gwynne, her only daughter, was adopted by Mary Pickford. Her sister's death leaves Mary the only surviving member of a devoted family. Jack and Mrs. Pickford died some years ago.

Spencer's illness was a serious one; and invariably the maid would reply that Master Spencer was very well, thank you; and invariably Mr. Fischer knew where to go.

On the days when Spencer saw fit to attend class his teachers were wont to sigh longingly for the peaceful times when he played hooky. Of the fat, self-flattening spitball he was indisputably master. He devised a special inkwell and put it in two of the front desks, so that when freshly laundered little girls dipped morning pens a spring released jetting floods of black liquid. His gallery of portraits on textbook margins was the finest in the school.

His grades were the worst. The only runner up in any of these activities was a youngster by the name of Pat O'Brien. At the age of fourteen they met, fought to the death behind the school fence, and with noses dripping shook hands in mutual respect. They've been pals ever since.

With adolescence the usual things happened to Spencer. His voice was ridiculous. He began to shave a year before there was anything to shave, he discovered sex (in the idealistic sense) simultaneously with a little red-haired girl down the street. She thought him magnificent.

They held hands and had ice cream and cake together at parties and were dramatically precise about the future. They had only just

decided on what sort of a house they would have, and how many bright-eyed tousle-haired children, when her temper met his in a blast of young fury and he forswore "wimmen" forever.

S OMEHOW, just before his family moved to Kansas City—following John Tracy's business—he managed to wangle a diploma, ribbon and all, from St. Rosa's parochial school. He brought it home in triumph and announced that henceforth he would earn his own way in the world, now that he was educated.

"No," said his father.

In quiet explanatory tone, first, and eventually in hot fury, Spencer pleaded. "You'll go on to school until you've learned the sort of things that make a gentleman," Mr. Tracy shouted, "and I don't want any more argument from you!" This was his last word, and thereafter Spence growled futilely in his locked room. When they were settled in Kansas City he enrolled at St. Mary's.

Shortly after (the reason would be a repetition here) he left that famous institution and went to Rockhurst, where a good thing happened. He met, there, two other boys who thought they were just as tough as he was.

And they were.

At home he nursed in silence his swollen jaw, his black eye and his loosened tooth, and faced himself for the first time. Tall for sixteen, splendid of shoulder, he looked in the mirror over his dresser and asked of the image there, with infinite scorn, "Who do you think you *are?*"

He dared to review the past honestly then. The egocentric spirit, the belligerent disposition, the conviction that either his fists or his charming Irish grin would carry him through —these his basic qualities. He had no thought for the sheer imagination or the creditable ingenuity, the personal honesty his activities had sprung from. The procession of his own personality was not a pretty thing to him that night.

He made to himself, during the next hour, two or three promises which he has always kept.

Whimsically John Tracy's home office moved back to Milwaukee, dragging the family with it; and Spencer entered West Side High School there with astonishing good grace. He still hated the requisite discipline, the study, the books—but his original attitude had changed completely.

Meanwhile Europe was explosively out for the hide of that mild man with the incongruously fierce mustaches named Wilhelm, Kaiser of unhappy Germany. In Paris a nervous populace awaited the sudden appearance of Boche Gothas, greeting them with darkness, the mourning of sirens seeking fingers of light; Loos, Amiens, Jouy were names in American newspaper headlines, and young students, when they had finished with local topics, discussed bitterly the outrages to Belgian babies by ogre-like Huns. Propaganda began early here.

Spencer was seventeen when official America decided to repay Lafayette's call. But the strange mob-inspired excitement didn't hit him entirely for a few months.

Eventually, however, it happened. Bands went by, playing. Young ladies with flushed

234

cheeks offered a carnation and a kiss to any young man who would enlist, and lines of khaki marched past through the Milwaukee streets, and glamour (synthetic, bought and paid for) was inexorably attached to war. It sounded like the most magnificent circus ever arranged in history and no Tracy had ever been known to miss a good show.

SPENCER left his last class of the day one cloudy December afternoon and caught a trolley that was headed downtown. He had tossed his books under a hedge with the happy thought that he would have no more use for them, now that he was going to substitute travel for education; he had decided on the Marines, you see. Naturally he had not taken the family into his confidence. It would be just like them, he knew, to point out that his age would prohibit enlistment and that a lie was a sinful thing.

"I found the enlistment station next door to the famous old Schlitz hotel," Spencer told me; "an occasional man straggled in and then wandered out again, between two very stiff-necked Marines on either side of the door. I went up, hesitated a minute, and walked right past—I couldn't get my face in any sort of form."

Fifteen times he approached the little station, and paused, and hurriedly went on down the street. Fifteen times the two uniforms, rigidly at attention, stared through him. Finally, on sheer nerve, he went in.

A courteous attendant asked him questions, gave him a blank to fill out, hovered over him as he scribbled.

"Your age, Tracy?" the attendant said, finally.

With eyes blank Spencer started to say, "Twenty, sir," but after so many years of the habit of honesty, his words seemed to speak independently and for themselves.

"Seventeen—and eight months," they said. The attendant tore up the enlistment blanks, smiling ruefully.

That evening Spencer sat moodily in his room, eyeing the books which he had retrieved from under the hedge on his way home. Rationalization was a tough project, somehow; the exchange of lessons for cannon fire, Milwaukee for all the world, had been too glamorous and too exciting to forget in a few hours. He was thoroughly disgusted with himself, too, for telling the truth when there were so many noble arguments to sustain the lie.

His mother knocked. "Whatever you're sulking about," her voice said, "I'd advise you to stop now. Pat O'Brien's here to see you."

Pat barged into the room grinning, over-brimming with news. "I've joined the Navy!" he told Spencer.

"You're a better liar than I am, if you did," Spencer said, frowning. He recounted shame-facedly his abortive attempt of the afternoon.

"But you crazy Irish Mug," Pat interrupted, finally, "that was the Marine Service. You're *old enough* for the Navy!" He shouted down Spencer's delighted yelps. "First the Great Lakes Training Station—and then overseas. Sounds pretty good, hmm?"

Spence was already clattering down the stairs, for consultation with his parents.

His mother wept, but surprisingly Mr. Tracy patted his son on the back and then flung up the evening papers as a barrier to argument. "Let the boy do this thing if he wants to," he said.

Spencer enlisted, and was accepted, the next day—and two days later left with Pat for Great Lakes, where together they fought the war.

A very few things happened. Spencer got a blister on his heel from too much drilling; he escaped the flu epidemic; and when, six months later, his company was transferred to Norfolk, he went for a cruise on a whale boat in the bay. Most important of all, his friendship with Pat O'Brien was cemented into a lasting entity, never to be broken. Before they could get into it, the war ended and they were mustered out of service. The two boys stood glumly in civilian clothes waiting for the Milwaukee train.

Pat lit a cigarette. "What now, have you any idea?" he asked, shaking the match languidly.

Spencer looked vaguely at the platform. "I hadn't thought of that, exactly," he said. "What—what would you think of our going to New York and becoming actors?"

"Actors?" cried Pat. "Actors? Holy Cow."

Spencer's ambition led him into strange paths. He stared starvation in the face looking for a job as an actor; then he fell in love with the leading lady! Don't miss next month's colorful installment of the star's life story

235

A very happy looking sextette are Harpo Marx (note the millinery); Helen Vinson and her husband Fred Perry, the tennis champion; Barbara Stanwyck, Groucho Marx and Gloria Stuart on the courts of the Beverly Hills Tennis Club which Fred Perry has recently bought, and will rebuild into a beautiful new clubhouse

BY EDWARD DOHERTY

MOTION pictures have done much to prove the truth of all the old saws concerning love and lovers. Over and over again they have convinced the world that true love never runs smooth, that love laughs at locksmiths, and that all the world loves a lover.

But sometimes the screen stars who bring to attention the verity of these adages must wonder about them—after their work in the studio is done, after the paint has been removed from their faces and the costumes have been laid away for the night, after the lights have gone out on the sound stages, after the players have come to grips again with actualities.

All the world loves a lover?

Yes, perhaps all the world loves Clark Gable, the suave and fascinating hero of the screen. And, no doubt, it loves Carole Lombard, the impish, kinetic, funny darling.

That is, it loves them as it sees them in rôles produced for them by some Hollywood writer. Of the real Carole Lombard, and the real Clark Gable, the world knows little.

And love laughs at locksmiths?

Many times, undoubtedly. And yet—how will love unlock the situation in which Clark Gable and Carole Lombard have become imprisoned?

Here is a typical moving-picture situation. It has been used over and over again. You have seen it developed hundreds of times. You have seen the problem solved in hundreds of different ways.

But this is a situation in real life—a beautiful blonde girl, witty and winsome and wise, in love with a debonair actor who has been married a number of years and whose wife is unwilling to divorce him.

What will happen? How will the characters react? How will the story end?

Will the wife step gracefully aside, someday, and allow her husband to marry the younger woman? Will she wait in patience, knowing that time oft withers infatuation, or feeling that even true love must give way to duty?

Or will the girl, tired of waiting, give the man up?

Will there be tragedy? Or will the last reel of the drama be played to the chimes of wedding bells?

HOLLYWOOD, dealer in love stories of all kinds, is eager to rush into print with the details of synthetic romances among the motion-picture stars.

Strangely enough, it is equally zealous to keep real romances from the knowledge of the press.

It may be that Hollywood feels something of awe, encountering the real thing, the romance it can neither buy nor sell, the love story that is written by Life.

At any rate, Hollywood has been chary of letting news of the romance between Clark Gable and Carole Lombard seep into print. It has, grudgingly, admitted that Mr. and Mrs. Gable have separated, and that Clark has often escorted Miss Lombard here and there. But that is all.

It has given no hint of the heartaches that must exist deep below the surface of the story, the anguish, the yearning, the bitterness, and the tears.

This isn't a springtime love affair; but it has poignancy and beauty for all that. Here are two people in the full splendid summer of their lives, with the sun of fame and fortune shining brightly on them—and autumn coming on apace.

And here is the wife, the charming, cultured, sophisticated Mrs. Rhea Gable, watching the two with what emotions no one knows.

What will the autumn bring her? Restored serenity, or gray despair? Loneliness, or peace?

Perhaps if Carole and Clark had met in the springtime of their lives they would have been merely infatuated with each other. But it is not so now. They have experienced too much of life to trifle with anything so enduring as real love. They have suffered too much, learned too much, to take love lightly.

They have a lot in common, these two stars. They both enjoy informality. They like to be themselves. They welcome anything simple and natural which will give them fun. They like getting into old clothes and going to some out-of-the-way place. Also they like dressing up now and then and visiting some public spot.

You may see them at an amusement park, laughing like a couple of kids at nothing at all, trying to be as inconspicuous as possible. You may run across them eating in some obscure little hole in the wall, enjoying the music of a four-piece Mexican orchestra. You might see them at Carole's home, playing bridge with friends. You might see them at the arena on fight nights, yelling with gusto "Sock him in the kish-kish, Abie; he can't take it there!"

BOTH have been unfortunate in their love affairs.

Carole thought that life and all its problems had been solved for her when she first met William Powell. She was twenty-two, and, though he was sixteen years older, there was a gay spirited youthfulness about him that appealed to her intensely, that promised her eternal happiness. There was a lightness, a breeziness, an impish joyousness in him, a tenderness no words could adequately describe.

And yet their marriage ended in divorce.

Carole obtained the decree on the grounds of incompatibility. Powell put no obstacle in her way. He is still her friend. She is still his friend.

But isn't it a major tragedy when marriage deteriorates into mere friendship—a glimpse of each other now and then; a little smile at meeting; a handshake or a pat on the back for old times' sake; a civil "How are you," uttered in the same voice that once thrilled with "Oh, my dear, my dear!"; a calm look in the eyes that once reflected only ecstasy in the presence of the other?

Marriage, made out of love and brightness and joy and singing hope, stifling in misunderstandings, struggling in incompatibilities, yawned and died; and was not greatly mourned.

But it must have left a scar. It must have left a lasting doubt—"Is love like that?"

And there was a second romance that ended not less tragically.

Carole had begun to think better of love. She had met Russ Columbo, the handsome young man with the golden voice. She had become his greatest fan, and then his worshiper. And

he died. Accidentally, cleaning his gun, he shot himself.

The death of Russ Columbo made Carole Lombard, Hollywood says, in its cocksure way. When she returned to the screen, after the long absence that followed his death, she was a better actress than she had ever been. She was actually a comedienne! Her comedy was of the highest type, that sort whose roots are planted in the deep, rich soil of sorrow.

Suffering and solitude had mellowed and softened her, shaped her character, enlarged her understanding and her sympathy.

They put her in "20th Century," and gave her free rein for her talents. And even those critics who had said she was little more than a gorgeous clothes horse and a mildly funny foil for bigger stars now admitted she was one of the outstanding personalities of the screen.

CLARK GABLE was ripened through tragedy of another kind, the tragedy of futility and disappointment.

Life, that now denies him little, was more than niggardly to him in his youth. It gave him hard work in various parts of the country. It made him a timekeeper, a lumberjack, a laborer in the oil fields of Oklahoma, an actor of sorts playing unsuitable rôles in one-night stands with theatrical companies that never got anywhere.

He came to Hollywood when he was young, and got little but rebuffs, an extra part once in a while, a day's pay, a door slammed in his face. Nobody in the film capital cared if he lived or died.

He married a woman much older than himself, a woman who helped him immeasurably along the rocky road to stardom. She spent hours teaching him, and he spent hours train-

On one side, Clark's wife, the charming Rhea, who watches this situation with what emotions no one knows

It's not a glittering Hollywood romance. It's just two human people in love, faced by a problem that might be yours. How will they solve it?

On the other, Carole and Clark, admired, as sophisticated screen hero and heroine, by all the world —for all the world loves a lover. Yet of these two people as they really are the world knows little

238

ing himself to be perfect in one rôle, in one scene.

Did he really love this woman, Josephine Dillon, Hollywood asks, and did she really love him? Was there more maternal than wifely feeling in her?

Clark was twenty-two when he married her. He was twenty-nine when she obtained her divorce. Mrs. Gable was in Los Angeles then. Clark was in New York. He had arrived in that city after a long tour of the south. He was playing in "Machinal," and he had met Rhea Langham, a wealthy divorcee from Kentucky, whose brother was in the cast of the play.

Scarce had Josephine divorced him than Clark married Rhea Langham. Like Josephine, Rhea was much older than her husband. They came west on their honeymoon. Clark was playing a part in "The Last Mile." Hollywood gave him a little more recognition on this second visit. M-G-M gave him a screen test. Eventually he appeared with Norma Shearer in "A Free Soul."

Mrs. Gable, who loves society, entertained lavishly, did all in her power to accompany her husband into the hectic life of Hollywood, and to keep pace with him as he walked through the glare of the light that plays on movie stars. Hollywood has a way of lionizing the star, and ignoring his family—especially if the family does not "belong." Yet Mrs. Gable attained the "inner circle" in her own right.

And, for a time, all seemed as merry as a wedding bell.

CLARK and Carole met in 1932 when they were selected to play in "No Man of Her Own."

Both were married then; and apparently happily married. There wasn't the faintest suspicion of any romantic attachment between the two, though they clowned together continually.

They were just having a lot of fun together, and everybody who watched them had fun with them. Either Clark or Carole always had some new gag, some new joke to spring. Where either was, there was bound to be spontaneity, laughter, honest enjoyment.

It was not until Jock Whitney's "gag party," on Feb. 7, 1936, that Carole and Clark took any serious interest in each other.

Powell had become just a friend by that time. Columbo was dead. Josephine Dillon was gone into obscurity. And Rhea Gable had left her husband and gone to New York.

She had left him once before, it was said, but later had come back to Hollywood. Everything had been well again for a time in the home of the Gables. And then everything was wrong again. Clark and his wife had definitely separated. There had been some attempts to effect a property settlement, it was said, but the terms of the settlement were in dispute.

The Whitney party was held at noon, and the guests were requested to appear in formal evening clothes. Carole had herself carried into the Whitney residence on a stretcher.

The guests rushed to her, horror-stricken, thinking she had been injured —and found her laughing at them.

The gag appealed to Gable. It attracted him to Carole more than anything else had done. And, somehow, Carole felt the attraction as much as he did.

The following week, on St. Valen-

tine's Day, she sent him the queerest valentine any man ever received.

It was nothing but a Model T Ford, dug up from a prehistoric burying ground, or enticed from a museum—a battered, shattered, tattered, and bespattered wreck of an auto.

It was horribly ancient, and terribly vulgar, and exquisitely unattractive. It had rheumatism in all its joints. It exhibited every symptom of St. Vitus' dance when it was in motion. Its glass was cracked, its fenders bent and gnarled and warped and torn and twisted into fantastic shapes. Its upholstery was mouldy and shredded. It had been patched and repatched, and the naked springs stuck through it here and there. Its paint had flaked off in places.

It was the most disreputable car in all the modern world. But it was covered with painted hearts, and so it was a valentine, unique and precious.

Much thought had gone into it, much bright laughter, and a great deal of tenderness. And Gable loved it.

He drove it over to Carole's home, and insisted on taking her out immediately for a ride. Carole consented gladly, and the two went bumping, galumphing, limping, jerking, wheezing, and blowing out great clouds of odorous vapors, down the principal thoroughfares of Hollywood to the immaculate Trocadero.

THAT'S a long time ago—two years and more—a very long time for lovers to wait. Thus far, time has held no threat to their romance. But, if the years pile up, and the hope of their marrying pales, may not their ardor and their passion languish and die?

Love never dies, says another old saw.

Many a super-epic in the films has preached the sermon of love's eternity; and one of the first love stories ever written deals with the timelessness of a man's affections. This is the story of Jacob who worked seven years for Laban, on the promise of winning his daughter Rachel. When the years were done Laban made a wedding feast. But the bride was not Rachel; she was Leah, Rachel's elder sister. Leah the tender-eyed, the cross-eyed. Jacob worked another week of years for the girl he loved.

Will Carole and Clark wait seven years if they must? And another seven thereafter if circumstances so compel them? Who can say?

Love never dies?

Stories in every newspaper every day indicate that love dies many deaths. Carole's love for William Powell died. Clark's love for Josephine died. His love for Rhea is dying, if it be not dead.

This story has never been written before. It isn't fully written now. Time is writing it. Time will furnish its climax and its end. It may be one of the deepest tragedies, one of the most poignant romances of Hollywood. The fans can only watch and wait, "with malice toward none; with charity for all" the principal characters.

How will the drama end? Will one of the lovers forsake the other? Will they both, someday, regard the cold ashes of their love, and sigh a little? Or will they wait patiently, chins up, brave smiles painted on their faces, never flagging in their romance?

True love never runs smooth?

Perhaps it never does.

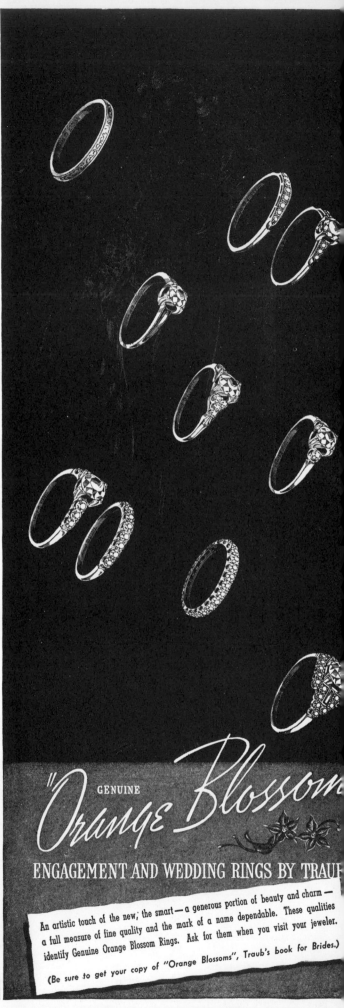

Bull

240

The beloved Will Rogers and his friend Wiley Post as they were about to start the ill-fated journey. The family he was so proud of: Will, Mrs. Rogers, and Will, Jr., Mary and Jimmy. Center, Will in his first movie—made at Ft. Lee, New Jersey, eighteen years ago— "Laughing Bill Hyde." Lower Left, in his last picture, with Irvin S. Cobb, noted humorist, "Steamboat Round the Bend," probably his greatest picture. He had just signed a new contract for ten pictures. Right, in "Doubting Thomas," with Billie Burke, widow of Florenz Ziegfeld in whose noted "Follies" Will went to his greatest stage comedy fame

TO A GREAT MAN

As we go to press, comes the appalling news of Will Rogers' death in an airplane accident when he and Wiley Post were forced down in a desolate corner of Alaska. Here, in deepest sadness, Photoplay shows you glimpses of that great star, Will Rogers. He hated formal portraits, so we give you "grab shots" he loved, taken in and about Hollywood a day or so before his fatal trip into the wilderness

EASY ON THE

ICE

Her name spells glamour in letters a mile high—Sonja Henie, 20th Century-Fox's orchid of the ice. Endowed with the beauty and poise of a ballerina, legs that were insured for $100,000 by Lloyds of London and a pair of silver skates, she flashed across the Hollywood panorama two years ago and proceeded to establish herself as firmly upon American celluloid as she had upon the ice rinks of the world. A brown-eyed little person with a Norwegian heritage, she is, primarily, the competent sportswoman who smashed all box-office records early this year in a now famous cross-country skating tour; secondarily, she is the dimpled movie actress, official siren of "My Lucky Star"

IT PAYS TO BE

TOUGH

BY IDA ZEITLIN

John Garfield expected the worst, got the best. "Four Daughters" (in which he appeared with Priscilla Lane) made him a Hollywood booster

AT five o'clock on the day "Four Daughters" was previewed in Hollywood, a young man slipped into the theater. He was short and black-browed, blunt features lighted by a pair of fine dark eyes. He found himself an obscure seat in the gallery, sat through two features once and one newsreel twice.

At seven or thereabouts he produced a sandwich from his pocket and munched it, the faint crackle of waxed paper drawing scowls from his neighbors. You might have gathered that a certain surreptitious air about him arose from the knowledge that all along he'd planned to eat a sandwich where none should be eaten. You'd have been wrong. He was simply intent on hiding out in the crowd.

At five, few would have recognized him. At ten forty-five—he sat slouched in the darkness for half an hour after the preview was over—it was a different story. A star had been born. Or, since Mr. Garfield frowns on the word star, a luminary. For a change, movieland was cheering a young man who could never have posed for a collar ad—cheering not a face, but a performance. Autograph-hunters, wise in the ways of their prey, nabbed him as he tried to sneak through the side door. Still unaccustomed to his movie-given name, he signed "Jules Garfield."

"Waddaya mean, Ju-leez?" snorted one indignant youth. "Ain't you the guy wuz ina pitcha, name o' John Garfield?"

"That's my grandfather," explained the harassed Garfield, and fled.

He'd gone to the preview to take notes on what he did wrong. By arrangement, Roberta, his wife, had sat downstairs. He preferred to be alone with his agony. "I'll twist my own fingers instead of yours," he'd promised.

He'd been warned against Hollywood previews. But then he'd been warned against other aspects of Hollywood and found his fears to be groundless. "I expected the worst and got the best—a swell part, a director who directed and still left me free to make what I could of *Mickey Borden,* plenty of good parts lined up so I don't have to moulder. No, I'm a Hollywood booster —so long as they don't star me. Anyway," he grinned, "I've got my sixty-day stage clause. So what can I lose?"

It was the stage clause that postponed his arrival in Hollywood. Movie scouts had been after him for a couple of years.

"No contract," said Garfield, "without a clause that says I can go back to the stage on sixty days' notice."

"You're crazy," they told him, "giving up all that dough. The theater's dying."

Garfield's answer, undistinguished by logic, was nevertheless effective. *"You're* dying," he

Introducing John Garfield—bright new luminary in the movie constellation

It Pays to Be Tough

said, and turned on his heel.

Garfield started the job of standing on his own feet at the age of seven when his mother died. The chief problem centered round his year-old brother and that was solved when a well-to-do uncle took the baby. Though his father worked all day in a garment factory, Julie offered no problem. He could walk and talk and go to school. A kindly old couple next door undertook to give him his meals. For the rest, he was left to shift for himself.

His life became the life of the streets in a New York ghetto. He grew adept with his fists and the sidewalk lingo, with the arts of cop-chivvying and fruit-swiping. He had no kick coming till his father married again.

His stepmother never had a chance with Julie. Julie was a wise guy. He knew all about stepmothers and how they treated kids. But he'd show this one. She happened to be a gentle, patient woman with no wish but to make life more comfortable for her husband and stepson. She found a sullen rebel, flint to all overtures, too old to turn to her for tenderness, too young to appreciate her qualities.

The family moved to the Bronx, and the boy was sent to Angelo Patri's school—not a reform school, but an experimental institution for difficult children. He didn't much care what school he went to, so long as his extra-curricular activities remained unhampered. He annexed himself to a promising gang.

"We were really fancy," he recalls. "Threw bottles from roofs and made war on other gangs. The classier kids crossed the street when they saw me coming. 'Don't hang around with Julie,' their mothers told them. 'He's a bad boy.'"

What was eating Julie, though he didn't know it, was the yen to be a hero. He wanted to be looked up to. The only talents he'd developed lay in being a tough guy, so he cultivated those for all he was worth.

He had another talent of whose possibilities he was still unaware. His friends called it "makin' crazy."

"C'mon, fellas," they'd yell, "listen to Julie makin' crazy."

Mounted on a box under the corner lamppost, Julie would improvise tall tales. The kids were all reading Frank Merriwell. Play by play he'd describe a thrilling football match, featuring his father who was a tailor but had somehow managed to make the Harvard team, and his brother who was eight but the star of the Yale eleven. The street rang with yells of laughter and Julie went home with a sense of warmth in his breast.

IT was Angelo Patri who diverted his energies into less anti-social channels. "He took me out of the gutter," says Garfield blandly.

Patri got wind of the boy's speech-making gifts. He pointed out that the school offered classes in dramatics and oratory and that any student could elect eighty minutes a day of any course that appealed to him.

Julie decided to enroll. Not long after, the *New York Times* sponsored an oratorical contest on the Constitution and the erstwhile strong-arm guy brought home the bacon—a hundred dollars in cash, assorted medals, honors for himself and the school.

Suddenly his world was looking on him with respect. Hitherto stony-faced teachers smiled and clapped him on the back. Boys who had ostracized him courted his nod.

To realize that he could achieve a place in the sun by using his head instead of his fists came as a revelation to Julie. More important still was the revelation that he had an absorbing aim in life. He was going to be an actor. Not that his turbulent heart was suddenly tamed. The itch to roam seized him just before graduation, so off he went to visit an uncle in Chicago. This fall from grace cost him the medal, already engraved with his name, which the school conferred on the boy of whom it was proudest.

Last year he returned to his alma mater to address the graduating class. On the platform Mr. Patri handed him a leather case. "Here's something you forfeited seven or eight years ago. We feel it's coming to you now."

It was during his years at the Patri school that he met a girl named Roberta Mann. The gently-bred Roberta was alternately chilled and fascinated by "that crazy Julie," whose hair was as wild as his ideas. "You're crude," she'd storm at him. "You don't behave like a gentleman."

"Who wants to be a gentleman? I'm a free spirit."

"What's so free about you?"

"Well, for one thing, I'm starting off tomorrow to see the world."

"Yes, you are!"

A week later she'd received a postcard from a distant city.

EXCEPT for some such occasional lapse, he kept his eyes fixed on the goal. A teacher advised him to apply to the Heckscher Theatre, a training school for dramatic students, where he was accepted and assigned alternately to the rôles of *Quince* and *Bottom* in "A Midsummer Night's Dream." Jacob Ben-Ami attended a performance and word reached Garfield that the actor had spoken well of him. So he sat himself down and wrote Ben-Ami a letter, asking where he could go for further training.

"To the American Laboratory Theatre," Ben-Ami wrote back.

This was an organization run by two graduates of the Russian Art Theatre, Richard Boleslavski and Mme. Ouspenskaya. Garfield made an appointment with the lady. For an hour he rehearsed himself in a casual rendition of his opening line.

"Jacob Ben-Ami, who happens to be a very dear friend of mine," he told her, "sent me here. I would like an audition." (Suppose she phones him, you dope, and finds out what a liar you are, he was telling himself meantime.)

Luckily, she didn't. He got his audition. "We'll give you a month's trial," said Mme. Ouspenskaya. "Then, if you've proven yourself, a seven months' scholarship."

He was earning five dollars a week, selling the *Bronx Home News* from door to door. He knew that, to take advantage of this opportunity, he would have to give all his time to it. He also had to have the five dollars a week. He couldn't tell his father he'd given up his paper route. So he took the problem to Mr. Patri. "I'll substitute for the *Bronx Home News*," offered Patri, and loaned him five dollars a week while, for eight months, Julie tried frantically to absorb all that the Russians could teach him.

Came autumn, and Garfield turned once more to Ben-Ami, for no good reason except that he'd turned to him before. It worked again and he found himself apprenticed to Eva Le Gallienne's stock company—no pay, but a chance to learn and, if he made good, to be given a job when his apprenticeship was served. He earned his keep as he could—running errands, washing dishes, pushing a handcart in the garment center. Meantime he was playing extras and bits in the training school.

THE apprentices put on "Journey's End" as their graduation play. Garfield made a distinct impression. This was the night of wild suspense and hope, the night when Miss Le Gallienne chose from among her apprentices a few of the most promising, to be made regular members of the company.

She called his name. "Garfield, I want to give you a little lecture. The discipline of the theater is as strict as the discipline of the army. Why did you take Mr. C's shoes and hide them?"

"What are you talking about?" he stammered.

"The night Mr. C gave a guest performance here, his shoes were hidden just before the rise of the curtain. Why did you do it?"

"But I *didn't*—"

"I'm sorry, Garfield. All signs point to you. And we have no room here for people who jeopardize a production to prove that they're smart alecks."

Garfield hadn't hidden the shoes. He had a notorious and well-earned reputation as a practical joker, but he confined his activities to the gentry abovestairs. His reverence for the sacred traditions of the theater was as deep as Miss Le Gallienne's.

But what was the use! He stood miserably silent while the jobs went to others. Later, he received a letter of apology. The culprit had been found. His chance, however, remained lost.

In a state of thorough disgust with himself and fate, he fell in with an artist friend. "The function of the artist," said his friend, "is to know the country he lives in."

"Let's go," said Garfield.

They left New York with six dollars between them. They worked in the coal mines of Pennsylvania and the wheat fields of Kansas. For handouts at kitchen doors, they paid as they could. Garfield recited "Gunga Din." His friend presented the lady of the house with a pen-and-ink sketch. Eventually they separated, because it was easier for one alone to get a lift than two together. They were to meet at a certain gas station, but missed each other.

ARRIVING on the coast, Garfield tried to join the navy. They wouldn't have him. He tried to join the marines. They wouldn't have him. So he started back east. In Nebraska he began feeling sick and drowsy, but he kept on moving, and ten days later stumbled into his stepmother's kitchen. Panicstricken, she phoned Roberta, who took one look at her friend and called an ambulance. He spent the next eight weeks in the hospital with typhoid.

As he convalesced, resolution took shape and hardened. On his second day out, he walked into a producer's office. "Give me a job," he said.

"What do you mean, give you a job? What job?"

"Any job."

"What are you, nuts? How do I know you can act?"

"How do I know you can produce? I'm taking a chance on you. You don't have to take any chance on me. Give me a part and I'll read it for you."

The producer was sufficiently tickled with this unorthodox approach to let him read a part in "Lost Boy" and sufficiently impressed with his reading to give him the job.

Success achieved is pleasant, but makes for a less varied story than the struggle to achieve it. An agent saw Garfield and presently he was playing the office boy in the road company of "Counselor-at-Law." The thrill of his young life came when he was called back to do the same part with Muni on Broadway.

Muni was his paragon. He met Victor Wolfson, who loved books and found Garfield drinking in all he could teach him with the thirst of a parched mind. For a while, indeed, he planned to interrupt his stage career for college, but things were happening too fast.

He met Clifford Odets, who had just finished "Awake and Sing."

"What it's produced, I think you're the one to play it," he told Garfield.

Odets did for him in music what Wolfson had done for him in literature. The fire was laid, waiting only for a match to kindle it.

He and Odets would spend hours drinking wine, listening to music, talking their heads off. The playwright told him, too, about the Group Theatre, about the young people who'd formed it, their hopes, their plans and ideas.

"Sounds like heaven to me," said Garfield.

It ended in his becoming an apprentice, then a regular member of the Group. A couple of flops were followed by "Waiting for Lefty." Next day they were the talk of the town.

It was then that Garfield and Roberta married. The ceremony took place at nine o'clock.

The groom dashed downtown to perform at a benefit and dashed back to stand beside his bride for the wedding reception at ten thirty.

"Awake and Sing" brought him still more brilliantly into the limelight and he began turning down his first movie offer.

"I want to be in the theater. I need more training."

Only after "Having Wonderful Time" and "Golden Boy" did he feel that he might be ready for a stab at Hollywood. He joined Warners, because they agreed to his "back to Broadway" platform. But he gets an extra kick out of being on the same lot with Muni.

He blushed like a boy when Muni visited his set one day.

"What are you doing here?" smiled the older actor.

"Just came out to see what it was like."

Muni nodded. "You'll be all right. Don't give up this for this," he added, pointing to heart and head.

"I won't," promised Garfield, earnestly.

HE was frightened by the advance raves on his performance in "Four Daughters."

"They've given me a hurdle too high to jump at," he groaned.

He needn't have worried. Now that the picture's released, no complaints have been heard.

There's a long list of what he calls "real people" waiting to be played by him. He's alive to his times and finds them exciting. He's using his talent well. He has his precious stage clause to hug to his breast.

The kid who composed comedy fairy-tales under a lamppost to entertain his gang hasn't "made so crazy."

Ferenc

THE dream of every young man's heart—to have such a girl as this waiting for him! Bette Davis—who registers twenty-four years but who looks like fifteen, off-screen—caught George Arliss' attention by her simplicity and won that splendid rôle in "The Man Who Played God." Since then she has appeared in six pictures.

"Why I Will Not Re-marry Margaret Sullavan"

Engaging young Henry Fonda explains the reasons why his future design for living does not include his ex-wife

By George Stevens

IF little Margaret Sullavan came to Henry Fonda tomorrow and said, "Let's try again,"—Hank Fonda would have to refuse. He told me so yesterday.

Not that she would, you understand. Not that there is the slightest possible chance that Margaret Sullavan would ever come to Fonda and say, "We were fools to end it. Maybe we could make-a better go of it now. . . ." She'd scream at the idea.

They're not in love any more. They don't want to live together any more. They're swell friends, they make a good screen team, they like to play checkers on the set. And that's that.

At least so Hank says. Naturally I had to ask him. With both of them starring in "The Moon's Our Home," with both of them meeting daily at the studio, laughing together, remembering together; and finally, with Margaret's sudden announcement of an impending divorce from Director William Wyler, Rumor lifted up her nose, sniffed the tense atmosphere twice, and swished off to her Hollywood duties.

In order to understand the situation and Henry Fonda's attitude in all completeness, you must know this boy; you must be given a portrait of his character and of his basic psychological type and of the dual personality that bewilders him. You must somehow be made to know Henry Fonda better than he knows himself, and that won't be hard.

In the first place, Hank isn't all of the extravagant, whimsical, even coy being so often drawn for you by casual observers who never got past the barrier of self-defense he has built around himself. Hank's new to this game out here, he's a little inarticulate in the face of America's hurrahs and Hollywood's glib tongue, and he scurries into his shell every other minute as a quite natural result.

Simply, he's a good guy not too long out of college, and he's the most normal person in the world with a nice extrovertive outlook on

"A good guy not long out of college, the most normal person in the world. Out of living he wants a little excitement and all the happiness he can get"

life, and out of living he wants a little excitement and all the happiness in the world.

He wants, above everything else, to be part of an average American family with no fuss or publicity about it; he wants, if he marries again, a wife and some kids and a good house.

YOU have to go back a little way to get the perspective of this Fonda portrait. But throughout, remember this; that Hank is two completely different and separate people in one—that half of him is the young careless what-the-hell fellow Hollywood knows, and that the other half of him deeply needs security, a family, and a trust-fund. For everyone to see is the one side of him, a personality predominant so far and one that Margaret Sullavan must have known too well. But beneath the events of the last five years you cannot fail to detect the mature, down to earth, strong character which has guided him basically, and which is only now making itself apparent in him and to him.

You know pretty well the story of his years in stock companies, on small stages in small theaters—the uncertain income, the crazy life of road engagements, the never knowing. . . . You know—everyone has told you—that he has gone hungry often.

But you've also been told that Hank didn't give a hoot whether he ate or didn't eat; whether he had any money or not; that everything was just a bowl of chrysanthemums to him, and life a big laugh, and that he didn't give a darn what happened. That isn't true.

"Of course, I didn't sit and brood when things were bad," said Henry Fonda to me. "I'm not capable of that. It doesn't ever do any good and you waste time in worry when you could be out trying to better your condition. But I didn't just laugh, either.

"I guess the worst time I've ever had was dur-

"Why I Will Not Re-marry Margaret Sullavan"

248

ing two months, a year or two before I met Sullavan. I'd sub-let my apartment to a friend while I went to Washington, D. C., for a few weeks' engagement, you see, and when I was through there I came back to New York with about two hundred dollars and no prospects. I found my landlord ready to kick this friend of mine out on his ear because the rent wasn't paid—the kid was broke.

"It was a swell apartment, and it took every penny I had to get it out of hock. My friend stayed on with me, and between us we cleaned out everything in the pantry before the first two days had passed. Then during the next week we didn't eat anything. Not *anything*," he emphasized when I smiled my disbelief. "We drank water. That's all."

"I've heard of people living on cigarettes and coffee for two or three days," I muttered, "but a whole week. . . ."

HANK snorted. "We didn't have any cigarettes. They went the first night and so did the coffee. I said we drank water. Of course in the second week people began to find out we were in town and would invite us to dinner occasionally. But starved as we were we couldn't go and gobble down enough food to last us until the next invitation—pride, of course; we had to arrive looking as if we'd had two big square meals that day, and didn't care whether the next course amounted to anything or not. Later we'd be able to pick up a nickel once in a while, and when we got one we'd spend it on rice and puffed wheat—five cents worth of rice swells up into quite a good-sized dish, goes a long way."

"It's a nice picture," I suggested: "You sitting there in splendor, quietly starving to death with a proud tight smile on your lips."

"What do you mean, *sitting?*" frowned Hank. "I didn't sit. I got up every morning and drank my water and went out looking for work. I stayed out all day, too, went the rounds and saw everybody I knew who might be able to place me. I confess I didn't worry myself into a decline over the situation, but I didn't just accept it either."

"But hadn't you friends who were good for a touch?"

Fonda said simply, "I didn't like to do that."

"Well, then, how about your family?"

"I've never asked them for a thing!" he said seriously. "Not ever. When I went to

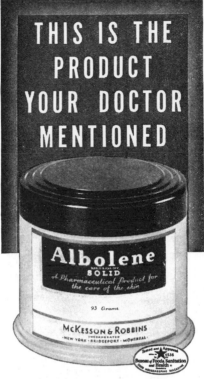

them and told them I was leaving home to try the theater, that was a definite break; I figured I was on my own, perfectly capable of taking care of myself, and if I did it so badly that I had to starve in the process then that was no worry of the folks."

Do you see? This was no irresponsible shallow personality going hungry in a smart apartment and making a game of it. Hank had character enough to eat rice when it would have been the easiest thing in the world to wire his father and get money for roast beef; Hank had character enough to keep up his prestige before his friends, and plod the theater by-ways in search of a job when he didn't know he was going to get this foot ahead of the next one.

He didn't groan all over the place, because he's congenitally unable to groan or worry. But he smiled at the spot he was in and went out to fix things.

In Easter week a Metropolitan florist hired seven extra men for rush delivery service; Hank was one of them. The forty-five dollars he earned lasted until the summer tour to Westchester.

Of his engagement and marriage to lovely little "Sullavan," you must know that they came together and looked up a minister because they couldn't help themselves. "I'd been in love before, certainly," Fonda told me. "Back in college I developed a heavy crush, the way you do in college, and I got the same way a time or two while I was batting around New York. But I never thought of marriage until I met Sullavan. Things were better then, I had steadier jobs and more money; she was in stock too, and together we made out pretty well. Of course, there were times when the going was tough—an engagement would be cancelled or something—but I couldn't worry even then. I'd take the bad breaks the same way I took those two months I told you about."

PERHAPS Margaret didn't understand. Anyway she is said to have explained to Hollywood that she couldn't go on living with Hank because Hank wouldn't take things seriously; because Hank laughed when they were broke, and made a game of things. And if that's the way it is—if beautiful little "Sullavan" must think of the future and if Henry Fonda must smile with the present—then nothing on earth, not even love, could make a successful marriage for them.

"When we found there was no show," he said to me, "we just talked it over and decided to call it quits."

Hank, true to his nature, is happy these days. He doesn't really believe that he's set in pictures or with the public, although all America sings his name; and as long as he's single he doesn't care.

"That's one side of me," he told me slowly, frowning in his effort at introspection. "Right now I haven't any ties, I'm having a good time, and I don't want security. If the movie industry finished with me tomorrow, I'd go right back to the stage and be just as content; if I go on making this money and have success, I'll travel a bit and hunt about for a little excitement.

"But that isn't what I want most, you understand. My home and my family were completely normal and average; I want the same thing. My sisters are married, having children—and every time I send one of them an anniversary present I feel as if I were failing to do my bit, as if I'd poofed out on them.

"If I could find the right girl tomorrow, I'd marry her and establish trust funds for my kids and I'd settle down. But you can't *make* things like that happen. I'm not going around peering into the face of every woman I meet, asking myself, 'Can this be the one? Would she be a good mother and a fine wife? Do I love this blonde, or that brunette?'"

"Then you're not in love now?" I pried persistently.

"No."

"Shirley Ross . . .?"

"A lovely girl and a good kid. We had a lot of fun."

"Jeanette MacDonald . . .?"

Hank grinned. "She's my next-door neighbor, you know." He pointed through a window. "Right over there. I think she's beautiful. But—well, I've taken her out once, to the Mayfair. At the beginning of the evening I called her 'Miss MacDonald," and by twelve o'clock Hollywood had us engaged. That's all."

That *is* all. You can't make anyone believe it, but there just isn't any more. Henry Fonda's having a swell time seeing the town, he's not in love with Margaret Sullavan or anyone else, and it may be years before he discovers the extraordinary woman who will understand his psychology and his viewpoints; who will be a wife to him.

At the time of this writing he likes Virginia Bruce, but there's nothing astonishing about that. So does every man in Hollywood. "James Stewart and John Swope (the fellows who live here with me) and I have a sort of contest every night to see who can get a date with her," grinned Hank. "We all took her to the preview of 'Trail of the Lonesome Pine' —she wouldn't make any choice that evening.

"Virginia has a sense of humor, you know. I think that's one of the most important things in any girl. The wife I'll have some day will be able to laugh. . . ."

Which explains much, if you will think back.

YOU may, then, conclude what you will. You may remember that famous actors and actresses have denied being in love before this; that they have carefully prepared a nice little story for public consumption, only to slip off in the dead of night a few weeks later to justify all the settled rumors.

But when Henry Fonda told me yesterday that he would never remarry Margaret Sullavan, I believed him. Because:

(1) He isn't in love with her.

(2) She isn't in love with him.

(3) Even if they had once more caught the elusive spark during those casual interludes on the set, they're both intelligent enough to admit one mistake is one lesson, not to be repeated.

(4) Hank is extrovertive, fundamentally unable to analyze or fuss; Margaret is obviously his exact antithesis. Wherefore they are, now and for-ever-more with no blame attached to either, incompatible.

(5) Hank, to the intense surprise of all who know him only through interviews and hearsay, is too strong a character to allow momentary sizzling (if any), sentimental memories, or any other fleeting impulse to lure him back into a relationship that has proved unfortunate.

And (6) Hank wants a marriage entirely apart from the glamorous hulabaloo and publicity which necessarily surrounds a Hollywood movie star; that would be impossible with famous Margaret Sullavan.

Somehow, in these six reasons why Mrs. Rumor is a liar, there are summed up all the various facets of Henry Fonda's personality.

They represent, in detail, the true portrait of "Hank."

PHOTOPLAY'S
Memory Album

Edited By Frederick L. Collins

Lawrence Tibbett's "The Rogue Song" raised the cry of "The movie-going public wants no hi-falutin' music!"

Garbo had the movie world jittery when she sprang her first "I tank I go home." Above, when she returned

Above, Charles Farrell and Janet Gaynor became the leading screen lovers in the film "Seventh Heaven"

Jeanette MacDonald, darling of the musical comedy stage, became Chevalier's partner

Warners set the world agog with talkies. Al Jolson and May McAvoy in "The Jazz Singer"

Above, the Farrell-Gaynor team scored again in "Street Angel." But within a year came a new order—the talkies

Probably the most popular screen pair of the day was Mr. Rin-Tin-Tin and his very comely spouse, named Nanette

Studio vied with studio in the new medium—articulate movies. M-G-M's bid—a dozen beauties as a living curtain in "The Broadway Melody"

Harry Carey and Edwina Booth in "Trader Horn," the film which sent Miss Booth on her daring adventure to Darkest Africa

Eddie Cantor, with the "It" girl, Clara Bow, in his first movie, "Kid Boots." Critics saw him as "promising material"

"Hell's Angels" introduced a sensation, Jean Harlow (with Ben Lyon), and platinum as a shade of hair

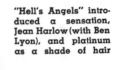

"The Tower of Lies" had in it the new star, Norma Shearer (with Bill Haines), and Lon Chaney without make-up

The prize picture of 1931 was the great epic "Cimarron," with Richard Dix in the leading rôle of Yancey Cravat

Right, Charles Rogers with Clara Bow in "Wings." He had not yet been nicknamed Buddy

Ruth Chatterton (above with Ulrich Haupt) in "Madame X." No less a personage than Lionel Barrymore directed her

Left, Doug Fairbanks, Jr., and Edward G. Robinson from the classic "Little Caesar." It made movie history

HOLLYWOOD SERVICE FLAG

"That this nation, under God, shall have a new birth of freedom . . ." *Abraham Lincoln*

252

Hardie Albright | Herbert Anderson | Russell Arms | Gene Autry | Lew Ayres | George K. Arthur | Roscoe Ates | William Bakewell | Richard Barthelmess | George Brent

Richard Denning | Roland Drew | Frankie Darro | Leif Erikson | Henry Fonda | Bramwell Fletcher | Doug. Fairbanks Jr. | Clark Gable | Richard Greene | William Haines

Huntz Hall | Dan Dailey Jr. | Jon Hall | Louis Hayward | Don Briggs | Tom Brown | F. Bartholomew | Macdonald Carey | Robert Cornell | Robert Cummings

Bruce Cabot | Alan Curtis | Donald Crisp | Jackie Coogan | Phillips Holmes | Alexander D'Arcy | Owen Davis Jr. | Stirling Hayden | Peter Lind Hayes | William Holden

Ken Howell | Billy Halop | Tim Holt | Nick Lukats | Jeffrey Lynn | Billy Mauch | Bobby Mauch | Ray McDonald | Robert Montgomery | Doug. Montgomery

Tim McCoy | Ray Middleton | Raymond Massey | Victor Mature | Wayne Morris | Burgess Meredith | Richard Ney | David Niven | Laurence Olivier | William Orr

George O'Brien | Edmond O'Brien | Tyrone Power | Robert Preston | John Payne | Gene Raymond | Buddy Rogers | Gilbert Roland | Cesar Romero | Ronald Reagan

Craig Reynolds | Jackie Searle | Robert Stack | Robert Sterling | James Stewart | Robert Shaw | Craig Stevens | Lyle Talbot | Frankie Thomas | Lee Tracy

Robert Wilcox | Henry Wilcoxon | Rudy Vallee | Douglas McPhail | John Shelton | Sid Silvers | Melvyn Douglas | Grant Withers | John Beal | Robert Coote

Richard Quine | Gabriel Dell | Guinn Williams | Van Heflin | Broderick Crawford | Gordon Jones | Tony Martin | Sterling Holloway | Wesley Barry | Fritz Feld

Jack Briggs | Buddy Pepper | George Holmes | Richard Arlen | Glenn Ford | William Tracy | John Carroll | Russell Hayden | Eddie Albert | Lewis Howard

Introduction to the Forties

Meatless Tuesday . . . V-Mail . . . Victory gardens . . . ration stamps. . . . Strange new words that would become a common part of our vocabulary by the second year of the forties. We were at war again, and the men we loved best were going off to serve their country.

Gable, recently bereft of wife Carole Lombard, was the first to go. A host of familiar faces would soon follow. Their "letters home" in *Photoplay* were our only contact with them.

For the girls back home, pining or troubled, *Photoplay* had an advice column written first by the undisputed queen of the movies Bette Davis, then by Claudette Colbert, the girl half America was in love with.

But *Photoplay* had lots of stars who were writing for them now. Humphrey Bogart had just blossomed into stardom and was already the irrepressible Bogey. The love affair between him and *Photoplay* was instant.

Meanwhile, new actors were piling into Hollywood like crazy. There were men to fill gaps left by departing heroes. Some were names that were forgotten at the war's end. Others, like Van Johnson and Alan Ladd, seem inseparable from the forties. And there was a skinny lad whose mere appearance was causing girls to swoon and perfectly sane people to riot—the fabulous Frank Sinatra.

But most fascinating were those dazzling new glamour queens the GIs called pinups. Rita Hayworth, who would soon marry the man of the hour Orson Welles, to begin a long line of impressive alliances. Sweater girl Lana Turner, who would tell *Photoplay* so hopefully, with every marriage, that this was the last. By the decade's end she would have married Artie Shaw, Bob Topping, and the father of her daughter Cheryl, Steven Crane. There were four more to go.

But the very favorite GI pinup, despite protest, was undeniably Betty Grable. Betty of the million-dollar legs and queen of the forties' musicals, for, as Hollywood had learned, musicals are indispensable in time of trouble.

But it wasn't just the new glamour queens who starred in the musicals. One of our own singing-dancing children had grown up. Judy Garland was a woman and marrying David Rose. Her musicals would forever be looked on as the best—her marriages not. By mid-decade she would be Mrs. Vincente Minnelli, posing for *Photoplay* photos with daughter Liza.

Within a matter of months, Judy's old pal Mickey Rooney would fall in love, marry, and have his heart broken by beautiful new starlet Ava Gardner.

What was it about the forties that made for such bad marriages and so many? The war had destroyed Carole Landis's first marriage, she told *Photoplay* readers. Later she would add, "Glamour Girls Are Suckers." And maybe she was right. By the next decade she would have committed suicide over Rex Harrison.

Appalled, happy couples in Hollywood protested and began giving advice on how to make a marriage last. One of those couples was Bogey and his battling bride Mayo Methot. Within years, it would be B and B—Bogart and Bacall.

But there was one lady who seemed to be in no danger of divorcing. The beautiful Ingrid Bergman, so pure, so clean, so natural, looked like the lady who could cure Hollywood. Beautiful, talented, her popularity would grow incredibly before the end of the decade. She would win an Oscar, and, together with Bing Crosby, she would win more *Photoplay* Gold Medal Awards than anyone had done before. She looked as if she was well on her way to being the biggest.

In 1945, a curious thing happened. An ad for a new movie appeared. But it was no ordinary ad and the message on it was magic.

"Gable's Back and Garson's Got Him!" it blared.

The King was back—the war was over.

They all started coming back now, and it was fantastic. But things had changed. Spencer Tracy was a full-fledged leading man by now—a star. And he and Katharine Hepburn were creating yet another show business legend. Release from the army was bringing some new talent to Hollywood. There were young Montgomery Clift and Burt Lancaster, and still more stars rising on the firmament. New legends were being made—and not all of them so friendly.

It was in 1941 that both Joan Fontaine and sister Olivia de Havilland were nominated for an Oscar. Joan won. Now it was Livvie's turn, but when Joan went to congratulate her, Livvie cut her dead.

It was on this note that the decade was dragging to a close. But the best and the worst were to come.

America, going through a postwar "Red" scare, began to look with suspicion on Hollywood, and the House Un-American Activities Committee began to investigate. "I'm no Communist," Bogey told *Photoplay* fans. But the scare would be a long one, and many would disappear.

Judy Garland wrote her very first fiction story for *Photoplay*. It was called "Lonely Girl."

Photoplay's own Louella Parsons was right there to see Rita Hayworth marry Aly Khan and become Hollywood's first full-fledged princess.

Ingrid Bergman—the favorite, the untouchable—had fallen in love with a man who was not her husband. Rumors were flying that she was furthermore pregnant by him. Ingrid sent her agent a telegram. "Sue anyone who says I'm pregnant." It was quickly followed by another: "Don't sue anyone."

It was true. The golden girl had fallen. And an America that had adored her was furious. They would not forgive her, they would not take her back. She was through.

And so, in a sense, was everything that had produced the movies, the stars, and, most importantly, the fan books. Within the decade all of them would change.

A letter to my Mother

This is a love letter, a different kind of love letter, one every woman will want to keep

BY JOHN PAYNE

ARMY AIR CORPS

"Mom" of John's letter: Ida Schaefer Payne

Dear Mom:

Looks like another Mother's Day is rolling around and it seems a little different than it ever has before. I feel as though I've started a lot of things all over again. I'm going to school again and, somehow, I feel as I did in high school. Today in this upset world, with everyone doing things he's never done before, you seem to kind of go back to all the things in your life that are most solid. It's nothing any of us here didn't know, but we seem to keep on discovering that mothers are the greatest institutions we've ever had.

You'd be surprised, but out of all the women the group in the barracks talk about, their mothers always top the list. Of course, they gab a lot about some blonde or girl they've dated, but that's half kidding and something that helps pass the time away. They're not kidding about the other. It sounds kind of serious, but I just thought I'd tell you, for the one thousandth time, that I love you very much.

I'm learning a lot here. You know how I always hated math and physics and how often I flunked. Well, I can't afford to flunk now, for math and physics are involved with something I'd like to do very much. Of course, I don't know for sure whether I will really get a crack at the job I'd like, but at least I've got a chance, a pretty good one.

Anyway, no matter what job I get in this war, I'll still be flying.

I read an article in the paper the other day and in it this guy had written a piece about why America and the United Nations couldn't lose the war. He was a German by birth and he'd been in a Prussian military academy for two years before he came to America and joined our Army. At the time he was writing he was a private with our Marines and had been injured at Guadalcanal. When he was injured it seems his best friend was hit, too. He died in his arms. The last words he said were to tell his name. The man writing the article said the Germans were taught to die, made eager to die for Hitler and for the Fatherland, but that that kind of fanaticism could never compare with the way Americans died for their home, for Mom and Dad and a girl.

The Americans died gallantly and without fanaticism. He said that was why we couldn't lose the war. I know he's right.

A LL this means such a big change for everybody, from the highest to lowest, the way we all are living, the food we eat, the places we go or can't go. I'm not sure, in part, that it's not a good thing. People have to look within themselves so much more than they used to for their pleasures and for the solutions to everyday problems. It's as though we were all growing up. We've always had so much of everything, everybody's had such swell chances to get what he wanted in this

For a last look at actor John Payne, see "Hello, Frisco, Hello."

256

A Letter to my Mother

country, that sometimes we ended up wanting a lot of things that weren't good for us. Unless I'm mistaken, when it's all over, we'll have a lot saner sense of values.

Not to change the subject, but I'm still looking for a pitcher you haven't got. Found a little Indian one the other day, but remembered you had two in your collection and didn't send it. Have made it part of my life's ambition to find somewhere one of these days a pitcher you don't already have. I was telling the fellows you have about 500 pitchers in your collection.

Remember the time, Mom, after I'd flunked solid geometry twice in succession and you and Dad were despairing about whether I'd ever get out of high school and I pulled the old gag about threatening to burn down the schoolhouse so I could get out? But you gave me a talking-to and tried to explain to me that in order to get a lot of the things you wanted in life, there'd always be a lot of things you had to do that you didn't like. I've found that increasingly true ever since I've been away, but I never expected it to be true about the same things. After ten years or more I wind up with solid geometry and math at flying school again only now, Mom, I've *got* to pass it. I got through the first stage and feel pretty proud about it and know that half of it must be due to the prayers I asked you to say. Maybe the things you slough off in life you have to go back to. It's even possible that the reason we're fighting this war is because we didn't finish the last one the way we should have.

Give Aunt Rosie my love and you two hold down the fort. I hear Brother Pete is in line for promotion. I hope he gets it. I was awfully glad to hear that Brother Bill got the job he wanted in the shipyards. Hope he likes the work. Tell him it's too bad he couldn't have been a little younger to join Pete and me and that I'm proud of him.

When I see my daughter Julie on my trips home from camp, she seems more beautiful and talkative each time. Did I ever ask that many questions, Mom? Anyway, I'm going to write you soon again for some answers when I run out of information for Julie. She sends her love and, naturally, Mom, you know how you stand with me though I still don't write as often as I should. I think of you and Godmother and Aunt Rosie and everyone at home every day.

I love you, dear, and God bless you.

John.

See-worthy: Ann Sheridan, who makes eyes at sailors in Warners' "Navy Blues"

Madison Lacy

Man who likes to laugh at himself: Sonny Tufts of Paramount's "I Love A Soldier"

Lady with ruffles:
Loretta Young, of
"Ladies Courageous"

Hard-working visionary: Orson Welles, who has given new ideas to the arts of Hollywood

Superb actor: He takes such stuff as dreams are made of and turns it into a great film—"Citizen Kane"

Master craftsman: He writes, produces, directs, acts; and his name is now a password in America drama

MAN
Of The Moment

Rita Hayworth

THE Little Foxes

Horace Giddens' soul turned over at the thought of Regina's forcing his lovely Zan to marry Leo

One of the most famous characters in the drama comes to the screen: Regina Giddens as played by Bette Davis

There is probably a woman like Regina Giddens in your town. You envy her her breeding, her position — but would you envy her her heart?

Fiction version by NORTON RUSSELL

Produced by Samuel Goldwyn. Directed by William Wyler. Distributed by RKO-Radio pictures. Screen play by Lillian Hellman from her stage success as produced by Herman Shumlin.

THE CAST

Regina Giddens........Bette Davis

Horace Giddens...Herbert Marshall

Alexandra Giddens...Teresa Wright

David Hewitt......Richard Carlson

Ben Hubbard........Charles Dingle

Oscar Hubbard....Carl Benton Reid

Leo Hubbard..........Dan Duryea

Birdie............Patricia Collinge

PHOTOPLAY COMBINED WITH MOVIE MIRROR

Girl on the cover

SHE sells magazines.
I don't mean that she actually stands on the street corner selling our wares, but it amounts to that. Here's why: Many people ask why an editor of a motion-picture magazine puts a star on a cover. Is it friendship? A desire to give a promising girl a break? The influence of the producing company? No, it is none of these. Box-office appeal is what matters, just as it does on a marquee. And Bette Davis on the cover of a motion-picture magazine means that that issue will sell more than if any other girl were on the cover.

Although that is true, I am fortunate to be one of Bette's friends. We met first in her platinum blonde days when she got her first break with George Arliss in "The Man Who Played God." I remember that she, Herb Crooker (then with Warner Brothers, now one of the important executives of this company) and I scurried through the rain to sit for hours in our favorite speakeasy and talk of many things. Today Bette is no different, unless perhaps more mature, more understanding.

She has that characteristic of great actresses: Intense preoccupation with her own work. And yet there is this difference: She always has time for yours; always makes it as much her problem as your own. When we planned to merge PHOTOPLAY and MOVIE MIRROR, she wanted to talk about it; she wanted to be helpful—and in one long recent discussion we had was very helpful. She was the first to wire me when the first merged issue arrived. She said, "Just previewed the copy you sent and enjoyed every page of it." While under ordinary circumstances I might suspect such a wire, since Bette sent it I believe every word of it.

ALTHOUGH in my opinion she is America's greatest movie actress, this is not her chief pride. On the contrary, she has said about one job: "This is the only thing I've ever done I'd like my grandchildren to know about." She was referring to her performance on the radio of the little Arch Oboler masterpiece, "Alter Ego."

The newest gossip rumor is that Bette will reconcile with her former husband, Harmon Nelson. I have never asked Bette about this, and I don't believe I need to. Every action of hers all her life contradicts the rumor. She and Harmon Nelson as intelligent people are good, close friends who see each other whenever they have an opportunity. I don't believe they will go back together because thus far Bette Davis has never gone back—she always goes forward. This is to me the secret of her greatness.

And wherever she pioneers it is always with an intensity and a sincerity that get results. Perhaps it is the raising of funds to buy a Seeing Eye dog for an unfortunate blind person; perhaps it is the slow, painful process of helping a young protegee find success; perhaps it is a game of charades—and I have seen her perform her part with all the spirit of a Big Scene. Always these things are done by Bette Davis with a whole heart.

I have admitted that she is on the cover of PHOTOPLAY-MOVIE MIRROR because "she sells magazines," but besides all that I am proud to have her there because I consider her the first lady of Hollywood.

Ernest V. Heyn

Riverbottom

In answering these letters I
am not seeking to set down hard and
fast rules of conduct. I am merely
giving my own personal opinion as to
the course I would follow, were I in
the position described by the letter-
writer. Of course, since I don't
know the actual persons involved, and
since I know that circumstances always
alter cases, under these conditions
my advice must not be considered
authoritative in any instance.

Sincerely yours,

Bette Davis

264

36

What should I do?

YOUR PROBLEMS ANSWERED BY BETTE DAVIS

Photoplay-Movie Mirror institutes the greatest advice feature of the year

BELIEVING that there is great need for wise counsel in this troubled world, Photoplay-Movie Mirror has persuaded Bette Davis, the woman who is Hollywood's famous advice star, to act as consultant to its readers. So every month Miss Davis will study the letters you send her and give her answers on these pages. Naturally she cannot cover every individual query; she will of necessity have to choose those problems which seem most universal. But you may rest assured your letter will be read personally by her and, as proof, each one of you will receive her acknowledgment. Address your letters to Miss Bette Davis, c/o Photoplay-Movie Mirror, 7751 Sunset Boulevard, Hollywood, California. And have no fear that your identity will be revealed to the world, for no names of towns are given and all names of persons are changed to protect the writers. From her personal mail Bette Davis has selected these letters as the ones to be answered this month through the pages of Photoplay-Movie Mirror.

The Editors

DEAR Miss Davis:

My husband has been drafted and sent to a training camp nearly 2,000 miles away. A good many girls have had to give up their husbands to the Army, but I wonder how many of them face the same problem that I do. You see, I had only known my husband six months before we were married. And we were married chiefly because he was going to be drafted and he said he couldn't bear to leave me unless he knew that I belonged to him.

He didn't know that for two years before I met him I had been going steady with a nice boy, Tom, in our town. Tom won't be taken into the Army because he was blinded in one eye during a hunting accident.

He has telephoned me several times, asking for dates. I told my mother at first that I didn't want to talk to him but she says I'm foolish.

I'm still in love with my husband and I write to him every day, but I'm only twenty-two and I'll have to admit that I think I'll go crazy sitting at home night after night.

What do you think I should do? Refuse to see Tom? Or go out with him on a strictly friendly basis? If I do that, should I tell my husband about the dates or just keep it quiet?

Eleanor J.

Dear Eleanor J..

You are probably only one out of the hundreds of girls who married in haste because of the war.

My deduction is that you are more in love with Tom than you are with your husband, in spite of what you say. However, let us suppose that you don't realize that fact yourself.

In a way, it seems selfish for a boy to want to marry just before he leaves for camp; this is a man's way of putting a girl on the shelf for the duration although he can do nothing for her, not even offer her companionship. It is, in fact, a type of hoarding.

I think you want me to say that it is quite all right for you to go out with Tom. Personally, that is exactly what I would do under the circumstance, being careful to keep our relationship entirely friendly—if you could manage it that way.

Every girl has to look down the road of the future and decide upon one of two paths for herself. She has to foresee the consequences of any given act. In this case there is a chance that townspeople are not going to understand your going out with Tom and that you may suffer from undue criticism. Also, Tom may get out of hand.

If you don't tell your husband you have been seeing Tom, he will learn of it in time, make no mistake about that. Then pray that your husband is an understanding soul.

Finally, beware of propinquity Being with Tom a great deal may create even greater problems than loneliness and boredom.

Sincerely yours,
Bette Davis.

DEAR Miss Davis:

This is not the typical "fan" letter. I have never before written a stranger a letter, but I suppose there is a first time for everything.

I'm a widow, Miss Davis. I'm only twenty-seven, financially independent, and I have a rather good education. But I can't seem to meet the right sort of man. I try not to be too particular; I've done all the usual little stunts such as going out with a perfect bore of a man just on the chance that I might meet someone interesting. Alas, I meet only more bores.

Worse, practically every man who takes an interest in me eventually works around to the old cliché—"Well, well, are you a *merry* widow!" In the town in which I am now living only a girl who will try anything once is considered a good sport.

I don't intend to sacrifice my ideals for cheap companionship. Yet I don't want to live my life alone. So my problem is this: How can I meet a "good" man?

How does one attract a man one meets casually? And how does a girl who *has* been married keep a man interested while refusing to grant him certain taboo favors?

I shall appreciate any advice you care to give me.

Most cordially yours,
Mary-Jo G.

Dear Mrs. G.:

In any woman's life, she meets only a few men who really appeal to her, so she must be careful not to drive those away. Life has a way of solving itself, if one doesn't push it too impatiently.

What Should I Do?

Apparently you are trying too hard to find a man to *marry*. Men sense this hunting quality instantly and are frightened away by it. A man friend of mine once said, "Why do women let that acquisitive gleam come into their eyes after they have known a man for an hour and learned that he has a decent job, has pleasant manners and is free?"

Let that be a warning. If I were you, since you have a good education and are only twenty-seven and financially independent, I should travel about the country.

For some reason, a newcomer to town has especial charm. If I were you, I'd take advantage of that fact. I think the only way to secure and hold a man's respect is to be good spirited company, interested in everything he says, but to keep him guessing.

The best of luck to you,

Bette Davis.

DEAR Miss Davis:
Please don't get the impression that I'm one of those girls who runs around complaining to all her friends about her woes. But I feel as if you were a member of my family, Bette.

Sometimes I think I'm going to tell Burke's mother right to her face what I think of her. The only way I could keep from it today was to sit down and write to you.

I'd better begin at the beginning. Burke and I have been married four years—we were both twenty-one on our wedding day. Burke explained to me when we were making plans for marriage that we would have to live with his mother.

For two years, things were really swell. Mrs. R. was very nice to me. She let us live our lives and she lived hers.

But at the end of that time, she decided that we should have a baby. She began to tell me about the mental troubles of some women she knew who had never had children. After that she began to hint that I should see a doctor because I might not be "normal."

Burke and I have talked it over and decided not to have children yet. Both his mother and I are self-supporting and he is likely to be taken into the Army. He told his mother that he didn't want to leave me with a child to care for alone. She scoffed at that and said she had raised him, she guessed she could care for a grandson. She said everyone had a baby during wartime.

I thought it was bad enough to live in a house with a woman who was sulking all the time, but the next thing I knew she was telling around town that I *couldn't* have a child. And she began to invite a young divorcee to the house practically every Sunday for dinner. This girl is very pretty and full of wisecracks. She has a little girl aged three that she brings along occasionally.

If you think that isn't something, you should see the performance. Mrs. R. hands the baby to Burke, saying that she can't get over how much the child resembles Burke. Then the baby's mother makes eyes at Burke and says he certainly could sire a handsome son.

I've tried to get Burke to move out, but the one time he agreed, his mother had a fainting spell. The doctor told me that she did have a tricky heart, but that she would live for years unless something unforeseen should happen. Of course, I don't want to do anything to upset her heart, but on the other hand I've nearly choked, trying to keep from telling her that I think she's a meddling old fool.

Forgive me, Miss Davis, for going on this way, but you can see that I have my hands full. I just can't see any way out. What would you do?

Janet R.

Dear Mrs. R.:
Your problem interests me very much. It seems to me that it is the right of every married couple to decide if and when they are going to have children, without interference from anyone.

By all means, go to your library and borrow a play titled "The Silver Cord" by Sydney Howard. This is the story of a managing mother-in-law and the trouble she caused in two households. The only solution to a problem of this kind, and the action I would take, is to explain to Burke how you feel about his mother's behavior, then to move out. Burke will soon see that his mother's attacks are phony.

If it were I, in this spot, I'd act—definitely, vigorously, and with full knowledge that one of two things would happen. Either I'd have my husband and home to myself, or I'd lose him entirely. That is a gamble I'd have to take for the sake of my peace of mind. Incidentally, if he doesn't stand by you, he doesn't love you.

Sincerely yours,
Bette Davis.

DEAR Miss Davis:
I just saw "The Man Who Came To Dinner" for the third time. I liked the way you played *Maggie Cutler* very much, probably because I am a secretary myself.

I am now doing my hair up high the way yours was done, but still I'm no prize package. A beautiful, famous, elegant lady like you probably has no idea what it means to be awkward and self-conscious. I just know, to look at your hands, that you've never bitten your fingernails. I'm ashamed to admit it, but I have an awful time keeping my nails above the quick.

I might as well tell you all the things that are wrong with me in hopes that you will be able to help me. Whenever a man pays attention to me—and that isn't very often—I can't think of a thing to say. I feel all tied up in knots and I just stand there sort of grinning and wishing the floor would open and drop me into a well.

I'm not exactly a dumb bunny because I got good grades in school and my three older sisters nag at me and say I wouldn't be bad-looking if I weren't such a goof.

I'm twenty-two years old, five feet, eight inches tall and I only weigh 115 pounds.

I won't take up any more of your time, dear Miss Davis, but I thought you might be able to help me. I get so blue sometimes. This is what I want to know—how can I gain poise?

Anxiously yours,
Ruth Ann W.

Dear Miss W.:
In the first place, since you are working and are, therefore, financially independent, if I were in your place I'd take a room in a guest house, so moving away from those three older sisters who, by their nagging, would probably give even a beauty like Hedy Lamarr an inferiority complex.

Paint your nails with the brightest red polish you can find and see if you aren't too pleased with the effect to spoil it by nibbling.

You are tall. Do you stoop when you walk? Some of the loveliest girls in pictures are tall—Alexis Smith, Gail Patrick and Rosalind Russell, for instance—and each of them is as straight as a ramrod.

Finally, the best way I know of gaining poise is to forget yourself entirely and to direct your attention at the person with whom you are talking. Wonder, if you can't divert yourself otherwise, how he or she would look in a bathing suit. Remember those celebrated lines:

When pompous people squelch me with cold and snooty looks
It makes me happy to conjecture how they'd look in bathing suits.

Develop a system of conversational topics to put the other fellow at his ease and you'll be surprised at your own resultant calm. Ask, "What picture could you bear to see once a week for an entire year?" or "What was the most frightening thing you ever saw?"

Relax, and you'll be all right.

Sincerely yours,
Bette Davis.

DEAR Miss Davis:
You've played the roles of so many girls in serious trouble that I thought you might be able to give me some good advice.

I am a country girl who came to the big city and met a very nice boy. Everything I have ever had I have worked for very hard; he has an elegant job that was simply handed to him on a silver platter.

What I am getting at is this, Miss Davis, he has always had everything he wanted. I've learned that there are some things out of reach. Now he is going into the Army. He asked me to marry him when he gets out and I said I would because I love him with my whole heart and soul.

The only trouble is that we are feuding all the time over a very important matter. He thinks I should give him the things that go with marriage right now, before he goes away to war, instead of waiting until he comes home and the wedding is held. He says he doesn't know what is in store for him and that I should be generous and noble instead of thinking only of myself.

I am seventeen and he is twenty-four. Please, please tell me what to do.

Your friend,
Betty L.

Dear Miss L.:
At seventeen, one is likely to think that the present love is the one and only, but take my word for it—life is just beginning. The argument that men use, "Don't be selfish; be patriotic, be generous—I may not live long," is not new. From my reading, I judge that stone-age men used the same type of persuasion.

A girl facing this decision, as I have said before, has to consider the consequences of action in either direction. The consequences, if she listens to her soldier boy, are likely to be extremely serious.

On the other hand, if she says "no" life will go on much the same for her—without regrets. Never forget this: It takes a frightfully strong character to be a weak woman.

And always remember, there are more ways than just one of showing love and devotion. The promise of daily letters, cigarettes every week, surprise packages of writing paper, razor blades and sweets, as well as visits to camp may not be as "all-out" for victory as he would like, but in that way you will be telling your soldier how much he means to you without endangering your own future.

Sincerely yours,
Bette Davis.

Bette Davis Faces Sorrow

Thoughts for this woman, for any woman, facing unhappiness today

THROUGH *this page each issue, Photo-play has brought you a feature of which it has been very proud—letters from you and wise answers to them from Bette Davis. This month, instead of these letters, Photoplay is bringing you some simply spoken and utterly sincere words from editor Helen Gilmore. The following issue, the magazine will publish those letters which did not appear this month.*
F.R.S.

BY HELEN GILMORE

TRAGEDY has come to Bette Davis.

Because of the God-given elasticity of human beings to meet incalculable sorrow and more particularly because of the quality of this woman's spirit, she will come through a finer person, without any words of ours to help her.

But friends cannot stand by and see a friend in trouble without reaching out a hand, without giving voice to the sympathy that fills them. And so we speak, not alone for ourselves and the days and hours of personal companionship we have known with Bette and the splendid man who was her husband, but for those thousands of readers who month after month through the pages of her Photoplay feature "What Should I Do?" have turned to her for help and advice.

It is now our turn to be the friend.

As friends, you will want to know what has happened to her. So let us walk with her through those last days of the life of her husband, Arthur Farnsworth.

It was Monday, August twenty-third. Farney, as she called him, had left their River Bottom home in Glendale for the Walt Disney Studios where he was acting as technical adviser on aeronautics for some Government films Disney is

doing. Seemingly he was in the best of health after their vacation in New Hampshire together and Bette promptly took advantage of the brief respite from costume and make-up tests for "Mr. Skeffington," her next picture for Warner Brothers, by calling her close friend, Margaret Donovan, formerly head of Warners' hairdressing department and now the wife of Perc Westmore. Together they sallied forth into the market place for some household shopping.

Bette had returned and was in the house alone with the servants when a call came from the Walt Disney studios in the latter part of the afternoon. Arthur Farnsworth, the voice said, had been found unconscious on Hollywood Boulevard, evidently suffering from a fall. He had been taken to the receiving hospital.

Through the numbing shock, Bette's mind functioned mechanically. Get their doctor . . . Dr. Moore said at once there was no point in her coming to the receiving hospital; that he would summon her as soon as he had his patient settled in the Hollywood Hospital.

In the endless wait for Dr. Moore's return call, she phoned the studio. This would mix up their schedules. They must know how to plan. So quiet and so desperate was the voice that said, "This is Bette Davis," and then went on with its message, that the studio's instant reply was that they'd do anything, regardless of schedules, to help her.

At the Hollywood Hospital the white figure on the bed was motionless. No flicker of recognition passed across the face as Bette leaned close and spoke low and urgently. Her mind flashed back to the day they had met scarcely five years ago, when a tall handsome man had come forth to greet her at the Lodge in Franconia, New Hampshire. What strange destiny had welded the course of their two lives into one?

What was it that had attracted her to him first? Perhaps the physical poise, the effect of controlled vitality that pervaded all his movements as you would expect in a man who had spent a lot of time flying planes; perhaps the quiet, dry humor, the mental balance that made him a constantly delightful companion; or his music—he had been a concert violinist and many an evening had been spent as he played and sang to her. Or perhaps it was the great love of the out-of-doors they both shared.

There had been the odd circumstance of her buying the Sugar Hill house which she was to love so much from the man who was one day to be her husband. The house had been a previous investment of Farney's and when she had spoken about buying a place there of her own he had shown it to her. In a gay mood they had swung up the long avenue of butternut trees and when the quaint little New England house came into view, Betty knew she had come home. Thus had it become a special bond between them, the very house that was to take him from her.

SLOWLY, her eyes focused again on the quiet figure. Here was the man who had stood beside her in the colorful living room of Jane Bryan Dart's ranch at Rimrock, Arizona, just three happy New Year's Eves ago during the simple ceremony that made them man and wife.

Then, as now, Bette's mother, lovingly known as "Ruthie," had been close to her side.

There was no room for Bette at the crowded hospital that night unless a sick patient were to be moved in with another patient. This she refused to allow. So she went home to the empty Glendale house and battled out her thoughts and her exhausted nerves alone.

The next day there was little change in Arthur's condition. He was still unconscious. Already they had sent for his people—his mother and brother Dan. There was nothing to do but wait—wait and ask the desperate question—how could it have happened? The police were asking the same question. One sinister angle of the case was that Farnsworth, a pilot himself, was the western representative of the Honeywell company in Minneapolis whose entire plant is devoted to the manufacture of important airplane equipment. Some one might have wanted to get at him. Offsetting this theory, however, was the fact that there was no external evidence of an assault and, what was still more conclusive, the brief case which he carried and which contained important confidential Government papers was untouched.

Wednesday morning Mrs. Westmore called Bette at home. What was she doing? Bette replied she was straightening out Farney's room, getting it ready for his return. Maggie's voice lifted—that meant things were better, didn't it? No, Bette answered wearily, it just meant she'd go out of her mind if she didn't think and act that way.

Sharing the outdoor life they loved so much: Arthur Farnsworth and his wife Bette Davis

Later that same day Arthur Farnsworth died. He never regained consciousness sufficiently to explain what had happened to him; he never had the chance to say good-by to his wife and family.

Science, supported by Bette's good memory, had supplied a solution to the first. For when the autopsy showed he must have suffered a previous fall or blow, she recalled a bad spill he'd had in June at their Butternut Lodge when he slipped and fell the length of the stairs as he was going down in stocking feet to answer the telephone. Thus for two months the injury within his head, seemingly nothing at the time, had been increasing until it struck him down that day on Hollywood Boulevard. For those two months, even while they had their last happy holiday in New York together, he was a man walking between two worlds.

The solution to the second must come from Bette's own philosophy. Thousands of men are leaving the world today without saying good-by to their families. Perhaps they wouldn't want to say good-by if they could. Perhaps it isn't really good-by after all, for certainly no man living has had the necessary experience to tell us that it is. And perhaps in Bette's own cry that came over and over again, "I can't believe it! I simply can't believe it," there is a true sign pointing the way; a sign which says, "Then don't. It's more important not to."

A simple service was held in the flower-banked Church Of The Recessional at Forest Lawn in Glendale for the immediate family and a few close friends. By a strange providence Jane Bryan and her husband were in town on a visit and had been seeing a good deal of the Farnsworths. Thus did Jane, who was Bette's devoted shadow in the days when they were both at the Warner studio, stand by her friend in the saddest moment of her life.

There also were John Garfield who had worked closely with her, not in a picture but in their mutual love, the Hollywood Canteen, Jack Warner, head of her studio, and Paul Mantz, noted stunt pilot and Farney's close friend.

Bette's uncle, a retired Episcopalian minister, conducted the services, reading in his quiet voice Arthur Farnsworth's favorite Psalm: "I will lift up mine eyes unto the hills from whence cometh my help. . . ." Then Bette started the long journey east to Rutland, Vermont, family home of the Farnsworths, for final services and on to Butternut for interment.

Perhaps in no way could Arthur Farnsworth have done more for his wife than by leading her back at this moment to the country which has always given her spiritual strength. "I will lift up mine eyes unto the hills . . ." There, from the rugged but not ungentle face of the mountains, flow power and peace. There Bette met again the undemonstrative kindness of the people—her people; felt again the strong, invisible hands that put her back on the road. Once more she set her face to the West and the work she had promised to do.

Fink

The Marriage Dilemma
OF JUDY GARLAND

A girl can count herself lucky if she's never had to meet the problems

Judy Garland is facing because of her romance with Dave Rose

BY CAL YORK

JUDY GARLAND is in love. Oh, certainly there isn't anything particularly startling or new in a nineteen-year-old girl's falling deeply in love; most of them do, in fact. Even young motion-picture stars as famous as Judy fall in love and marry the boy of their hearts. Deanna Durbin, Judy's age, will marry young Vaughn Paul just a day or two before Judy herself becomes nineteen.

But Judy's love is different. The man of her heart, Dave Rose, is much older than the little girl who played *Dorothy* in "The Wizard of Oz" just a year or two ago. Dave was Martha Raye's former husband, a gentle and understanding person, talented in music and growing more and more successful in his radio work.

So, after all, it isn't quite the simple problem of a boy and a girl in love.

It's the case of a girl young in years, who has wisely remained just a youngster, and of a man, older, wiser, more experienced.

Furthermore, it's a problem that concerns more than just Judy and Dave, for it vitally touches Judy's studio, which has so carefully groomed her for stardom. So much misinformation seems to have been spread concerning this romance which the whole world is discussing that it seems

only fair to both Judy and Dave to reveal the true facts. Here for the first time is the full story of the dilemma that faces Judy Garland.

To begin with, Judy has known Dave Rose, a man in his early thirties, for years—so long, in fact, that even Judy herself fails to recall just when she hasn't known him. Dave is a musician, a man who has always been vitally and tremendously interested in music, although he never had any formal musical education.

"It just sort of came to me," he says with a smile.

Music just sort of came to Judy, too. She cannot read a note nor can she play a single instrument. Only recently has she displayed an interest in learning to play the piano "by note," as we say in the hinterlands. Her mother is now teaching her.

It was this mutual interest in music that first drew the pair together. After Dave's divorce, the casual friendship ripened into something deeper.

In order to understand Judy's attachment for a man advanced beyond her group of close kid friends—Jackie Cooper, Dan Dailey Jr. and Mickey Rooney—one has to understand Judy. And so few people do.

Judy Garland is a girl faithful to old friends, the ones she knew all through her childhood and adolescence. That she never forgets is illustrated by this little story. Judy attended grade school in Los Angeles, making the usual young school friends. She grew up, came to Hollywood, became a famous star. But only last month she went back to Bancroft Junior High School to visit the boys and girls who were with her several years before in grade school. We make this point to emphasize the fact that once a friend, always a friend to Judy. Dave Rose has before anything else been a friend to Judy; that is an indissoluble attachment as far as the girl with the warm eyes and the exciting voice is concerned.

Little freckled-face girl who grew up to be the white hope of a million-dollar studio: Judy Garland, of M-G-M's "Ziegfeld Girl"

The Marriage Dilemma of Judy Garland

Judy is a person of dreams and moods —the kind who needs older companionship to understand those moods. She expresses them best on paper and already has written a volume of poems, a limited number of which is being bound into a book for distribution among her closest friends.

We begged Judy for just one verse to bring you. She refused, and then she went on to give her reason. Used in such a fashion, her poems would not be serving the purpose for which they were written—to be enjoyed and understood only by those who knew her best—for others might not understand her motives in such a medium of expression. So you see within her, welling up and seething over, is the urge toward self-expression in various fields. And that's where Dave Rose comes into the picture in bright, clear focus. He is giving understanding and aid to that self-expression.

HE'LL go over to Judy's new white house in Brentwood of an evening. The two will work together for hours over a song—a new one, perhaps, or an arrangement of an old one. Together they'll think out the arrangements for Judy's Decca records, Dave writing out the music for Judy's songs.

Dave Rose is the release through which Judy's moods and thoughts find escape. No one else, no one nineteen, at least, can offer that to Judy Garland.

He understands. When Judy first wrote the story "Love's New Sweet Song" she was almost afraid to show it to her own young gay companions. It was a skit, incidentally, that revealed the tug of war in Judy's heart, for it, too, concerned a young girl's love for an older man. But Dave saw merit in the sketch and sat down with Judy to work out the musical arrangements to accompany the story. The results you may have heard on a recent Sunday afternoon broadcast. The day following the broadcast several major studios telephoned about the story. Was it for sale? Had Judy written others? Could they see them?

Dave Rose shared that success and that glory with her; for he had helped to make it all come true.

In fact, his influence goes even deeper. Through the earnestness with which he approaches his music he has made Judy want to learn more, to know more. This significant little incident will illustrate. Just two short years ago Judy was a happy-go-lucky kid with a youngster's typical attitude toward her studies. "When I'm eighteen," she kept telling her studio teacher, Miss Rose Carter, "I'm through with these books. Not one more day do I spend with your old geometry!" And she longed for the magic day in June of 1940 when she would be no longer a schoolgirl but a grown woman.

However, before that day arrived, Judy's friendship with Dave had begun to blossom and take root. On the morning of June tenth she walked into the schoolroom for the usual lessons and found to her astonishment that things were different. Miss Carter was busy packing away the books and papers.

"What are you doing?" Judy asked.

"Why, you're eighteen now," Miss Carter replied. "You don't want these any more."

Judy burst into tears. "I do though," she sobbed. "I want to take the examinations and graduate with my class."

Truly, the gentle handiwork of Dave Rose was then plainly to be seen.

Graduation night arrived and Judy, in a simple organdy dress that matched but did not surpass the other dresses, stood up with the girls and boys of University High School. Suddenly a friend dashed down the aisle to Judy's mother, returning the bouquet she had sent her daughter. The note that was attached said: "Dear Mother, please do not be angry about my returning the bouquet, but all the girls are carrying corsages alike and they even had one for me. I want to be just like them."

Yes, there is a certain humility about Judy in everything she does that seems to reduce to its proper importance the query occasionally put to her: "But, my dear, Dave isn't well-known. Why, you should be going with someone equal to you in fame."

Judy Garland wouldn't understand that. She simply hasn't the capacity to understand that sort of snobbery. Nor does she crave elaborate gifts or luxuries. Her own bedroom is simple but tastefully fixed as a den or sitting room where the gang can congregate.

Her prize possession is a charm bracelet given her by Clark Gable for singing to him the song written by her own studio arranger, Roger Eden, "Please Mr. Gable."

AS to the fame of Mr. Rose, we can say that no musician in Hollywood is rising faster in his work than Dave. He is now musical director of four radio programs, arranging the music in his own style—which is good.

We watched him one afternoon during a Tony Martin radio rehearsal as he sat on a stool, microphones over his ears, directing the orchestra.

"Strike out that B natural," he'd call, or, glancing toward the quartette, he'd say quietly, "Bad note there."

We noticed how carefully Tony listened

Judy Garland and Jackie Cooper: A team-up that fits in with Hollywood's teen-age theory but misses out when it comes to romance. For the "why's" see story on page 27

to his every suggestion and how quickly Dave could detect the slightest off-note of any one musician.

He came down between numbers to chat for just a moment. When Judy's name crept into the conversation, he spoke of her without fluster or embarrassment, giving the impression their relationship was one of good friendship. But beyond generalities he would not go.

He spoke of his hobby—a train, not a miniature, that runs on its own track in his back yard, arriving nowhere but just where it started.

"In England where I was born, trains of this sort are quite common as a hobby," he said. "Perhaps that's where I gathered the idea. Or perhaps I got it from my ancestors, for I've been in this country since I was four years old.

"Yes," he added, "I am an American now."

All through his boyhood, he explained, he had been torn between wanting to run a train and write music. He does both now. And he admitted Judy is one of his most frequent passengers, riding round and round and getting nowhere.

SINCE the plans for Deanna Durbin's marriage have become so widely discussed, rumors have been rife in Hollywood that Dave and Judy would next trek to the altar. Don't believe it.

"I want Mr. Mayer of my studio to be at my wedding if I get married," Judy once said, "and I want it to be in a church with flowers and music. And I want my mother to be happy about it."

There you have the story in a nutshell. Judy recognizes the debt of gratitude she owes to the studio that has made of a plump, freckle-faced little girl a glamorous star (and we say glamorous after seeing Judy in "Ziegfeld Girl") and will do nothing against their wishes.

Her mother means the world to her and Judy will do nothing against her wishes, either.

So, there is her mother, dear beyond words to Judy, her studio, the work she loves, her career, all at stake. And we do mean at stake because it can truthfully be said Judy's marriage would be a disappointment—to put it mildly—to all but the parties of the first and second parts.

It would be ridiculous even to suggest that Judy does not adore Dave Rose. Seeing them together at Ciro's with Judy's heart shining through her eyes as she looks at him would convince the most incredulous.

But forced by the dictates of her affections, this girl finds herself faced with a decision, the momentousness of which few eighteen-year-olds of our generation are called upon to make. What will she do?

"I won't marry yet. Not for three or four more years," Judy said not so long ago.

But Dave Rose becomes a free man in March. (See page 17) What then? Will the bright and glowing prospect of a paradise no longer forbidden be too much for the heart of a girl in love?

We have tried to explain why Judy cares for a man older than herself, a man beyond her circle of happy kid times. We have tried to explain Judy and her soul. But we cannot explain the future and say what will come of this love.

The crossroads lie ahead. Only Judy knows which road she will choose and at what price.

HEARTBREAK FOR MICKEY ROONEY

For the first time in his life Mickey, with his marriage to Ava a failure, faces defeat. Was he to blame? Was she to blame?

THE Mickey Rooneys are divorcing. Barely eight limelighted months after the simple wedding ceremony at the little Santa Ynez Valley Presbyterian church, Hollywood's most talented boy and the beautiful girl from North Carolina are calling it quits in the court of domestic relations. So say the little ink words on Case Number —; charges, extreme cruelty; signature, Ava Gardner Rooney.

Behind those words lies more than the usual disillusionment story of a man whose home has failed and a woman who bleakly faces emotional bankruptcy. Acute as may be the sense of personal disaster to these two, there is a farther reaching drama involved. For in his marriage failure

Mickey's mother, before the wedding, gave his marriage to Ava Gardner three weeks. She knew then what everyone is just finding out

BY SARA HAMILTON

to make a home for Mickey, cooking and tending the house, but he would have none of it. Then when Ava went home for a visit to her mother in Wilson, North Carolina, the grapevine started up afresh with word that she was leaving him, a report which was quashed not so much by Mickey's hot denials as by Ava's early return to Hollywood.

But the peak of the rumors was reached on the anniversary of their first six months of marriage. On that occasion the reports said there had been a downright battle in which Ava came out the loser.

As in all such affairs, the truth lies somewhere in between. But on one point—why they are divorcing—there can be no doubt.

The true reasons are obvious and simple. They were too young, and completely unsuited. The girl from Wilson, North Carolina, might as well have been an immigrant from the steppes of Russia, so far was she removed from Mickey Rooney's world.

Remember she had been in Hollywood only a few short days before she met Mickey. She had come West with her older sister Beatrice, who gave up a New York job and gambled her savings to make sure that Ava was properly cared for until they saw if her stock contract at Metro came to anything.

Mickey Rooney is facing his first major defeat. And make no mistake —it *is* major, just as everything else about Mickey has been, since *Andy Hardy* made a star out of him. He can put on the best performance of his life to fool his friends; but this time it won't get him an Oscar. He can write a symphony, play the drums, jive with the jitteriest; but it still hurts.

Mickey isn't the only one. There's Ava, young, beautiful, asking a lot of her marriage—too much, perhaps. For there came a day when the little Southern girl could stand no more bewilderment and unhappiness. Two of the few friends whom she came to know in her brief stay in Hollywood

were Jimmie Fidler and his wife. To this reporter she gave the news of her decision to file suit for divorce and that very night listened with her heart pounding as he made the announcement over his broadcast. . . .

That was the first authentic word the public had of the marital differences of the Rooneys. But it was by no means Hollywood's introduction to the possibilities of a split-up—not in this town where grapevines are more prolific than the city water mains. Rumors had come seeping through from neighbors in the beautiful Wilshire Palms apartment where Mickey ensconced his bride that she could be heard nagging him. Other reports had it that Ava was desperately attempting

Heartbreak for Mickey Rooney

What they had seen from that point forward had been mostly Mickey. There had been no opportunity for Ava to become acquainted with the peculiarities and customs of America's great foreign city of Hollywood which, by the very nature of its industry, compels an irregular way of life; no chance to acquire a new set of values. To her, Sunset Boulevard was essentially no different from Main Street in Wilson.

In all Hollywood the most undomesticated, un-Babbitty individual is Mickey Rooney. And this was the man she married.

We hope we aren't betraying a confidence in mentioning this startling prediction made by Mickey's mother, Mrs. Panky, a few days before the wedding. "I love Ava, she's a grand girl, and naturally I want Mickey to be happy. But I give the marriage three weeks before it's over."

And despite her effort to keep the pair together her words were almost uncannily true. Three weeks of happiness and then the deluge! The quarrels, the bickerings, the fights!

WHY? Why would the boy's own mother make such a prediction? Because she knew Mickey. Knew his restless dynamic spirit that cannot be chained by a series of bride's home-cooked dinners or a wedding ring. He can't help it. It's just Mickey. It has been from the day when as a baby of two he toddled out on a vaudeville stage and became an actor. It didn't stop there. His amazing ability spread to dancing, sports, music, composing. He plays practically every instrument in the band and has since he's been able to reach a piano stool, hold a drumstick or finger a brass instrument. His compositions have been widely published and publicized. His acting rates him a place among the first ten in all box-office polls. As a tennis player, he's considered one of the finest amateurs on the Coast. He's an ego-ridden, dynamic, disturbing genius.

And to Ava, genius was just a word in a dictionary. To find it suddenly part of her intimate life would have staggered a far more experienced woman than this nineteen-year-old.

IT is generally believed in Hollywood that Ava Gardner was not genuinely and deeply in love with Mickey Rooney; that she may have thought so, but that in reality she was enamoured of him and flattered by his attentions, blinded by his fame, though honestly convinced she could make him a good wife.

In the beginning she treated Mickey exactly as she had her dates back home and Mickey liked it. No doubt of it. Shortly after their marriage we spotted Ava and Mickey at Charlie Foy's cafe. Mickey was jumping attendance on his beautiful wife. Her cloak had to be adjusted just right, her wants relayed to the waiter, her chair adjusted. Once or twice, Mickey leaned over to kiss his bride behind her dainty ear. Mr. Rooney got politely shoved away and put into his place for his pains. Or perhaps it was embarrassment on Ava's part, since she was little used to the ways of Hollywood swains.

But the novelty of this sort of treatment soon wore off for Mickey, and when it did what in the world did these two people, at the opposite poles of life, have in common? Mickey loved the jam sessions on Monday nights at a local cafe. Ava didn't. Mickey loved the wild rhythm of jitterbug music and dances at Little Pico Boulevard cafes. Ava didn't. Not that she didn't enjoy music and dancing, but she liked to take hers in more moderate doses. Mickey liked crowds and excitement and fun. Ava was more interested in quiet home life and a serious career. Mickey's career was already established and he craved fun. Ava didn't. They were too young to understand the law of compromise. Wide open were the rifts and battles that carried them further and further apart.

SEVERAL weeks before the divorce, when the separation rumors were growing strong, Ava suddenly left Mickey and went home to North Carolina. The actor went wild at the merest hint that all was not well between them and Ava re-echoed the denial.

The truth about that is the kids had been quarreling and Ava, anxious to see her mother who is ill, seized the opportunity to go. The short separation helped things along for a while until the night of their six months wedding anniversary. And even Ava admits that quarrel was the beginning of the end.

Another point of difference, small on the surface, but deep-rooted psychologically: Ava Gardner is taller than her husband. That's a handicap for both of them.

Then, Ava came to Hollywood for a career. Most people do. As Mickey's wife she wasn't having it. Whether Mickey objected or not we can't honestly say, but Hollywood claims he was bitterly opposed to it. Certainly the opposition didn't come from Ava.

On the other hand, she claimed she wanted a home more than anything in the world. There is certain touching evidence to support her efforts to establish a home life for Mickey. Believing that if they had a piano, Mickey would be more content to spend his evenings home with his own music, she wanted to buy one. But this could not be done within the tight budget which Mickey is alloted by his business manager. Most of the budget went toward their apartment in the exclusive and beautiful Wilshire Palms.

Ava is leaving this apartment. It holds too many unhappy memories for her. Mickey has, of course, already left and is living with his mother.

Concerning their private troubles, the pair have wisely refused to discuss the matter publicly. There was, however, a distinct note of unhappiness, a sort of catch in the heart, when Ava said over the phone, "I'm not very happy. Conditions are such I cannot continue to accept them."

Our heart goes out to this little Southern girl who tried so hard. As some wag suggested, living with Mickey would be like living in the midst of an electric fan, with no way of getting out or turning off the current.

Ava chose the only way—the divorce courts. She claims that in the eight months they were married Mickey's community property amounted to $200,000, half of which she has a right to under California law.

She also asks alimony to the amount commensurable with Mickey's $5,000-a-week salary. Whether this will be granted remains to be seen when the decree is given. She has a sick mother to whose support she contributes and she is still paying back her sister Beatrice for the money advanced to keep them going the five months before she married Mickey.

WHAT of the future of these kids? Ava is under contract to M-G-M, Mickey's own studio, and has had several small parts in "This Time For Keeps," "Calling Dr. Gillespie" and the unreleased "Pilot Number Five." The studio has just renewed her contract for a year, but Ava feels her future is very uncertain. For once the Rooney name may prove a handicap. One paper openly stated the studio might keep her under contract whether they used her or not in order that no other studio would bill her as Mrs. Mickey Rooney.

Mickey's military classification is 2A, which means he is exempt for the time being as a worker in an essential industry. There seems to be no anxiety on the studio's part that he will be leaving soon. It's all up to the draft board and Mickey's height, or lack of it. One never knows about that.

Thus ends married life for Mickey and Ava. Tragic when you think that the girl herself does not deny that she still loves Mickey or that she believes he still has some feeling for her. But reconciliation? No, she says, it wouldn't last a month.

And that is what has stopped Mickey. For the first time in his life since he became a star he is confronted by something he can't lick—his marriage. And it still hurts.

Heartbreak for Mickey Rooney? We're afraid it is.

The End.

A serious-faced Mickey Rooney shows up at the Tennis Tournament shortly after the announcement of his separation from Ava Gardner

274

Gentlemen to ladies: Request granted, if you look like this. Linda Darnell of "The Loves Of Edgar Allan Poe"

The Bonita who has had to grow up fast these days, realizing that it isn't too simple to be an unattached girl today

MORALS

Thoughts like these must be spoken very

frankly. They are for every girl,

thinking of the man she'll love

BY

Bonita Granville

Bonita met Tim Holt when they made "Hitler's Children" together. "Tim and I could have made a serious mistake . . ." The boy who had her first love was Jackie Cooper (right). She says now: "Our love had been so sweet we couldn't quite bring ourselves to relinquish it."

I THOUGHT my generation was smart. Now I'm not so sure. I read these days about girls who jeopardize everything that matters most to women for a cheap thrill. Last week, for instance, I read of girls who pick up sailors on Times Square in New York and go to Coney Island beach with them. When the sailors leave to return to their ships these girls sleep under the boardwalk. The next day they are back on Times Square again—in quest of another date. One would think every man was about to vanish from the earth and any emotional experience that wasn't crammed into these days would be lost forever.

These girls are extreme cases of war hysteria. I grant that. But I hear about less flagrant examples of the same sort of thing all the time. I even see girls I know discarding standards which are as necessary to the preservation of a woman's happiness as helmets and guns are to the preservation of a soldier.

I know how easy it is to be tempted to risk everything for a boy you love, or think you love. I suspect it's only normal for a girl to be tempted to forsake her chastity at one time or another. Especially in these times when life is uncertain. More especially still if the boy is in uniform and likely to depart any day.

However, this is the very time we should not complicate our lives. Events—and emotions with them—are moving so fast that we must guard against any mistake that will make us as truly war casualties as the boys who are killed and wounded. There are things like blood plasma and sulfa drugs to save our fighting forces for the good years which lie ahead. Our salvation, however, lies solely within us, in a hard-boiled code of wartime morals.

For when this war is over and the boy we believed would be forever wonderful is forgotten (unless we so mess up our lives because of him that we remember him bitterly) there will come into our life, with peace, a man whom we'll truly love, whom we'll wish to marry, whom we'll want for the father of our children.

It's a good idea, I think, to dream about that man these days; for dreaming about him we guard against doing anything which might remove us from the social circles in which we would be likely to meet him or make us less likely to attract him.

I know what I hope the man I love will be like . . . I hope he'll have a crazy, mad sense of humor, enjoy funny little things and never be one to make a grim production of life. Whether he's short or tall or dark or fair won't be important at all. It's only important he be clean and honest and sincere—which means, of course, that he'll be good-looking too because, inevitably, he'll have that good look about his eyes.

I have a fair chance of being the girl for him, I think. I'm not taking a bow when I say that. I'm rejoicing because Life got in at me during the past year with first-hand knowledge that should serve me very well right now.

It isn't too simple to be an unattached girl these days. Everything moves so swiftly you begin reaching out for something, anything, so you won't be passed by and find yourself empty-handed. If you're young it's natural, of course, to reach for romance. It's dangerous, too. Because boys today—whether they're in service or about to go into service or rejected for service for one reason or another—are overstimulated and mixed up the same as girls are.

Jackie Cooper was the first boy I ever loved, the only boy I ever loved, really, even though it was a young love.

We knew each other for years, Jackie and I. We shared everything—friends, good times, the bewilderment of the early 'teens, the demands of careers and the joy of an ever-deepening emotion. For years we always could be sure of the same quick response from each other. But when we came to our late teens it was different. Personality traits which had bound us together began receding. Personality traits which found us basically at variance—for the first time in our lives—began strengthening. Quite literally as Jackie and I grew up we also grew away from each other.

Neither of us would admit this at first. Our love had been so sweet we couldn't bring ourselves to relinquish it. Actually, trying to hold on to what no longer existed, we lost for a little while the quiet affection which should remain forever for two who loved each other as we did.

Because of Jackie I know that emotions change. And if the commonplace adventure of growing up can shift a deeply rooted emotion, surely the violent adventure of war not only can change a sudden war romance but is exceedingly likely to do so. I'll be suspicious, therefore, of any romance that comes swiftly, as romances are likely to at this time. And should I find myself caught up in something before I know it I'll keep away from solitary places where I might be tempted to yield to emotional duress. It's so much better to warn yourself, "I shouldn't do that," than to be obliged to say later on, "I wish I hadn't done that."

It never makes sense to me when girls excuse something they have done by saying they were swept off their feet. We usually are responsible—to some extent, anyway—for the ardent moments. Usually, by one feminine device or another, we ask for what we get. Boys aren't likely to sweep us off our feet without encouragement.

I'm grateful for my religion, too. I happen to be a Catholic, but I know it isn't the form of religion that is important. It is just the simple business of believing in God and trying to do right in His eyes. It's all right to make exceptions occasionally—for others, not yourself. All of this takes self-discipline which can be most uncomfortable when it's in operation. However, the dividends of self-discipline are decidedly worth while. It makes you strong. And to be realistic—and this is the time for it—those who are strong always have a better chance of finding happiness and holding on to it than the self-indulgent and weak.

IT WAS after Jackie and I faced the fact that it was over for us that I thought for a time I loved Tim Holt.

I'd seen Tim around Hollywood for years. It wasn't, however, until we worked together in "Hitler's Children" that we really knew each other. Tim had separated from his wife. He was sad over this, feeling lost, too, because his marriage meant a great deal to him. The Army had given him a stay until our picture was completed and his uniform hung, waiting, in his closet. He was eager and emotional over this. I, no longer wrapped up in my love for Jackie or his love for me, was unhappy and lonely. Not only were Tim and I sorry for ourselves; we also were sorry for each other. I'll never smile again—as you do at an old bromide—when I hear anyone say, "Sympathy is akin to love." I found out! I know now this has been sold over and over because over and over it has been true.

Tim and I came close to making a serious mistake.

Our first date was a drive out to his ranch. When he stood at the ranch fence telling his horses good-by I wanted to put my arms around him, hold him close, assure him the war would be over one day and he would be home again. It's natural enough to want to put your arms around a boy and comfort him, these days

particularly. However, right now that instinct—good as it is—is likely to cause trouble. Boys, lonely and frightened underneath at the moment, are likely to respond to an arm around them with more emotion than it's simple to handle.

Tim and I prepared in advance for the night when we must say good-by, the night he was leaving for camp. By this time we were firmly convinced we had been made for each other.

I'm naturally emotional. This, of course, puts it up to me to guard against the dangers involved.

IT was in self-defense that Tim and I agreed to pretend that the night he left wasn't a special occasion at all, that he was saying good-night as he had dozens of times before. However, just in case our make-believe didn't take too well, we asked Mother to spend that last evening with us. Mother likes Tim tremendously—she's knitting him a sweater as I write—and she also had sympathy for our fondness for each other. With her present, however, we obviously couldn't work up the same emotional quality that would have been likely had we been alone. Not only did this make those terrible last few minutes easier but it also saved us the possibility of regrets later on. It isn't a mark of weakness to protect yourself from yourself. It's the smart thing to do.

It wasn't long after Tim left for camp that I started out on a personal-appearance tour with our picture, "Hitler's Children." I was away six weeks or more. It was then Tim and I began to wonder if it hadn't been the emotional state we both were in—to which the picture, too, had contributed—rather than emotion for each other that had thrown us together. Neither of us ran away from this possibility, fortunately, but faced it squarely.

Some of the doubts which assailed us and some of the questions we had begun asking ourselves crept into our letters. It was not, however, until I returned to California and Mother and I drove out to camp to see Tim- that we actually got around to saying, "This isn't it!" While Mother visited with friends in the Service Club that day Tim and I went out and sat in my car—this held no danger now—and talked honestly, fairly.

That wasn't easy to do. It's never easy to admit there is no romance where you thought one existed. It means giving up something for nothing. Momentarily it's quite impoverishing. But only momentarily.

Because of Tim Holt, then, I know how confusing emotions can be. And since this is true I know how smart it is to respect conventions. Suppose Tim and I hadn't. Neither of us could be as happy as we are now. Especially Tim, for otherwise it wouldn't have been possible for him and his wife to have their chance at the reconciliation which enriches them today.

WHICH reminds me of a man I know who works on airplanes. He was telling me recently about an air show his factory had staged to celebrate the thousandth plane off the line.

"Those ships were so pretty and so powerful!" he said. "You should have seen them, one after another, as—with a roar—they soared almost straight up and disappeared into the low ceiling. A tough guy standing next to me had tears running down his cheeks. He had helped build those planes and he loved them."

That "tough guy" didn't really love those planes, of course. What moved him was the design and work that had gone into them and the missions for which they were destined.

No harm is done when we mistake our feelings about inanimate things, like planes. But we are asking for unhappiness when we are mistaken in our feelings for human beings, when, for instance, we attribute the emotion we have for the

collective men in uniform to a boy who comes home on furlough or a boy we meet at a camp dance.

I'm going to do my utmost to see that I don't enter any relationship lightly and, when and if that relationship doesn't pan out, go on to another and another. Leave the moral equation out of it. On a hard-boiled basis promiscuity doesn't pay.

A California girl I know, hurt when a love affair to which she had given everything didn't prove all she thought it would be, has been on an emotional binge for over a year. There are no more tender curves in what used to be her beautiful mouth, only bitter, straight lines. There is no more shine in what used to be her lovely eyes, only cynical doubts. I see her everywhere with boys who once wouldn't have been nearly good enough for her.

I don't mean to give the impression that I'm standing clear of boys these days. That would be as unwise and as unhealthy as an emotional binge. I see boys all the time, especially boys in uniform. I'm captain of the Junior hostesses at the Hollywood Canteen.

At the Canteen I've learned boys who are away from home like to talk about home and the girl they left behind them. So often when I'm dancing with one of them he'll say, "Gee, you have eyes just like my girl's," or "How tall are you, about five feet two?" And when I answer "Yes—how did you know?" he'll grin, a little embarrassed sometimes, and tell me, "My girl back home is just five feet two—and her head comes to the same place on my shoulder."

It's safer, among other things, to talk to the boys about their home and their girls than to try to become their girl. Because they are lonely and emotional they may very well forget their girl temporarily; but this won't mean their true heart doesn't belong to her still.

I wouldn't want to face that—if I'd gone emotionally overboard about some boy. It's that sort of hurt that sends a girl into another man's arms—to prove to herself she is attractive, to prove to everybody else she isn't carrying a torch.

I THINK sometimes it's because of an urge to be part of the war that we girls attach ourselves to men so easily, to men in uniform, to men about to go into uniform, and to men behind the war in one way or another. It's a stupid thing to do. And wasteful! There are so many urgent things which need doing. There are so many ways in which we can go to war, too. We can roll bandages for the Red Cross, in our spare time if we have a regular job. We can help turn out planes and tanks and ships and guns and ammunition. If we're in school we can join the Victory Corps and really do something in it. We can gather scrap. By taking any one of a hundred jobs we can release some man to fight. We can become a nurses' aide—nurses' aides are desperately needed right now. We can care for some woman's children so she can work in a defense plant.

This is a different war. When it is over those who picked crops or spotted planes or cared for war workers' babies will have been as vital as all the rest. Victory when it comes will be a mosaic of millions of people doing millions of things.

"Think straight! Be strong! Don't act like an emotional fool! Remember, if it is important it will last!" That sums up my wartime morals. I have an idea I'll get along much better with this code than I would without it—chart a far straighter course to the man I'll love. Where is he now, I wonder? I like to dream about him—laughing at perfectly silly things, with that good look about his eyes—that good look our sons, too, will have one happy day.

The End

Junior Miss Miracle

BY SALLY JEFFERSON

Siren in socks, wistful Margaret of "Journey For Margaret," the pigtailed Miss O'Brien, Hollywood's newest and truest love

★ MARGARET O'BRIEN is a name that's two things in Hollywood—it's new, and it's known. For Margaret O'Brien is the wistful, pigtailed little "Margaret" who outshone even Robert Young and Laraine Day in "Journey For Margaret." A miniature acting genius, she is still a small-fry representative who wears two smooth, brown braids down her back, draws pictures by following with a pencil the numbers from one to two to three and loves to play a screen role that "chokes her throat." The little girl she portrayed in "Journey For Margaret" "choked her throat" so badly she could hardly cry.

The greatest test of her ability came when Margaret was called upon to play "a genius" in "Lost Angel" when there wasn't the slightest trace of genius, except her acting ability, about her. For the picture she rattled off Chinese like mad, "O nee loo la, O Yoo doo pao kwan," recited calculus problems, mathematical theories and what not without knowing the faintest thing about them.

As a matter of fact, there are few nursery rhymes that Margaret has ever met personally. She can print her name and does, a dozen times a day, in fan autograph books, but she can't read, spell or do sums, except for counting the picture-book numbers.

Margaret is just six, is forty-four inches tall and weighs a hefty forty-four pounds. Her tiny face is ethereal in its glowing sensitiveness. Her gestures, especially when she speaks of the play she's writing—well, printing—well, just "making up," as she finally amends with her two small arms circling gracefully in the air—bespeak the artist that Margaret will one day become. That's why she stands today, a tiny mite of a person, in an open doorway and looks back longingly at the children who will never pass through that door with her. She is trying so desperately, too, to stay one of them just for a little while.

"Mother, mayn't I have brown shoes instead of white this time?" she'll ask. "All the school kids down our street have brown."

Yet, when it comes to her screen work, she is as wisely confident in her ability as a Davis. When the weeks of testing for

Junior Miss Miracle

a little *Margaret* went on and the matter remained unsettled, her mother tried to prepare her for disappointment. "It's my role," Margaret insisted, "no one else shall have it. I've got to have it."

A summons one day brought Margaret and her mother to Twentieth Century-Fox Studios to talk over a role in "My Friend Flicka." Margaret, or Maxine as she was then called, was finally chosen to discuss the part with the director and Roddy McDowall. They liked her instantly and chose her from among some twenty others. "Can you and Maxine go to Utah for location?" they asked. Yes, they would go, said Mrs. O'Brien, provided the *Margaret* role came to nothing.

That night, when Margaret got home she went straight to the telephone in the hall and knelt down on her knees. "Oh God," she cried passionately, "please, please give me the part of *Margaret.*"

She got it the next morning.

IT was she who insisted upon the legal changing of her name from Maxine to Margaret. The screen child had become so much a part of her she wanted to carry it with her always.

"But suppose you play in a picture called 'Tea For Susie'?" the judge asked facetiously. "Wouldn't you want to change your name again to Susie?"

She was horrified. "Oh no, I'll always be Margaret." And so the name was given her for her very own.

She came into pictures through an accident. Her mother had gone to see her sister's agent and taken Margaret along. All through the interview the agent's eyes kept turning to the little girl listening so earnestly to the conversation. "Say," he said finally, "how about this little one's going into pictures? They're looking for children for a sequence in 'Babes On Broadway.'" So Margaret went, got a small bit and was completely lost in the beruffled cuties surrounding her.

After the "Margaret" role she made the now famous short "You, John Jones" and played ten little girls of different nationalities. And because they were desperate little girls of Europe, each one "choked her throat." In "Jane Eyre" she played a small part with Orson Welles and then went over to M-G-M again for her "Lost Angel" role.

Margaret was born in Los Angeles, January 15, 1937. Her mother had been a dancer who gave up her career, when Margaret came, to devote herself to the career of her younger sister, Maissa Flores, also a dancer. Before Margaret was five, she had made four transcontinental flights in passenger planes and several trips in trains. She always insists upon an upper berth on trains because, as she says, it's higher, which seems to be reason enough. Because she lived so much of the time from babyhood in various hotels she's a quiet child who easily conforms to her surroundings. A wretched case of whooping cough, when she was just six weeks old, has kept her tiny and underweight. She's finicky about food, but simply adores pears and cottage cheese salad.

Once, when she was stubborn, her mother slapped her hands. She's never forgotten it and the one word "punishment" is enough to settle any problem. It's her own idea about her hair. She's "partickle" about its being plain, but the eternal feminine vanity creeps out in the angle of her hat. Margaret insists upon giving it a slightly rakish tilt to one side.

SHE'S not the least bit affectionate, giving and demanding no kisses or hugs. Maggie, a dog of dubious character, is the victim of her dressing-up for play, attending tea parties in weird bonnets and ill-fitting garments. Maggie puts up with it beautifully.

Margaret isn't much for toys, a woolly dog being her favorite next to Maggie. Her three fully furnished doll houses interest her but little. But let the school kids next door come home from school with a small hand loom and Mrs. O'Brien is driven wild until she buys Margaret one exactly like it so that she, too, may be one of them in play.

Luncheon in the studio commissary is her big delight. She sits quietly in her corner thoroughly fascinated, not with the stars, but the other children from other sets. The schoolroom on the set is her special delight, although Margaret won't start her education until she's seven. She tries hard to keep the others from seeing the talent that will eventually set her apart. After a terrific crying scene before the camera that left the crew "choked in the throat," she dashed for the schoolroom, her smile bright and eager. "Why, Mar-

garet," cried her little stand-in, "you've been crying." Margaret shrugged. "Oh, it's just work, you know how it is," and instantly she diverted her attention to the drawing lesson.

She learned early the lesson of attention to business. Once she lost a small role to a little girl who listened more attentively to the director. For days after she wistfully wondered about the little girl to whom she had lost the role. "Is she having fun, do you think, Mother?" she'd ask. Never again did Margaret's attention stray when a director spoke to her.

Her dialogue, once memorized, is forever fixed in her mind. Her mother begins by reading her the entire script so Margaret can understand the character she plays. Once, at the end of a scene when the director had called "Cut," she turned to him and asked, "What happened to my line? I speak after he finishes."

The director looked at her. "You sure, Margaret? Well, let's see." So they looked it up in the script and, sure enough, her line was there. They reshot the scene for her dialogue.

Since the death of her father in her infancy, Margaret, her mother and aunt have lived in modest circumstances in an inexpensive apartment building. There is no car for traveling and no maid for cleaning. While Mrs. O'Brien washes the dishes in the evening and Margaret dries them, they discuss the events of the day. The set is Margaret's dream castle. She adores the atmosphere, the people, the work. When her contract with M-G-M was signed, Margaret was thoroughly happy. "Mother can use a million dollars," she commented. A quality of swift understanding and the ability to know what people are thinking about are the attributes that set apart this amazing bit of humanity.

EXPRESSIONS flee across her tiny face like living things as she listens to her director or a friend. Their every thought finds true response on the plainest of little faces.

She can be stubborn. Her persistency in rising at six and disturbing her mother's rest is one habit that places her in the O'Brien doghouse. "Please, Margaret, I didn't sleep all night," her mother will beg. The chatter keeps up regardless.

Persistence and determination march along beside her. Sitting on the sidelines while other children were being tested for Margaret, she watched one child through a crying scene.

"He never tested me in that scene," she cried. "He never did and I could do it too." Before her mother could restrain her she'd popped off her chair and gone to the director with her complaint.

Over the telephone her mother asked us to listen to the new poem Margaret had learned at the studio schoolroom. The little voice came over the wires repeating in the sing-song tones of the other children, "What do we plant when we plant a tree? A desk, a ship that sails the sea," and on and on.

"You know why it is, of course," her mother said, "that Margaret wouldn't say it differently for the world?"

We knew. They mustn't know, for just a little while longer so she can stay in their world, the world of little children who recite sing-song rhymes and play with hand looms and wear brown shoes and don't cry out a heartbreak when a director says softly, "All right, Margaret, cry now, dear." Little children who might not accept a movie actress as one of them, though the world will see her as Hollywood's Junior Miss Miracle.

The End.

Service-star wife, service-man husband: Ruth Hussey and Lt. Bob Longenecker having a Mocambo leave dinner date

280

VERONICA LAKE

Center of current Hollywood talk: Veronica, top-draw star of "So Proudly We Hail"

FABULOUS

Jitterbug jam: Typical of Sinatra's arrival everywhere was this California scene

At the Canteen with author Parsons ("Louella" to Frank) to entertain soldiers

This is what the singular Sinatra admitted to his famous friend—about his wife, his life, himself

BY LOUELLA O. PARSONS

Women in the Sinatra life: His wife and small daughter Nancy

FRANK SINATRA, crooner of intimate love songs, the American-Italian boy who has turned Hollywood upside down and who has women swooning at his feet is just as unspoiled and unassuming as if he were still singing in the Demerast High School Glee Club in Hoboken.

If that sounds a little press-agenty, the truth is—and I might as well confess it: Frankie got to *me* before he got to Hollywood.

At least a week before the 20,000 Bobby Socks overran the sacred Hollywood Bowl to listen to his concert of "bedroom" lyrics that had the musical intelligentsia pulling out long hairs by the roots, I was, you might say, "in a spin" along with the other Sinatraites.

When I heard Frankie was coming to 'Hollywood I wanted to beat the competition to his first Coast interview (it's an old habit with me). So I called him in New York.

It was a terrible connection. It rattled and jangled and sounded as if the Japs had got at least as far as Kansas City where they were bombing the telephone wires.

I kept yelling into the clash-banging, "Mr. Sinatra—Mr. Sinatra—this is Louella Parsons in Hollywood." And then over the din, or perhaps under it, came the old black magical voice saying gently, but with all the stops out: "Hello, Louella. This is Frank." That did it. It wasn't what he said. It was the intimate Sinatra-way he said it!

So, anybody who is not a dyed-in-the-wool Sinatra fan can stop reading this story right here and leave the rest of it to us girls who are going to have a fine old heart-to-heart talk about Frankie in Hollywood.

In the twenty years I have been covering Hollywood I've never seen anything like the Sinatra craze. Bing Crosby can cross the street without bringing out the reserves. Some of the boys can even appear in public without their "top pieces" without being embarrassed—because nobody is looking, anyway. But Sinatra—!

It isn't only the girls. The night he appeared with me at the Hollywood Canteen I've never heard such a reception as 750 soldiers, sailors and Marines turned on for Frankie. The cheer that went up from nearly a thousand masculine throats was a particular kind of a tribute to a boy who looked dead tired after what he had been through in his first two days in Hollywood. Frankie's unruly black hair was more unruly than usual. There were lines of fatigue around his mouth.

Within forty-eight hours he had gone through that unbelievably hysterical scene at the station . . . he had sung his regular "Hit Parade" program before going on to that highly disputed concert at the Bowl . . . he had spent all day Sunday in a huddle with Tim Whelan who is directing him in "Higher And Higher" at RKO . . . all day Monday he had been before the cameras in his first acting role which must have been a strain. Yet, Monday night, in his first "free" moment—there he was all ready to turn it on for the boys at the Canteen.

FRANK SINATRA

Fabulous Frank Sinatra

So they turned it on for Frankie by picking him up on three Marine shoulders and carrying him in.

I NOTICED that as he and Harry James were playing "All Or Nothing At All" they were clowning through it like a couple of young colts. "What was so funny about that?" I finally asked Frankie when we snatched our first quiet moment of the evening.

He laughed: "'All Or Nothing At All,' is the song that gave Harry and me our walking papers out of the old Victor Hugo cafe and, incidentally, out of Hollywood a few years ago, Louella. It was just four years ago this month that we were thrown out—right in the middle of that song. They didn't even let us get through it.

"The manager came up and waved his hands for us to stop. He said Harry's trumpet playing was too loud for the joint. He said my singing was just plain lousy. He said the two of us couldn't draw flies as an attraction—and I guess he was right. The room was as empty as a barn.

"It's a funny thing about that song," Frankie went on. "The recording we made of it four years ago is now in one of the top spots among the best-sellers. Most people think it is a new one we've done. But it is the same old way we made it four years ago when we got thrown out for our trouble!"

SINCE that night at the Canteen I've seen a lot of Frankie and I've heard a lot of discussion about him. Some of the Hollywooders who do not think he is as good as Crosby wonder how he got where he is. They'll tell you that he isn't particularly good-looking and that he is just plain lucky—a happy accident evolving out of "war hysteria" and shattered feminine nerves. When Frankie personally is concerned, they diagnose his boyish manner as naïveté.

If you are asking me, I don't think that Sinatra is naïve. I think from the beginning he has known where he was going and how he was going to get there. He practically told me as much the day I dropped by the Garden of Allah to see him. It was the first day he had had off the picture and he was taking it easy. For Frankie that means that he had slept an hour longer than usual, had given out only six or seven interviews and played only a couple of sets of badminton.

He was wearing one of those coats of his—a not-too-subdued sports coat—and I suppose the Best Dressed Brigade would say it was too long for correctness. His hair was not slickly in place because it never is. But outside of that he was spick and span. Frankie sets great store by his wardrobe. We talked about everything including:

His favorite dish: Spaghetti. He will get up in the middle of the night to eat it and has been known to polish off a dish for breakfast.

His favorite melody: "Night And Day"—just because.

The way he sleeps: Lightly—and on his face.

The way he feels about emoting before the camera: It doesn't bother him. Nobody expects him to be Charles Boyer. And everybody—Michele Morgan and Jack Haley and the rest of the cast—is treating him fine.

His favorite human being: Nancy, his wife.

AND then, of course—we got around to how it all happened.

I think I learned a lot about Frankie that afternoon. He not only talks easily about himself, he talks with complete honesty.

He wasn't boastful, he was merely stating a fact when he said: "I guess everybody is surprised about me—except me. I've always had an enormous amount of self-confidence, Louella. Perhaps I never dared to hope it would be this much—but I have always believed I could get there.

"When I was a kid, living in Hoboken, everybody thought I was cocky, including my parents. My folks are of Italian descent, you know, though born in this country.

"My mother used to say, 'That Frankie—he's as fresh as paint!'

"I was, too. I thought I could do anything I set my mind to. I guess I still think so," he laughed, suddenly. "I've just recently started playing badminton and I'm already looking for a tournament to get into here in Hollywood. When George Evans, my pal and press agent, told some of the experts that I wanted to play with them, they asked, 'Is Sinatra that good?' George said: 'No—but he thinks he is!'

"When I was a kid I liked to sing—not enough to study and seriously apply myself, you understand—and to this day I can't read a note. But when I got to high school and found they had the best glee club in town I made up my mind to get in it, and I did.

"Call it self-confidence, call it cockiness—call it anything, but it has always been true of me that when I get an idea by the coattails I can't let go. I choke it to death."

"Why not call it perseverance, Frankie?" I asked.

"Most people who know me well would say it is too polite a term," he grinned widely, "and that includes the person who knows me best—Nancy."

You don't talk to Frankie very long without hearing about Nancy, his first and only sweetheart. They have been married since 1939. They have one daughter and another child is expected in the late winter. It is one

★ ★ ★ ★ ★ ★ ★ ★ ★

of the little ironies of his career that with the world of femmes at his feet, the one girl Frankie has met and fallen in love with wouldn't marry him for three years because she thought he was a pain in the neck!

"We met at a beach resort, Long Branch, New Jersey," Frankie explained. "Our families were down there for the summer. The Barbados, like my family, were of Italian descent, born in America. Nancy was about sixteen and I was seventeen.

"Nancy couldn't see me for dust—most of it kicked up by her other beaux."

NANCY gave Frankie an awful runaround. She would put her hands over her ears when he would show up strumming a ukulele and singing all the songs Bing Crosby was making popular that year. She would say, "Let Crosby do it. You listen."

Well, Frankie listened. But he wasn't entirely willing to leave it all up to Crosby. In fact, Bing's success had given birth to a big idea with Frankie—and you know about Frankie and the way big ideas affect him.

He started "choking the idea to death" by getting himself a job, practically gratis, on the radio in New York. They gave him seventy cents and carfare—and a *great* spot on the air! "I did my stuff at the stroke of midnight," Frankie remembers. "While everybody else was in the night clubs listening to the stars, Sinatra was crooning privately into the ears of the New York taxi drivers, lulling them to sleep."

There was a brief interlude with a Major Bowes unit before Frankie landed a job at $25 per week at a place called the Rustic Cabin in Jersey. In addition to singing for his supper, Frankie was also encouraged to usher the paying customers to their tables.

Maybe it was because for the first time in his life Frankie was a little blue and discouraged that Nancy finally gave in and married him. It was the first time she caught him in a modest mood and it turned the trick.

It would just be taking up good space

to recount what came after that. There was that stint with Harry James (also unknown at the time) on the Coast, followed by another job at the Palladium which was a little more successful. Then came his solid sending with Tommy Dorsey—who still chunks out thirty-three and a third percent of Frankie—and then the Paramount stampede in New York.

What happened there, or *why*, is still being discussed by psychiatrists. They say Frankie became the "love object" of girls swept by war hysteria. Other experts say he appeals to the maternal in woman. All that is definitely known is that when Sinatra sang the ushers were equipped with smelling salts to revive the slick chicks who swooned in the aisles because he "will never know how much I love him."

NOW he is right back to the scene of his first "flop." But what a difference. He wouldn't be human if he didn't feel it—not much, but a little. So many people wanting to meet him—asking him everywhere. The same people who had never got around to showing up when he was playing at the old Victor Hugo.

But don't think for a moment that there is any bitterness in Frankie even if he does spend most of his time with pals of his entourage who accompanied him from New York.

He doesn't know a great many people in Hollywood—yet. His closest friends are Harry James and Betty Grable and he likes Lana Turner and Steve Crane. He also feels an everlasting gratitude to his friend Morris Stoloff, the symphony conductor, for the graciousness of his speech to the men in the orchestra before Frankie sang in the Bowl. Stoloff said:

"You men know *your* kind of music and play it as though you loved it. Now," he went on, "tonight I want you to play the kind of music Mr. Sinatra sings and loves with the same feeling." And they did. "I'll never forget that," Frankie says. "Never!"

As Frankie says—"They sent it solid"—and so did he!

THE END

285

At the CBS Command Performance: Command Performers Alice Faye, Frank Sinatra, Ginger Rogers giving off some special glamour

Last month Photoplay-Mov[ie] Mirror went to artist Paul Hes[s,] Doctor Mary Halton, showm[an] Billy Rose and designer Ire[ne] and asked them to select the b[est] figure in Hollywood. Betty Gra[ble] won the race, leading a field [in]cluding the following stars [:] Claudette Colbert, Ginger Roge[rs,] Ann Sheridan, Paulette Go[d]dard, Carole Lombard, Sus[an] Hayward, Loretta Young, Oli[via] de Havilland, Martha Sco[tt]

HOW I KEEP
MY FIGURE
BY
Betty Grable

She was judged by four professional critics as the girl with the best figure in Hollywood. Now she gives you her own rules for the perfect figure — so amazingly simple that every woman can measure up to the Grable mark

287

THE first time I was ever asked, "What do you do to keep your figure?" I answered immediately, "Why, nothing. Nothing at all!" And I meant it. Certainly I had never "dieted," as many girls do. Certainly I had never done a "daily dozen" in my life. The whole idea of watching over and worrying about weight seemed pretty boring to me and if I considered it at all, it was to think, "Well, Betty, my girl, you are lucky you don't have to go through all that!" It was swell, I opined, to be able to eat what I liked without worrying about calories. It was swell to be able to get into a size twelve any time I felt the urge for some new clothes. Yes, I was very lucky!

But lately, I have come to the conclusion that my not having to pay any attention to weight is, perhaps, not wholly a matter of luck. I have decided, in fact, that this happy state of affairs is due, also, to certain habits acquired, thanks to my mother, a long time ago.

In the first place, Mother always wanted me to be a dancer and saw to it that I had dancing lessons from the time I was five years old. I loved it from the very beginning and I believe it is safe to say that I have danced anywhere from half an hour to several hours a day, at least four days of the week most of my life. And I suppose that is one very good reason why I have not had to "watch my weight." I don't think anyone could get very fat dancing as much as I have. Also, I am certain that dancing is a good thing to help develop symmetry. You exercise just about every muscle of the body and should just naturally find yourself proportioned as nature intended you to be.

And so, while I am on the subject, I heartily advise every girl, fat, thin or in between, to give dancing a good try. Tap dancing, ballroom dancing, acrobatic dancing — anything that appeals to the imagination. Even though you don't want to dance professionally, try it, anyway. You'll love the good healthy way you feel all the time and the way you can wear the clothes you were meant to wear. And I should like to advise you, too, to go in for it wholeheartedly. I mean, while you're doing it, do it for all you are worth—when you are night-clubbing with your boy friend; when you're dancing to the radio at home. I don't mean you have to turn into a jitterbug. I simply mean to let yourself go and enjoy the music and the rhythm and motion. The more you kick and twirl and jig, the better you'll like it and the better you'll look, too. And, probably, the happier you'll be.

LET me tell you a story. It happened here in Hollywood. A certain girl I know met a producer at a party. He was discussing with some of the other guests a role in a picture he intended to make which required a rather difficult-to-find type of actress. He looked at my friend and said, "You'd be the type, if—"
He hesitated and she challenged him. "If—what?"
So he let her have it. "If you weren't thirty pounds overweight."
Well, of course she was. She had dramatic talent, but she loved to eat and hated to exercise. She hadn't worked for months because she was so fat. But now she told him, "I'll lose those thirty pounds in thirty days if you'll give me a chance at that role!"
He looked skeptical, but he promised.
A month later, she went to see him. He didn't recognize her at first, but when she'd persuaded him she was the same girl, he tested her for the role and she got it. She had lost the thirty pounds, all right—and easily. *She had simply taken a lesson in tap dancing every day.*
Of course, I realize that no girl, even though she exercises extensively, can keep her weight normal if she doesn't eat properly. That, too, is a habit which my mother helped me to form early. Yes, I have an excellent appetite. And—hold everything—my favorite foods are steak, mashed potatoes, fried chicken, good old southern biscuits and chocolate milk shakes. Moreover, I eat them whenever I want to. But the point is, I don't seem to want to more frequently than is good for my figure. That is my mother's training again. Even as a child, I was never allowed to eat between meals and I was never allowed to "gorge" at meal time, as you've seen some children—and grownups, too—do. So, as a result, I have never developed an over-craving for food.

When I get up in the morning I drink one or two cups of coffee, with cream and sugar, and as much orange juice as I want—usually a large glassful. If I am working, I have this breakfast around seven o'clock so that by noon I am hungry and eat a fairly hearty lunch. In the summer, too, if it is a hot day, I have an ice-cold milk shake in the middle of the afternoon—not, however, if the weather is cool. Iced drinks don't tempt me then. At dinner time, I eat a lot of any one thing. I seldom take a second helping of anything and I think that alone helps keep one's weight down. I know a movie actress who is one of those persons who gains between pictures. When she is working, she is able to keep slender easily. She "burns it off," so to speak. But on vacation she'll gain anywhere from five to fifteen pounds. But she doesn't mind, because she has a sure way to get these pounds off when she wants to. She simply never eats a second helping of anything; never eats between meals; never eats a "snack" before bedtime. Losing weight is a little slower this way, but you might try it sometime. Always leave the table just a little hungry. You'll lose that slight hunger in half an hour and will just feel wonderful. Most people eat too much, I think.

Another diet I know of is an all-liquid diet. You can drink any liquid you want—milk, orange juice, tomato juice, clear soup, at any time you want it, but you must eat nothing solid. A man I know took off a pound a day, that way, for ten days, and could have kept on indefinitely, he insists, although his doctor wouldn't let him. Incidentally, dieting can, I guess, be very dangerous if you go at it too strenuously without a doctor's advice. That is why I think the idea of eating a balanced meal, but small helpings of everything, is such a good one. You are sure, that way, to get all the vitamins you are supposed to have. And, by the way, after you've gotten used to this smaller sized meal, you probably won't want

288

so much food in the future. You won't be able to eat too much, even though you satisfy your appetite at every meal.

Another sane habit into which my mother guided me is not to sleep too much. There is nothing, according to my observation, that will cause anyone to gain weight quite so readily as more sleep than the average human being requires. I was always encouraged to sleep eight hours out of every twenty-four and I don't feel exactly right if I don't get that much. But I never sleep any more than that, even though I should like to, sometimes. Instead, I get up and play a game of badminton, golf or tennis.

YES, I like out-of-door games very much and they, too, are quite certainly good insurance against overweight. I have never chosen my games, though, with reducing in mind. I play golf, eighteen holes once or twice a week (when I am not working; I haven't time for much golf when I am), because I like it; tennis about twice a week, because I like that, too. I am crazy about bowling and usually bowl three nights a week.

And—no, I don't eat a "snack" right after my "athletics." I wait until mealtime. Thanks to Mother's training, regular eating is a habit too strong for me to break now. Incidentally, when I am not working, I often stay up later at night and therefore get up later the next morning. Which schedule works out so that I have breakfast around the middle of the morning and then usually don't eat again until dinner time. I don't seem to feel the need for so much food between pictures.

Do you know what I should do if I ever found myself in danger of "losing my figure"—if the tendency to gain weight should "rear its ugly head" in my own scheme of things? Well, first I should check up on my normal measurements, with relation to my weight, and if the latter were even a pound over normal, I should lose that pound. It shouldn't be so hard to lose one pound! Going without lunch or a few desserts or potatoes or cream in your coffee for a day or two should do it. Next, after I had my weight just where I wanted it, I should buy myself, if at all convenient, a new dress which fit *perfectly* . . . not one loose enough to allow for a few extra pounds, but one which would tell the sad tale if even half a pound came on! *And then, using that dress as a sort of gauge, I should keep myself slender enough to fit it!* I have a dress, now, which is smooth-fitting enough to be such a gauge. I wear it every once in a while. And believe me, if it ever begins to get tight, I'll know what to do!

Of course, a set of bathroom scales is an awfully good thing to have, too, if you are weight-conscious. I have one and while at present I have become sort of negligent in using it because my weight seems never to vary, believe me, I shall weigh myself regularly if I ever develop a tendency to gain! It is so easy to step on the scales after your morning shower and to plan your meals or your athletic program for that day according to what you read there.

You could even do some "daily dozens" right there in your bathroom. I have always felt I should find routine "daily dozens" very uninteresting, but they are good for one's health as well as one's figure, certainly. For instance, I don't suppose there could be any better way of keeping your waistline intact than bending over front and sideways and touching your fingertips to the floor without bending your knees. But surely you know that one already.

And—don't forget dancing! I am sure you'll find that a lot more fun! After you learn a few basic steps, just turn on the radio or phonograph and go to it, remembering, always, to do it wholeheartedly. Because "keeping your figure," like everything else, is scarcely worth doing unless you give it the best you've got!

•

Cue as to how Betty Grable, now dancing for a star-studded living in Fox's "Miami," keeps her award-winning figure is the dress at the left. Facts behind the figure are her measurements as given below

•

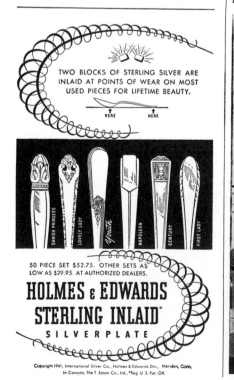

Height	5' 4"
Bust	34½"
Waist	24"
Hips	36"
Neck	13½"
Headsize	22½
Weight	112 lbs.
Wrist	6"
Thigh	20"
Calf	12½"
Ankle	7½"
Upper arm	10¼"
Shoe size	4C
Glove size	6

JUDGE FOR YOURSELF—
WE QUIT!

Several issues ago, Photoplay-Movie Mirror made the innocent mistake of asking noted experts to pick the best figures—male and female—in Hollywood. Ever since Betty Grable and Errol Flynn were announced as the winners, we've wished we had been smart enough to mind our own business.

It seems many of you weren't inclined to agree with some of the candidates.

As far as you were concerned, our noted experts shouldn't have limited the field just to Betty and Errol. The stream of protests suggesting other star contenders for figure honors is still flooding our desks.

We open letters like these every day:

From Norton Buckley,
Minneapolis,
Minnesota

Was interested in your story the Best Figure in Hollywood but your judges sure went sour when they didn't even mention Carole Landis!...

Betty Grable is plenty okay with me, but when it comes to the best figure you must have been blind when you didn't put Rita Hayworth at the top of the list...

From Alfred Comstock, Klamath Falls, Oregon

From Gwenn Findley, Atlanta, Georgia

Where does Vic Mature come in on your list? I should think he'd have beaten the field and you didn't even mention him!

From H. C., New Haven, Conn.

...If John Payne doesn't have a better physique than several stars who placed, I'll eat my hat!... Why not give readers a chance to vote on the feminine star with the best figure and the male star with the best build?

From Caroline Nohl, Chicago, Illinois

So you put Loretta Young in the top ten! Well, give me Jinx Falkenburg the personification of the outdoor American girl.

So We've Thrown Up the Sponge!

Now it's up to you to select the best figures in Hollywood. And just to make the job easier, we're publishing four eye-filling figures on the next two pages. (Also, to show that our experts weren't so far off the beam, we've included Betty Grable.)

Next month with the October issue as your reviewing stand you will find more contenders on exhibit. Remember, this is only the beginning. Keep on watching until you've had a complete lineup of potential winners. Then we'll give you the signal to send in your vote for the winners.

Good luck—and good looks!

Photoplay's

PHOTOLIFE OF ALAN LADD

Here is the colorful panorama of the life of Alan Ladd—the second in this exciting new series—letting you in on the odd facts that have gone into the making of a versatile man. You'll agree when you see "Salty O'Rourke"

BY LYNN PERKINS

THE story of Alan Ladd is a drama of one battle after another, of a buffeting, tough climb up the stairway to fame. There were many small and valuable successes—more failures. Alan had a brutal time of it—until a really brutal role catapulted him into the Olympian heights of success. When Paramount needed a handsome young killer to play opposite Veronica Lake in "This Gun For Hire," they gave him the role and made a long term deal. This first picture starring Alan Ladd made movie history. It also made Ladd. Alan Ladd and movie audiences can never forget the scene on the stairs in "This Gun For Hire" when he found a child playing after he had killed a man. You will remember the terrible, tense moment when Alan seemed to hang between killing the child . . . and returning her ball.

N. HOLLYWOOD
H. S. 'MIKADO'
WINS ACCLAIM

Students Win Much Praise In Gilbert, Sullivan Operetta

NORTH HOLLYWOOD, May 13. —Their performances declared as outstanding among those offered by the other members of the North Hollywood high school student body cast, Alan Ladd and Lavine Myers last night evoked tumultuous applause from the nearly 1000 persons who attended a concluding performance of "The Mikado" in the school auditorium.

Ladd's interpretation of the part of Koko in the favorite Gilbert and Sullivan work was acclaimed by critics as such as would have done much credit to a professional. Miss Myers' work as Katisha placed her high among the feminine members of the cast, it was declared.

Bill Roode as "Pooh Bah," Eileen Wilmer's grace and convincing acting, and Lester Mortensen's hilarious and natural comic touches, gave them high rank.

Spirited Performance

Only scattering applause was accorded Ladd during the first act, but in the second, the entire cast joined him in a spirited performance which caused the delighted audience to demand endless encores.

Miss Isabel Gray accomplished an excellent dramatic direction and beautiful staging. Mildred Hughey and Bernice Sheets were responsible for the music.

2

3

Back in 1932 when Alan was a senior at North Hollywood High School he won the above acclaim. Significantly, he played the role of *Koko*, Lord High Executioner!

Though a good beginning toward his preferred goal, the "Mikado" did not lead to immediate acting. Alan went to work on the *Sun Record* as a cub reporter. He was then twenty years old. He has always had a yen to play the part of a newspaper man in pictures. When the newspaper changed management, Alan left it

... and concentrated on the cafe which he had run on the side. The restaurant was Alan's baby. He owned it. He operated it and worked behind its counter, too. This was wonderful experience but it wasn't getting him anywhere—in his consuming ambition

4

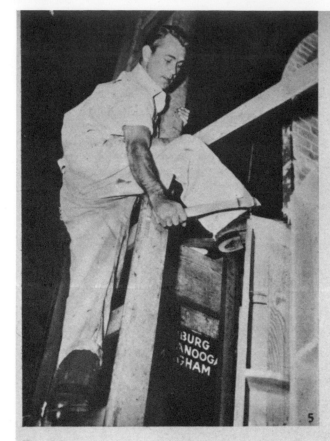

Then followed a job selling cash registers, a brief and unsuccessful period of picture training for Universal. Finally he landed at Warners as a grip. Because he had been a high diver Alan got high work. Then he fell twenty feet from a scaffold.

Luckily he wasn't hurt, but that did it. He quit and enrolled at Ben Bard School For Acting. He had little money and what he had was soon gone so his sole diet became doughnuts and coffee. Today he can't even look at a doughnut.

Success was fast coming and so was happiness. On March 15, 1942, Alan married Sue Carol. He went into the Army Air Corps and won his corporal's chevrons. However, his fan mail kept right on flooding in, reaching record proportions.

His greatest disappointment came when he was medically discharged. Back to pictures, still acting as his own double, he dived from a bridge, played with real fire. Asked how he practiced for such scenes he said, "I just go ahead and do it."

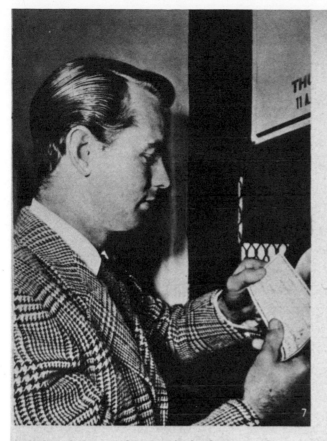

Radio brought him a wide range of roles, but not much money. One weekly program which shared revenue among the cast netted him fifty cents a week. When things looked blackest a local Los Angeles station gave him a spot as a one-man show.

The experience was invaluable. Came the angel of his life. Sue Carol, an actor's agent and former star, heard him and was so impressed she sent for him. She signed him immediately. Two weeks later he made his screen debut at Paramount.

The Ladd career continued to skyrocket. His home in Los Feliz Hills was a place of warmth, understanding and comfort. His faithful partner, Sue, whose unflagging effort and unshakable belief in her husband brought him stardom, stood squarely behind Alan in all that he did. On April 21, 1943, a junior partner was added to the Ladd-Carol team—a little daughter that they named Alana. It is symbolic of the marriage that the name Alana is the Celtic for beloved. So now the circle is complete.

294

Glamour Girls
ARE SUCKERS!

by
Carole Landis

as told to Gladys Hall

Men marry her: Carole at the time she was the wife of Willis Hunt

Men like her: Enthusiastic cadets at Fort Ord gave her a puppy after a personal appearance

They let men hurt them because they don't know how to handle men. A startling confession by a girl who sees her mistakes

A SUCKER? Me? Listen! A great, terrific constant thing came into my life. A man, of course. For obvious reasons I can't use his name, but he is an actor and—it was love I felt. Real love. I knew it and I still know it. There I was, there was little Carole being so happy, so ecstatic, so delirious, so willing to forsake all others (again) and all that!

Glamour girls are hard, eh? Glamour girls are self-sufficient, vain, pampered, flattered, foolish, spoiled, popular, too popular to care whether Tom walks out or not because Dick and Harry, twenty of each, are lined up to take his place?

Let me tell you this: Every girl in the world wants to find the right man, someone who is sympathetic and understanding and helpful and strong, someone she can love madly. Actresses are no exceptions; glamour girls are certainly no exceptions. The glamour and the tinsel, the fame and the money mean very little if there is a hurt in the heart.

Most of us have hurts in our hearts —don't you think otherwise.

Why all you have to do is think us over . . . think of Marlene Dietrich, Hedy Lamarr, Lana Turner. For all of Marlene's beauty and exoticism, for all the adoration she has from men, what is her deepest concern, her dearest love? Her daughter Maria, as everyone who really knows Marlene will tell you. Hedy is simply lacquered with loveliness and acclaim, but what does she do? She adopts a little son who is her whole life. Take Lana—the romances she has had! Yet I know she really wants marriage. She's told me so. Marriage and home and stability, that's what Lana talks about when we're just two girls together.

If glamour girls are so smart, so shrewd, so devastating to men, why don't we have home and love and marriage? Or, having them, why don't we hold them?

Glamour girls are not smart with men. In many other ways, yes, but not with men. I give you the story I started to tell as proof: There I was, as I said, but in love. This went on for months. We were constantly together every possible moment. I felt this, at last, was it. I saw no one else, didn't want to see anyone else. I lived in a dream when, suddenly, a little girl, a nonprofessional, not pretty really, clothes just so-so but not chichi, vivacious perhaps, but that was all, stepped in and—here I am!

No such thing as a broken heart, the medicos say. Well, maybe not. . . .

To continue my demonstration of how un-smart I was, when I first met X., as I'll call him, I was going with another fellow who was simply magnificent. He was fine, substantial and devoted. So I meet X. and, bang, out the door goes the other fellow! I threw out a wonderful future and (here is where I show myself up as a candidate for the giggle-house) I told X. what I had done! That's not being very smart, that's being very dumb. For the minute you let a fellow know so completely that he's the whole floor show, you're sunk.

Then, when it happened, when this other girl moved in, I was as deaf, dumb and blind as any novice in a nunnery could ever be. When, instead of his saying, "Dinner tonight?" he said, "I have a conference," I believed him. The same old homespun line, without so much as a gold tassel at the end of it, and I let him hang me with it!

When it began to be one of those things where the phone just doesn't ring, the flowers don't come any more, I still believed in—well, I don't know in what I believed. Perhaps I should say I still hoped.

Then the good old grapevine of Hollywood began to give out code messages: Other fellows would tell me they'd seen X. with this girl, dining and dancing here and there, what fun they were having, how "serious" it looked. I said the usual banal things: "Well, why tell me about it? We were just good friends." No one believed me any more than I believed myself.

I swear that I have never in my life been so terribly unhappy as I was during the X. interlude. I have been married twice and my marriages have failed. Twice before then, I had felt let-down and miserable, but this hurt me more than I can find words to say.

I married, the first time, a boy I'd known at home in San Bernardino. It was an average everyday-girl marriage, but it didn't work. Then, when I had become a so-called glamour girl, a "rising star," I married Willis Hunt. That wasn't a success, either. Let the blame, if any, fall where it may; we won't go into that. But I do say this: If I had been the super-smart gal a glamour girl is supposed to be, I would have made my marriages successful.

So you might rightly hail me, "Hi Sucker!" because, as the nicks on a gun indicate how many men a killer has got, nicks on the heart of a glamour girl indicate how many men she didn't get!

There is very little I can do about it, either. Being a glamour girl doesn't help any. I can only do what other girls do, cry my eyes out at night, hope and pray, pretend I don't care, do the best acting job of my career for the benefit of friends and family, for the sake of my own pride.

I THINK I have always been a sucker. By a sucker I mean someone who is very vulnerable, who wears her heart on her sleeve, who is easily hurt, who, in fact, almost asks to be hurt.

I was brought up, most of my life, in San Bernardino, here in California. My folks moved from Fairchild, Wisconsin, where I was born, to San Diego and then to San Bernardino where I lived until, at the age of sixteen, I climbed aboard a bus for San Francisco to make my fortune as a torch singer.

You always hear a lot of talk about all the people, usually men, who "discover" glamour girls. Well, let me tell you this: Carole Landis "discovered" herself! She even rechristened herself. Born Frances Ridste, I figured that Ridste would be a hard name to pronounce. I wanted something sort of flowy and graceful and made up Carole Landis.

From the age of seven I was stagestruck. Since that time when I knew I wanted to be an actress to the present day when I am one (I hope, I hope) in "Hot Spot" at Twentieth Century-Fox, I

Head of the sirens-in-socks bicycle brigade is Jane Withers. Fink catches her starting out on a bike hike, with her mother helping pack lunch — and kitten. The Withers has three bicycles in her barn, one equipped with a radio

painstakingly made me what I am today, take it or leave it.

I worked in the dime stores, waited on table in cafes after school (my father was a machinist, not a millionaire) until I had saved enough for my bus fare to San Francisco—and a job. I didn't try Hollywood then because I thought I wouldn't have a chance here. Glamour girls are vain, you think? Oh, little do you know!

I landed in San Francisco with $16.72 in my dollar purse. I stayed at a cafe job in San Francisco until I had saved $100 which, I decided, was enough for a siege of the screen ramparts. In Hollywood, I was a little hungry. I made friends (not with millionaires, as fiction would have it) but with chorus girls, extras and bit players who would be able to tell me where to go for work. That's how I landed in the chorus Busby Berkeley was training for "Varsity Show" at Warners. I finally did a solo dance in that, not because I was a smart little glamour-digger who knew her onions but because the star didn't want to do it and someone had to.

That's how I began. Then I tried the stage. Being seen in a Los Angeles company of "Roberta," featuring Bob Hope, gave me a break at a Broadway show which was a flop. Eventually, after a lot of crying-far-into-the-night routines, I returned to Hollywood.

D. W. Griffith, the old Maestro, was seeking a cavewoman for "One Million, B.C." I didn't think I looked much like a female Tarzan, but D. W. hired me. Then I landed in "Turnabout," "Road Show" and "Topper Returns." Then Twentieth Century-Fox bought up half of my contract, I made "Moon Over Miami," "Dance Hall," now "Hot Spot" —and here I am!

HERE I am. That's the way one "glamour girl" got that way and I tell it hoping to prove that I discovered me. I trained me in the way I wanted to go and, with the exceptions of one topaz bracelet and one diamond wrist watch, I covered me with such diamonds, minks and other luxuries as I possess.

Glamour girls, to smash another popular misconception, are not so dumb about getting along in the world. But they are dumb with men.

We "do" for men rather than demand from them. When I was married to Willis Hunt, I give you my word I'd up and light his cigarettes for him. I'd come home from work and rub his back when it hurt him. I should have been the one to be pampered. I wasn't. Marlene, I know, does the same sort of thing. After hours of work, instead of being entertained, she often takes the pains of entertaining men at her home, mixing the drinks, waiting on them.

WHAT is more, we not only do not demand attentions from men, but we don't demand gifts. In fact, we make it very clear we don't want them. We make it even clearer that our affections are not to be had by bribes, however costly.

Instead of "demanding" to be taken to Ciro's and other expensive places, we say —I've said it myself a hundred times— "Oh, no, no, let's have a quiet little dinner at some tired little drive-in somewhere and just go to a show."

But we are constantly seen at Ciro's and similar places, you may say. Yes, we are, quite a bit. But not always of our own volition or choosing.

So many men in this town want to go out with us just because we are glamour girls. That's another reason why we're suckers—we go out with them! They want to go out with us, not because they are fascinated with us, let alone in love, but so they will get their names in the papers the next morning. It's like a man's buying expensive champagne not because he really likes or appreciates the wine but because the label is impressive.

I had an experience of this kind that is really something. A wealthy New Yorker called me on the phone one night, mentioned a mutual friend in the East who had asked him to call me, asked me if I would go out with him, seemed to be a very nice person. No reason, surely, why a man like that would take out a girl for any ulterior motive.

Well, we went to Ciro's. He didn't

like to dance and so, when someone asked me to rhumba, I asked to be excused and accepted. When I came back to our table this man said, "Look *I* brought you—remember? But if you dance with another man, no one will know I am with you!"

I should have known. After all, he couldn't have been attracted to me personally; he had never laid eyes on me before. I certainly should have known, but we fall for it time and time again.

We fall for it because, I think, we so much want to believe we are not just make-believe to men, not just mannequins, not just the equivalents of shiny, chromium-trimmed cars, sleek yachts, Chauvet ties or other expensive accessories with which men advertise their importance to the world.

Who wants to be an *accessory?*

Well, I've learned one lesson now— these days, unless I go out with someone bigger than I, a bigger name, someone established (Gene Markey is an example of the kind of man I mean), someone who can gain nothing by being seen with me, I don't go out!

Now that I have convinced you, I hope, that glamour girls are suckers, with men at any rate, I'll give you my opinion of why we are:

I THINK it is because we want so badly to have some sort of natural, normal life, to be just Two People who are just two people. Because we want this so much, we overdo it, we overdo everything —the wrong way. When we are publicized glamour girls a man expects us to be exotic, aloof and expensive. Wants us to be, I bet! But we bend over backwards, if we like a guy, to be just a person, an average girl. Believing, wanting to believe that's what he really wants. We are as simple as curds and whey and hence the little girl who doesn't have the glamour buildup can walk right in —and does.

If we were not suckers, we would learn to play the parts men seem to expect us to play and put the sucker's shoe on the other foot. But no, not us, we never learn.

And another thing: Glamour girls, you may have noticed, marry and keep on getting married. Other women have one, at most two unfortunate experiences and, very often, remain single thereafter. I've heard many such women say, "No more marriage for me, I've learned my lesson!" But glamour girls keep right on altar-hopping and hoping.

Maybe, too, the men have a great deal to do with the lack of luck-in-love sustained by glamour girls. They are never natural with us. They figure, Here's a glamour girl. I must handle her differently from other girls. So many men want her. She is so sure of herself, so flattered and spoiled.

Men are afraid. So they act indifferent to us, cool, casual or downright cruel, thinking not only to "handle" us by these means but also to demonstrate their own dominance and superiority. And in the "handling" everything gets mixed up and unhappiness for all concerned is the result.

But results mean nothing to us. We can't read the writing on the wall. So listen! Listen hard and, so help me Hannah, you'll hear me falling in love again! You'll hear marriage bells ringing out again one day, sure as shooting. For here is the pay-off. Here is the tag line. Here, heaven help me, is the truth: Right now I want marriage more than I want anything in the world. I want love, marriage, home, children.

. . . A sucker? Who? Me?

THE END

FIRST THING I SEE—
In a Man

Says Ellen Drew:

His mouth. Many people think eyes are the most important thing. I don't. A man's eyes change with his thoughts. His mouth doesn't. It's the result of all the things he has been and thought all his life.

Says Mary Martin:

His speaking voice. When a man pays you a compliment it isn't always what he says that is most important—but his way of saying it, if he has a charming voice!

Says Dorothy Lamour:

His dignity. We all go through a phase when we like a man to give us a million laughs and don't care about anything else. But eventually we want a man to be dignified and to treat women as if they were women.

Says Joan Fontaine:

The expression of his eyes; whether he looks at you steadily or whether he gives you a side glance—things like that. I must say I always like frankness in a man's eye. A steady gaze is admirable. (See Brian Aherne's eyes.)

Some confessions about first impressions—with an eye
to giving you the lowdown on what to look for in looks

In a Woman

Says Tyrone Power:

The general stance. Often when a girl turns around you think, "Oh, oh, not so pretty!" But she's still attractive if her figure's good. I remember a photograph of ten girls . . . only one stood well, and right away you looked at her.

Says Jackie Cooper:

The face. I don't like anything pasty but I don't like this pancake of make-up everybody's wearing. Across the room it may look all right but not when you get close. The main thing is I don't like the way it smells.

Says Bob Hope:

It depends on the woman . . . on how close you are to her! Men notice a woman's figure first, I think. Then they move in closer and get a little of the eyes . . . and move in closer . . . .

Says Brian Aherne:

Her hands! You get a good impression of a person from hands. I think hands are more indicative of character and breeding than anything else. I like my wife's hands. (See Joan Fontaine's hands.)

You belong TOGETHER

Photoplay-Movie Mirror makes this plea to recently divorced Anne Shirley and John Payne: That they stop and read this story. It is something both of them should know

BY MATILDA TROTTER

For John to think of now: The words he penned on the picture he gave the author, and the way he felt when he wrote them

REMEMBER, John Payne, the day I read your hand? Ginny Wood left us alone in the little reception room off the publicity offices at Warner Brothers.

You had laryngitis that afternoon and couldn't speak above a whisper. Remember how we laughed when I suddenly discovered that I was whispering right back at you?

You weren't very important then. You had been working hard and making pictures, but no one was particularly aware of you. Oh, you did have an exceptionally good voice and your acting wasn't too bad, but all the magnetism and vitality and warm charm that are yours somehow hadn't penetrated the silver screen and gotten through to the movie-going public.

As a matter of fact, I wasn't too keen on analyzing you; wanted to save myself for bigger and better stars, such as George Brent and Bette Davis and Livvie de Havilland, but Ginny (as usual) talked me into seeing you—said I'd love you, you were such a swell person, so thoroughly unspoiled and definitely not Hollywood.

As soon as I felt the grip of your strong hand and looked into your eyes I knew what she meant, but I didn't realize just how right she was until I had talked with you.

Perhaps you don't even remember writing these words on the picture you gave me: "To Matilda: There was only one thing wrong. Ever— John Payne."

Well, I am sure they will come back to you now and with them the memory of how you felt when you wrote them.

And I wonder if you will recall that when you put away your pen and gave me the picture, you asked me not to publish or tell anyone the thing I had seen in your hand. I promised. How could I help it? And I have kept my word ever since, just as I have to many another star whose future and private life is an open book to me. I have kept my word because I felt that it wouldn't be fair to talk. But now that news has come of your separation and pending divorce I am going to talk —not to you but to Anne Shirley.

ANNE dear, I have liked you and followed your career ever since you were a little girl and I wanted so much to meet you when I was in Hollywood, but it seemed that each time we made an appointment to meet something always happened to break it.

Perhaps you know—or perhaps he never told you—that I analyzed John's hand back in 1938. I want to tell you just exactly what happened that afternoon. Even though he made me promise not to tell anyone what I saw that day there is no reason for me to keep silent any longer and a very good

reason for me to talk now—or so it seems to me.

Well, in reading John's hand I went through my usual routine, noted his strong character, honesty, determination, magnetism and talent for music and acting, also his career line which did not promise any particular success until around the latter part of 1941. Then, at last, I came to the love and marriage lines at the side of his hand.

As I read, we had discussed his character, health and career and were not too serious about it, but when I glanced up at him and said, "You will love twice and possibly marry twice," he

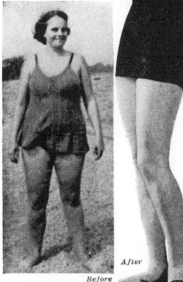

You Belong Together

looked solemn, almost angry, and he said:

"That is one thing you are wrong about. There is only one woman for me and there will never be any other."

And, what is more, Anne, he meant it. I didn't contradict him as I might have another type of man. He was too upset, too sure that I must be wrong; so I let it go at that. But my letting it go didn't satisfy him.

He said firmly: "I am going to ask you not to use this in your article. I am not going to have Anne hurt and worried. Whether one believes in palmistry or not he can be hurt by such a prediction. There isn't going to be any second marriage. There is just one woman for me and I am married to her now and for always."

Well, ever since the news of your pending divorce was given out, the memory of that day has kept hammering away at me. Something kept telling me, "You must do something. Whatever the trouble is, or seems to be, John Payne loves Anne Shirley. She ought to know about that day."

I MAY be one of the fools who rush in where a wise angel would fear to tread, but I have to tell you two what a terrible mistake you are making. No matter which one of you is at fault (and perhaps you both are) he or she should be forgiven. Life is made up of give and take and compromise. And your particular marriage *was* made in heaven.

Anne, *you belong together*. Your stars almost defy you to try and separate.

John Payne is now at the gravest point in his whole life. He is passing through a period which comes once in a lifetime to some of us and fortunately never to many of us. The transiting Uranus, Saturn and Mars are passing through his 12th house, house of self-undoing, secrets, imprisonment and sorrow, and these transiting planets are conjuncting Venus, Mercury and Saturn, which were in his 12th house at birth. In simple words then, these aspects warn John Payne of danger, loss, tragedy, sorrow and self-undoing. Right now he is in danger of bringing the whole world crashing down upon his head unless he and those of you who love him do all in your power to get him through this crisis. No one in the whole world knows what he has been going through by himself and no one understands.

These dynamic astrological aspects can be used for good or bad. They are dangerous as radium in the hands of a novice and beneficial as radium in the hands of an expert. They spell sensational publicity, emotionalism, temperament, excitability and foolhardiness, depending entirely upon the use they are put to, and can take the person in whose chart they appear to the heights of fame and popularity or fling him to the depths of destruction.

This danger period for John Payne continues until around the middle of June. After May fifteenth there is a lull, but June fifteenth to eighteenth marks some sort of crisis in his life and, Anne, I want you to stick to him through this period, no matter what he has said or done, or what he says and does until this crisis is past. It *is* a crisis and you are the one person who may be able to help him.

I can assure you you will not be happy without him, nor can you ever be happy knowing that you may have failed him when he needed you so much. You are too loyal a person and fine a friend to rest comfortably knowing that you

have failed one who needed you, no matter how black that person's moods may have appeared, or how difficult it may have been to understand some of his actions.

Your stars bring you trouble and sorrow through love; and Mars in opposition to your Venus tells you of danger of separation. Jupiter squaring Venus, planet of love, suggests the same trouble. Your stars also warn you against unscrupulous people who pose as your friends, only to take advantage of your kindness and generosity. Just to prove the similarity in your horoscope, John's chart, too, tells of secret enemies who make trouble for him and cause gossip and slander which lead to scandal and probable divorce.

BOTH of you are stubborn and somewhat secretive and inclined to keep your troubles to yourselves; and both of you are idealists who find it hard to accept life and human nature as they are.

Apart, there is unhappiness and suffering. Together, there can be happiness and understanding born from the trouble you have just been through and a willingness to compromise, tolerance for each other's weak spots and the certain knowledge that your stars favor love and marriage to one another but warn each of you against marriage to someone else.

So harmonious are your charts that they even favor success together in the entertainment world and if you make a picture or a series of public appearances together it will bring you both great popularity and acclaim.

According to your own chart, around July fifteenth of this year, you should be able to settle the problems that have been besetting you for so long a time. This aspect will cause you to face realities, to look deep within yourself and find yourself and with this discovery will come true values and the true meaning of life.

It will be a period, Anne, when you can make a fresh start and find a happiness far greater than any you have ever known.

I hope for your sake and John's that he will come safely through his crisis and that this fresh start will be together, with the past months filed away under the heading, "Experience." You belong together, not for a little while but for as long as you both live.

The End.

Fabulous film inspires some fabulous jewelry: Rosemary DeCamp, star of Korda's "Jungle Book," is the smart-set wearer of new Indian-type jewels

New Face

In this bright corner—Maria Montez, she of the red hair, the Spanish-Dutch temperament, the bright personality that's made her known in Hollywood. Latin-American born, convent-bred she spent three years on the Universal lot watching the stars go by, was suddenly chosen to join the procession herself will probably end up, in Wanger's "Arabian Nights," as a leader of the Hollywood glamour-girl band

Recruit of recent vintage: Turhan Bey, young Turkish nobleman who has boomed Universal business by way of a velvet voice, dark eyes, a hint of a foreign accent. Born in Vienna, he grew up in a silver-spoon atmosphere, came to California with his mother just for the climate, came to Hollywood just for a lark. His name, officially, is Turhan Selatthettin Schaltavy Bey. Don't bother to say it. Just echo the words "polished" and "poised" and "sophisticated" and you have the new ace man of "Ali Baba And The Forty Thieves"

304

Looking into the Fink lens: Kathryn Grayson of "Thousands Cheer"

Bing Crosby, whose "Silent Night" echoes 'round the world

A welcome to Gene Kelly, newcomer from the Broadway stage, male magnet in M-G-M's "For Me And My Gal"

Spencer Tracy

308

Hollywood's most

She's the famous big sister of the world's socialites—and she can tell a phony from

HOLLYWOOD'S most successful human beings . . .

They aren't necessarily those you think. . . .

A mink coat, the biggest star sapphire in town, the longest roadster with the brightest red leather seats and the shiniest chromium trim on the Boulevard, a show-place among the show-places of Holmby Hills, a name glowing on theater marquees all over the land add up only to professional success. Many in Hollywood, possessed of all these things, are failures as human beings. They are not happy. They have little to bring to any personal relationship. Their marriages fail and their friendships do not endure. Which is a great pity.

You can be successful professionally and personally too, of course. One or two of the citizens I rate as Hollywood's most successful human beings have great wealth and fame.

That, however, is more of an accident than an integral part of success as a human being.

First I name Orson Welles. I also name Orson as one of the most successful human beings in the entire world; for to consider him as belonging to Hollywood is fantastic. Hollywood is only a slight episode in his life. He is more articulate, lucid and clear in his thinking than anyone who ever went to Hollywood before. Everything electronics is to the General Electric Company he has been to Hollywood. He shook Hollywood by the shoulders, rattled its teeth, horrified it, almost ostracized himself socially from it—if you can mention such a thing in regard to an open place like Hollywood.

Orson, I believe, could be anything he chose to be.

He is the greatest living democrat, the greatest humanitarian, the greatest living intellect. He has the great-

est personality over the radio. He has the greatest speaking voice of our time, finer by far than President Roosevelt or Mr. Churchill; also a greater choice of language than either of these very important men.

Orson is a Stukker dive bomber, a Liberator, a P-38. . . .

Recently Orson married Rita Hayworth, one of Hollywood's younger and extremely pretty girls. "A glamour girl and nothing more," I thought; until Orson put me right, explaining Rita is intelligent and sensitive, and a very fine actress without vanity or pretensions.

"Where did you meet her?" I asked.

"Well," he said, "I met her at a radio show over two years before I married her. I groaned when I heard she was to be on the show. 'What have I got to do with Rita Hayworth?' I asked myself. 'How in the

BY *Elsa Maxwell*

successful human beings

a faithful any day. That's what she's doing here—and maybe you're in for a surprise!

world can I tone down my natural overtones to meet the tiny theme of her charm song?'

"Believe it or not I didn't have a look-in on that show. Rita stole it away from me, clean as a whistle. Which caused my confidence and inner man to take a terrific tumble but also made me respect Rita more than any woman I have ever met.

"Then," Orson confessed, "we got to be better and better friends. When I put on my Wonder Show for men in the armed services I asked her to be my leading lady.

"After I had sawed her in two for a couple of weeks—on the stage—she took my heart away from me. I found it uncomfortable being without a heart, so to get it back I married her. And we have lived happily ever since."

I include Orson in my list not because he is a genius but because he is an intelligent idealist.

Right now, he is too interested in the job there is to be done in the post-war world; the great job of breaking down politics so the will of the people will really have an opportunity to operate in the choice of the men they would have in government; so the peoples of the world may get face to face with each other and work out a simple and fine way of life.

MY SECOND choice of a successful human being is Betty Hutton.

Betty has more professional success—for which she fights and in which she revels—every day she lives.

She is listed here, however, for an entirely different reason; because she had a terrific kicking around by life, knew humiliation, sometimes did not have enough to eat—and instead of being embit-

tered or crushed by this emerged hard-boiled, perhaps, but generous and kind.

When people are as poor as Betty and her sister and mother were after her father went away, they do not talk about it. As Betty says, "All they have left is their pride."

The mother, an upholsterer in a Detroit automobile factory, never earned enough to save a penny. Therefore, when slack seasons came around and she was laid off, they lived on crackers and did anything that came to hand, from singing in barrooms to slinging hash in restaurants.

When Betty was in her teens she and several girls and boys somehow saved enough, out of the money they earned singing and playing in local cafes, to besiege Broadway. They lived in little uptown apartments, the boys in one apartment, the girls in another. They ate together and Betty was cook. It was when the musicians' union refused to let them work together as a band until they had been in New York for six months and they had practically quit eating that Betty went looking for a job on her own.

She took one discouragement after another until, at Christmastime, a manager sent her home. "You're a sweet kid who should be celebrating these holidays with your folks," he told her. "Why are you here anyway?"

"Because I'm hungry," Betty answered with angry honesty.

This, in a way, was her turning point.

He gave her coach fare home and money enough for milk and sandwiches en route. That New Year's Eve the boy friend of her sister, who was working as a waitress, urged her to go with them to a local night club. The club manager asked her for a song. She sang. But, chagrined and desperate, she threw everything around in her now famous manner. Vincent Lopez saw her there and signed her to sing with his band. She was on her way.

She has come far, but never having forgotten what it is to go without, she doesn't spare herself when she sees others are in need. When she does camp shows, for instance, she doesn't sign up for camps adjacent to large cities where she can return to a luxurious hotel every night to entertain the press and garner first-page stories about her camp experiences. She sings and dances for boys in remote, outlying camps who have infrequent entertainment or no entertainment at all; even though this means she must travel in jeeps over incredible roads, eat at camp mess and put up at hotels which often aren't even clean.

THIRD, I name Robert Montgomery. . . .
Bob was born to riches. He has spent his life in luxurious surroundings, those in which he was reared and those to which his Hollywood fame has entitled him. He long has enjoyed holidays at famous spas and world capitals. He always has contributed to and appreciated brilliant conversations. He always has admired beautiful women beautifully groomed. His love of all these things has in a way contributed to his charm. But his charm is as great and permanent a thing as it is because he loves other things more—things like freedom of speech and worship, freedom from want and fear. As he has so well proven.

Long before we entered the war Bob turned his back on the luxurious life he loves so well to drive an ambulance in France. While there he saw and heard many things; and being an accurate observer he told us then and there exactly what we might expect to happen. Upon his return Government heads here interviewed him privately and saw the moving pictures he had taken.

Immediately after the United States entered the war Bob enlisted in the Navy. Now, in the South Pacific, attached to Admiral Halsey's fleet, he commands his own boat.

"I don't know much about Germans," he says, "but I've learned to know the Jap at pretty close quarters, for everything there is head-on. It's all close-ups—no long shots at all."

After one battle between Bob's ship and a Jap sub, in which the sub was sunk, its captain came to the surface. When he saw Bob and his men trying to rescue him with nets he tried to drown himself rather than submit to such humiliation. So one of Bob's men knocked him out with a boat hook and dragged him up on deck. One of his heels had been nibbled by a shark and his arm was badly crushed. Bob watched him intently. The Jap's fluttering eyelids indicated consciousness, but he wouldn't open his eyes. He lay there waiting for death at the hands of his "savage American torturers."

"Bandage his foot and arm," Bob commanded the ship's doctor. "Give him some hot tea." (The Japs' preference when they are wounded.) "Shove a cigarette in his mouth."

Then the Jap captive, realizing that what was happening to him was the reverse of torture, instinctively sucked in a large puff of the cigarette and exhaled ecstatically; and, slowly opening one eye, looked up into the friendly faces looking down at him.

"Well," said Bob, "that's one member of the suicide squadron who learned Americans are very different from the way they've been painted by Jap propagandists. For when that Jap was finally shipped ashore to join the other prisoners, as he lay on his back in the boat, he feebly but definitely, saluted our ship."

Bob explained the Japanese officer prefers death any time to capture by Americans. "The common Japanese soldier," he added, "is different. He folds up at once when things look hopeless—all the fight knocked out of him."

I saw Bob last summer at the time when he was returned to California on leave after a bout with malaria and tropical fever. He came to a party at my house and I could see his nerves had been a bit stretched, but, smooth and suave and polished as ever, he danced every dance. It was plain he had hungered for the relaxation and escape of dancing with girls again, including, of course, his charming wife, Betty.

Betty had to leave my party at midnight but she wouldn't let Bob accompany her. "This," she told him, "is better medicine than any rest cure."

That, I think, was a pretty swell attitude for a wife whose husband had been away and in danger for nearly two years and soon would be off again.

For that evening, the horrors he had been through were forgotten. Sometimes parties are more than just parties; they are cure-alls for the soul and spirit.

So I give you Bob Montgomery—gay and brave and true to himself and those things in which he believes!

THERE is, fourth, Diana Barrymore. . . .
You have seen Diana on the screen, no doubt, and have not liked her. She hasn't liked herself. Diana, of the theater's royal family, has been a spectacular failure in Hollywood. The way she has come through this failure, which must have been torturous to one born to the purple, so to speak, proves her fortitude.

I first knew Diana when she was three weeks old in a bassinet. Her bringing up lay between the psychological rivalry of the Great Profile, John Barrymore, her father, and the beautiful, brilliant Michael Strange, her mother.

Think of the difficulty of being born of two such people!

In 1938 when I came back from a visit to Hollywood I remember saying to Diana, with the condescension you use toward a small child you do not know very well: "I saw your father while I was on the Coast."

She seemed very unmoved.

"Aren't you happy to hear about your wonderful father?" I continued. "He sent some very nice messages to you."

"I don't know very much about my father," she replied. "How can you be terribly impressed by a man, who like a Greek bas relief, is always seen in profile? I would like my father to be full face. I don't really know if he has one."

It was always understood Diana would go on the stage. She was weighted down by her fateful name.

George Jean Nathan, that disdainful dean and maestro of the critics, and I saw her in "Lord Byron," her first appearance on the stage. There was something very lovely about her and I thought she held great promise, as did my companion.

Later Diana did George Kaufman's play, "The Land Is Bright," a saga of a Western miner, playing first a young girl and in the end a woman her mother's age. During the second intermission I met my friend, Walter Wanger, the Hollywood producer and husband of Joan Bennett, in the lobby.

"How do you like this opus?" I asked.

"Not very much," Walter said, "but I like the kid."

"To me," I said, "she's the only thing in it."

"I'm going to put her under contract and take her to Hollywood," he told me.

"How can you do that?" I protested. "You'll ruin her. She's not for pictures. No Barrymore should be in pictures—really! Remember Jack and Lionel in 'The Jest' and 'Peter Ibbetson' and consider what they had to offer the stage! What has Hollywood done for them—except promote a comfortable living for Lionel and bad debts for Jack?"

"Well," said Walter, "I'm going to do it." And he did it. And Diana went to Hollywood—alas!

She has made money in Hollywood and invested it well, apparently. But her pictures have been poor and she has not appeared to advantage in them. However, at no time has she allowed this to defeat her. Through all of it she has managed to hold firm to her belief that she has something fine to give the theater—to which she has now returned. When, for instance, she came to a party I gave in Hollywood there was no sign of defeat or failure about her. Her life on the screen was static and insecure but she walked into my drawing room with her head high, personally vivid and compelling. That, in Hollywood, takes quite a bit of doing.

FIFTH, I name Jean Pierre Aumont. . . .
One night in the summer of 1941 I was going to see the debut of Ty Power and Annabella in "Liliom" at the Westport summer theater, with Jack Wilson and his wife. When I entered the Wilsons' living room, instantly I was aware of a fair young man looking out of the window. There was such an attitude of desperate depression about him! When he turned I recognized

312

Jean Pierre Aumont, whom I had seen last in 1939 in Paris.

I had heard reports that he had been awarded a Croix de Guerre just before the fall of France for throwing his tank into a dangerous gap and holding back the onswarming Nazis long enough for the rest of his unit to escape. I had also heard he was in a Nazi prison camp.

"Jean Pierre," I said, kissing him on both cheeks, "I have been wondering about you!"

"I got out," he said. "I can't tell you how. I'm an immigrant or whatever you call them. I haven't any money or passport. But it doesn't matter . . . all I want to do is go back and fight with De Gaulle."

He was so sweet and serious and sincere that tears rushed to my eyes.

Then I met him last year in Hollywood. As always, I was happy to see him. His eyes look so seriously into yours. And his manners are the most beautiful I know. He sends flowers at the wrong time; which is really the right time—when you have done nothing to earn them, when you don't expect them.

He had, after a struggle, gotten work. And his first picture, "Assignment In Brittany," had put him over with a bang as a great male personality. With his future so bright, he might well have felt he had done his share in the present war and was entitled to take advantage of the thinning male ranks in Hollywood to clinch his position, at least until such time as he was called upon to bear arms for this country.

Moreover, he had fallen radiantly in love with Maria Montez and had made her his bride in July. He would have been only human had he begun to think less about De Gaulle and France and more about Aumont and Hollywood. However, he still talked, above all, of getting into the fight again.

The last time I saw Jean Pierre was last autumn at a supper party at the home of George Quevas. (Mrs. Quevas is John D. Rockefeller's granddaughter.) He had just finished his second American film, "The Cross Of Lorraine," reported to be a personal success for him, and I wondered if now at last Hollywood would get him.

Instead, he walked in wearing the khaki uniform and red cap of the Free French, looking more the soldier than any man I have ever seen.

"I have it!" he cried excitedly. "I'm off tomorrow to join General De Gaulle as liaison officer!"

My hat is off to Jean Pierre for turning his back on the fortune and fame his new career promised and his beautiful bride, Maria Montez, whom he loves dearly, to go to his Générale and do his job as a real fighting Frenchman.

SIXTH and last on my list is my first and foremost successful Hollywood human being—Mary Pickford—because of many qualities I hope to illustrate for you.

Twenty-five years ago Mary Pickford was the greatest of stars and the sweetheart of the world. In her house, "Pickfair," every potentate and every visiting fireman was a guest, as a matter of course—Lord Louis and Lady Montbatten . . . the Duke of Alba, Spanish Ambassador to England, who is trying to bring a monarchy back to Spain . . . great bankers . . . politicians . . . ministers of state . . . duchesses and dukes . . . labor leaders.

BESIDES being a great and gracious hostess, Mary Pickford also is an humanitarian, always ready to lend herself to anything done for the uplift and welfare of mankind. No one ever taught Mary to live in this beautiful way. Her manner of life is an emanation of her true self. For she is great-hearted, with dignity and the inspiration of religion. And she has held firm to firm standards at all times, not an easy thing to do when you are rushed by life.

Mary loved Douglas Fairbanks and made every effort in behalf of her marriage with him. When he returned to Hollywood in 1935 after a long absence, Mary, in a pathetically sweet gesture, had a special room built to surprise him, a replica of an old Western bar, with sand on the floor and cowboy hats and saddles and old pictures.

This bar, a strange note in the center of beautiful Pickfair, was the scene of the now famous costume party where the guests came in dress appropriate to the scene. Douglas was a virile, swashbuckling gaucho, very handsome. Mary was a poke-bonneted pioneer girl, very lovely.

It was soon after this party that Mary and Doug, realizing the light had gone out of their marriage, decided parting was best for them. Mary still loved Douglas but she gave him up to Sylvia Ashley with dignity and resignation, without scandal or recriminations. And a year or so later when I entertained Douglas and Sylvia Fairbanks at a party where Mary also was a guest she was graciousness itself to Sylvia.

TODAY, as you know, Mary is married to Buddy Rogers. Buddy, too, has a room planned by Mary as a lovely surprise. It adjoins her rooms on the second floor and is a fine man's music room, sound-proofed, where he can practice and study.

Last summer when Evalyn Walsh McLean and I were in Hollywood, Mary gave a party for us. It was everything Mary's parties have been for the twenty-five years I have known her. Mary, too, is unchanged, with the same little modesty, simple charm and lovely gaiety. Supper was served on a long glittering table. There was a band playing. You wouldn't have known there was a war. In her daily life, however, Mary well knows there is a war. She never relaxes in her efforts. And her pride in Buddy, doing so well in the Navy Air Force, is boundless.

I find Mary Pickford a completely good woman. She is, however, gay about it, never gloomy or grim. Those who embrace the cheap, garish, so-called "modern" ideas which have come into the world may say the code Mary represents belongs to another age. But let these selfsame people get into trouble and you will find them at Mary's door, where the latchstring is always out.

Orson Welles . . . Betty Hutton . . . Robert Montgomery . . . Diana Barrymore . . . Jean Pierre Aumont . . . Mary Pickford . . . six of Hollywood's most successful human beings, in my book, for six and more most human reasons.

The End.

313

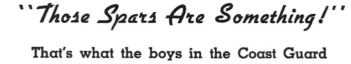
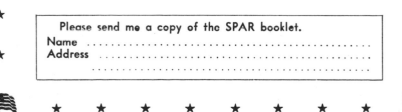

What every woman wants to be, Fred MacMurray's Lillian is—a successful wife. Her formula calls for a lot of talking on the woman's part

A nine-years "happy marriage" is that of Eloise and Pat O'Brien. Her theory is based on the right answer to that famous wrong question, "What did he ever see in her?" Know it?

How to stay married

BY MARIAN RHEA

ELOISE O'BRIEN said, "You must never be jealous. . . ."

Lillian MacMurray said, "Forget your own ambition and be a wife, first, last and all the time. . . ."

Mayo Methot said, "I never let the sun set on a quarrel. . . ."

Joan Blondell said, "Home and children are everything. Careers must come second. . . ."

They call Hollywood "Heartbreak Town." They call it that not only because it so often spells broken ambition and shattered ideals, but because—or so they say—no happiness can live there long. They say love can't walk hand in hand with careers built on fame. When a star gets married, especially a male star, people shake their heads and say, "Too bad. He was going good. This will hurt

him at the box office." Or, "It won't last. She'll never hold him. Too much competition."

Well, maybe they're right. The problems of a movie star's wife are tough, sometimes—tough as they come. Still, Hollywood *has* its happy marriages! The only thing is, we don't read about them much because they aren't exactly news. Or perhaps not the kind that makes headlines. Because they are news, all right—news that is good to hear about, too, and from which every wife can learn a lesson. Because if a movie star's wife can make her marriage go, with all its problems and difficulties, other women can make a success of theirs.

So we give you the experiences of four wives of Hollywood screen stars, whose wisdom and tact have made

their marriages ideal and enduring! Mrs. Pat O'Brien, Mrs. Fred MacMurray, Mrs. Humphrey Bogart, whom you know as Mayo Methot, and Mrs. Dick Powell—Joan Blondell.

Eloise O'Brien, happily married for nine years, sat curled up in a great, deep chair in the library of the O'Briens' new home in Brentwood. She wore an exquisite ice-blue satin negligee. Her hair was as shining and as smartly coiffed as any glamour girl's. She was camera-slender. You wondered why she herself wasn't in pictures. She had been successful on the New York stage. She was charming, pictorial. But—she was telling you why not.

"Perhaps you know that, just as we were about to be married in New

It's not the quarrels in marriage; it's the making-up that matters. Promoter of a novel plan is Mayo Methot, clever wife of Humphrey Bogart

Girl who knows how to keep her husband dating her every evening is Joan Blondell, wife of Dick Powell

to a movie star
—OR TO ANYBODY FOR THAT MATTER

York, Pat was offered a contract to star in the screen version of 'The Front Page.' Well, he came to me and said, 'Honey, shall I go to Hollywood?' and I said, 'Of course.' No, I didn't hesitate. I was sufficiently in love to let Pat's interests come first. And besides—" honestly, "I thought that I, too, might find a place in pictures. I didn't know—then—that if you want a real break in pictures you must let Hollywood come to you.

"And so," she went on, "although I was happy in Pat's success, I was miserable, too, those first two years out here, because I could get nothing to do. I wept bitter tears and devel-

oped an oversized inferiority complex before I finally realized that, after all, it was nothing but vanity that made me want a career for myself, when Pat was doing so well. Now I would not go back to the other life for anything in the world! We have our home and children and—well, life seems very full and very good."

"And easy, too?" we asked her.

But she shook her head. "No, not easy. I don't believe being married to a celebrity is ever easy for any woman. There are always problems."

"Such as—?"

"Well, fans for one thing, especially women fans. You go to a premiere,

for instance, and they recognize your husband and think, because you are with him, you are Somebody, too. They ask for your autograph, but when you obligingly sign it, they say, 'Oh, that's nobody!' Or maybe, 'For the love of heaven, what does he see in her! He ought to be married to Hedy Lamarr!'

"I used to get furious over things like that," she went on. "But Pat would be so upset and anxious and solicitous that—well, one night I suddenly made up my mind to stop being so silly! We had been to a preview. 'Why did he ever marry her?' some fresh little snip had said and I had boiled over as usual. Then, as we were driving home and Pat was trying to console me, I remember the street light shone on his face. He looked so worried and harassed and unhappy that I stopped being sorry for myself and was sorry for him! He couldn't help it if the fans had mobbed him. It wouldn't have been very flattering if they *hadn't!* I stopped fuming and laughed.

" 'Incidentally, how do *you* feel about being married to a nonentity and a frump?' I demanded.

"Well, his relief at this new attitude of mine was so obvious I was thoroughly ashamed of my former tantrums. After all, any man loves peace and in my opinion, the surest way to lose one is forget it!

"Yes, of course, funny things have happened to me since. One night after we had been to the fights a woman caught me by the arm and whirled me around, demanding, 'Well, dearie, just what did you do to get him?' "

"And what did *you* say?" we asked Eloise.

"I told her I had baited a trap with cheese!

"After all," she added, "jealousy has no place in the lexicon of a movie wife. You might as well get used to that fact. Not only is your husband going to be mobbed by feminine fans, but he is going to be thrown with beautiful women in pictures. And if you can't laugh off that situation, too, you're lost.

"For instance, during the filming of a certain picture Pat was exceptionally helpful to a new player who showed a great deal of promise. Whereupon followed a period during which she was hovering around him every chance she could get, telling him about her progress, asking his advice, until at last she got a contract.

"As it happened, the next night or two Pat and I saw her at a night club. Immediately she sallied over to our table; spoke directly to me.

" 'Oh, Mrs. O'Brien! I want to thank you for your husband, but now I give him back to you. I won't need him any more!' "

Eloise laughed, just, she said, as she had laughed that night. "Time was," she admitted, "when I probably should have wrung her neck. But I had learned restraint. And when I saw the relieved look on Pat's face, relieved because I hadn't said something nasty, I realized how much a man can suffer from his wife's jealousy, innocent though he may be. No, I am not one of those blind wives who would believe in her husband's faithfulness though contrary evidence

were flung in her face. But I do know that the average decent, self-respecting man is not going to chase around after every woman who makes eyes at him, be he in pictures or not. And I believe that he is still less likely to do it if his wife has faith in him!"

Lillian MacMurray, a happy wife for something over five years, says that her formula for a successful marriage is twofold: "Forget your own ambition; two careers in a family don't jibe." And . . . "Never neglect your appearance. *Never!*"

Like Eloise, Lillian had a career once upon a time. She was one of New York's most beautiful show girls. When she came to Hollywood (because Fred was out here), she had offers to go on the screen. But she

HEDDA HOPPER

braves the Hollywood lions

by choosing

"THE THREE NICEST MEN IN HOLLYWOOD"

In next month's Photoplay-Movie Mirror

and Fred were in love and were to be married soon. So she let her own career slip by. "And I've never been sorry," she says. "You see, husbands like to take care of their wives."

Rather tragically, fate put this theory to the test right after the Mac-Murrays were married. Lillian, still ailing from an appendectomy, became quite seriously ill and was in bed for months. But, she says, now that she is well again, she has never regretted it.

"Fred was so sweet to me. He took care of me as one would a child. And I have a theory that when a man must work extra hard for his wife, whether it is against financial odds or because she is ill and requires special attention, or for any other reason, she becomes extra important to him—that is, if he is the right kind of a man. And Fred is.

"Our marriage," Lillian said, "is rather peculiarly remote from Fred's work. To us, his career is a business at which he works as hard as he knows how. But we don't worry about the box office or whether his

leading lady is going to steal the show or whether his latest picture was good or bad. He comes home at the end of a day and we sit in the garden, if it is summertime, or by the fire if it is winter and perhaps have a cocktail and talk about the news of the day or how the garden is doing, or maybe about the new Duncan Phyfe table I found in an antique store. I usually do most of the talking and he just stretches out in his chair and relaxes. I remember one day last summer, during some very hot weather . . . I had a change of clothing laid out on his bed upstairs and the cocktail shaker and glasses ready on a tray in the garden. He came home, went upstairs, showered and changed and came back to me. We just sat there, not saying much of anything until I caught him looking at me rather strangely. When I asked him what was on his mind, he came over and dropped a kiss on my head.

" 'I'm glad I'm married to you,' he said.

"Well, it was a little thing, but that quiet moment was worth all the careers I might have had. It made me feel happy and *safe*. Because I knew that he was happy."

Lillian smiled. "I don't think the wife of a movie star should ever feel too safe, though," she added, "competition being what it is. Therefore, I pay a lot of attention to my appearance. I don't forget that my husband meets dozens of girls, far better-looking than I, makes love to many of them on the screen. I believe it is very foolish for any wife to neglect herself. A man is attracted to her in the beginning for a certain set of reasons. Quite possibly her appearance is one of them, and she shouldn't ignore this the minute she has him 'hooked.' "

Mayo Methot, blonde, voluptuous, intelligent, sophisticated, sat before the Bogart fireplace and admitted frankly, without crossed fingers, that her marriage is ideally happy. "And I mean to keep it so," she said simply.

Mayo believes that a marriage is a wife's responsibility. She believes in the essential decency of the average man—that decency which keeps him from philandering, "cheating" if you will, if all is right with wife and home. Furthermore, to her, "Bogie" is not a "celebrity" to be handled with kid gloves. He is just a sensitive, sentimental, attractive man—and her husband. But she doesn't just "blunder along" in steering her ship of marriage—not Mayo. She has a Plan. One of its mainstays is preventing the bitterness which colors every domestic quarrel (and she admits that she and "Bogie" have them, even as most married couples) from taking root.

"There is nothing that cannot be ironed out between two people who love each other," she told me, "and I never forget it. But I don't forget, either, that for most men it is difficult to say, 'I'm sorry.' So, I say it. Sometimes I say it even though in my heart I don't think I'm to blame. I remember one time in particular, although (and isn't it often the case?) I don't remember now what we quarrelled about. Anyway, Bogie was sorry and I knew it, even though he never put it in words. You see, his manner told me so—the way he looked at me, the way he spoke to me, the way he did things for me. So, after dinner, as he was sitting before the fire, I went over and sat on the arm of his chair.

"'I'm sorry,' I told him. And his arms around me and the way he said, 'Mayo, you're sweet,' told me I'd made things right in a way that a dozen apologies from him might not have.

"You see," she added, "I don't think pride—the kind of pride that needs must save its face at any cost—has a place in marriage. I know it's trite—but give and take has got to be the rule!"

ANOTHER old-fashioned rule of Mayo's for a successful marriage—and particularly a successful marriage to a movie star—is to make him a home. She has done that; you know it the instant you walk into their small but lovely living room. It's not so grand as half the homes in Hollywood, but it kind of reaches out and welcomes you.

"Bogie loves his home," Mayo said with quiet pride.

Yes, a success on the New York stage and in screen character roles as well, Mayo Bogart has, since her marriage, relegated her career to the background. "I learned that would be necessary not more than two weeks after our honeymoon," she said. "I had gone to work upon our return and it seemed I was late getting home every day. When I would finally arrive, there would be Bogie wandering around like a lost soul. Our houseboy told me, 'Mist' Bogart not enjoy hisself until you here.' And it came over me that a wife whose husband 'not enjoy hisself' until she is with him is luckier than the most successful 'career woman' in the world. So, now I work occasionally—this because I like to have my own money to buy Bogie's Christmas and birthday presents with—but that is all.

"Meanwhile," she went on, "I find my time as full as it ever was when I was working steadily. I plan the meals and do the marketing. I take care of Bogie's clothes—attend to buttons and mending like a most admirable *hausfrau*—" she smiled—"and I garden like mad. Bogie, who, until we were married, didn't know a chrysanthemum from a carnation—well, scarcely—is as proud as punch over my horticultural achievements. Just the other day, I heard him talking to Boris Karloff about them. 'That Mayo,' he was saying, 'she's a wonder. She grows petunias seven feet high!'

"Yes, he meant hibiscus, but it gave me a warm comfortable feeling to hear him bragging about me. 'It's hard to be married to a movie star, isn't it?' some movie wives say to me. 'You never know when you might lose him to a more beautiful woman.' But I sort of think that as long as your husband is bragging about your seven-foot petunias, you're safe."

Star Finds
IN THE STORES
BY MARION HAMMON

MONOGRAMANIA: Anne Shirley goes in for monograms in a big way. Most original are the initials on her slack suit. Letters are made with rows of tiny white pearl shirtwaist buttons. Cute idea, and inexpensive, too.

*　*　*

MOCCASINS—that wash! It's an old American custom—wearing moccasins—that goes back to the Indians. The new, trim, wall-toed moccasins are designed for play clothes, slacks and sports dresses. They're comfortable, but not sloppy. Best of all, they wash as easily as a hanky. Called Kedettes, you'll find them for about $2 at your local shoe or department store.

*　*　*

BE A SISSY: A froth of ruffles and dainty bows make Sissykins a charming bit of summer whimsy. It's a trim little pantie that controls your curves and fits your figure as if it were moulded on. It's cute and oh-so-feminine. Won't make a dent in your budget, either. Only 59c at your local store.

*　*　*

SUMMER SORCERY: Summer means a new shade of lipstick—one that makes your eyes brighter, your teeth whiter and your tan deeper. If you're the golden-girl type, Pond's Honey lipstick is a shade you'll want to wear and wear. It's a bright, sunny red. Creamy smooth in texture, it will endear itself by staying on for hours and hours. Pond's Honey lipstick is 55c at drug and department stores and there's a trial size at the dime store.

*　*　*

NATURALLY: Practically every star you see has healthy, natural-looking eyebrows—heavy, even a bit shaggy. Evidently, Hollywood has turned "brows down" on thin, plucked-out-painted-in eyebrows. But you'll notice that the glamour girls of the screen are careful to tweeze out all straggling hairs. Try professional Twissors if you want to pluck out those offending hairs with hardly a twinge. 50c at department stores

AT the Dick Powell residence in the Hollywood hills fully fifteen square feet of floor in front of the fireplace had been taken over by toys, including a most intricate electric railway system. "Dick's present to himself," Joan told us, "he says it was for Normie on his birthday, but you see who's playing with it."

I saw. Normie was engaged in piecing together a jigsaw puzzle. Miss Powell (Baby Ellen, aged two, is known in the household as Miss Powell, being too robust a personality for a mere Ellen, Joan and Dick contend) was scooting an automobile across the floor.

"I can't imagine a real home and real married happiness without this sort of thing," said Joan above the din. "Children are everything.

"No," she went on, "I don't lie awake nights figuring out rules and regulations to 'hold' Dick. We are just here in our home, with our children, and it is impossible for me ever to see us anywhere else. I can feel our roots digging in every time I see Dick put a caressing arm around Normie's shoulders or speak of him, proudly, as 'my son.' I feel it when I see him take Miss Powell in his arms and hold her close; when I see him look at her with love and pride written all over his face. I feel it when he reaches out a hand to me to draw me into our family circle.

"'It is our home,' this gesture says. 'These are our children. And it is our love that is responsible!'

"No," Joan explained, "I don't think children can or should keep two people together who no longer love each other; who are quarrelling constantly; whose marriage has become bitter and hateful. But I do think that in a marriage made by love, children are the cement that strengthens and beautifies it.

"It seems to me," she said, seriously, "that it is little things building into big things which ultimately spells divorce. And it seems to me that children, the sense of responsibility they give any normal father and mother, is the greatest safeguard any marriage can have.

"Yes," she admitted, "the wife of a movie star has her problems. I remember one night when we were in Cleveland and Dick was acting as emcee at some sort of convention. During the evening, he introduced a young girl who had won a beauty contest.

"Of course, he took her hand and told the audience: 'Here is a very lovely lady whom I am privileged to introduce—' or something like that.

"Whereupon," Joan said, "a woman in the seat back of me gave me a whack on the head. 'Aren't you *jealous?*' she screeched. Everybody turned and stared at me. Well," Joan admitted, "this wasn't so very long before Miss Powell was born and I undoubtedly didn't look my best. It was a little hard to see those stares and to hear such remarks as, 'So that's the girl who got him!'

"Still," she recounted, smiling, "I wasn't too upset. I knew how Dick felt about our having a baby. I knew he wanted one more than anything. I wanted to turn around and announce to those assembled, 'Yeh. I'm the girl who got him. And watch me! I'm the girl that's going to keep him!'

"Of course, nothing ever is certain in this world," she concluded, "but"—with eyes on Dick and his electric train, Normie working on his jigsaw puzzle and Miss Powell throwing gleeful monkey wrenches into the whole setup—"dollars to doughnuts, if I had made that little speech, I would have been speaking the truth!"

Liza, Liza Smile at Me

Don't look now, Judy, but your

happiness is showing. How come? Just

listen to what an old friend has to say

BY ELSA MAXWELL

SURPRISING what a difference a little thing like Liza can make in a life.

One year you're still the Judy Garland whom Metro put under contract at the age of twelve because your voice had an odd habit of flying straight from your heart to the heart of your audience. You're the Judy who—before you had a chance to think of the things you wanted for yourself—had become a part of Hollywood's golden saga and, shy and sensitive, found yourself with the wrong people.

The next year, Liza! And you're the real you. Only, like most personal metamorphoses, yours has been so gradual, it's only now that you, or your friends, catch on to what's been happening.

At least, that's the way it looked to this reporter the other day as I watched Judy with her baby Liza in her arms. At the risk of sounding like last year's Valentine, I must report on the discovery I made that afternoon. We were in Vincente Minnelli's old study which has been transformed into the nursery because it is the room into which the sun shines all day.

Liza, I must tell you, is enchanting. She loves being alive. She cannot yet walk but she bounces on her feet trying to dance. Music, unless it is very gay, makes her very quiet. And Judy has started a collection of recordings for her, including several lullabies. She cuts a disc for Liza every time she makes a professional recording and included in the collection is the lovely "Liza, Liza."

Liza flirts boldly, aided and abetted by big dark eyes and long black lashes. Usually she's sunny. But, denied

Judy Garland, starred in "Till the Clouds Roll By"   Engstead

Every day is Mother's day since Liza Minnelli came to stay with her mother, Judy

Judy's teaching Liza not to be afraid. What's a tumble or two among friends?

Liza flirts boldly—is sunny most of the time —until she's denied something she wants

what she wants, she gets as mad as a hornet. Also, because she's interested in everything, her wants are not few. Judy, of course, dresses her in the most divine little-girl clothes.

On the day of which I write, Liza, who is teething, grabbed the soft folds of Judy's dress and stuffed them into her mouth. With gentle authority Judy freed her dress from the baby's determined grasp. And I became aware Judy had changed. For only those with personal security, only those who are self-sufficient and self-contained can have gentle authority.

Judy used to remind me of a startled fawn, with her restless eyes, her quivering nose and her little awkward leggedness. With her wildness too. For, a typical bobby-soxer, she went for hot

Liza, Liza, Smile at Me

bands and jam sessions. Now her lovely eyes lie quietly in her face. And, no longer running away from anything, no longer searching, she has no need of the old nervous activities.

Vincente helped Judy find herself, I'm sure. Actually, it would take a man like him, a genuinely sensitive artist to understand her. Beyond her recklessnesses and young brashness he felt her depths and her beauty. Like that unforgettable time she sang "Dear Mr. Gable" at a Metro convention. Two thousand members of this organization, fairly worldly human beings, sat, tears on their faces, trying to divide their eyes between the little figure on the big stage and Clark Gable who sat with tears on his face, too.

Judy singing "Dear Mr. Gable" wasn't one star singing of another star; she was a kid singing of a great idol. She still has that ability to lose all sense of her own importance in her appreciation of others. At a party last autumn, for instance, I asked Vincente to create a costume for Irene Dunne from odds and ends out of the five and dime store. Then I apologized to Judy for not having thought to ask Vincente to dress her. It was, after all, the first party she had attended since her illness following Liza's birth.

She looked at me with her velvet eyes. "But Elsa," she said, "I am proud to have Vincente dress Miss Dunne! She's my favorite actress. She's so talented!"

WHEN Vincente won a prize for his costume she beamed upon every one, Vincente especially. And he beamed upon her. For this is a real love match, one I predict will last. Of course they have spats. Isn't it one of the oldest human laws that those who love will quarrel?

"Judy's learning to cook," Vincente told me that night. "You must come for a spaghetti dinner on our cook's night out."

This was news! I thought of Judy's first marriage, at nineteen, to David Rose. It lasted less than two years. I don't know what he did or didn't do that was wrong. But I do know that Judy at this time was completely unfitted to be a wife. In the studios—and her work dictated her life—she had just been cast as a thirteen-year-old in an *Andy Hardy* picture. In fact, it was the knowledge that she would be a married woman by the time the picture was shown that influenced the studio to let her grow up.

One time, I remember, dinner guests arrived at Judy's house to find Dave out and her having dinner in bed. She had invited the guests, then forgotten them. Other times, because she never did keep the engagement book necessary in a family with two careers, she and Dave would discover they had accepted dinner dates or asked separate groups of friends for the same evening. The servants, who had seen her as *Dorothy* in "The Wizard of Oz" called her Judy. And if she went into the kitchen and said, "We'll have clams and a roast, a mixed green salad . . ." her cook was not impressed at all.

It's different now. Vincente's bachelor house, with its acres sprawling down the hillside in gardens, a tennis court and a pool, has been redecorated as a family home. Like all beautifully managed menages it runs as if it ran itself. Whiskey and soda, for a gentleman guest, tea and sandwiches, a pot of coffee for an early morning caller, appear as if by their own accord. The silver always is shining, bath towels and linen are always fresh and ashtrays always clean.

Also, I delight to report Judy's spaghetti dinner is worthy of a husband with Italian ancestry. Her meat is savory and her spaghetti is *al dente*, not limply overdone.

"You know, Elsa," she told me that day as we sat in the nursery, "we mothers have a great responsibility. We must guide our children and we must discipline them—yet, above all, we must be a friend. . . ."

I never in the world thought Judy would be such a wonderful mother. "The Pirate," a Technicolor production in which Vincente will direct her and Gene Kelly, will be the first film she has made since months before Liza was born. At first there was her illness. Then there was her wish to get Vincente's house in order and see Liza started in the way she should go. For the first time in her life, you see, since she sang in her family's vaudeville act at four years of age, the personal demands upon her time, thoughts and energies have been so many that her professional life hasn't had a chance.

The most important thing she is teaching Liza is not to be afraid. She even seeks to free her of the two fears with which an infant comes into this world—the fear of loud noises and the fear of falling. If there is an unexpected noise everyone acts as if nothing had happened. If Liza falls everyone laughs.

A few days before I saw Liza, Judy and her nurse had taken her for a drive. When the nurse had accidentally let the car door slam with a frightful noise, Liza had practically leapt into her mother's arms. Then she had laughed. And Judy had wept with pride and joy.

JUDY, who loves jewelry, used to buy pieces that befitted her position. Now she thinks of Liza. "She'll love this when she's older," she said, admiring the heavy coral necklace and earrings which, I'm sure, were Vincente's choice. With his artist's eyes he would see the great complement they would be to Judy's frail dark beauty.

It's good to see Judy these days . . . being herself. It used to be only infrequently and briefly she knew this pleasure. I remember how she used to talk about the few months she once had in high school while Metro were deciding what to do with her. "I wasn't known," she always says describing this interlude, "and I didn't tell that I'd done a few small parts in pictures and been in vaudeville. So I was just like the other girls! It was wonderful!"

Another time, in 1943, after her marriage to David Rose, Judy tried to crash a party I gave at Romanoff's. However, since she was with two sailor boys, was wearing old sport clothes and had no invitation, the doorman didn't recognize her and would not admit her. "I know Elsa Maxwell," she told the boys. "I'm sure she'd let us in; then you could see the stars. Let's wait—maybe we'll catch her . . ." So they stood with the crowd and waited. They didn't catch me. But they had a magnificent time. For, in slacks with the collar of her coat turned up and her hat pulled down, Judy was not recognized and the crowd's comments were unconfined.

"I never had a better time," Judy told me afterward. "I kept wondering what they would have said about me had I arrived all dressed up. I had more fun than I would have had at your party, Elsa. I was one of the people as never before!"

Always, I think, Judy has longed for a place in the world without benefit of her name in electric lights. At last she's found it. And from the slightly reckless, slightly wild, jam session devotee there has emerged an old-fashioned girl who finds her pleasure in the simplest things.

Vincente started her transformation, no doubt. Then, there was Liza.

Liza, Liza. . . .

THE END

HOLLYWOOD'S
Newest Pin-up Girl

CHERYL CHRISTINA CRANE SPEAKING

I HAVE navy blue eyes and black hair. I weigh ten pounds and thirteen ounces so far, and I was born on July twenty-fifth of this year. My name is Cheryl Christina Crane.

I probably inherit my looks from my parents. I don't know whether you've heard of them or not—they're Mr. and Mrs. J. Stephen Crane, and my mother's acting name is Lana Turner. But considering how old they are (she's twenty-two years older than I am and he's twenty-eight), I think they are stunning people. She's about a foot shorter than Daddy, with soft blonde hair that falls around her face, and she wears a size ten dress; and he's six feet one, with big shoulders and brown eyes and dark curling hair like mine. And aside from being good-looking, they're the two happiest people I've ever seen.

Not that they've always been happy. They had a bad spell for two weeks, just before I was born—because of Daddy. You see, he was just determined to have a son. In fact, he even told Mother he'd disown her if I were a girl and he got very touchy whenever anyone kidded him about it . . . and one time, a week before I was born, he even walked out on a party to cool off because he got so angry when someone said I might be what I am.

So you can imagine how my mother felt when I finally appeared, at 5:14 Sunday morning on July twenty-fifth. She'd been conscious all the time I was arriving, because she'd taken something called a spinal anaesthetic; so the minute she was told about me she said, "Oh, how will we ever tell Stephen?"

One of the nurses said she would, and she went out into the hall and said very quickly, "Congratulations—you have a lovely daughter!" Then I hear that my father turned milk-white with disappointment. But he came into the delivery room right away and kissed my mother, and then couldn't help snarling when he said, "Well, where is she?"

The nurse took him over to where I was, in a hotbox in the corner . . . and he took one look at me and changed his whole attitude right then and there. Mother says he got the most foolish look on his face—and now, whenever he thinks she's not around, he comes into my room and tells me a lot of pretty foolish (but very wonderful) things. If anyone makes me conceited, he will. He says I am the most marvelous baby girl in the whole world and he wouldn't change me for anyone. Even a boy.

What I wouldn't change is the life I lead. I lie all day long in the prettiest room you can imagine, which my mother designed herself. The walls are pale, pale blue with fleecy white clouds painted on them—and pink cherubs pulling the clouds along, and riding them, and pushing them. My furniture is all pink and blue and white, too—and outside my room is a one-story white house on a hill overlooking the whole Pacific Ocean and the city of Los Angeles. A swarm of people live here—seven altogether. There's my grandmother, and Daddy and Mother, and two maids, and my nurse and me. Only I sometimes wonder what the nurse is for—because Mother likes to do everything for me. She feeds and bathes me, very gently, and talking to me all the time. If my Daddy were here alone, of course, I could understand the nurse—because, even though he likes to come in and make love speeches to me, he's scared to death to touch me. And whenever he does, Mother says he's so clumsy that she's terrified he'll drop me.

Before I was born a lot of hubbub seems to have gone on. Like Mother's yens, for instance. She got a strawberry yen, when she ate strawberries for breakfast, lunch and dinner and in between meals too—and she insisted that everyone else in the house eat them with her. She got so strawberry-conscious, she even bought a strawberry-print maternity dress—and Daddy just stopped her in time before she had

Her mama is Lana Turner; her papa is Stephen Crane; she's just herself, talking the most unexpected baby talk you've ever heard!

"Even though my daddy likes to make love speeches to me, he's scared to death to touch me."

all the wallpaper in their room changed to a strawberry pattern. She even had the paperhangers arranged for before Daddy argued her out of it. As he said, once I'd come, strawberries would be out—and he was quite right.

Then there was her thriller yen. Every night when Daddy was up from Fort MacArthur (he was a Private in the Army until just recently, when he got an honorable discharge for medical reasons), he had to take Mother to the Hawaiian Theater to see "The Wolf Man" or "Frankenstein's Sister," or some other horror picture. Mother was crazy for them. They went so much (and loaded down with popcorn, too!) that the ushers began to say, "Hello, Lana and Steve," just the way they said hello to each other every night. But now that I'm here, she says she doesn't have to have movie thrills any more—she's all excited just staying home with Daddy and me.

That's all they seem to do, I must say—is stay home. Sometimes when they're talking over my bassinet, I hear them remembering their courtship, which seems to have been carried on in every night club and restaurant in Southern California. They went to a lot of parties while I was on the way, too. But now they are a couple of home bodies. Mother says, "Darling, why go out?" to Daddy, and he says, "Why indeed?" . . . so then they pull out the gin rummy board and begin trying to beat each other at it every night. Or else Mother reads her beloved biographies and Daddy reads the paper or listens to the radio. And a lot of the time they just talk, about me.

AS YOU can see, we lead a very simple life—there's only a lawn and a white picket fence outside my window, no pool or tennis court. When Daddy and Mother feel like exercising, they go someplace else for him to swim or play golf or tennis—and for her to bowl. (She says she'll have to wait 'til I grow up to have a bowling partner, because, as she says I will find out in time, husbands won't play games that their wives can beat them at!) We hardly know any other actors, any more than most families do. And Mother isn't the kind who likes to sit for hours at lunch with other women—she'd rather grab a sandwich in a drive-in when she's not home. And when she goes shopping, she takes Daddy with her because she says she's dressing for him anyway . . . which means she's usually in blue or black and *every* dress has a sweetheart neckline! I can't wait to get old enough to try on her clothes, because I like all of them—the dresses, and the tailored suits, and the long-sleeved dinner gown (Daddy doesn't like real formals), and the slacks she wears around the house. And I also can't wait to grow up so I can help fight for the funnies on Sunday—which is a regular ritual with Daddy and Mother!

But mostly I can't wait to grow up to see if I turn out the way they plan. Because they have lots of plans for me—big and little. The first thing they hope for me is good health, maybe because I've had such a hard time so far. I've had nine blood transfusions, you know. However, I've gained three pounds already since I came into the world, so I'm not worried.

But to get on with their plans for me: They say they're going to prepare me for anything in life I want, and nothing I don't want. College, for instance, is up to me. Mother never went past Hollywood High School and doesn't think college is necessary for a girl; but Daddy says college is fun, if not necessary, because he's an honor graduate of Wabash University in Indiana. Mostly, though, they want me to be good at anything I do, whether it's

college or a career. They don't care whether I'm an actress or not.

"We just want her to be happy, to be loved, and to have a nice and normal life," I hear them saying to each other. They don't want me to be deluged with luxuries —just to have the average amount of clothes and toys and friends, the way they both did. They both stress honesty, too. When I begin asking questions, they'll answer all of them—nicely but completely. They think that truthfulness is the most important thing in the world—and next to truth, tolerance, and patience, and self-control. They want me to know how to control my temper at all times, because they think uncontrolled people are at the mercy of themselves and the world; and they want me to have patience because they themselves didn't have it at times—and in the end, after all their impatient worrying and sadness, things worked out just the way they would have anyway. Also, they want me to have a sense of humor. Which Mother says Daddy has, and Daddy says Mother has—so between them, I certainly should have one too!

Those are their big plans for me. Then there are their little plans, which are very cute, I think. Daddy carried out one the other day, when he came home with a pair of pink booties for me with my initials C. C. C. on them—matching my fa-

vorite pink coat, which Norma Shearer gave me. When Daddy brought them in he said, "I knew I'd have to buy the shoes in order to woo you, because you take after your mother and she's a shoe fiend!"

But his and Mother's main little plan is to have a miniature bracelet and ring made for me, just exactly like the ones they wear—made like the Army identification disks, only in silver. Hers says on the front, "Lana Crane," and on the back, "Return to J. Stephen Crane." And his is just the opposite—and mine will say "Cheryl Christina Crane" on the front and to return me to both of them on the back.

Usually, when they're talking about me, it's Daddy who breaks up the discussions. He always ends by saying anxiously, "Darling, at what age should we let Cheryl go out on dates?" And then Mother laughs and says, "Don't you think that's something we can worry about later?"

And then she almost squashes me by hugging him, with me in between, and she says, "You know, if someone gave me a wish, and said I could have anything I wanted in the world—I couldn't think of a thing to wish for. Because I have everything now. I have a wonderful husband, a good life and a precious baby. I couldn't possibly ask for anything more."

Then Daddy says he feels the same way. And I, Cheryl, do too!

324

For Rita Hayworth and Victor Mature the muted strains of a Strauss waltz, recalling the past

It happened one eventful night when a chance remark

led Photoplay's photographer to a candle-lit corner

where two people were meeting again, just like old times

What I think about

Flynn, portrayer of America's heroes: Above, in "Dodge City" . . .

. . . and as a Union Army officer in the rousing "Virginia City" . . .

. . . a West Point officer in "Santa Fe Trail" with de Havilland . . .

America's most famous woman reporter brings you the honest, plain-spoken truth about the grave accusations this Hollywood favorite now faces

AS nearly as I can remember, it was about twenty-three years ago that I wrote my first story for Photoplay Magazine. Because I believe that motion pictures are the most vital influence upon public thought in the world today, I have always felt an obligation to carry out the editorial policy of Photoplay which at all times has been to speak the truth to the public about motion pictures and the truth to the motion pictures about the public.

Which brings us to the case of Errol Flynn.

To begin with, it is manifestly impossible for any magazine devoted to the works and people of the movies to ignore a case which occupies the front pages of newspapers all over the world and which is discussed wherever people gather, no matter how difficult to achieve fairness and impartiality in so delicate a situation.

In my own personal experience I have heard the Errol Flynn case discussed and I have been questioned about it at an important tea in Washington; at an aircraft plant; at a military academy; during a delightful evening with the publisher of a highbrow literary review; at my hairdresser's; and on trains.

In these times that may seem strange, but it is true.

Photoplay has had hundreds of letters asking why it doesn't come to the defense of this screen favorite who they say has been accused by publicity-seeking girls crazy to get into

Flynn with his attorney, Jerry Geisler, at the preliminary hearing

the movies and by others demanding in justice to the rest of the Hollywood stars, who behave themselves and sell War Bonds, that Errol Flynn be cast into outer darkness. Upon one thing they all agree. They want the opinion or judgment of Hollywood's foremost motion-picture magazine.

As nearly as we can come to that in justice and fairness we now propose to try.

But we must ask your consideration of one or two problems, First, Photoplay finds itself up against that arbitrary tyrant called the deadline, of which the reader seldom thinks. A certain length of time must pass between the writing of this story and its appearance in your hands. Much may be revealed of which we could not know at the time I write. But this should reach you three or four days before Mr. Flynn is called into the Superior Court of Los Angeles County to answer the District Attorney's charge against him of statutory rape upon two girls under the legal age of consent, which in California is eighteen.

It is now so grave and far-reaching a matter that it must be faced. First because it necessarily involves all Hollywood, which has too often been called upon to suffer en masse for the sins of its individual members. But most of all because Mr. Flynn has become part of America.

For Errol Flynn has had the great good fortune to portray upon the screen the heroes of our country. He

the Errol Flynn case

BY ADELA ROGERS ST. JOHNS

has worn the West Point uniform, he has been a brave officer of our Union Army, he has done the epic deeds of our pioneer forefathers. We have come to identify him with the men to whom we Americans owe so very much, we Americans who are once more fighting to the death for those things they bequeathed to us. It is Errol Flynn who made Custer's last stand come alive for many of us.

As a whole we are richer, we are warmer, for the way in which Errol Flynn made these men come to life, made them into real people and thus inspired us to feel a closer brotherhood with them.

The boys who a short time ago yelled and whistled and stamped to cheer on Errol Flynn's rides across the plains are today in the African desert or on the Solomon Islands or in camp somewhere in the U. S. A., getting ready to go over there. And Flynn was their idol. Let's not kid ourselves about that. I sat through too many Errol Flynn pictures with my own sons.

That is why it seems so essential to get at the truth, the whole truth and nothing but the truth of this controversial matter—for controversial it must be upon whichever side the truth now is. It is a tragic thing to lose any hero right now—or any man who has portrayed those heroes and identified himself with them in our eyes. But the times are too realistic for whitewash to stick.

When I get just this far I am overcome with a desire to smack Mr. Flynn. Honestly. Whether or not he is guilty of the crime with which he is charged—I for one do not believe that he is guilty *as* charged and we'll go into that in a moment—he had no business to get himself into such a spot. He had no right not to protect us all from such a mess. He's old enough to know better.

For Mr. Flynn now stands charged with a crime at the mere suggestion

of which that great sportsman whom Flynn has just brought to the screen, James J. Corbett, would have poked him right in the nose.

Sometimes you can hurt just as many people and get yourself in just as bad a jam by being dumb as you can by being bad.

However, I think that in view of all these things there are a number of matters which it is essential that we consider at this time.

If our timing on the deadline is right, you will read this before Flynn comes to trial in the Superior Court of the County of Los Angeles, prosecuted by District Attorney Dockweiler and Assistant District Attorney Cochran and defended by Jerry Geisler, who is not only a fine trial lawyer but a man whose integrity and honesty are highly respected by our judges and law enforcement officials.

There and then Mr. Flynn will be charged and tried by a jury of his peers.

But in his case, that courtroom widens to take in most of the English-speaking world and the jury grows until millions will sit upon it.

FOR Errol Flynn must also be tried at the bar of public opinion and you are the jury of his peers in that vast court which is so vital to him— and to you. Your verdict is the most important thing in life to this man whom you have lifted to movie stardom. You will not be present in that small courtroom when Errol Flynn answers "Not Guilty." You will depend upon eyewitness accounts through the newspapers of what takes place and upon printed testimony of the two girls involved and the other witnesses. I know that is always difficult. I have read the transcript of court cases that I have covered and been amazed to find the difference: the ring of truth or the knell of guilt in a voice, the appearance and posture of a witness,

... an upstanding Naval doctor in the stirring "Dive Bomber"

... as General Custer in "They Died With Their Boots On"...

... and as James J. Corbett in his latest, "Gentleman Jim"

What I Think about the Errol Flynn Case

the signs of nervousness or of calm, the way the eyes of the accused look at a jury.

You will have the accurate account of proven reporters when the case goes to trial. But to this account you will need to add as full a knowledge of the scene behind the scenes as you can possibly acquire if you are honestly to prepare yourselves to serve as members of the jury of public opinion.

Aside from denying all charges, Mr. Flynn has made only one statement to you. He has asked that you withhold judgment until all the evidence on both sides is in. He has a right to ask that. It is the spirit and the letter of American law that a man is innocent until he is proven guilty. The burden of proof rests upon the prosecution. They must present evidence to prove their charge and in reviewing that evidence you have a right and a duty to judge the credibility of the State's witnesses, when and why they first told their stories accusing the defendant, their general character and reputation for honesty and integrity.

BUT for that jury of public opinion of which the readers of Photoplay make up so large and vitally interested a part, there are other things which may, in fairness, be taken into account. Whether that jury in the courtroom finds the testimony of the two girls true or false, it makes up only one part of those things concerning Errol Flynn by which you will judge him.

Lest you think that I, as an old-time resident of Hollywood, am in any way a special pleader in this, I would like to say that I have met Mr. Flynn only three or four times in my life, two of these on a movie set, and that I never formed any opinion of him either way. I knew and liked his ex-wife, Lili Damita, but Lili was a small and very ornamental package of dynamite and Hollywood always figured insofar as the Flynn-Damita love story and marriage, with its brawls and jealousies and passionate reconciliations was concerned, it was strictly fifty-fifty.

My only personal interest is a young son who has been an Errol Flynn fan for years, which is why I have seen all the Flynn pictures. So far his comments have been about as follows: He does not believe a word of it because no guy like Errol Flynn who could take out Betty Grable would be caught dead with those girls who got their pictures in the papers. He says none of the older fellows at his school would have bought those girls a coke, so why should Errol Flynn have taken them out? He adds, impersonally and offhand, that so far the Errol Flynn case just confirms his opinion that some girls are dopes and that they do not think anything of getting other people in trouble and that I ought to know by this time in my business that girls will do anything to get in the movies.

That is a loyalty to the man who played Custer that I would not like to see destroyed.

He also mutters darkly that it looks

pretty silly for a girl who had her picture taken walking up Hollywood Boulevard with her stomach showing to start wearing pigtails and who does she think she is fooling?

SO it is no use saying that Mr. Flynn's private life belongs to him. It does *not*. Nor does the life of any other man or woman who accepts the rewards and fame of public popularity. He owes us all a great deal and he must pay for it by conducting himself so that no disillusionment can result. In other words, he needn't be an angel, but he must be a right guy.

There are points to be reckoned with upon both sides of this case.

For instance, there seems little question that Mr. Flynn has been guilty of lack of taste and discretion in his associations. In not protecting himself from either temptation or possible frame-ups, as the case might be, Mr. Flynn took chances with our confidence and his employers' money apparently for his own amusement. That's silly. And of that he must already stand convicted, I think.

However, that's slightly different from the crime of which he is accused and for which he can be sent to jail or even, if he escapes a prison sentence, be ruined in the public's eye for all time.

As Tallyrand once remarked, sometimes a blunder is worse than a crime. There are a few facts about Mr. Flynn and his life in Hollywood which I think it is only fair that you should know. They are pretty generally known in the movie capital and have had a great deal to do with the fact that as a whole Hollywood would like to see Mr. Flynn get a break—at least a fifty-fifty one—on this present trouble.

HOLLYWOOD hasn't said much and for a reason that does it credit, though it may be hard on Errol Flynn. Right now, the motion-picture industry has plenty of troubles of its own and Mr. Flynn is merely a personal headache, as they see it. Hollywood is honestly and deeply wrapped up in the war effort. They are more aware than ever before of the job they can do for their country—both as entertainers and as propagandists, in the best sense of the word. The casting problem with young male stars going into the service is one so serious that unless something sane is done about it, it won't be long until those of us at home and our boys in the service won't have any more motion pictures. The $25,000 salary ceiling is a desperate one for people who have assumed large obligations, support half a dozen families, keep up farms and homes and are faced with no time in which to adjust to smaller incomes.

Above all, right now, the movies want to serve in the war — want to get credit for the job they have done toward unity and war spirit with "Mrs. Miniver" and "Wake Island" and pictures like that. They dare not go all out, even though they may understand and sympathize greatly with Mr. Flynn for many reasons, for fear their defense will be misunderstood and put down as condonement and folks somewhere will say, "Oh sure—you'd expect Hollywood to defend a guy like that—look at 'em—they haven't any morals themselves." And right now Hollywood—to do its job—dare not risk any part of a scandal, any part of a defense of a man accused as Errol Flynn is accused. It isn't selfishness, it's a true desire to keep their name clean so that they may better serve. So much I *know*.

So, to a large extent, Mr. Flynn is going this part of the road alone.

Yet only Hollywood could understand how often a man in Flynn's position is in a spot, how dangerous his every step, how much safer he probably was out on that little boat with the sharks than as a matinee idol among a lot of movie-mad, career-hungry, publicity-crazy girls.

I have watched it for a good many years—in the days of Wallace Reid, of the incomparable Valentino, of Jack Gilbert and many others. And sometimes I have had good reason to be ashamed of my sex. I have seen things you would hardly believe—diamond necklaces handed to a star's valet, very clever badger games, girls of good family hiding under beds after climbing in windows; every possible effort to rope in a movie star made by women of much higher education and much more knowledge of right and wrong than the girls in the Flynn case can possibly have.

A man in Flynn's position if he is unmarried and foot-loose is always headed for trouble with forms of female persecution, with every known form of blackmail and frame-up. Every detective who ever worked in Hollywood and every reporter who ever covered it will bear me out in that. It sounds fantastic, but it is necessarily true.

BEHIND this case of Errol Flynn lies the peculiar dangers of Hollywood fame and fortune.

And above all, in this particular instance, the special dangers to Errol Flynn.

In the first place, Mr. Flynn has never been a real favorite with people. When he first came to us and made an overnight success, he was a pretty cocky young man. He was very handsome, and gave the impression of thinking well of himself. He had lived a totally undisciplined and adventurous life, and he had an unfortunate superiority of manner and accent for which possibly he was not to blame.

Anyhow, he never made a great many friends on his own lot and he did make a number of enemies. His methods with people who played in his pictures were highhanded to say the least. Of course, he was young and spoiled and he *had* done amazing things.

Somehow, he never won the hearts of his equals, the way Gable and Cooper, for instance, have always done. However, be it said in his favor, he has the loyalty and affection of a good many great friends whom he has chosen because of his own liking rather than for anything they could do for him.

Now if you know anything at all about the Irish you know what happens in that case. And it happened in the case of Errol Flynn. Hurt inside, he started putting his worst foot forward with a sort of brittle defiance. It wasn't in him any more than it has ever been in any other Irishman to attempt conciliation, or to try to make himself better liked. Under the general opinion that he was an arrogant pup, he proceeded to get worse and because of his success people had to like it.

But in the last year or year and a half everybody in Hollywood tells me that Flynn began trying to change. His marriage broke wide open and there is no question that he loved Lili at one time. Perhaps he had begun to get the unexpected accumulation of his own carelessness. But above all, came the war—and Errol Flynn, the great fighter, the man who played Custer, the adventurer, couldn't get into service.

As nearly as I can find out, he wanted to get into the fight two years ago. His courage has never been questioned and he was born a British subject. Everything about him led to the sure conviction that he wanted to be in the thing, even if you rule out the fact that a man of his age and reputation would feel he had to go. He *wanted* to go.

Totally unprepared, never having had to learn what it means to fail, Errol Flynn got a real body blow. He wasn't physically fit. Like a good many athletes, he had overdone his endurance stuff. Anyway, it is a definite matter of record that he couldn't pass his physicals.

His pride was slashed to ribbons, his whole philosophy of life failed him at the greatest and most crucial test. He'd gone all over the world looking for trouble. He'd fought his way through every picture he'd ever made. He'd been Hollywood's best rider, fisherman, sailor, tennis champ. But now, when the real thing came, he was—burned out.

I guess, at that, it must have been pretty tough to take on top of the fact that his wife had left him. He hadn't created that warmth, that affection which would now have brought him consoling sympathy and friendships. Perhaps there were even people glad to see the swashbuckling Mr. Flynn getting it right in the eye.

The fact must be faced that Flynn was always a ladies' man. He liked —and what man if he is honest doesn't— female admiration. I think with the bitterness that came upon him he got careless, he got utterly restless, he got a sort of a what-the-devil-does-it-matter attitude.

He tried. He started thinking about other people on the lot. He went to the powers that be, for instance, and fought to have Miss de Havilland's part in "They Died With Their Boots On" built up—an unheard-of thing for Flynn. He fought to give Ronald Reagan equal billing on "Desperate Journey." He did a lot of nice things for people before all this happened. I heard all that last time I was in Hollywood. Folks said, Flynn acts as if he's trying to convince people he's a right guy.

WE HAVE, upon the statute books of our various states, a great many laws. Some are good, some not so good. Some have had to be repealed. There are laws intended for one purpose which have been so drawn that they can be used for personal ends having nothing to do with their original intent. The Mann Act was drawn entirely to prevent the commercial horror of white slavery, yet it began to be used on sheer technicalities against men who obviously had no such intentions but had bought a middle-aged lady a meal while crossing a state line. Breach of promise and heart balm laws, once used to protect innocent girls against seducers, became instruments of blackmail.

The law of statutory rape is one that has caused considerable controversy among intelligent people. I do not know myself whether it is a good law, but I know its basic purpose was good. But it is possible that it can be used technically for ends that are not so good. It deals, as you know, entirely with the age of consent. A girl may not only give her consent, she may do everything humanly possible to attract and vamp a man, she may look twenty, she may have had several years of worldly experience, she may lie to a man about her age, and yet the law may be invoked against him. The matter must be in the hands of the judge and the prosecutors and the jury to decide whether the intent of the law has been violated, and though ignorance of the law is no excuse in the eyes of the law, it some-times is in the eyes of human beings. In other words, there is a great difference between the action of a man who meets a singer from a night club, who runs around in revealing costumes and who says she is past eighteen and who not only shows knowledge of men but uses her charms to entice him, and the actions of a man who by physical violence attacks a young girl who is obviously under age.

The whole thing boils down to a fairly simple matter.

We must wait until the courts have decided the guilt or innocence of Mr. Flynn insofar as the crime with which he is charged is concerned.

That is a legal, technical matter.

We can by no means on earth escape the fact that he has been foolish in the extreme, whether criminally foolish or not we don't yet know, but certainly foolish.

He has not realized his obligation to protect his own good name and to live up to the admiration of his fans, as long as he spends the money they make for him and takes advantage of the fame they have given him.

But our verdict rests upon this: Are we prepared to give Errol Flynn another chance?

Granting he's been foolish, do we feel that he has given us enough on the screen and maybe will in the future so that we can overlook these mistakes and let him come back?

If he's been let in for a rotten time by nothing more than careless lack of good taste, that's one thing. If he has used his name and glamour to entice little girls with offers of movie success, that's another. If he's been "joe" for someone's shrewd little ambition, that's still another.

That the girls were injured in any real sense of the word does not seem to be the case. Even in their accusations against Mr. Flynn, both say they gave consent so that the whole case is based upon the law that they could not legally have given that consent.

If we acquit him, I think we must wipe the whole thing out of our minds. Its great danger lies in nasty rumor. That's just foul for everybody. If we convict him, we must do it with care and with a real purpose, the purpose of reminding all those who occupy high places that the price of fame and the love of the public is a very high one always.

Nobody can have the cake of stardom and eat the bread of freedom to do wrong at the same time.

Out in California, there will be a verdict by twelve men and women of Guilty or Not Guilty of the crime as charged.

Throughout the country there will be a verdict of a Second Chance or No Second Chance for a man who has been a great favorite and contributed some fine chapters to our history.

Like every member of every jury, it's up to you. Remember how much is at stake.

The End

329

Why the news of Lana Turner and Steve Crane's separation was a bit of a surprise to Hollywood: This is the way they looked just a few short weeks before at the Trocadero

CASE AGAINST CHAPLIN

By Adela Rogers St. Johns

This is the page on which editors usually speak to you, PHOTOPLAY's readers. This month the editors make an exception. They allow a famous writer to speak to you. The words she speaks are strong words, angry words. They are spoken on a subject of such immediate concern to Hollywood that, although PHOTOPLAY does not necessarily agree with everything that is said here, we believe they should be brought to you. . . . Fred R. Sammis

FEEL very sad about Charlie Chaplin, our lost genius.

Always I've said proudly, "Nobody can come up to Chaplin." Of late I've said, "Now that America is in the war, Charlie will make us laugh again through our tears."

Instead he has written his wartime comedy on the back fence with a piece of chalk. Minus the baggy pants and the famous cane, he has crossed that thin line between the funny and the ridiculous and the kids of today don't laugh at him any more, they snicker with a sort of knowing embarrassment painful to hear.

His arrogance has denied us even the privilege of silence, those of us who tried to cling loyally to old memories.

For it has to be faced, doesn't it? With every front-page record, he has helped to destroy our sense of decency, the way every man and woman does who fails in these days to exhibit self-control and self-discipline in order to uphold that of our men at the front. We can't dismiss it all carelessly, because Chaplin has been a great figure, he has borne a great name, and every questionable action of his sabotages something of the dignity and steadfastness of the home front.

Fully as important, there is this stab in the back which he has dealt Hollywood, the Hollywood that gave him fame and fortune. No loyalty made him careful of his good name and theirs, no gratitude inspired him to protect his honor and theirs with much-needed watchfulness. For in a limelighted community like Hollywood it is the glaring exceptions which stand out in the minds of outsiders and color their judgment of the town.

The beloved clown is gone, the beloved clown who with comic mustache wriggling and trick hat bobbing nevertheless was always the gallant knight rushing to succor betrayed damsel or homeless pup. We now have the man Joan Barry has accused as the father of a child she is soon to bear.

Of course it is human nature to judge a man on past performance, to recall those others who stand silent beside Joan Barry out of the past—Mildred Harris . . . Lita Grey . . . stories too well remembered to be ignored now. Yet, whether Joan Barry's accusation should prove true or false, whether in the final outcome Chaplin proves himself innocent of the charge leveled by this girl who says that she was driven away from the house of the man where for a year and a half she had been his student, his friend at least, it remains true that at exactly the psychological moment when his friends expected him to act with the dignity and honesty that went with the reputation of genius, Chaplin instead flaunted decency and good taste and made new headlines with his runaway marriage to Oona O'Neill, debutante of the Stork Club set.

IT seems to me that Chaplin needed to wait for a verdict; he should have met this charge before he married another girl. Chaplin's record certainly doesn't outlaw the possibility of the charge's being true. Every law of self-respect should have made him wait to marry until he was vindicated by the court in the event that no overwhelming proof of the girl's story developed.

Chaplin brushed aside all that. He put himself beyond reach of Joan Barry's hope by marrying. We can disregard Oona's statement that she was the one who urged the marriage. Chaplin was still the one to decide.

After all, Chaplin is not a young man, subject to the fevers and uncontrollable temptations of youth's hot blood, or a lad bewildered by all that goes with sudden fame. Chaplin has been on those dizzy heights for thirty years. He ought to be acclimated by now.

Life has been very good to the man whose hair has grown silvery with honors and acclaim seldom won by any man of genius in his lifetime.

Yet with the land of his birth and the land of his

Case against Chaplin

golden opportunity both fighting for the very kind of liberty and pursuit of happiness he has always enjoyed, Charlie Chaplin has chosen to sit by rather than give his services. For all we have given him in this nation he has returned us not one laugh since the need of humanity called us to battle after Pearl Harbor.

We are reminded of the striking contrast between him and another little English clown, whose early story was much the same as Chaplin's but the end, oh so different. Stanley Lupino—father of Ida—who knew as Chaplin did what it was to go hungry in the streets of London when he was young. Knew what it was to turn his gift for making people laugh into stardom and fortune.

While the bombs fell upon London during those long dreadful days and nights of the Battle of Britain, Stanley Lupino was up there on the stage making people laugh so loud they couldn't hear the scream of bombs. And when the curtain went down Stanley Lupino put on his helmet and went out to his duties as an air raid warden. All England remembers and always will that Stanley Lupino was killed at his post by a German bomb.

HOLLYWOOD, however, is not without its record of a great comedian today. Nobody has ever thought to call Bob Hope a genius and I daresay he would not like it much if they did. Well, if Hollywood's Bob Hope has missed a laugh he could bring us since this war began I don't know how or when or where, do you? If there is a camp he could get to, a soldier or sailor or marine he could entertain, an hour he could devote to laughter for our people and he failed to find it all—I'll be surprised. Actually, it is Bob Hope who represents this generation of Hollywood laugh makers as king, and of him Hollywood can be proud, believe me.

When you think of Hollywood in war time you can think of Bob Hope and Bing Crosby and Abbott and Costello, of Carole Lombard and Captain Clark Gable and Lieutenant Commander Robert Montgomery and Bette Davis of the Hollywood Canteen and Betty Grable and Dorothy Lamour and all the troupers who have never faltered from any chance to serve.

It has been said that Hollywood is afraid of this Chaplin case. I don't think so. I think it is sick and sorry and ashamed. Through all his years it has allowed him to remain on the throne. He has been Hollywood's one authentic genius, and Hollywood has been proud of the recognition given him by the great. It is very difficult to cast out the man who has been hailed as a genius. Hollywood as a whole wants to turn away its eyes and weep at the spectacle of their genius, their great artist.

I think it is necessary that we forget Charlie Chaplin, as we must forget the others who have failed the great task. He doesn't belong to wartime Hollywood.

"I must have peace, I must be let alone!" cried Mr. Chaplin beside his swimming pool.

Who is Charlie Chaplin that he out of all this war-torn world dare demand peace?

I don't think we can give Mr. Chaplin peace.

But his other request it is within our power to grant. Sadly, but without bitterness.

We can let him alone.

THE END

We Won't Forget

In memoriam to Leslie Howard: The editors feel that there can be no better tribute paid to a great star than these sincere words from a Photoplay reader

When I first read of Leslie Howard's tragic "killed in action" death, my main thought was what a terrible loss it is for the screen. There are so few actors capable of expressing a whole emotion by just a gesture of the hand or an expression in the eyes and he was one of that few. But then I thought of how much the screen has *gained* during his lifetime . . . of the many memorable characters he has created. . . . A young crippled doctor who, as he was caught by the wiles of a cheap little tramp named *Mildred*, broke our hearts as surely as he did his own . . .

A broken, tragic old man, sitting alone in a garden mourning for his lost *Moonyean*, the beautiful bride killed on their wedding day . . .

A gay and dashing nobleman rescuing aristocrats in the very shadow of the guillotine, while his enemies searched on for "the demned, elusive *Pimpernel*" . . .

The selfish, maddening and utterly charming professor who taught a little flower girl to be a great lady and fell in love with both of them . . .

They're all vivid characterizations, enriching the screen a hundredfold and for which we are all deeply grateful even as we recognize our great loss.

Forget him? How can we ever—for he left with us all those vibrant living memories, portraits etched by the hand of a master artist—bright, eternal, defying time itself.

C. Frisbie

A personal story on Clark Gable

by Adela Rogers St. Johns

This friend has found the keynote of the change that marks Gable today

IT goes without saying, I suppose, that Clark Gable came back to America after combat flying over Germany a changed man.

When I saw him in Hollywood, where he was concentrating upon cutting the many reels of fighting film he brought back, I was aware first of the change in his eyes. The twinkle with which he'd always faced life until the tragic death of his wife, Carole Lombard, was back. But behind it was something I had not seen before. Something strong, steady and utterly sure.

To tell you the truth, I kept looking for the keynote of that change among Clark's close friends in Hollywood and in my own thought for quite a long time. I kept wondering why I had such a true and enormous admiration for Captain Gable. It couldn't be because he is a movie star. In my years in Hollywood, I have known a good many movie stars and, to be frank, have not admired all of them. I have also known a good many men who have been in battle, who have flown combat over the enemy in the face of death.

I admire all of them, naturally, but not with the same deep and solacing feeling that Gable gives all of

This was once his gateway to happiness—to the ranch where Gable lived with Carole Lombard. During his Hollywood stay it is still "home"

us who know him rather well.

Then it came to me in a rush and I pass it on to you because I think there is comfort in it for all of us in these hard days.

The keynote of that change in Clark Gable is humility.

Not that Gable was ever conceited, ever high-hat, ever arrogant.

But this new look is one of a man who has pushed back many horizons, who is humbly grateful for the gift of life, who has seen men so brave and so fine that he can thank God for having created man at all.

And in that he has found for the first time, I am sure, some comfort for the grief, which went deeper than most people realized, at the loss of Carole. There was a long time when he couldn't even talk about her. A long time when his friends feared the bitterness that came into his soul at her accidental death. That bitterness is all gone. In its place is a quiet and unspoken faith that fills your own mind as though somebody had turned on a light. It isn't necessary for him to say anything. You know that he knows that somewhere all is well with Carole and that has given him back peace.

Over there, in the little island

which stood so firmly and so alone for so long against the enemy, Clark Gable, Captain in the U.S.A.A.F., saw a lot of the men who fly and fight in this war.

They liked him. And they liked him because he was literally one of them. Clark Gable went into the Air Corps the hard way. He didn't take—more than that, he refused to accept—anything except by the hard way. He wanted combat service and nothing else.

Once in the early days when he was fighting to get in, he explained that. He wanted to do a job, he wanted to earn equality with the other men and he felt pretty sure that he could do it only by following their path. They might tolerate him if he became a major in public relations or recruiting or something like that. Fighting men are apt to be tolerant of lesser mortals; they can afford to be; they can look down and pity the men who refuse the call for greatness. You will know what I mean if you bring up strikes with Marines who have fought in the South Pacific. In their anger is a true note of pity for the blind and limited thought that rejects service, glory, patriotism.

So Gable took the hard road and when he got to England he was just another combat member of the Air Corps, ready for any combat service. He got it.

On those first raids, he tasted fear for the first time. Years ago Captain Eddie Rickenbacker told me that real courage was the courage of the boys who went ahead and did a great job in spite of fear; he said that was courage far beyond that of the few individuals who were born fearless. In this war, there must at first be fear, as I see it. A Marine gunner who was at the battles of Midway and the Coral Sea and at Guadalcanal told me once that at first you were scared silly, with a sort of paralyzing stage fright, it was all so new and so strange. But he said after a little while you just got so darn busy you didn't have time to be afraid. Then, he said, came the great inner surge of something that made you want to fight and fight hard, because you were fighting against everything you had always been taught to hate.

Combat mess halls, which are sacred to the men who do the actual fighting and extremely exclusive, so I am told,

334

Great memorial to a great lady: The liberty ship, "Carole Lombard," is launched with Irene Dunne as christener. At the left: Clark Gable; right, rear, L. B. Mayer

A Personal Story on Clark Gable

received Captain Gable with open arms. Even the famous Polish squadron, those fliers whose memories drive them to heights of combat few others achieve, welcomed Captain Gable.

For months he saw the real thing. Saw it with eyes trained to know men, to understand drama and emotion, older eyes that knew life pretty well.

That experience gave him humility. When he talks about the men of our Air Corps—about the men of the RAF and the RCAF—he does it with a respect, with an honestly awed admiration that sends your own heart racing up to meet that tribute. You can't match it, of course, because Captain Gable has seen, he has been there, he has flown in great bombers attacked by German fighter planes, he has been "in trouble" up there in the skies.

A GOOD many honors, a lot of applause and success, have come to Clark Gable in his lifetime. I can tell you now that he is prouder of the friendship of the bomber crews with whom he flew than of anything else that has ever happened to him, that he values their unexpressed-in-words acceptance of him more than he has valued the cheers of millions of fans, though he's always been grateful for those, too.

Those kids. Those kids who fight and win and fight and die. Those American kids, the roughest, toughest two-fisted fighting men in the world. Those kids who live in the skies, who fight in the Universe, no longer earthbound humans but part of the Army of St. Michael himself. Why—to have been one with them, to have flown with them, heard their careless, sure, unswerving faith, seen their courage—it's done something for Captain Gable and you can see it plainly enough.

There is, pilots tell me, something between a bomber crew that probably exists nowhere else in the world. A friendship, a love, an understanding that doesn't happen except up there in the sky. They belong together in a way other men know nothing about. They think as a unit, fight as a unit, face death and danger and know the measure of each other's ability to take it in a way that is unique. That's an experience that will last a man a whole lifetime. Gable's had that. And when he talks about it, you'd think every member of the crew had done him a favor to accept him and approve him. That's what I mean by humility.

The whole story cannot be told now, we all realize that. Moreover, Captain Gable wouldn't tell it anyhow. Not yet. Someday he'll pay his tribute to his fighting

brothers but right now he doesn't want, above all things, to be an exception.

That has been the only fly in the ointment; it's been the thing he has fought hardest against. He doesn't want to do anything any other captain in the Army Air Corps of the United States wouldn't and couldn't do.

But this much can be told:

You judge a man by the measure of his temptations. You know what manner of man he is by how he lives when great demands have been made upon him. It is no disrespect to call attention to other men who have been in somewhat the same spot that Gable occupied before he went into the Air Corps. Valentino, Wallace Reid, Jack Gilbert—or even to a few of today like Errol Flynn.

BUT it's only fair for us to put Captain Gable where he belongs, not so much fair to him as fair to ourselves. We need to look up to somebody, we need very badly to have those we have thought well of measure up to all we hoped they were, we need to see clearly how much of a man a man can be. It helps.

When Carole Lombard went to her death in an airplane accident, Clark Gable actually hit the lowest ebb of his life.

He had found the one woman and they had found together a fine, clean life. Her loss shook the very foundations of his being.

Yet today with all the new sadness that is in his eyes, I think he is happier than he has ever been. He has found men to look up to, he has found that at its best the human race can be great. That's why he's living in a new world. There has to be immortality because, as he himself says, you couldn't possibly kill a spirit like the one he has seen in fighter pilots. You might kill the body, but nothing could kill such a spirit; it has to be deathless, immortal, everlasting. This life becomes only part of the great, vast, never-ending life of the Universe.

DON'T get the impression that Clark is serious or sad or solemn about all this. His tales are lusty, strong and often very merry.

The film he brought back from his missions and which he's now cutting for release is human film intended to make you and me see and know the little things, the daily, hourly, ordinary things as well as the great moments. He has the same virility and personality he's always had.

But—the change is there.

Gable didn't have to go into the combat service. He didn't have to go into service at all.

Lots of people didn't want him to. Certainly he didn't have to fly in actual fighting warfare. Certainly he had a great deal to lose, if position and money and fame and opportunity mean anything.

He was and is just one of those guys who quite simply saw it as his job and the only job that could content him. Saw plainly that a man in these days must offer all that he has and all that he is to preserve the rights of humanity upon this earth.

Out of his service over there, he has brought the conviction that he was right. Humanity is worth preserving, free and untrammeled.

All that he has gained makes you pity those who have hidden from service under some alibi or other. Or who have given less than their best.

It seems to me we ought to appreciate a guy like Gable. Ought maybe to make him a promise. I know I made mine, when I saw him and talked with him.

I promised myself that I'd try to live up to him.

THE END

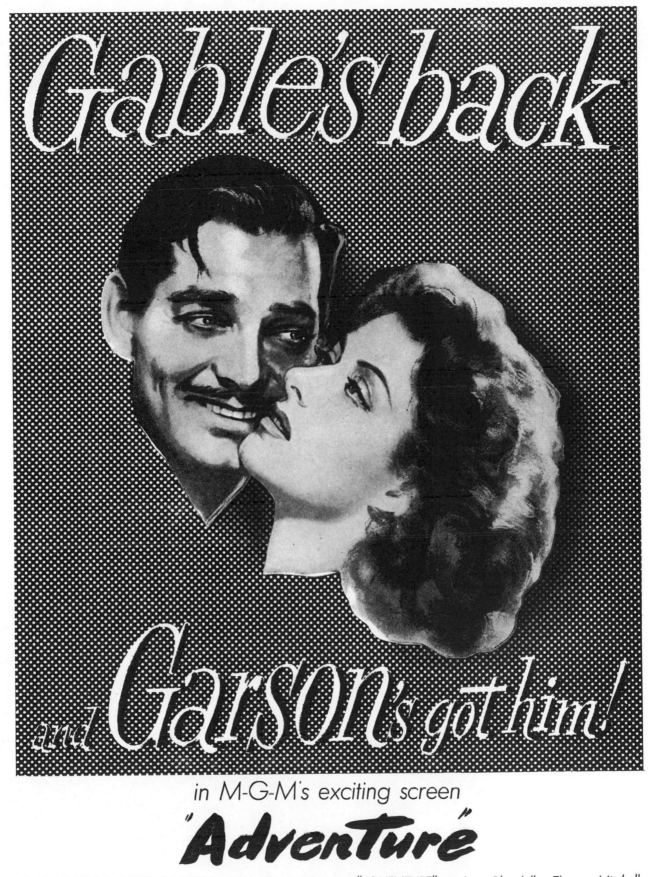

in M-G-M's exciting screen

"Adventure"

CLARK GABLE • GREER GARSON in Victor Fleming's production of "ADVENTURE" with Joan Blondell • Thomas Mitchell
TOM TULLY • JOHN QUALEN • RICHARD HAYDN • LINA ROMAY • HARRY DAVENPORT • Screen Play by FREDERICK HAZLITT BRENNAN and VINCENT LAWRENCE • Adaptation by
Anthony Veiller and William H. Wright • Based on a Novel by Clyde Brion Davis • DIRECTED BY VICTOR FLEMING • PRODUCED BY SAM ZIMBALIST • A METRO-GOLDWYN-MAYER PICTURE

NORDIC NATURAL

Number-one new rage in Hollywood today is Ingrid Bergman of "Adam Had Four Sons" and "Rage In Heaven"

BY KIRTLEY BASKETTE

"Better keep quiet about those things!" said the publicity men. But Ingrid Bergman, victorious newcomer, doesn't see why she shouldn't discuss what is closest her heart

IT TOOK a World War to bring a new deal in feminine charm to Hollywood. Ingrid Bergman is a Nordic natural who is going to make things a little tough for Hollywood's synthetic glamour girls from now on out.

Ingrid doesn't use make-up, false eyelashes, trick hair-dos, seminude evening wear, or a so-tired-of-it-all face. She doesn't need them. She's fresher, more beautiful in her unredecorated state, more unspoiled and real than any screen newcomer in a year of Sundays. She's a beauty who blushes, smiles and twinkles her eyes without realizing it—and the effect is devastating.

After "Intermezzo," two years ago, Ingrid Bergman was vaguely disturbing to Hollywood. But outside of that one picture she was only a lovely legend. No one knew her when she made it and she vanished back to Sweden the day it stopped shooting. But by now, after "Adam Had Four Sons," "Rage in Heaven," "Dr. Jekyll and Mr. Hyde" and the war-isolated state of Sweden have kept her around long enough for a good look, well—

Hollywood knows something has indeed hit it.

Ingrid Bergman is the number-one new rage in Hollywood today. And the current movie parlor pastime is analyzing just why. It's a little baffling to the home folks why this twenty-three-year-old foreign mother with long limbs and dairy-maid cheeks who has no pretentious tricks or publicity poses has lifted the limelight right over to her natural light-brown waves. For lack of a better answer they're saying she's a second Garbo.

We've just spent a swell afternoon with Ingrid Bergman and for our two cents worth on this pressing question, let us say that if she is the second coming of Garbo then Ernest Hemingway—who likes her too—is Little Boy Blue.

Ingrid Bergman (who calls it Eeng-reed Bare-mahn) is slim and tall and straight, with deep blue eyes and a throaty voice that registers, the sound men say, like Greta's. She can act like divinity and she's also a native daughter of Stockholm. But if she is another Garbo, she is a Garbo who laughs, a friendly Garbo who's full of

fun and a good sport. She's a Garbo with genuine frankness and womanly charm. She's a Garbo with a heart.

A picture of Ingrid Bergman's heart is pasted on the inside cover of her make-up kit, ready to smile up at her every time she powders her face. She rushed from the last take of "Intermezzo," in costume and with tears streaking her cheeks, to board a train and journey to it. She came back to America last year carrying her heart off the boat in a little wool-lined knapsack slung over her shoulder.

Ingrid's heart is named Pia. The "P" and the "a" are for her father's first two names, Paul Aaron, and the "i" is for Ingrid. Pia is Ingrid Bergman's daughter, two years old now, golden-haired and sunny.

Nothing explains Ingrid's warm, natural charm more than her devotion to Pia and her husband, Dr. Peter Lindstrom. At the same time, nothing symbolizes more acutely the heart-rending conflict her Hollywood success has persistently posed between Ingrid's career and her private happiness.

The other

Says Spencer Tracy of co-star Bergman in "Dr. Jekyll and Mr. Hyde": "This girl is great—and you know how seldom I use a two-dollar word like that!"

338

day in Reno, where Ingrid had flown on her first Hollywood vacation for some mountain skiing, reporters besieged her en masse. A few blurted, "Are you in Reno to get married?" and others, "Are you in Reno to get a divorce?" Ingrid blushed, speechless, and her eyes filled. It shocked her to realize that, despite her new Hollywood fame, the greatest thing in her life was still unknown in America, in fact, almost a secret.

INGRID BERGMAN is an orphan. Her parents died when she was a small girl. She grew up in girls' schools—one, prophetically enough, called "Flickor" (although the term is Swedish and has nothing to do with the movies). Her teens were spent in the Royal Theater of Dramatic Arts and within the walls of the Swedish film studios. Although Hollywood thinks of Ingrid as a discovery, she made eleven Swedish pictures before she was twenty and starred in nine of them. "Intermezzo," which brought her to Hollywood, was originally made in Sweden.

All her life Ingrid has been storing up the maternal affection denied her in childhood. When she married Peter Lindstrom, a young Stockholm surgeon, success and fame were old stuff to Ingrid. She yearned, as every actress yearns, for more and greater triumphs. But she also desperately wanted the undisturbed happiness of motherhood and the arrival of her daughter was set to seal her happiness.

At that point Hollywood interrupted.

Of course, David O. Selznick had no idea Ingrid was about to have a baby. He'd merely seen her in the Swedish "Intermezzo" and decided that both picture and actress were what he needed for Leslie Howard. Ingrid's first urgent Hollywood summons arrived almost in the maternity hospital. Naturally, she never considered accepting it. It was impossible.

But after Pia arrived, the cables grew more insistent. And soon Selznick's representative, Katherine Brown, showed up in Stockholm personally to apply her persuasive powers. "I have a home, a husband and a wonderful new daughter," Ingrid told her. "Why should I ever leave them?" She honestly thought she never would.

But seven months later she was traveling alone, bound for a fantastic, frightening place she had never seen, thousands of miles from what she loved most in all the world.

Her bewildering struggles with American, as she is spoke, make her chuckle today. On the funny side, too, were Ingrid's ghastly fears of a Hollywood remodeling job on her features. Hadn't every European star returned practically unrecognizable? "I walked trembling into the studio the first day," Ingrid grinned, "and when the make-up man said, 'Step this way, please,' I almost fainted. I knew they were going to pluck my eyebrows, dye my hair, lift my chin and do all sorts of horrible things. I resolved to fight to the finish. Imagine my surprise when Mr. Selznick looked me over and said, 'H-m-m-m-m! You won't need any make-up.' This couldn't be Hollywood!"

In Sweden, mothers are proud of their babies and love to talk about them. Here in this strange Hollywood studio publicity men frowned slightly, shook their heads and said, "Better not." Ingrid couldn't understand. When something lies always on your heart it's hard to keep it forever

to yourself. Ingrid was puzzled but she said nothing. She would soon leave, anyway. She was in Hollywood, all told, three months, and then she went home—to a Sweden isolated from the world, almost, by Hitler's hostilities.

The local picture industry, never exactly big-time, had shrunk under the shadow that hung over Sweden. Ingrid did one picture at home, discovered that both husband Peter and daughter Pia had thrived very nicely without her, and wondered, on second thought, if it had been Hollywood that was so lonely—or just herself. When David Selznick kept cabling for her to return and do "Joan of Arc," a part she had always been dying to do, Pia was old enough to travel and husband Peter confessed he had always dreamed of studying medicine in America.

Adding all that up explains why Ingrid Bergman is in Hollywood apparently to stay. For her, it is indeed a wonderful new career, a thrilling new life. In a few short weeks she has become the talk of all the movie-conscious world. Not through "Adam Had Four Sons" and "Rage in Heaven"—her cheering section in America, while vociferous and solid enough, was still small until Ernest Hemingway wrote a phenomenal book called "For Whom the Bell Tolls" and the movies snapped it right up like a second "Gone With the Wind." Parlor casting parties gathered all over the land. Then Mr. Hemingway had his official say. He said Gary Cooper was his idea of *Robert Jordan,* one central character in the book. For the other, *Maria,* the only girl in the world was Ingrid Bergman. In fact, Hemingway allowed that he wouldn't cooperate with the filming of his masterpiece unless Ingrid played the part. And he sent her a copy of FWTBT inscribed thus on the flyleaf, "To Ingrid Bergman, who is the *Maria* of this book."

But after all Paramount paid $150,000 plus for the novel and they'll have something to say about who plays *Maria.* Already they're testing every actress in town.

Meanwhile, everywhere she goes in Hollywood Ingrid is making friends and influencing people. What particularly appeals to everyone is Ingrid's natural humanness, if that's strictly correct grammar. She's naïve and girlish, and at the same time worldly. She sees the funny side of everything, but her heart is sensitive. She can break into tears at the tiniest sadness and giggle like a schoolgirl the next moment. She's a great actress and a wonderful sport at the same time—something you very, very rarely find.

As for the acting:

A gentleman who should know, Spencer Tracy, told us this about Ingrid. "When you see 'Jekyll and Hyde' you're not going to know I'm in it. This girl is great —and you know how seldom I use a two-dollar word like that!" That's the sentiment all over Hollywood. But Ingrid isn't letting it throw her. If you mention salaams like that to her now, she just chews her blackjack gum (which she adores) a little more furiously, blushes and changes the subject.

She dresses her five feet eight-and-a-half inches and 130 pounds in smart feminine fashions which she adores, slipping into slacks, sweaters and plaid sports coats only in her at-ease moments. At the same time she can laugh at her size without self-consciousness. Ingrid has taken quite a beating in "Jekyll and Hyde." In one scene she wrestled around with Slats Wyrick, a

former UCLA football tackle. "Look out, Slats!" the camera crew yelled. "Don't get hurt!" Ingrid thought that was very funny.

Yes, it would take plenty to make Ingrid Bergman good and mad in Hollywood at this point. She has both Pia and Peter with her now. She's only a few hours from the best ski slopes (she's swell on skis) and the outdoor life she loves is all around her—swimming, tennis, riding and the sea. She has a brand-new bright red roadster which she drives herself and a cozy apartment. You aren't going to hear any beefs out of Bergman. Nor is her sensible head likely to turn with time in Hollywood.

King-size appeal:
Clark Gable of "The Hucksters"

Fink

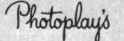

Photoplay's

PHOTOLIFE OF

Gregory Peck

SURELY you've heard of the "young man of the mountain"? His name is Gregory Peck—and he's on top of the world in more ways than one.

You see, Greg really lives on a mountain, in a home he built for himself and his family.

From the time when his life began at La Jolla as the son of a druggist until he hit his star stride, there were some tough climbs for Gregory. Yet once he reached Hollywood he made the astounding record of starring in his first two pictures and starting his third before the public ever saw him in "Days of Glory."

He climbed to movie prominence with such film triumphs as "Valley of Decision," "Spellbound," "Keys of the Kingdom," "The Yearling," "Duel in the Sun." His latest picture, not yet released, is "The Paradine Case." Where did he get all his energy? The answer lies perhaps in this panorama of his life.

BY LYNN PERKINS

1. Greg Peck's love for mountain music began when he was twelve and accompanied his dad on trips to Yosemite—he learned to ride and shoot

2. This is that gay college blade, Stroke Gregory Peck, in 1938—before a fall on a slippery pier put an end to his athletic career. Greg's energies turned elsewhere

4. Back in college as an English major, he earned tuition looking down throats of cars for insurance underwriters. No stethescope was needed for this job!

3. Two years of study convinced him he'd never be happy as a doctor. So he took a truck-driving job, which meant eating hot dogs at roadside stands most of the time

6. On tour with Katharine Cornell in "The Doctor's Dilemma," he met—a beautiful blonde, of course. She was Greta Kukonen from Finland, Miss Cornell's make-up artist. He married her

Photoplay's

PHOTOLIFE OF *Gregory Peck*

5. After graduation Greg decided to become an actor. A two-year scholarship at New York Neighborhood Playhouse eventually led to a role with Jane Cowl in "Punch and Julia" in Washington, D. C.

8. He learned Chinese for "Keys of the Kingdom," skiing for "Spellbound." At heart he's still an English major—his hobby, of all things, collecting words!

7. Then Greg heard the siren song: "Go West, young man," so the Pecks went to Hollywood. He made such a hit that when Jennifer Jones decided to pull a gun on her boy friend in "Duel in the Sun" it had to be Greg

9. As the staid, dignified English barrister in "The Paradine Case," Gregory Peck gives one of the most outstanding performances of his career

10. In some ways life is pretty much the same —whether you are the son of a La Jolla druggist or a famous Hollywood star—you chop wood when you want to keep warm

11. Mr. and Mrs. and the Pecks' good boys. Steven the baby gets all the attention these days. But watch young Jonathan; the son of the "young man of the mountain" won't remain in the background all his life

June Days

It's a dog's life. Madame Allyson-Powell thinks
Heathcliff should take his fiancée, Heidi, a posy

June Allyson, self-styled hillbilly from Westchester

Junie likes to cook by instinct, but it takes a book to learn to sail

I'm in LOVE with 10 men

BY SHEILAH GRAHAM

—who has plenty of
hard-headed reasons for
her soft-hearted condition

Fink-Smith

Remembering the right things at the right times is the reason
why Monty Clift of "The Heiress" remains on most girls' minds

Burt Lancaster of "Criss Cross" doesn't dress up to
many girls' expectations—but he's worth cultivating

If you love strong men, Richard Widmark of "Down to the Sea
in Ships" rates, but it isn't muscles that make him a menace

Jones

Kornman

Handsome is as handsome does. What Frenchman Louis Jourdan of "Madame Bovary" does—is mow you down with a look

Smith

THIS story should really be titled: "Confessions of a Columnist!" For twelve years, I have been surrounded, or vice versa, by the most publicized and palpitating men in the world. Sounds wonderful, doesn't it? (P.S. It is, and being a bit on the frail side, when it comes to gorgeous men I've had a heck of a fight to keep my perspective, so to speak. After all, a girl can't fall in love with *all* her masculine paragraphs.)

So, after carefully weeding the wolves from the wonder boys, I give you the movie men I really love—all ten of them.

When I first came to Hollywood, the man I yearned to meet above all others was Gary Cooper. I even had (Continued on page 82)

It's hard to catch up with the real James Mason but when you do you'll find the star of "Caught" well worth the chase

Fink-Smith

He breaks most of the rules and routines but Victor Mature of "Interference" has *the* way with all women

Smith

I'm In Love With 10 Men

an auto accident on the way to the first interview—I was in such a hurry! Well, I still love Gary, but twelve years of struggling to make printable conversation with a sphinx have dimmed my ardor, to put it printably.

So, when I first saw Montgomery Clift in "The Search," I said: "Hold on, Graham—he seems sensational, but remember Coop." But business is business, sometimes monkey business, so I put on my best dress and most fetching hat, and dashed to the set of "Red River," where Mr. Clift was making love to ten thousand head of cattle. Between moo's, I was introduced to the new number one heart-throb of Hollywood.

My first reaction was surprise. Montgomery is much shorter than he appears on the screen. Then I was amazed. The boy was *thanking me* for the praise I had given him in the column!

In Hollywood, it is the custom for stars to forget the nice things you write about them, and to scream over the items they don't altogether like. Like Peter Lawford, for instance. When this writer once intimated that Pete was not exactly extravagant with his cash, a fact well-known in Hollywood, he was most indignant, and chased madly across the cafe at Metro to tell me so. That would have been okay if Pete had ever bothered to say "Thank you" for the hundreds and hundreds of nice items from this corner. But Montgomery said "Thank you." He also discussed his career intelligently and modestly. I am still swooning from him.

NO ONE could call Bob Hope the handsome lover type (forgive me, Bob, but I'm trying to explain honestly why I love you!). But here is the kindest man in Hollywood. And yet you don't love a man only because he is thoughtful and careful not to hurt you. There has to be something more. The "more" in Mr. Hope's case is the intriguing build-up he gives me and every woman he talks to.

I watched him recently with a girl who was doing some technical advising. Bob didn't do the obvious thing—praise her for her work. That's nice, too, but it's nicer to be admired for the simple unbrainy fact of being a woman. Bob made her feel attractive as a female, not only with words, but by attitude and approach. So that when the not-too-beautiful girl walked off his set she actually *did* look beautiful.

You notice I do not include Bing Crosby in my list of the lovely ten. Sure I like him, but Bing is too intangible—like a pastel piece of air—he slips hurriedly through your fingers. Women (I know *I* do) like someone they can hold, even if it's only theoretically.

If Mr. Hope is in a hurry, and he must be sometimes, because he has almost as many business interests as side-kick Bing, it doesn't show when you talk to him. "Come into my dressing room," he'll say. "What do you know?"

I have a rival for Burt Lancaster—Margaret O'Brien! Our passion will do us no good, because Burt's happily married. Maggie is less restrained and more audible about Burt than I am. At last year's big circus charity event, Miss O'Brien shamelessly waited outside Burt's dressing room for half hours at a time to get a glimpse of her hero. I, being a few years older than Margaret, merely strolled casually by once every five minutes, hoping to bump into the boy, accidentally.

I've tried to analyze why I love Lancaster. If it comes to looks, Tyrone Power is handsomer, and yet Ty leaves me colder than yesterday's newspaper. If it's a tough guy quality I'm susceptible to, why does Humphrey Bogart fail to thrill me in private as much as he does on the screen? Of course, Bogey has lost most of his hair, and in a year and a half he will be fifty years old. But that really doesn't explain it. I guess it's something chemical.

And that brings me back to Burt. There's an earthy quality about him that appeals to me. He doesn't dress too well and sometimes he can't be bothered to shave. Burt hasn't too much sense of humor, he is more on the earnest side. But he bothers to take time out to explain whatever you ask him. He is always polite, pleasant, always on a well-balanced keel, never an exhibitionist like Bogart, never hard to reach like Tyrone.

The first time I talked with Richard Widmark, I said, "Please laugh for me." Dick grinned, then gave with the cackle that made him famous in "Kiss of Death."

Widmark is probably the most obliging of all the bad movie boys in Hollywood. No matter what difficult scene he is rehearsing, he'll stop in a minute to answer questions and give a columnist a good story. Like most of the actors who play cruel men on the screen, Dick is very kind in real life. But behind the quiet affability you see a flash of steel. You don't take liberties with Widmark. And don't ever mistake his gentleness for weakness. It is strength. I love strong men!

WHEN I say I'm in love with Victor Mature, don't get me wrong. I would never want to marry him. I like him too much and a quiet home life even better! But for fun, a sympathetic pal, and for down-to-earth horse sense, Victor is my man.

Very few women, or men for that matter, can resist the Mature brand of charm. His gaiety is infectious. His energy is irresistible. And come clean, Graham, he's a very good-looking man! Rules and routine were invented for Victor to break. He eats hamburgers for breakfast and breakfast cereal for dinner. He never makes plans. And that's fascinating for a girl like me who always does things by rote. Well, *nearly* always!

Mature is sensible with money. "I'd like to leave this picture business with $250,000. Half a million would be even better," Vic told me recently. He has bank accounts all over the United States. But that isn't why I love him. You don't love a man for his money, anyway. I love Victor because he's such a crazy, attractive, friendly son-of-a-gun.

When Dan Dailey took off for Dallas, a few months ago, without first telling his wife or his studio, I was the most surprised gal in town. Dan just didn't do things like that. Errol Flynn, yes, but not Dan. So when he returned, rather sheepishly, to Hollywood, I drove over to Twentieth Century-Fox to take another look at him. But it was still the same Dan. He hadn't sprouted horns or wings. He was still friendly, still grateful to Lady Luck for the big breaks.

Mr. Dailey's chief characteristic is a wide grin that stretches square across his rather homely face. It always gets me. Ditto, the Dailey chuckle. He's like a small boy who wants you to like him. And I do!

Dan is the best-natured lamb in Hollywood. I've never yet seen him take offense, even though some of his replies to questions get him in trouble with trouble-seeking reporters. Like when he was asked, "How is your marriage?" and Dan replied, "Fine, I only beat my wife three times last week." Dan, who was only being funny, had his knuckles rapped for that one on a coast-to-coast hookup! Was he sore? Not Dan. He just chuckled.

Gregory Peck may not know this, but every time he talks to a girl he makes mad love to her! I used to believe he did it for me alone (hopeful creature that I am!). Then, happening to be on his set one day, I saw him giving that old, always new and always wonderful, routine to another girl. It's nothing he says, it's what he *doesn't* say, a sort of inching close to you with his eyes. Brother, those eyes!

You know, it is sometimes quite difficult for a reporter to keep her mind on her questions. Especially when Mr. Peck says, "What is it you want to know, Sheilah?" in that smooth-as-silk, crooning half whisper. Sinatra does it a little bit, but with less attention to the girl receiving the line. You feel that Frankie's real thoughts are not with you, but with himself. Not Greg. When you are with him, *you* are the only important object in his world. That's how he makes you feel, anyway. And I'll settle for that!

FARLEY GRANGER is the youngest of the men I love in Hollywood. But don't get your nouns confused with your adjectives—youth is not necessarily inexperienced. Farley is hep. Even though, when I asked Shelley Winters who is hepper, if you get what I mean, "Are you and Farley getting married?" she replied with a flurry of exclamations, "Gracious no, Farley is too immature for a girl like me."

Well, he wouldn't be for a girl like me. (How'm I doing, Farley?) And he isn't for Ava Gardner. And before that, there was Pat Neal. And at about the same time there was Geraldine Brooks. And earlier I used to listen to June Haver swoon for the boy. So I am in good company. Although young Hollywood actors, like very young men anywhere, usually bore me, not for what they don't know, but for what they think they know. Mickey Rooney is better now, but when he was twenty, boy, oh boy, he knew every answer to every question and he did not wait to be asked, either. Farley is a boy who can wait.

When Louis Jourdan came into the Metro cafe a few days ago for lunch, every woman, except a couple of octogenarians, sat up and took notice, including yours truly. Audrey Totter, who was sitting next to me, said excitedly, "Bring him over to this table, Sheilah." "Not on your life," said I and, camouflaged with pencil and notebook, I walked (hurried) to Mr. Jourdan's table and said breathlessly, "How do you do."

Louis is so good-looking, it almost hurts to look at him. But a man, as I said before, needs more than a classical profile to win my, believe it or not, non-susceptible heart. Ronald Reagan's nose is probably straighter than Jourdan's. And Rory Calhoun has darker eyes than Louis, but the Frenchman's are soft, they don't go through you, they mow you down.

James Mason was recently described as "The small Clark Gable." And that's a pretty good description. James looks a lot like the Gable of fifteen years ago, when his face was leaner and his waistline was pencil slim. I'd like to see James in some of Gable's old roles, although, as a screen lover his wooing is less obvious. But the underlying ruthlessness is the same. Why women love ruthless men I'll never know. I only know that they do.

The real-life Mason is not at all the man you see on the screen. He is gentle, rather shy, intelligent and utterly nice. He is hard to catch up with. That is the number one priority I have promised myself for this summer.

And now I am dashing to the beach for a long cool swim!

THE END

A Christmas Prayer

How close the narrow circle of embrace
Can hold a world of love, made manifest
In starfish hands, and flower-textured face,
In rosy flesh, by innocency blest,
By nature, vulnerable; the child, at birth,
A legatee of joy and grief and pain,
Also inherits wonder; and the earth
Aware, in patience, of both sun and rain.
Therefore, oh Child, who once from Mary's breast
Smiled to see dawn, and did not fear the night,
Christchild and Saviour, grant our Christmas prayer,
Give to all mothers, wisdom; dwell, as Guest
Within our homes; and shelter, in Thy Light,
All little children, always, everywhere.

FAITH BALDWIN

Engstead

Love encircled—Jeanne Crain Brinkman and baby Paul, inspiration for Faith Baldwin's prayer

"FOR WHOM THE BELL TOLLS"

—and for whom the plaudits ring: The Year's
Most Romantic Lovers, Gary Cooper and Ingrid
Bergman as American Robert Jordan and Spanish
Maria in Paramount's picture of the year

Candid of the month: **Tense moment caught by Hymie Fink just as Olivia de Havilland turned away from the outstretched hand of Joan Fontaine at the Academy Awards.**

Talking behind Lauren Bacall's back are Humphrey Bogart, one of top five men, and Claude Jarman Jr.

Al Jolson, with Hollywood editor Ann Daggett, received a special tribute from the violins, too

The white and gold brocade walls, red velvet drapes and crystal chandeliers in the Crystal Room of the Beverly Hills Hotel. . . .

Photoplay's

The Larry Parkses had reason to be happy. He won a Gold Medallion for "The Jolson Story"

There was champagne and candlelight, the soft

strains of violins and Al Jolson, standing before the

Gold Medal plaque, singing old, nostalgic songs

... made an impressive background for the gay and glittering ensemble. Crowds jammed the hotel lobby to watch the stars enter

June Allyson, chatting with Claudette Colbert, was almost too excited to eat! June was in-winning five

Ingrid Bergman, with "Joan of Arc" haircut, receives her Gold Medal from Jack Benny

Jeanne Crain, with husband Paul Brinkman, was star of "Margie," one of ten top films

Gold Medal Party

LIGHTS! Cameras! Action! The Photoplay Gold Medal Awards Dinner was on. Celebrities and motion picture executives, three hundred and fifty of them, thronged the Crystal Room of the Beverly Hills Hotel.

This room, with its white and gold brocade walls, red velvet drapes and crystal chandeliers, was a glamorous background for the gowns of the women and the formal dress of the men. There was champagne and candlelight, and the soft sentimental strains of the famed l'Aiglon strings, "Mischa Novy and his violins." And the large Gold Medal plaque, that was the center of the decorations, symbolized *you*—the people who voted for your favorites in the Gallup Audience Research Poll, on which these awards were based.

You will be able to see all this for yourself at your local theater incidentally, for Ralph Staub's Screen Snapshots titled "Photoplay

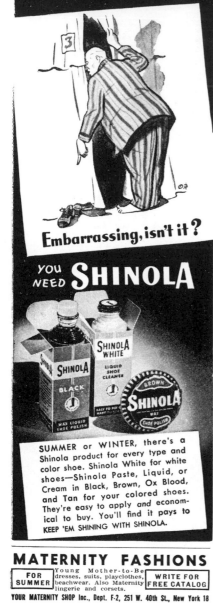
Gold Medal Party

Magazine's Gold Medal Awards," is being shown in 5000 theaters throughout the United States right now.

Crowds jammed the hotel lobby to watch the arrival of Ingrid Bergman, Claudette Colbert, Loretta Young, June Allyson, Lauren Bacall, Dick Powell, Humphrey Bogart, the Alan Ladds, the Larry Parkses, the Bill Holdens and many more.

The crowds cheered loudly for Al Jolson whose life was the basis for the winning picture, "The Jolson Story."

With other honored guests, Al and Larry Parks were seated on the dais; the "Face" and the "Voice" of "The Jolson Story," a unique team in the annals of motion picture history and a winning one.

There, representing Macfadden Publications, and to give the awards, were Herb Drake, Vice President, and Fred Sammis, Photoplay's Editorial Director. In a brief welcoming address Fred Sammis reminded those present that the Gold Medal Awards, which started back in 1919, are the oldest awards in the film industry and that they represent the choice of 60,000,000 people—the movie-going public—You.

Officiating as master of ceremonies, Jack Benny presented the awards . . . and bon mots.

By way of introduction he remarked that he didn't really know why he was present. "I'm getting nothing . . . nothing but the little I make on the concessions . . . and that's not much . . . what with the high cost of towels and whisk brooms." He reminded all that his pictures, too, were not without distinction. " 'The Horn Blows at Midnight' is still playing . . . in Palestine. The Arabs are using it for propaganda," he said.

INGRID BERGMAN graciously accepted her Gold Medal, the second she has received. Loretta Young was delighted with the citation for "The Farmer's Daughter." And June Allyson, cute as a pixie in a "Gibson Girl" evening gown, went forward for her award as one of the winning five actresses. Claude Jarman Jr., taller but with the same sincere, winning smile, accepted the citation for "The Yearling." The screen's "Tough Guys," Alan Ladd and Humphrey Bogart, approached the stage modestly for their awards, each politely willing to allow the other to go first.

To Larry Parks and Evelyn Keyes went honors for "The Jolson Story." Sidney Skolsky, received an award as producer of the picture. Harry Cohn, President of Columbia Pictures, accepted the Gold Medal for the winning film. Describing his part in the production as "Just an innocent bystander," he paid tribute to Larry Parks for his excellent performance, to Skolsky, for his endurance and drive throughout the entire production, to Sidney Buchman for his invaluable assistance and to Al Jolson, for living the life that made possible "The Jolson Story."

In a voice choking with emotion, Jolson said this was the first time in all his years in show business that he had been honored with an award; that he was especially appreciative because it came from you . . . the people.

There against the background of statuesque white columns, red velvet drapes and the big Gold Medal plaque, Al sang the same nostalgic numbers that made him the hit of the Winter Garden back in 1911.

It was a golden anniversary for Al Jolson . . . and another for Photoplay's annual Gold Medal Awards, thanks to you, the public, whose votes decide this, the only yearly poll which expresses the People's Choice.

THE END

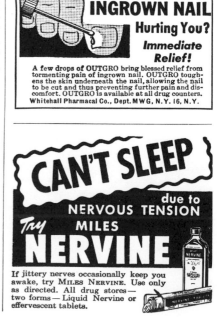
354

We All Have To Grow Up

BY DUDLEY NICHOLS

DOES the public really want grown-up motion pictures?
Let us face the fact that we in Hollywood, in trying to make films for that difficult audience, *Everybody,* find ourselves catering to the very young. There is something of the child in all of us. Youth and its gaieties and shenanigans are ever fascinating. So older people will attend motion pictures addressed to the young. Conversely, however, the young-in-mind have small interest in the grown-up world and its conflicts and problems which are the fountainhead of mature theater and literature. All great comedy and tragedy present mature characters in conflict with themselves and each other—or young characters in conflict with a mature world.

By reason of the enormous investment that every film represents, Hollywood naturally attempts to reach the largest possible audience. Occasionally, however, some misguided producer will attempt to do Dostoevski or O'Neill.

I remember when John Ford made "The Informer" many years ago (I doing the script) all the sensible people called it a crazy gamble. They said it had no entertainment value. They meant of course for the young audiences—and they were right. The film was not a profitable one until a handful of people saw its importance and it won some Academy Awards. Then it fared handsomely. But without the luck of winning awards and so garnering unexpected publicity a hard-headed man might have called it a failure—even though it was an advancement for the screen and opened many gates for new achievement.

Eugene O'Neill's great tragedy, "Mourning Becomes Electra," is the latest mature, grown-up film. As such, of vital importance to the motion picture industry and to you, the public, it needs the support of all thinking people who realize that even the young must grow up.

The great value of literature and of the theater—besides their taking us out of ourselves and giving us pleasure and entertainment—is that they extend our experience of life. We have multitudes of sleeping beings inside us and imagined experiences projected on the screen enable these wraiths within us to wake up and live lives—and so make us larger people.

You cannot keep on making pictures by repeating the old story patterns without growing senile and sterile. I believe there is an audience for "Mourning Becomes Electra" if it can only be reached—a large audience that can make the film more profitable even than a best-selling piece of nonsense—and I believe you readers are a part of that audience which will respond to new adventures on the screen.

I'M NO COMMUNIST

"Bad man" Bogie of "The Treasure of the Sierra Madre"

A plain-talking star

answers his critics—and leaves

no doubt about his meaning

BY HUMPHREY BOGART

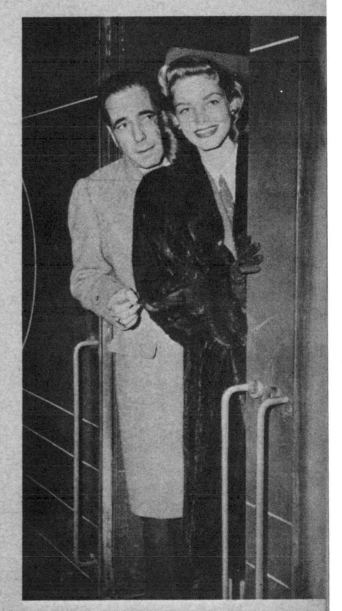

Bogart and Bacall: "We're about as much in favor of Communism as J. Edgar Hoover"

A S the guy said to the warden, just before he was hanged: "This will teach me a lesson I'll never forget."

No, sir, I'll never forget the lesson that was taught to me in the year 1947, at Washington, D. C. When I got back to Hollywood, some friends sent me a mounted fish and underneath it was written: "If I hadn't opened my big mouth, I wouldn't be here."

The New York Times, the Herald Tribune and other reputable publications editorially had questioned the House Committee on Un-American Activities, warning that it was infringing on free speech. When a group of us Hollywood actors and actresses said the same thing, the roof fell in on us. In some fashion, I took the brunt of the attack. Suddenly, the plane that had flown us East became "Bogart's plane," carrying "Bogart's group." For once, top billing became embarrassing.

And the names that were called! Bogart, the capitalist, who always had loved his swimming pool, his fine home and all the other Hollywood luxuries, overnight had become Bogart, the Communist! Now there have been instances of miscasting, but this was the silliest. I refused to take it seriously, figuring that nobody else would take it seriously. The public, I figured, knew me and had known me for years. Sure, I had campaigned for FDR, but that had been the extent of my participation in politics. The public, I figured, must be aware of that and must be aware that not only was I completely American, but sincerely grateful for what the (Continued on page 86)

I'm No Communist

American system had allowed me to achieve.

It was in that comfortable frame of mind that I reached New York City. I first learned how wrong I was in my reasoning through a newspaper pal of mine, Ed Sullivan. He and I have been friends for close to twenty years and when we met, at Madison Square Garden during a big charity show, he called me aside and bawled the life out of me. "Stop it, Ed," I told him. "Suppose I have lost a few Republicans—likely as not, I've picked up some Democrats." Sullivan looked at me as if I had two heads. "Look, 'Bogie'," he said, "this is not a question of alienating Republicans or Democrats—this is a question of alienating *Americans*. I know you're okay. So do your close friends. But the public is beginning to think you're a Red! Get that through your skull, 'Bogie'."

Me a Red! That was the first inkling I had of what was happening. Impossible though it was to comprehend that anyone could think of me as a Communist, here was an old friend telling me just that. If it had begun and ended there, okay. But it didn't. Letters began to arrive. There were local newspaper stories and word of mouth spreading rumors across the country. Something had to be done quickly. But what?

I was in the position of the witness who suddenly is asked. "Have you stopped beating your wife?" If he answers "Yes" or "No" he is a dead pigeon.

Let me set it down here, that in this crisis, the newspapermen and the radio commentators of the country were standouts. A few of them, polishing apples for managing editors, acted like imbeciles, but the bulk of them went to my defense. My first statement turned the tide. It read:

"I'm about as much in favor of Communism as J. Edgar Hoover. I despise Communism and I believe in our own American brand of democracy. Our plane-load of Hollywood performers who flew to Washington came East to fight against what we considered censorship of the movies. The ten men cited for contempt by the House Un-American Activities Committee were not defended by us. We were there solely in the interests of freedom of speech, freedom of the screen and protection of the Bill of Rights. We were not there to defend Communism in Hollywood, or Communism in America. None of us in that plane was anything but an American citizen concerned with a possible threat to his democratic liberties."

We may not have been very smart in the way we did things, may have been dopes in some people's eyes, but we were American dopes! Actors and actresses always go overboard about things. Perhaps that's why we play benefit shows night after night, why we contribute money so freely to causes we believe just and good, why we volunteer our time and services to help sell bonds or just sell America to the rest of the world. So why is it that as loyal American citizens and taxpayers, we shouldn't raise our voices in protest at something we believe to be wrong? It was our belief, and it still is, that the House Committee easily could have identified the very small percentage of Communists in Hollywood through the records of the FBI. There was no necessity for the vaudeville show—the Klieg lights, newsreels, coast to coast radio broadcasts—and the dirtying of many good names with no right to speak in their own defense.

Why single out Hollywood? As Bob Montgomery and Ronald Reagan said, we have a minute percentage of Commies, but they are under control. Why didn't Washington single out the auto industry, or the coal industry or the Newspaper Guild? Why smear Hollywood?

It seems to me that the thing to be kept in mind is this: On the left, in America, we have the Communists, not many, but tightly organized. On the right, we have the bulk of our population, who believe with me, that cures can be effected within the framework of our democracy. In the middle, however, there are a great many Americans, liberal in thought, who are stoned by the unthinking, who don't realize that these liberal-minded folks are pure Americans. Let's realize that these liberals are devoted to our democracy.

Let us trust that what happened to us, in Washington, does not discourage actors and actresses from taking active, constructive interest in our form of government. It would be tragic, if, because circumstantial evidence created the wrong impression at Washington, actors should withdraw to the political sidelines. That would be downright cowardice. So long as we are opposed completely to Communism and do not permit ourselves to be used as dupes by Commie organizations, we can still function as thoughtful American citizens.

In the final analysis, this House Committee probe has had one salutary effect. It cleared the air by indicating what a minute number of Commies there really are in the film industry. Though headlines may have screamed of the Red menace in movies, all the wind and fury actually proved that there's been no Communism injected on America's movie screens.

As I said, I'm no Communist. If you thought so, you were dead wrong. But, brother, in this democracy, no one's going to shoot you for having thought so!

THE END

Gallant Comeback!

Richard Quine, in a story you will never forget, reveals the courage and faith that brought his wife Susan Peters back to the screen in "The Sign of the Ram." DON'T MISS IT—IN APRIL PHOTOPLAY!

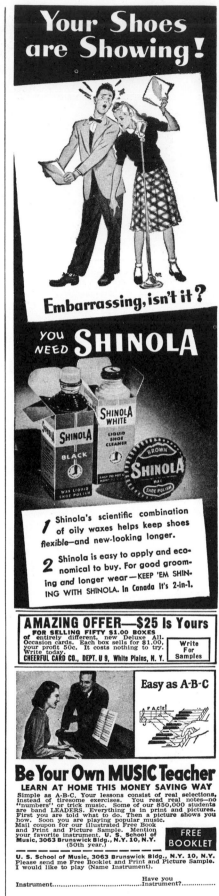

THE BERGMAN BOMBSHELL

BY LOUELLA O. PARSONS

The story behind the gossip that began as a Hollywood whisper and exploded into international headlines

WHENEVER anyone in Hollywood has become involved in any great scandal, always we have said, "Well, thank goodness there are those stars upon whom you can count." And, invariably, we have added, "Stars who live with the greatest personal dignity and propriety—Ingrid Bergman, for instance."

That's why it is so heart-breaking that Ingrid should have been involved in this Stromboli incident with her fiery, tempestuous director, Roberto Rossellini. And I think it a great pity that not once did he make any effort to protect her from a situation which he must have known would be headlined around the world.

Had stories and photographs similar to those circulated about Ingrid and Rossellini been circulated about Rita Hayworth or Lana Turner, or any one of the other glamour girls who have been in and out of love so many times, no one would have thought much about it. Ingrid is different, a gracious and dignified woman with a clever business brain. No other producer or director ever has been able to prevail upon her to commit herself to a production minus a story, cast and, in the beginning, financing.

Along with everyone else, I can only ask what happened to change her so much. Is this an overwhelming love story? Or could it all have sprung only from Ingrid's great and complete confidence in the genius of an artist she has known for such a short time?

Ingrid's association with Rossellini began innocently enough. About a year ago when she was in England, having seen Rossellini's fine films, "Paisan" and "Open City," she wrote him a letter. A friend to whom he showed this letter says it was very simple and direct, that it read in essence: "Dear Roberto Rossellini: I love your pictures and your direction. So if there's ever a small part for a little Swedish actress, please think of me. Ingrid Bergman."

Rossellini, described as a fascinating but arrogant man and a law unto himself, not only accepted this letter as a fine compliment, but considered it little short of a promise to make a picture with him.

He flew to London to see Ingrid who was highly amused and no little embarrassed by his interpretation of her impulsive note. However, Rossellini, with his flashing brown eyes, was not to be put off. When Ingrid returned to Hollywood, he

Stromboli volcano, never quiet

Fishermen here face danger

Houses crack from eruptions

Beyond reach of telephones, Rossellini and Ingrid on Stromboli

Island life is primitive

The Bergman Bombshell

followed her.
And no one who saw her believed that she was displeased. In fact, both Rossellini and Lopert, his business manager and great friend, were house guests of Ingrid and Dr. Lindstrom. And Ingrid, who has been considered by many as something of a recluse, went out of her way to show her guests the town. She and Rossellini were everywhere together—sometimes in parties, sometimes alone.

The press, which has frequently been accused of disliking Bergman because of her aloofness, handled their appearances with more discretion than many stars would have received. I, myself, ignored many "tips" called into my office that Ingrid and Roberto had been seen dancing or dining together.

Soon after this, what previously had been mere whispers about Ingrid's marital status with Dr. Peter Lindstrom became open talk.

Rossellini and Ingrid certainly were not exactly inconspicuous. He was very much by her side when she attended Hollywood's spotlighted and flashlighted premiere of "Joan of Arc." Cameramen had a field day—or night—snapping pictures of the party, which included Dr. Lindstrom and Lopert.

AND THE night after Howard Hughes signed a contract to take over the financing job of their picture, "After the Storm," an unfortunate incident took place. Ingrid and Rossellini, very happy and excited over the deal, decided to stage a celebration in a Sunset Strip cafe. But they stayed so long congratulating themselves, that Dr. Lindstrom strode in and had a few thousand annoyed words in Swedish and English to say to his wife. This story was printed only as a "blind item" (no names used), but all Hollywood heard of the ruckus that had taken place.

From the beginning, everything that happened to these two was splashy and sensational. Samuel Goldwyn, the first producer who planned to put up the do-re-mi for the Bergman-Rossellini production, soon found out that Rossellini is an artist who cannot be pinned down to facts and figures. One evening at a dinner party, Sam discovered the distressing fact that Roberto "works in his head" and frequently goes on fishing jaunts in the middle of a picture. Amused eavesdroppers in adjoining rooms report the ensuing battle, about which "boss" was going to boss the job, as loud and most interesting. And following the argument, Bergman and Rossellini departed without ever joining the other guests.

Any disappointment they may have felt, however, was short-lived. For, almost immediately, Howard Hughes took over the financing job.

The next thing anyone knew, the great Anna Magnani, Rossellini's terrible-tempered Neapolitan girl friend and screen star—when she heard that Ingrid was to follow Rossellini to Italy—threw a private tantrum. Then she took more tangible steps about the "importation" from America. She called a rally, enlisting the aid of 3,000 Italian actors to "protest" the appearance of "outsiders" in Italian movies. As several other American players, including Cornel Wilde and Louis Hayward, were appearing in native movies (minus outbursts from Magnani), it was obvious that Anna had one particular "outsider" in mind.

On every hand was heard, "What will happen when the great Magnani and the great Bergman meet in Rome?" Well, nothing happened. Because someone prevailed upon Anna to absent herself in London at the time of Ingrid's arrival. Even so, Bergman's advent in Rome was not without excitement.

The press party Rossellini staged in her honor turned into a free-for-all. The printer, who had been given the job of turning out the invitations to accredited correspondents, decided to print an extra 300, which he sold to friends and curious mischief-makers.

The result, well played up in gossip columns all over the world, was that Rossellini traded a few blows with the impostors and took a few sideswipes of his own, before he could get Ingrid out of the place.

Following this, he hurriedly moved his movie headquarters and his Swedish star to location at Stromboli where he quartered his troupe on boats in the harbor and took over a little pink stucco house —to which he added the much publicized plumbing facilities, unique on this primitive volcanic island—for Ingrid, her companion, his sister and himself.

All apparently was quiet—momentarily, at least. Just a little too quiet to suit the taste of Howard Hughes. Weeks went by with expenses mounting and still he had seen no script, not even a story idea, in fact, other than a vague outline about "a woman in a concentration camp."

An emissary was dispatched to see what was going on. Apparently, nothing, because the report came back that everyone seemed very happy lolling in the sun, content to talk over the angles and problems.

It was about this time, you'll remember, that the pictures of Ingrid and Rossellini walking hand-in-hand on desolate lava-covered Stromboli began flooding the newspapers. Headlined stories accompanied them. "Will Ingrid divorce Dr. Peter Lindstrom to wed Rossellini?" In one way or another, they all asked the same startling question.

I called Dr. Lindstrom, still in Hollywood at this time. I had met him previously, admired him and always found him a direct thinking and speaking person. When he heard my name on the telephone he was very gracious. But when I asked him if the first rumor printed was true, he froze below zero and said, "No comment."

"Surely, Dr. Lindstrom," I said, "you will want to deny this story which is gaining so much momentum in talk and print, if it is not true."

"Nothing to say," he repeated.

But, two hours later, I received a call from him, this time with a laconic statement, "As far as I am concerned, the story is so ridiculous I can say nothing about it."

I then cabled Ingrid, putting the question right to her. She replied: "Peter en route. Will make statement after he arrives. Best regards. Ingrid Bergman."

Peter indeed was en route, although I am reliably informed Ingrid told him, before he sailed, of her feeling for Rossellini. However, he refused to take it seriously. Lindstrom is a man who knows what he wants and there were those who, from the beginning, insisted that he had no intention of consenting to a divorce and that he would not change his mind.

He first met Rossellini. They conferred on a sloop off Messina, Sicily. Originally, it was planned that Ingrid would be there, too. But, at the last minute, she changed her mind. The day following, however, both Ingrid and Rossellini conferred with Lindstrom at a hotel at Milazzo, Sicily. It was then her statement, that she would rejoin her husband, in Sweden or the United States, upon the completion of the picture, was issued.

Now, Dr. Lindstrom is back in California with charming ten-year-old Pia, the little daughter whose private life Ingrid always has guarded so jealously. Because she wants her "to be like other little girls."

The Stromboli incident—if that is all it turns out to be—with Ingrid returning to her husband when her picture is completed—is, however you look at it, most unfortunate.

Ingrid is not just another Hollywood *flutterbrain* to be gossiped about. She has always stood for the finest and most dignified type of artist.

But still to be reckoned with are all the weeks she must spend at Stromboli in Roberto Rossellini's company. Everyone who knows him agrees he is a charming and fascinating man. Those who respect and admire Ingrid hope she now will be able to stand clear of his spell, reclaim the high place she has so long enjoyed both as an actress and a woman.

THE END

361

Ingrid and her husband Dr. Lindstrom before an island came between them

MOVIES ARE
THE BEST ENTERTAINMENT

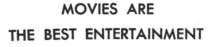

Then: Margarita Cansino, age 12

I SAW RITA

BY LOUELLA O. PARSONS

**But she saw more than that. For she saw
Rita as she is today, the fabulous life that is
now hers, the obstacles that must lie ahead**

NEVER was there a more exciting assignment than mine—to see the wedding of Rita Hayworth and Prince Aly Khan, as their guest as well as a reporter. As I flew over the Atlantic, I kept reviewing the fabulous love story of the Spanish dancer who grew up to be a motion picture star and marry one of the richest young men in the world. I thought I knew how luxurious her new life would be. But when, a few hours after my arrival at the Carlton Hotel in Cannes, Rita and Prince Aly called to take me to their now famous Chateau de l'Horizon—I realized I hadn't even begun to visualize the luxury of Rita's new life.

However, whether she will be happy I am not certain.

Now: Margarita, Princess Aly Khan,
wife of an Indian prince

For Rebecca Welles, on lap of Aly's former stepmother, the Princess Khan, the attentions of new stepbrother, Prince Karim

Prince Aly and Rita in the sumptuous Italian car he gave her before their celebrated marriage

Can any American girl, much less one as spoiled as Rita has been, adjust to any such existence as she has set for herself? This I know—it isn't going to be easy. Her Prince, who is most fastidious, will be no lenient American husband. Rita will have to dress to perfection when she appears in public with him. And she will have to hold her own with his European friends, who chatter in French, are at home all over the world and have the advantage of leisured Continental backgrounds.

The wedding itself in the little town of Vallauris was, in spite of the crowds and fanfare, most charming. Rita looked very lovely in her blue dress and big blue hat. And she did not appear unduly nervous. Neither did Prince Aly. But Paul Derigon, Communist Mayor of Vallauris, who performed the ceremony, was nervous indeed. No wonder! Not only were the bride and groom important people—so were the guests. It was a colorful scene with the Ismaili women wearing nose diamonds and beautiful rich saris. The Ismaili men, curiously, wore business suits; but carried handsome gold turbans.

After the ceremony Rita gave her two stepsons a kiss, American style. Her daughter Rebecca did not attend

I Saw Rita Hayworth Marry Aly Khan

the wedding. She arrived at the reception later, however, in time to see her mother cut the beautiful wedding cake. The sword of antique glass which Rita used had been bought by her and Aly in Paris. Rebecca was brought to the reception by the Princess Khan, Aly's stepmother. Princess Khan, who was married to the Aga Khan prior to his marriage to the current Begum, practically raised Aly after his mother's death and he adores her. Rebecca does too, begged to live with her, in fact.

PRINCESS KHAN told me that Rebecca was terrified of the photographers who tried to take her picture everytime she left the house. Because of this, Aly, who loves children, felt she should not be subjected to such experiences.

The wedding gifts were worth a King's ransom. The Aga Khan's gift to Rita was a choice of heirloom jewels. And her gifts from the Prince were a $12,000 car, a twelve-carat diamond ring, a case of silver, paintings and jewels of moderate size.

Even more lavish gifts came later from the Ismaili guests who attended the Moslem ceremony. No one but the family and a handful of guests knew that the Moslem ceremony was to take place at the Chateau de l'Horizon the night following the civil ceremony. To it the Ismaili guests came bearing the gifts of diamonds as big as walnuts, gorgeous silks, cloths of gold and golden coins.

Rita's title of Princess is a courtesy one. But in India, when Aly succeeds his father, she will be called Her Royal Highness.

The Aga Khan who, I thought, looked like a lovable kewpie, is regarded as a god in India; his image worshipped by the Moslem natives. And when he passes on, Prince Aly, his successor, will become Imam or spiritual leader of the Ismaili branch of the Mohammedan religion.

The angle of Aly becoming a god has been much discussed. And Rita has been jokingly referred to as a future goddess.

Many of the stories told about Rita's thirty-eight-year-old Prince Aly are completely false. As the eldest son of the Aga Khan, he has been raised in the greatest luxury. However, he is greatly annoyed when it is intimated that he is very dark in color. As a matter of fact, his mother was Italian. He is only half Persian. His mother's brother, incidentally, a delightful Italian gentleman, is major domo of l'Horizon, manages the dozens of servants, among them the chef formerly employed by the Duke and Duchess of Windsor.

Prince Aly has blue-gray eyes and wears his hair rather long. And he still walks with a limp as a result of a broken leg he received while he was playing with his sons. He drinks little, smokes practically not at all and frequently takes a cigarette from Rita's lips, puffs on it, and returns it to her mouth.

The day Prince Aly showed me over the chateau, Rita brought him a plate of cherries. He looked at her, smiled and said, "Thank you, my darling." As he spoke, I'll confess, my thoughts flew backward. To the bitter young tears Rita shed during her marriage to Edward Judson and her unhappiness when she was married to Orson Welles.

The Chateau de l'Horizon has fifteen bedrooms and baths, each with a balcony overlooking the Mediterranean. There is a swimming pool, the water of which is piped in from the Mediterranean. I have seen more elaborate pools in Hollywood but none with any such background. A chute goes from the terrace to the blue-green sea and Aly's two sons, who adore Rita, use it when they are at the chateau.

The house is white with green shutters. And inside, the decoration, supervised by Prince Aly, is in pastel colors, all very bright and gay.

Rita's boudoir is in delicate shades of pink with white. The salon, which opens on the sea, is done in buttercup yellow and soft greens and blues. Utrillo's latest painting, gift of Aly to his bride, hangs in a conspicuous place. There are bookcases all around this room which also boasts an Aubusson rug and a grand piano. The formal drawing room is in French Renaissance, with pink satin and pale gray furniture. And the dining room is in powder blue. It has antique chairs and an old Italian marble dining table. Most of the time, however, the Prince and Princess have their meals served on the terrace overlooking the sea. This, however, is only one of Princess Rita's residences. There are also eight places in Ireland, one in Norway, a house in Paris and a country place in London.

IT WAS walking through the fabulous rooms of Rita's new home that I remembered the first time I ever saw her. It was 1935. With her father, she was a dancer at Agua Caliente then. But she was Margarita Cansino then, sweetly pretty, with black hair, painfully shy and a little too plump.

At l'Horizon many languages are spoken. When you see Rita there you know at once the sophisticated life she will lead as Princess Aly Khan. At the moment she is studying hard to master French. Her knowledge of Spanish should help her, of course. Nevertheless she hasn't progressed as quickly as her little Rebecca who, with the facility that is natural to children, now speaks the language fluently.

The day I lunched at the chateau I realized Rita had acquired some of the poise of Prince Aly's set; comprised almost exclusively of men and women who are widely traveled, cultured and devoted to him. But she went a little overboard, I felt, in her reticence and carefully modulated sentences. The only thing faintly reminiscent of Hollywood about her was her costume. In contrast to the cool, quiet prints worn by the other women present, she wore a blue jacket over a bathing suit that was so short you could see only her legs.

Her hair was a very dark brown and not nearly as becoming, I thought, as the glamorous red hair she has worn for so many years. When she makes a picture she will have to become a redhead again. And she does intend to keep her career, which is still precious to her.

John Hyde, vice-president of Beckworth, Rita's own company, has conferred with the Prince about Rita continuing to make pictures. Prince Aly says Rita has worked so hard to attain her popularity that he will not ask her to retire. He is not—he makes this very plain—interested in the financial end of her business. And Rita need not be either. The dowry settled upon her provides for her handsomely.

The Prince would not, he says, be averse to living in Hollywood during the time Rita makes a picture. However, he would prefer this to be some time during the racing season. Then he could let Hollywood see his thoroughbreds. And Rita could show her stable, another wedding gift, which she will race under her own colors of red and green.

Rita and her Prince are now madly in love. If this continues she will, at last, have the happiness she deserves.

I say with her father, Eduardo Cansino, the Spanish dancing teacher, "I want her to be happy." Happiness is better than all the wealth and power in the world.

THE END

The rolling Hollywood hills back-
drop Paramount's great sound stages

HOLLYWOOD TOUR

The guarded doors to a great
movie empire swing wide—
with this Photoplay pass
to Paramount Studios

Genius at work: Here Charles Brackett and Billy Wilder, Paramount
producing team, dream up hits like "Emperor Waltz," "Foreign Affair"

THE Paramount Studios are just beyond the Hollywood hills. Most movie companies, having departed from the town they made famous long ago, are now situated in the Valley or out Culver City way. But Paramount remains in Hollywood, not far from the corner field where the old barn—in which the studio had its beginning—used to stand. The executive buildings face the streets surrounding the studio acres. But only the few for whom the big iron gate, policed day and night, swings wide ever see the heart of the studio—the big stages, the commissary, the dressing rooms, the make-up department, the dressmaking salon or the busy streets peopled with actors and actresses wearing the costumes of many ages and many countries.

When the Gages get together it usually means a gag for Ben's radio show

Esther's charm lies in her naturalness—there are no barriers between her and people

Easy

When they feel sentimental, they wisecrack. When they're together, it's a sideshow. But wherever Esther goes, it's home

BY BEN GAGE

I FIRST dated her when I was a GI in the radio division stationed at Santa Ana.

I had only just met her. But I had gotten her phone number. I was a sergeant and sergeants have a lot of confidence. So I phoned her and said:

"Hey, pretty girl, are you busy tonight?"

She said, "Yes—but actually it's none of your business."

I said, "Madame—you are addressing a sergeant of the U. S. Army and it's your patriotic duty to keep up the Army morale."

Since she was a very patriotic girl and also a girl with a sense of humor, it was a date.

I loved her on sight. She is easy to love. Practically everyone, up to millions, have the habit. I not only loved her, I liked her.

On our first date I took her to the Pit Barbecue in Glendale and a movie afterward. The movie was "The Song of Bernadette." She enjoyed the picture tremendously. She cried all through it. I didn't like it and she said it was because she had cried so hard and didn't look pretty enough to be seen and go get something to eat afterwards. I was hungry. When is a GI not so?

We were married in Westwood and our reception was at the home of our friends Melvina and Ken McEldowney. Esther's family home wasn't big enough to hold our relatives. It was a tiny house. Esther was born in the living room. There wasn't room in the bedrooms, they already were full up with babies.

That's my Priority One for liking her. She's a family lover, as

to Love

Esther Williams, of "Take Me out to the Ball Game," is still a kid about surprises—especially honeymoons. Ben is planning their sixth!

Easy to Love

I am. Everything she is and all the happiness she enjoys, she credits back to her wonderful parents. I like that, because the pivot of my life has always been my old home with my dad, mother and brother.

Right now, as I dream up these notes beside our pool, she is tearing off in her car for the village of Pacific Palisades to buy a birthday gift for her mother. It is now five-twenty. She will arrive at the store two minutes before closing—or two minutes after—and go round to the back to pound on the door. She will buy several gifts for the house and a present for me.

"What you buying for me, sweetie?" I yell as she leaves. "Nothing," she yells. "I'm just going to the hardware store."

Well, I muse, she'll probably buy me just what I've always needed—a new Boy Scout knife.

We've never stopped buying presents and dating one another. And whenever we get a week or two free, we go on another honeymoon. With her picture schedules and personal appearance tours, my radio programs, we have had to scheme to match time for trips. But we have had five honeymoons in three years, since our wedding day, November 25, 1945.

When she is away on personal appearance tours I like to surprise-date her by airplane. She's like a kid about surprises.

It was a surprise date that acclimated me to being a star's husband. I had no idea how carefully a star is protected. All telephone calls are screened. No visitor gets to her without running a line. She is guarded like a precious piece of porcelain, surrounded by press agents, secretary, maid, dicks, harness cops and motorcycle squads. All this precaution is most gratifying to a husband until he finds she is protected from him, too.

Esther was doing five shows a day in New Haven, Connecticut, with "This Time for Keeps," when I made up my mind to see her. After my Saturday evening Joan Davis broadcast, I grabbed a plane and arrived next day in New Haven.

I called her hotel as soon as I landed. The alerted operator at the switchboard asked who was calling Miss Williams, please. "Her husband," I said.

"Her husband, oh sure," said the operator suspiciously. "That's a new one. What's Miss Williams's husband's name?"

I said, "Ben Gage."

"I know," said the operator. "And Mr. Gage is not in New Haven, he's in Hollywood, because I heard him on the air with Joan Davis last night."

Click! I was cut off that line.

I called back and explained I had flown 3300 miles just to date my own wife; surely the operator would reward such devotion by letting me say hello.

"Well," she said doubtfully. "I'll call her room and let you talk to her secretary." Her secretary proved just as skeptical. Sorry, Miss Williams had just left for the Yale gymnasium.

"The Yale gym?" I honked. "My wife doesn't attend Yale."

"She is being made Honorary Water Girl by the Yale team," the voice said. "You might see if you can gain admission to the Yale gym."

"What do I have to do, get on the Yale team?" I howled.

I WAS getting a little worried. I only had a few days to be with her and one of them was rapidly disappearing. I sped to the hotel and joined the crowd that watched her as she came out and got into a big limousine.

"Hi, Esther!" I yelled. "Look."

"Move along, bud," said a cop.

I decided to cool off with a Coke. This was going to take some fast action. I knew I couldn't make the Yale team in time to see her become their Water Girl.

After the third Coke, I had an idea. I skipped around to the theater where she would appear after Yale honors had been bestowed. The stage entrance was guarded and no Mr. Gage appeared on the day's agenda.

My coked-up scheme was to bribe an usher to let me carry flowers down the aisle to the footlights. The usher wasn't interested in the offer of my autographed photograph but responded to Lincoln's likeness on a fiver autographed by John W. Snyder, Secretary of the Treasury.

At the conclusion of Esther's show, which I was permitted to watch from the rear of the house, I waddled down the aisle, my six-feet-five's worth of arms and legs telescoped as far down into the bouquet as nature permitted. For once, Esther's being a little nearsighted came in handy, but I was afraid she might recognize my bulk. I wanted to surprise her up close where the cops couldn't give me the bum's rush again.

Covering my face with the roses I walked upon the stage. She graciously thanked me and started away. When she saw I remained on the stage, she turned to look again. "Yeeeeee. Ben!" she screamed, with a beautiful double take.

The audience took it large though some of them probably suspected it was a gag for the show.

Fun is the basis of our married life. We put on our best shows for one another. I get lines for my radio show while kidding around with her in our little pool. It's just a three-stroke pool, but it's a good joke basin for a couple of happy performing seals.

When I say I not only love Esther, I like her, people ask what I like most about her. She laughs at my jokes, I say.

But above all, I like her because she loves people as I do. This afternoon a guest of ours called a taxi. When it arrived, Esther sang out to it, "Hello, driver, come on in." We get to know the best people that way. As with the Mexicans whom we love, our house is your house. A while ago, I heard a motorcycle come putputting up the road and stop outside the hedge which screens our garden.

"Who's that?" I said.

"Oh, that must be my little man in the hedge," Esther said.

"You got a little man in the hedge, darling? How long has this been going on?"

"Oh, for several weeks now. I saw him there in the hedge, while I was swimming in the pool one day," she said. "I asked him what he was doing there in the hedge and he said, 'I am watching you swim. Is it all right?' I said, 'Yes, it is all right but don't step on my begonias'. The little man said he would be careful."

While Esther was working in "Fiesta," on location in Mexico, we celebrated Christmas there and went all out for the country, especially for Acapulco with its grand swimming and fishing. We saved up pesos and bought a cottage—not a

The love scene all Hollywood is talking about: In "The Fountainhead," Pat Neal stares into mirror as Gary Cooper . . .

enters her room. Destined to fight the attraction they feel for each other, Pat runs from him, falls against the bed . . .

but she cannot escape the great magnetism that exists between them. Even as she resists, she yields to his embrace . . .

hacienda, *please*—but a very small cottage way up on the cliffs overlooking the sea. Just a couple of bedrooms, kitchen and vast porch that serves for a living and dining room.

This Acapulco place is our second honeymoon casa. The first is a small brown shake cottage that hangs by its brows to a hill in Pacific Palisades. It was an old house hidden in acacias, two stories with two bedrooms on the entrance floor, a living room, dining room and kitchen below on the garden level. We reshaped the interior with our own hands, making it comfortably early American—American as rocking chairs and flapjacks.

ON OUR last honeymoon trip to the casa at Acapulco, we went exploring down the Mexican coast. We had heard of a fine white beach, thirty miles away, where there was fine bass fishing at the mouth of a rivulet. The manager of a hotel at Acapulco assured us the roads were excellent and that we would find showers and bathing facilities at the beach.

We hired a beat-up old car. Esther had met two American girls who were spending their vacation in Acapulco and she invited them to come along.

The excellent roads lasted three miles. Then we started boulder jumping, the car shuddering and the occupants churning like ingredients in a cocktail shaker.

When we got to the fine white beach, it was mud. A hurricane had preceded us. The surf was so high we couldn't swim. We took a dip and then went for a shower. The shower didn't give. We remained coated in brine and barnacles.

"We might try fishing," Esther said brightly.

The fish obliged. They had been landlocked by the surf in the mouth of the rivulet and were probably bored. Anyhow, six or seven climbed onto our hooks.

Night came down before we were aware of it. The thought of jeeping back to Acapulco on those rocky roads caused me to scrounge for a telephone. I called the Acapulco airport and they agreed to send a plane. When it bounced down on the little clearing, we found it could accommodate but two passengers. Esther insisted that our girl friends must take it because they had only one day of vacation remaining. The plane promised to

return for us. It returned all right, made three passes over our heads and flew away toward Acapulco. Landing in the dark was too hazardous on the small field.

Esther and I hippity-hopped back to Acapulco in our jeepy-heap. It took us two hours. We were coming apart like the car when we arrived. But not a nasty word from my wife. The nearest she came to it was when she walked up to the hotel manager and said: "About your roads . . ." But she smiled when she said it.

We were to be guests at a party that night.

"Shall we call it off?" I asked.

"We can't," Esther said. "We promised we'd be there and they'll wait dinner for us."

The party went on past midnight. I comforted myself with the thought of sleeping a solid day. My comforting dream was short. Esther recollected we were due as honor guests aboard an American naval craft that had arrived from the East. Her old refrain: "We promised!"

After a few hours sleep, I still felt worn and torn but Esther looked fresh as a daisy. She was the only woman among the fifteen enlisted men aboard the ship. I could see them standing back, waiting for her to be a movie star. Their language and manners were guarded and formal. Three minutes after she came aboard, she was looking at pictures of the cook's wife and babies. They forgot themselves, it became a family party. That's Esther, she makes it home wherever she goes. Someone has defined good manners as just showing your good heart. Esther is more than natural; she's transparent. There are no barriers between her and people, her heart is there to see and it's a good one. The best definition of her is herself, up there on the screen.

Late that afternoon we loafed together on the beach. The day was dreaming off into twilight. White wings of birds flecked the blue sky. It had been a perfect day and I had been awfully proud of her on shipboard. Now we were alone at last, relaxed, on our *playa encantada*—enchanted beach. The surf made music like Lohengrin and I looked up to her and said, "How many honeymoons can you have?"

THE END

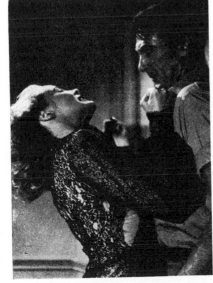

With their kiss, Pat and Gary acknowledge the love that makes theirs the stormiest, most exciting romance ever screened . . .

But, as the kiss ends, Pat fights again, fiercely. Yet, even as she runs from him, she knows she cannot escape her destiny

369

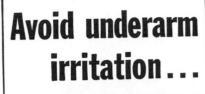

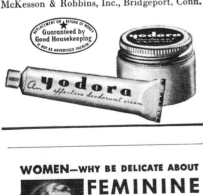

Wendy and her guest Kirk Douglas take direction from George Wallach

INSIDE TELEVISION

BY WENDY BARRIE

THE editors of PHOTOPLAY have asked me to report what goes on behind the cameras when "Inside Photoplay" brings Hollywood to your living room.

A literal statement, that! For the gossip on this show comes directly from Cal York. The pictures are hot from Hymie Fink's camera. Sometimes there's a preview of a film. And many movie stars appear as guest stars. It's exciting and fun. I know. I'm Mistress of Ceremonies.

Always we start out sanely enough. But we rarely end that way. I've had stars turn the tables and start interviewing me! After one such session when I didn't have the right answers, I spent an entire day with the boys in the engineer's booth being briefed. "Be-prepared-for-anything-Barrie," they call me now.

But one thing for which I wasn't prepared happened the evening that Kirk Douglas was on our show. In the audience of the telecast preceding ours was a club of twenty girls in their teens. One of them spotted Kirk in the hall. She stood transfixed. To break the spell, Kirk planted a big-brother kiss on her cheek. With a squeal of glee, she cried, "He kissed me." Whereupon the other nineteen girls streamed into the hall and lined up. And I got on the end of the line myself.

We've had our share of beautiful ladies before our cameras, too. Nina Foch looked so beautiful and chic when I interviewed her that I had to hide my head in shame—behind a handkerchief. The sound man told me that my voice through the hanky sounded like a fog horn—but better than comparison with the extraordinarily lovely Nina.

I'll never forget our pre-telecast conference with Edward Everett Horton. He wouldn't say a thing. He'd just smile and nod pleasantly. Would he, I wondered, just nod and smile while the show was on? My fears were groundless. He was witty, charming, wise and completely wonderful. "Why wouldn't you talk before the show?" I asked him later. Eddie smiled. "I have a dreadfully sore throat—and didn't want to lose the benefits of the spray in conference."

See you Inside Photoplay.

Tune in Inside Photoplay, Monday, Wednesday, Friday. See your local newspaper for time and station.

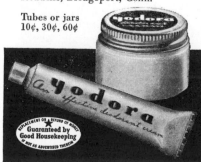

List of Pieces from Photoplay

(Page reference is to present volume)

The Thirties

The Forties